PUBLISHING AND MEDICINE IN EARLY MODERN ENGLAND

PUBLISHING AND MEDICINE IN EARLY MODERN ENGLAND

Elizabeth Lane Furdell

UNIVERSITY OF ROCHESTER PRESS

University of Rochester Press
668 Mt. Hope Avenue, Rochester, New York, 14620, USA
and at Boydell & Brewer, Ltd.
P.O. Box 9, Woodbridge, Suffolk IP12 3DF, UK
www.urpress.com

Library of Congress Cataloging-in-Publication Data

Furdell, Elizabeth Lane.
    Publishing and medicine in early modern England / Elizabeth Lane Furdell.
        p.   cm.
    Includes bibliographical references and index.
    ISBN 1-58046-119-0
    1. Medicine—England—History—16th century.   2. Medicine—England—
History—17th century.   3. Printing—England—History—16th century.   4.
Printing—England—History—17th century.   I. Title.
    R487.F867 2002
    610'.942'09031—dc21   2002032363

British Library Cataloguing-in-Publication Data

A catalogue record for this book is available from the British Library

This publication is printed on acid-free paper
Printed in the United States of America
Designed and typeset by Straight Creek Bookmakers

To Barbara and Joanne,
Sisters for an Only Child

CONTENTS

ILLUSTRATIONS

PREFACE

Political theorists have traditionally identified the origins of democratic culture with the philosophical debates of the Enlightenment. Perhaps no one has excited scholars of early modern Europe more than Jürgen Habermas, a sociologist who situates the development of a public sphere of interest in Great Britain after the so-called Glorious Revolution of 1688. Habermas attributes the genesis of this public sphere in large part to the burgeoning English press, liberated from stifling governmental control by the post-revolutionary expiration of the oppressive Licensing Act. But since Habermas' theories became popular, even conventional, a new generation of academics has begun to question the chronology of his analysis, if not his general thesis, pushing the origins of a public sphere ever earlier in English history—as early as the 1540s, a hundred years before the Civil War. These revisionists argue that our liberal heritage did not arise from the lofty words of enlightened sages, but from post-Reformation populist and technological metamorphoses associated with the spread of books and pamphlets among a broadly literate audience.

Print-led progress affected more than patrician politics; other elitist conventions encountered similar misgivings addressed directly to public opinion and propagated by bookmen and women. This book considers one of the most important of those areas altered by the presses of early modern England: medical publishing, especially in the capital, both stimulated and chronicled momentous theoretical and jurisdictional changes in health care. Twentieth-century historians have postulated hypotheses explaining the dramatic collapse of medical orthodoxy when control of medicine in London was lost by the Royal College of Physicians. Surgeons and apothecaries, deemed by physicians as little more than tradesmen, vigorously contested the monopoly over health care held by university-educated doctors and refuted the philosophy maintained by those doctors. Historian R. K. Merton has connected middle-class Puritanism to the rise of scientific empiricism; Charles Webster has extended the nexus between merit-obsessed Puritans and these new methods to include the sort of efficient, clinical medicine espoused by reformers.

Because many London publishers of medical texts were republicans and dissenters, it has been assumed that they deliberately undermined the elitist, Latinate, and Galenist College of Physicians by printing health-related information in the vernacular. However, the evidence shows something else: that it was profit, not political, religious, or even Paracelsian principle, that drove publishers to spread medical knowledge to an eager readership. Radical printers produced both inexpensive iconoclastic medical literature and costly tomes aimed at rich professionals. Ironically, even conservative publishers who put out works by famous Fellows of the College of Physicians were unintentionally disseminating the secrets of the trade and diminishing the cachet those Fellows possessed.

After appraising the multiple controversies within the medical community, we will then investigate the book trade and the role it played in the transitional medical marketplace. Subsequent chapters analyze the politics and religious preferences of publishers along with their printed titles; chapter 5 examines gender as a factor in medical publishing, while another essay looks at the location of London printing houses for clues to the medical marketplace. Advertised medical specialties and products, surveyed in chapter 7, became common in seventeenth-century England; publishers and bookshop owners sometimes held the rights to proprietary medicines, thereby undercutting licensed doctors. The College Fellows were not oblivious to their challengers; indeed, by the late seventeenth century many of the Fellows had studied Paracelsian-Helmontian curricula at continental universities and supported a more accessible program. They founded a Dispensary to reach out to the London poor with medicines usually prepared by apothecaries.

Chapter 8 studies medical illustrations of all sorts and their effect on the changing relationship between patient and professional. The book's epilogue considers the English medical scene leading up to and following the famous *Rose* decision of 1702, when the House of Lords recognized the right of apothecaries to practice medicine.

I owe many people and institutions gratitude for helping me complete this work. The University of North Florida gave me time to devote to research and writing, funds to travel to collections and conferences, and library professionals like Barbara Tuck and Alisa Craddock to manage the maze of information-gathering. I wish to thank the staffs of the British Library, the Public Record Office, the libraries of the Royal College of Physicians and the Royal College of Surgeons, and the Wellcome Institute in London. Timothy Madigan of the University of Rochester Press encouraged me to continue with the Press after the success of our previous collaboration, *The Royal Doctors*.

Earlier versions of certain chapters were floated at conferences filled with unselfish scholars who offered sound advice: chapter 3 first emerged at the 1999 DeBartolo Conference on Revolutions in Print; chapter 4 saw the light of day in Montreal at the Northeast Conference on British Studies; and I read a variant of chapter 5 at the 2001 Southeast Conference on British Studies in New Orleans. Work that I did on Stuart-era doctors and publishers including James Welwood, Walter Harris, George Bate, Peter Cole, and George Sawbridge will appear in the forthcoming *New Dictionary of National Biography*, whose section editors like Ian Gadd, Henry Summerson, and John Cooper offered important advice and knowledge. Maureen Bell, Margaret Hunt, Elizabeth Eisenstein, William Eamon, James Carrier, Kevin Siena, Robert Martensen, Mary Rhinelander McCarl, Jonathan Sanderson, Barbara Brandon Schnorrenberg, David Reid, and Eric von der Luft provided me with useful information on female printers, medical advertising, and anatomical illustrations, as did other generous scholars via the on-line networks H-Albion and SHARP.

Finally, family and friends buoyed me with their love and support. In particular, I owe thanks to my husband and colleague Theo Prousis, to my sons James and Andrew and my daughter-in-law Kimberly, and to Barbara Hageman Sarvis and Joanne Liberty, dear friends to whom this book is dedicated.

For the reader's ease I have modernized some, but not all quaint spellings from the Tudor-Stuart era, and adjusted Old Style dates to begin the New Year on January 1. In early modern England, money was calculated in units of pounds (£), shillings (s.), and pence (d.): twenty shillings to the pound, twelve pence per shilling. Actual currency included coins of various metals and mints with many names and nicknames. Ascertaining the worth of money for a long stretch of time is complicated, but multiplying seventeenth-century pounds by a hundred will give a crude approximation to amounts understandable today. Probing the motivations of men and women dead for centuries can be an even more daunting task, as is challenging the solid theses of generations of scholars. One must be careful with the hearts and minds of those in the foreign kingdom of yore, for as Samuel Butler reminded us in *Erewhon Revisited*, "though God cannot alter the past, historians can."

Chapter 1

ENGLISH MEDICAL ORTHODOXY AND ITS CHALLENGERS

Among the many political and religious controversies discussed with passion in the sixteenth and seventeenth centuries, the practice of medicine stands out as an issue burdened with complexity. Because of exuberant public interest in health care, medical practitioners found voice for their convictions in the flourishing world of print, where they could promote their ideologies, their associations, and themselves. Published speculation stimulated further discussion among family and friends, creating yet more demand for information about various therapies and the available practitioners. The healing arts in early modern England split along intricate theoretical and jurisdictional lines. Doctors trained in classical medicine fought with those taught more experimental and clinical treatments. University-educated physicians opposed efforts by surgeons and apothecaries to compete with them for patients, regarding these competitors as subordinate in professional preparation and occupational status. In the midst of this turmoil, "irregular" practitioners, neither credentialed by colleges nor trained through guild apprenticeship, plied their trade among the sick poor, while bishops asserted their traditional privilege of licensing as healers whomever they wished. Patients of all economic strata faced bewildering choices among various medical doctrines and categories of specialists, choices shaped by what they could afford, by what they knew of the practitioner's skills, and by whom they could find willing to tend them. In all cases, published materials informed their choices and enlivened debates.

Let us first survey the dispute over medical creed in England, particularly the battle between the followers of the Roman physician Galen and their adversaries. While many historians of medicine and science have branded proponents of classical theories in the Tudor era as old-fashioned, in fact sixteenth-century Galenists embraced reform of medieval medicine as part of the Renaissance rediscovery of a better, more refined existence in Greco-Roman times. Classical knowledge and pure medicine had been distorted and defiled, it was thought, by incorrect medieval texts and translations; reformation in medicine depended on the accurate rendering and editing of the words of its founders, especially Galen.[1]

Galen was the Greek-born court doctor to Marcus Aurelius who wrote over 500 treatises on medicine and philosophy, studies he adjudged intrinsically intertwined. He submitted that four "humors" or bodily fluids govern the body's

1.1. Galen in concert with Hippocrates, Plato, and Aristotle. From Symphorien Champier, *Symphonia Platonis cum Aristotele, et Galeni cum Hyppocrate* (Paris: Badius, 1516).

health: blood, phlegm, yellow bile (choler), and black bile (melancholy). Galen embraced the Aristotelian notion of harmony and moderation, postulating that human beings are a balance of warm, cold, dry, and moist, and he saw disease as a product of humoral imbalance (See Fig. 1.1.). Too much or too little of any these humors led to instability and illness. Furthermore, disease or contagion could corrupt the humors, poisoning them and causing sickness in the patient. Galen's works, brought to full glory by humanists of the Renaissance, inspired and excited philosophers, creating the medical philosophy of Galenism, which "more or less cogently described principles, doctrines, and concepts . . . used in thinking about man's body in health and disease, and shaping the physician's attitude to his profession and to human life."[2]

According to the Galenic method, a physician must prescribe ways of redressing the humoral balance, either by removing a surfeit or adding to a deficit, or by ridding the body of contaminated humors that caused infirmity. If a person is feverish, flushed, or hot, he has an excess of blood. Too much blood required bleeding; purging via vomitories, laxatives, or emenagogues eliminated other superfluous or putrid humors.[3] Moreover, the dominance of one humor over the others affected personality and disposition: too much phlegm, for instance, made one phlegmatic. Galenists scorned common simples and administered complex concoctions containing great numbers of ingredients, surmising that if one component would not help, another in the recipe should. Galenic medications promised restoration and rejuvenation, though usually taken by a patient denied fresh air or sunlight.

Galenists considered food medicinal if prepared properly, reflecting the classical conviction that internal medicine was a specialized construct of dietetics and that meal preparation was akin to preparing medicines; cooking ought to mirror the Galenic ideal of equilibrium. Edibles fell into four distinctive groups: wet, dry, cold, and hot. A tempered diet must include nourishment from each Galenic category; for example, beans were considered cold, so they should be balanced by hot spices. Febrile patients should eat predominantly cold foods, since opposites were presumed to cure opposites. Even John Archer, an advertising empiric who treated Charles II, voiced a Galenic truism when he labeled hare "a melancholy meat, and therefore not good for those who have dry bodies."[4] Auxiliary to these concepts was the idea that each person had a unique makeup and therefore needed to be treated individually. Particular treatments in one case might not be good for someone else, and since disease could change over time as the physiology of the patient changed, treatment needed to be varied according to the current state of the illness. Galenic physicians therefore emphasized a patient-centered practice and took into account the constitution, lifestyle, and circumstances of their patients when relating treatment to disease.

The worlds of medicine and print converged throughout the early modern era in England, inciting commotion in one another and providing a publishing gauge of iatric theoretical dominance. The ancients dominated sixteenth-century print.

Between 1500 and 1600 approximately 590 different European editions of Galen were published, and in England humanist medical scholars like Thomas Linacre (1460–1524) and John Caius (1510–73), both royal physicians, spurred what they envisioned as the renovation of medicine through the propagation of Galenic teaching.[5] Linacre used salaried lectureships at Cambridge University to assure regular medical instruction in selected texts of Galen translated by himself (See Fig. 1.2.). He strongly supported the Medical Act of 1512 which castigated "ignorant persons . . . smiths, weavers, and women (who) boldly . . . take upon them great cures . . . in which they use sorcery and witchcraft . . . to the damage and destruction of many of the king's liege people."[6] No one, subject to a fine of £5, should practice physic or surgery who was not a graduate of Oxford or Cambridge.

Although responsible for the well-being of the court, royal doctors like Linacre pledged to ameliorate bourgeois medicine; in fact, they spearheaded reform, becoming the driving force to begin licensing and monitoring of health care in the capital. The College of Physicians in London, created in 1518 by Henry VIII at Linacre's instigation to supervise the practice of medicine in the capital, compelled its Fellows to comprehend classical Latin texts and to distinguish themselves from ignorant empirics.[7] Henry VIII granted the College its first charter, ostensibly to improve the professionalism of health care providers, but also to give control of doctoring to university-educated physicians, who were then all Galenists. By the terms of the College's charter, no physician was permitted to practice within seven miles of the City unless he had been elected a Fellow or held the College's license. The College also safeguarded the quality of medicaments within London according to Galenic principles: among the College's officers was a Board of Censors, Fellows whose task it was to burn impure drugs found in the grocers' and apothecaries' quarters.

However, the number of Oxbridge medical graduates was chronically inadequate, and, while the Henrician regulations aimed to upgrade the quality of care under the College's licensing management, they also exacerbated the shortage of practitioners, especially in London.[8] Things got worse with the passage of an Act in 1542, commonly called the Quacks' Charter, which allowed unlicensed men and women to practice the healing arts, but only out of humanitarianism and not for a fee. Even those unlicensed healers who declined compensation faced danger, such as the poulterer named Grig from Surrey, who in 1550 treated an array of diseases with prayer; he was pilloried in Croydon and Southwark on the order of the king's council.[9] Biases, philosophical and patronizing, spawned by the Reformation, sharpened the problem of doctor scarcity in the kingdom as the College took it upon itself to suppress medical ventures by the clergy, "arguably the most common type of practitioner in the nation."[10] Moreover, despite Henry VIII's intention to ameliorate the health problems of his subjects, the king inadvertently aggravated the medical situation in his realm when his government confiscated ecclesiastical properties, including church hospitals and other facilities for the sick poor, as a result of the break with Rome. London citizens had to petition in 1538 for restoration

1.2. Portrait of Thomas Linacre, artist unknown. Department of Prints and Drawings, British Museum, London. Reproduced by permission of the Trustees of the British Museum.

to them of St. Bartholomew's and St. Thomas' hospitals, but the Henrician regime responded slowly and incompletely, granting St. Bartholomew's to the City in 1544 and other religious properties in 1546.[11]

There was great need for medical expertise during the reigns of Henry VIII and his three offspring. Chronicler John Stow recorded numerous epidemics and sicknesses during the last half of the sixteenth century, including diseases bewildering to helpless victims and physicians alike. Pestilence broke out in London in 1548, sweating sickness (still unknown but perhaps an arbovirus that killed in twenty-four hours) in 1551, "hot burning fevers" in 1555, and "quartaine ague" in 1558; more epidemics ravaged the city in 1563, 1578, 1593, and 1603.[12] Perhaps ten percent of an afflicted population in the sixteenth century would die in a year of plague outbreak, but nearly one-fifth of London's population died in the calamities of 1563 and 1603.[13] Beyond the mortality of plague, typhus, the "pox" (which included modern syphilis), and other new diseases added to the uncertainties of Tudor urban life.

Despite the chaos caused by the dearth of legitimate professionals and the inability of London physicians to deal with pandemics, the Galenists pressed their humoral theories virtually unchallenged for several decades, thus inhibiting, according to their critics, much medical investigation and experimentation. Then came Paracelsus. It is hard to exaggerate the impact of the sixteenth-century Swiss physician and educator on medicine and science, not just the laboratory aspect of his studies, but on their political and institutional aspects as well. Born Philippus Theophrastus Bombastus von Hohenheim in 1493, Paracelsus impugned Galenic teaching and the omnipotence of the medical establishment in ways often described as analogous to Martin Luther's defiance of the Roman Catholic Church. The links between Protestantism and Paracelsus were evident during his lifetime; he was an "evangelical dissenter who felt at home among reformers" questioning authority.[14]

Medical modernization was the exclusive province neither of Protestants nor of the challengers to Galenic physicians. The Catholic Counter-Reformation also produced institutions that hoped to remedy urban ills and minister to the sick poor. New religious orders and confraternities dedicated themselves to public health care and medical charity. Historians have had difficulty explaining this paradox, but similarities surface in Protestant and Catholic spiritual renewal.[15] Economic decline may have delayed the building of new institutions in southern Catholic Europe by over a century, but vibrant localized examples of health care reform and poor relief commenced throughout Italy. Likewise, in other Catholic areas in Europe the Counter-Reformation "gave an impetus and a direction to the care of the sick."[16]

Nonetheless, Paracelsus presaged that impending Catholic energy by a generation and took on historic medicine headlong. He ridiculed humoral calculations, instead advocating chemical and metallurgical experiments combined with a sort of mysticism to attack disease. He upset the medical profession with his unorthodox ideas, monumental ego, and insistence on writing in German

1.3. 1625 Plague Bill printed by William Stansby for the Worshipful Company of Parish Clerks. Reproduced by permission of the Guildhall Library, Corporation of London.

rather than Latin. As fate would have it, Paracelsus got his start as a healer through a patron in the world of print, Johann Froben, publisher of Erasmus and a satisfied patient of Paracelsian cures. Froben acquainted Paracelsus with the Erasmian circle in Basel, which led to his appointment as the city physician in 1527, a post which included the right to lecture at the University.[17]

Unabashedly, he issued an invitation to students across Europe to come and study with him. Followers of Paracelsus, he cautioned, should not expect to get wealthy by being doctors, for he enjoined compassion and charity towards the indigent. For him, it was insufficient merely to refrain from charging the penniless fees; Paracelsus demanded from his disciples the vigorous pursuit of Christian policies on behalf of the destitute.[18] Exiled from his post at the University of Basel after about ten months, he subsequently led an itinerant life, practicing medicine, writing books, and studying diseases of miners.

Paracelsus subscribed to the Neoplatonic cosmology taught by Marsiglio Ficino in Florence, with its tenets of macrocosm and microcosm: the body and soul of man replicate in miniature the body and soul of the world, a correlation that the philosopher or magus can comprehend and master. Since Paracelsus believed that the universe was chemically controlled, it followed for him that the human body could be altered and cured by the chemical treatment of a medical magus, rather than by trivial herbal remedies or bleeding to syncope.[19] Paracelsus built a bridge between magic and science; there are elements of both in his endeavors.[20] Because of this peculiar amalgam, Paracelsus is neither ancient nor modern. Physician to Erasmus, he defined the bases of medicine as philosophy, astronomy, alchemy, and ethics. As an anti-Aristotelian, Paracelsus contemptuously discarded the four humors of Galen, impugning the lack of patient examination and symptom observation he believed to be characteristic of Galenic theory. Paracelsus argued instead that disease emanated from external causes and became localized in particular organs. He termed his urine analysis "chemical dissection" and carried his patient's weighed urine in a gauged cylinder shaped like the human body.[21] Albeit famous for his use of chemical remedies such as mercury, lead, arsenic, and antimony, he did not neglect vegetable simples or mixtures made from them. Despite his affinity for laboratory experimentation, Paracelsus endorsed certain mystical treatments such as an ointment made of usnea (moss from skulls), bear grease and boar fat, dried boar brains, red sandalwood, calcined worms, and bone or tissue matter from a mummy. The ointment, called weapon-salve, was a treatment for injuries; it was to be applied not to the wound but to the instrument that had caused it. Healing would occur by the power of sympathy.[22] Paracelsus' sanctioning of cabalistic remedies underscores the complexity of Renaissance thought and the interrelationship of magic, science, and religion. Like other Neoplatonist magi, he grounded his iatric beliefs in Hermetic philosophy which he valued as more authentic than Galen and closer to God's initial revelations to Adam than to the pagan Greeks. Hermetic books emphasized the complete community of beings and objects. Using the forces of nature through magic, astrology, and alchemy, wise men could achieve a closer union between the world of things and the world of the mind. Denigrating academic doctors, Paracelsus declared that the "physician derives from nature, from nature he is born; only he who receives his experiences from nature is a physician, and not he who writes, speaks and acts with his head. . . ."[23]

According to Paracelsus, disease was a material entity that could be made apparent and detectable. In chemical terms, disease emerged as the product of coagulation caused by some exogenous substance, introduced with food or drink, and specific or fixed as a process, doubtless influenced by some local environmental factors.[24] Among other things, his convictions provided him with a new explanation for gout, which he advanced in 1531. Water supply, he argued, could cause chemical deposits like bodily tartar to cluster around a joint.[25] Paracelsus also touted the natural healing processes of the human body, recommending milder doses of medication and opiates like laudanum, a word he invented, to relieve pain. Whether his theories were correct or not, his patients and those of his followers recovered and handled their recoveries better.

Paracelsus fits no more easily into a sectarian category than he does into an ideological one. Although he directly confronted institutional authority with his seditious ideas, he did not always agree with the man to whom he is frequently compared. He disliked Luther for embracing secular authority as much as he disliked the Roman Catholic ecclesiastical hierarchy; Paracelsus made no secret of his blessing on the German Peasants' Revolt in 1525. While city physician of Basel, he lectured in German rather than Latin, suggesting a popular audience for his views. Paracelsus disdained traditional medicine and tossed the works of Hippocrates and Galen, as well as the canon of Avicenna, into the St. John's Day bonfire in 1527.[26]

Though ownership and access to medical books had become crucial to academic Galenists, Paracelsus published very little himself by the time of his death in 1541, apart from a surgical treatise and pamphlets on the pox and astrology.[27] Nevertheless, his influence was profound, especially during the so-called Paracelsian moment of the 1570s, which revolutioned medical training on the continent through a more empirically based course of study tied to the observation of patient symptoms and the insistence on better nutrition.[28] Myriad diseases, his followers held, revealed themselves through fairly constant symptoms easily recognized by the patient and easily diagnosed by any observer. Once diagnosed, exact countermeasures could be prescribed. Paracelsianism became as much a social threat as an intellectual heresy, especially to privileged practitioners with vested interests to protect. It "encouraged the subject classes of the medical profession, the surgeons and apothecaries, to claim rights above their station."[29]

While lesser luminaries within medicine envied or condemned the towering social standing of physicians as they perceived it, the English gentry appraised doctoring as not dignified enough for its sons. Historian William Birken has discovered that "non-gentle, plebeian, or clerical" descent characterizes a majority of the Fellows of the College of Physicians.[30] Nevertheless, the Fellows behaved as though they were a distinctly privileged group within medicine, not just another guild, and associated the College with the idea of service, monopolizing the right to define its own national duty. Of course, they were extraordinary, the first collective of medical professionals to license doctors, unlike the usual system of church, state, or university licensing. Claiming authority to regulate all aspects of health care, the Fellows capped the "first vertical differentiation in medicine."[31]

Although many continental universities endorsed the more experimental medical theories of Paracelsus and his followers in their curricula, throughout the Tudor-Stuart era Oxford and Cambridge, the only places where medical education was available in Britain, still rated the traditional Galenic theories of sickness and health more authentic for study by would-be doctors. Oxbridge faculties emphasized reading and disputation, not anatomy, dissection, or surgery. Medical historian C. Donald O'Malley harshly described the quality of sixteenth-century Oxbridge instruction in medicine as "medieval in character and in some respects below the level attained at the great northern Italian universities in the fourteenth century."[32]

Interest in chemical therapy began in Great Britain with the 1559 publication of Conrad Gesner's *Treasure of Euonymus*.[33] The following year, when College of Physicians Fellow John Geynes spoke out against Galen's teachings, his colleagues summoned him to justify his criticisms or face imprisonment. Geynes asserted that he found twenty-two errors in Galen, but after three days of debate the Fellows remained firmly on the side of the ancients, and Geynes repented.[34] Despite the outcome of that imbroglio, physicians trained in the Paracelsian-influenced curricula began to make their way to England. The Oxbridge majority in the College of Physicians responded by tripling its fees for Fellows with foreign degrees.[35] Historian Allen Debus terms Richard Bostocke, practicing around 1585, the first English Paracelsian. Bostocke wrote *Difference between the Auncient Phisicke . . . and the Latter Phisicke*, which noted the historical antecedents of chemical medicine, from Adam to Hippocrates, and pointed out that herbs and plants comprised a valuable part of a doctor's repertoire when treated chemically before being administered. Bostocke warned, however, that doctors should not experiment on men.[36] Leading English surgeons like John Banister and William Clowes found aspects of Paracelsianism appealing, and Thomas Moffett (or Muffet), a prominent Fellow in the Royal College of Physicians, transmitted "the sophisticated form of Paracelsianism into England."[37] Moffett, an Anglicized Scotsman, transferred in 1578 from Galenist Cambridge, where he studied under Caius, to the University of Basel, where he absorbed the new medicine. Upon his return to England, he cultivated noble patrons, sat in Parliament, and joined the College of Physicians. He presented Paracelsus as "the Hippocrates of a new age."[38] Spurred by a spate of publications after 1570 and the lobbying of Dr. Moffett, the College flirted with Paracelsianism in the 1580s and contemplated a section on chemical medicine for its proposed pharmacopoeia.[39]

The passion for chemistry as the touchstone of a healthy regimen affected amateur pharmacists as well. Elizabethan courtier and explorer Walter Raleigh fancied himself a "chymist," and his earliest biographers enumerated his chemical competence with all his other talents. In the early 1580s, the distiller John

Hester, an enthusiastic Paracelsian, dedicated a book of medical recipes to Raleigh. While in the Tower of London from 1603 to 1616 on charges that he conspired with Catholics against James I, Raleigh passed the time in chemical and medicinal work. Praise began to resound for his eponymous cordial in 1605, and James's queen, Anne of Denmark, became a devotee of Raleigh's tincture after recovering from a dangerous fever in 1612. The recipe was lost, however, after Raleigh's failed second voyage to South America and his execution on the orders of an ungrateful king in 1618. Paracelsian Nicolas Le Fèvre, Professor of Chemistry to Charles II, provided the fullest account of the cordial's ingredients after trying to re-create it for the king and diarist John Evelyn in 1662.[40] Among the components he specified: decoctions of hart's horn, bezoar stone, musk, pearl, ambergris, bole of Armenia, and white lodestone, all brewed with a gardenful of herbs, roots, and fruits, and steeped in a syrupy suspension of sugar and wine.[41] Even adventurers could find excitement in the laboratory.

But, as the College did not complete its plans for an Elizabethan pharmacopoeia, no chemical segment could be included. Notwithstanding the desire of the Fellows to monitor the drugs apothecaries dispensed, as their foreign counterparts were doing, the project involved so much work that inertia won out. Committees studied particular categories of medications on and off for five years, but the College Annals show no progress on the crucial job of actually editing the whole work and the project languished for a generation.[42] A period of conservatism in the College ended the Tudor century, although by 1589 fully one-third of the Fellows had graduated from universities with chemical therapy among their requirements, and their numbers would only increase in the next age.[43] Toward the end of the Elizabethan era, an implicit doctrinal truce existed within the English medical profession; the seventeenth century would bring new impetus for change in the person of royal doctor Theodore Mayerne.

Geneva-born, Mayerne studied medicine at Paris and Heidelberg, and then iatrochemistry at the sophisticated Huguenot university in Montpellier, where he received his M.D. in 1597. While insisting that Galen was still the master of physicians, Mayerne strongly defended chemical remedies and the more experimental curriculum of continental practice, endearing himself to the neo-Paracelsians who held sway at the French court, if not to Parisian Galenists. Mayerne traveled to Italy and Britain for purposes of finding new cures, and while he sojourned in Oxford in 1606, his degree was incorporated there and he became physician to Queen Anne. Mayerne eventually developed a large practice in England that included important personalities, and in 1611 he became first physician to King James. Mayerne kept detailed case notes on both his English and French patients; one historian has called those the "medical annals of the Court of England."[44]

An apostle of the chemical school, Mayerne engaged in countless experiments, bringing the purgative calomel (mercurous chloride) and a mercurial lotion called "black wash" into use. As part of his chemical repertoire, Mayerne advocated the taking of unpalatable "steel" in powdered form for "the spleen" or melancholy; his other, nonmetallic treatments could be just as fearsome. For stupor and numbness he invented a balsam made of twelve boiled bats, three snakes, two suckling puppies, one pound of earthworms, hog lard, and white wine applied to the backbone; he advocated drunkenness once a month, probably one therapy to which the king did not object.[45] He believed that "the bitterest medicines . . . work the best," prescribing for a patient with respiratory problems "a syrup made with the flesh of tortoises, snails, the lungs of animals, frogs and crawfish, all boiled in scabrous and coltsfoot water, adding at the last sugar candy."[46] At the same time, Mayerne sustained faith in the Galenic expulsion of undesirable humors through bleeding—opening veins and keeping them open by means of "issues" or incisions prevented from healing by the insertion of small gold pellets.[47]

The College of Physicians welcomed Mayerne as a Fellow in 1616, comprehending that his Paracelsianism was eclectic, compatible with much traditional practice. The College felt his influence immediately with the long-awaited publication in 1618 of the London Pharmacopoeia, a potpourri of chemical and mineral medicaments as well as Galenic standbys. Mayerne was responsible for much of its contents, including the description of Thomas Moffett's Paracelsian medicines, which Mayerne had acquired after Moffett's death. Mayerne continued his service to the Stuarts under Charles I and later, inspiring other Huguenot physicians to follow him to England. His case books carefully document treatments given King Charles and his queen; for the latter he prescribed cosmetics and a dentifrice made from pumice stone, cuttlefish bones, powdered coral, pearl, and deer horn.[48] Medical historian Norman Moore called Mayerne "one of the three great clinical observers in England."[49] Mayerne was also adroit at preserving the quiet syncretistic compromise effected by the College Fellows in the late sixteenth century and preserved until the Civil War.[50]

After 1640, the theoretical conflict in medicine again grew overt as chemical doctors denounced Galenists in print, challenging their knowledge of the latest therapies and adding a new name to the pantheon of theoretical medicine, Jan Baptista van Helmont, pioneer chemist and mystic.[51] Van Helmont studied philosophy at Louvain and earned an M.D. there in 1599. During the several years of travel and research that followed, he was sought out by the leaders of ecclesiastical and secular courts as a physician and an adept. Drawn into the weapon-salve controversy in 1621, van Helmont insisted that his Roman Catholicism did not prevent him from endorsing the magic of sympathetic healing, and he praised Paracelsus for his disclosure of natural magnetism. Van Helmont's enemies cited heretical elements in his propositions and brought his work to the attention of the Inquisition, which condemned van Helmont for heresy and magic. Chief among the charges brought against him was his support for Paracelsus and chemical philosophy. In 1634 he was arrested and his books seized. After displaying abject contrition, van Helmont won his release and spent his final years writing on fevers, plague, and the errors of ignorant doctors who adhered to humoral pathology. Van Helmont died in 1644, but his son collected his papers and had them printed in 1648 as *Ortis medicinae*. Medical historian Allan Debus calls van Helmont's oeuvre "among the most influential medical and scientific publications of the seventeenth century."[52]

Van Helmont's iatric and chemical theories posed a threat to existing medical practices as well as to religious and collegiate precepts. He considered the ancients heathens, chiding Aristotle and Galen for their unwarranted conclusions and lamenting that medicine had been cultivated by enemies of Christianity—Greeks, Arabs, and Jews.[53] He rejected the doctrine of humors and bloodletting altogether, insisting that only through chemistry could the nature of medicine be understood. At the same time, van Helmont disavowed the metaphysical basis of Paracelsianism.[54] Concurrently execrated or embraced across continental Europe, Helmontianism was promulgated in England by Robert Boyle. Ignoring the strictures of his conservative professors at Oxford, Boyle engaged in experimental science., eventually playing a large part in the English acceptance of Helmontian chemistry through his analysis of corpuscular theory. Although he found fault with some aspects of van Helmont's work, he influenced a second generation of Helmontian disciples, many of whom were thrilled by the frontal assault on Galenism.[55] More chemical books were published in translation in the 1650s than in the entire preceding century; Paracelsian-Helmontian interpreters produced most of the new renderings of foreign medical authors' work, coloring themes with their biases.

Home-grown Protestantism also reproached the medical establishment and the English Galenists at its apex. Besides the Puritan welfare scheme begun in London in 1647 with the Corporation of the Poor, concerns for urban health care and medical provision found voice among Christian samaritans of all stripes. John Cook, Solicitor-General and public prosecutor at the trial of Charles I, penned a 1648 pamphlet, *Unum Necessarium or the Poor Mans Case*, which argued that physicians should do one-tenth of their work for the poor without receiving any fees. He espoused total deregulation of the medical market and advocated the use of the clergy in handling medical responsibilities, policies at odds with the College of Physicians' formal and informal supervision of health (See Fig. 1.4.). Moreover, Cook advocated basic training in medicine for the poor, so that they could produce simple drugs for their own use. No less unpalatable to physicians, another tract in 1649, *The Poor Mans Advocate* by Peter Chamberlen III, a committed Protestant whose family specialized in midwifery, urged confiscation of church lands to finance the situating of poor families, who in return for their labor would be extended free medical services from doctors and hospitals.[56]

Traditional Galenists were not generally clinicians, so proposals to advance clinical teaching threatened the substance of their medical customs while disparaging classical theory as insensitive to patients' needs. The poor especially had to make do with minimal care and cheaper medicaments, be their own doctors, and rely on the kindness of their parishes to pay practitioners' fees. University-educated physicians were seen as high-priced, venal, and uncharitable, adding to an acquisitive reputation condemned by rich and poor alike. In the 1650s, Dr. William Petty, a graduate of Leiden and proponent of bedside instruction, recommended the idea of a teaching hospital in London to be staffed by unmarried men—physicians, surgeons, and apothecaries—all devoted to public service and not to their own affluence. Envisioning a place where the recovery of needy patients could be combined with the improvement of knowledge, Petty, part of the circle of medical reformers close to Polish-born merchant Samuel Hartlib, proposed that the steward of the hospital be a mathematician, that apprentices be given to all younger personnel, and that widows be employed as nurses.[57] Notwithstanding the attention of Paracelsian and Helmontian reformers, no such charitable institution aimed at alleviating the chronic need for medical care in the city was set up until the end of the seventeenth century, when the College Fellows launched a Dispensary. As late as the reign of George II, only St. Bartholomew's and St. Thomas's hospital formally taught novice surgeons.[58] So, despite the Christian ethic of altruistic duty toward the sick and the obvious need to train more medical personnel, the plight of the London masses without health care did not appear to move Galenist doctors.

Historian Owsei Temkin, however, reminds us that "the extinction of Galenism was not a sudden event, but a process" with multiple milestones and no single cause. Andrew Wear parallels that cautionary note by drawing attention to the "continuities" within English medical practice.[59] The career of Thomas Sydenham illustrates the transitional nature of medical science in early modern England. A clinician taught at Montpellier, a leading European school of medicine, Sydenham created a novel tripartite method: describing the disease before him, determining the praxis or remedy, and using that specific treatment. He wrote monographs on febrile disorders, dysentery, and syphilis, all the while telling his pupils to "go to the bedside; it is there alone you can learn disease."[60] Regardless of his training, however, Sydenham did not abandon Galenic methods altogether; he advocated bleeding, especially for epidemic fevers and apoplexy. At the same time, he often blamed over-treatment by doctors for spreading disease. Sydenham never acknowledged the implications of the circulation of the blood and, as a Puritan, he rejected the need for postmortems.[61]

Despite the substantive rebuke represented by Paracelsianism and Helmontianism, as well as the pressures for improvement of health care brought by Puritan reformers like Sydenham, the universities of Oxford and Cambridge continued to embrace a largely Galenic curriculum until the mid-to-late seventeenth century. The Caroline Code, instituted at Oxford in 1636, strictly required students to attend Hippocratic or Galenic lectures or be fined.[62] Hampered by their collegiate structure, neither Oxford nor Cambridge showed any proclivity until the last Stuart decades to update their anachronistic pattern of medical training. A man could collect a doctorate in medicine fundamentally

1.4. The Doctor's Dispensatory, ca. 1650, a broadside sold by Nathaniel Brook. Reproduced by permission of the Bodleian Library, Oxford University.

for book learning, after having observed only two anatomical dissections and participated in none. Moreover, English doctors resisted phasing out humoral bleeding and purging; the intellectual defense of bleeding persisted tenaciously in Britain until far into the eighteenth century. Samuel Pepys regularly visited his surgeon, Thomas Hollier, to be bled because Pepys was "exceedingly full of blood;" both the diarist and Hollier subscribed to the belief that periodic ven-esection promoted well-being.[63] Royal physician Walter Harris, writing in 1699, thought Dutch practitioners were peculiar since they "bleed so sparingly and seldom."[64] Because nearly half of the Royal College of Physicians by 1670 had trained on the continent, it is not surprising that English universities finally started to reshape their curricula to acknowledge that trend.[65] English medical degrees began to reflect a new emphasis on finding specific cures for specific diseases; familiarity with human anatomy and the observation of patient symp-toms were also stressed. Repercussions from the scientific revolution produced additional conflict between the old-fashioned gentlemen physicians of the Oxbridge establishment and the ambitious, utilitarian products of the latest continental curricula. There were many Englishmen like Thomas Withers, M.D., who believed that the "character of a physician . . . cannot be main-tained with dignity but by a man of literature," and on that score the university curricula at Leiden, Utrecht, and even Padua were found wanting.[66]

As if these theoretically based divisions within English medicine were not sufficiently rancorous, fault lines separated university-educated physicians from the more practically trained surgeons and apothecaries, who were in turn voca-tionally superior to the myriad of unlicensed, unregulated men and women to whom most people turned when sick. For a variety of reasons, these nominally discrete, specialized categories of health care lingered, albeit blurred, in early modern England. No profession was in a more active state of flux than medicine, the borders of its occupational categories smudging and variegating so often as to diminish reliably genuine distinctions among them. For instance, "surgeon-apoth-ecaries" like Robert Hitchcock and John Harris plied their trade in London, and even more of these hybrids practiced in the provinces. Furthermore, With the help of some sympathetic physicians, the tactically astute apothecaries, who were traditionally the lowest rung on the medical ladder, usurped the middle ground from the surgeons in the first decades of the seventeenth century and became a political powerhouse by the end of the Stuart dynasty.[67] The complications of this many-runged ladder of medical rank further debilitated the efforts of traditional physicians to maintain supremacy in the battle for both respect and customers. Let us now examine the jurisdictional battle in early modern English medicine.

Physicians, degreed and expensive, ruminated about illness and cures. They were the philosopher-kings of medicine and their palace was the Royal Col-lege of Physicians of London (See Fig. 1.5.). Members of the College, the only licensed practitioners in the metropolitan area, grouped into Fellows and can-didates; there were also nonvoting honorary Fellows and licentiates in the as-sociation. Unless one had a full seven years of arts study at an English university

1.5. The College of Physicians, "Long Room, Warwick Lane," by Thomas Rowlandson and A. C. Pugin. Reproduced by permission of the Wellcome Library, London.

or had one's foreign degree incorporated there, obtaining a license to practice proved arduous. Candidates had to undergo a three-part Latin examination in physiology, pathology, and therapy; even an superior applicant like William Harvey, M.D. from Padua, had to undergo a lengthy testing and waiting period, watching as lesser aspirants with English diplomas passed him by.[68] Because of the College's restricted membership and control of licensing, the ratio of lawful doctors to Londoners in the seventeenth century was startling, about 1 to every 4,000 residents, making a medical marketplace of enormous opportunity.

The College monitored medical activity in the metropolis, prosecuting unlicensed practitioners who violated the law. Between 1550 and 1640 alone, the College pursued well over seven hundred medical scofflaws, fifteen percent of whom were women.[69] Although the Fellows avoided political controversy whenever possible, the exodus of royal authority from London during the Civil War left the College incapable of enforcing its regulation of medical practice, and by 1649 the triumph of Puritans contemptuous of Galenism persuaded the Fellows to set up a laboratory with a chemist, William Johnson, in charge. Such a defensive endeavor would probably have come about in any case, since a significant number of the Fellows were active supporters of the parliamentary cause and because some of their younger colleagues developed close links with the government of Oliver Cromwell. For its part, Cromwell's administration came to view the College as a stable element in a volatile medical world and did not interfere with it as an institution; the cautious policies of the Fellows enabled it to withstand a successful if transitory crusade among the College's professional opponents to establish a rival college of chemical-physicians.[70]

In 1660, hoping to curry favor with the restored Stuarts, the College welcomed Charles II back to England, likening him to a phoenix. The Restoration advanced the careers of some doctors over others, raising complaints among candidates of long standing leapfrogged by new men of the king's choice. The Fellows erupted in a chorus of disapproval when Charles raised a charlatan, Cornelius Tilborg, to the station of royal physician in 1682.[71] To raise money for the College, honorary Fellows, many suggested by Charles II, were admitted upon payment of £20, later £100. (In 1681, regular Fellows paid a fee of £4.) Though some of the Fellows grumbled that the king ought not intrude in their professional brotherhood, the College acquiesced when he reconfirmed its ancestral privileges. In appreciation, the king exempted the College from some of the usual civic responsibilities exacted from the guilds, such as providing men for the night watch or providing arms to the city.

The College continued its compliant relationship with the Crown in the 1680s; nevertheless, it was not held in universal esteem within the City, primarily because of the institution's perceived arrogance and pretensions. Especially aggrieved were London's other health care providers, of whom there were nearly 3,000 in the 1680s. In October 1685, as part of James II's sweeping plan to confirm his control of London's corporations by rebutting their privileges, a quo warranto was issued against the College charter. James sanctioned a comprehensive yet hierarchically controlled pattern of medical practice in the capital, one which circumscribed the opportunity for many to practice medicine. Rather than fight confiscation, the College delivered the charter up to the king, effectively surrendering its previous rights. The new king wanted to pack the College with men of his choosing, and Thomas Witherley, former physician to Charles II and President of the College during James' reign, suggested increasing membership from forty to eighty Fellows. Given the need to include all London physicians who were fit to be Fellows, this was real reform, even if flavored with political purpose. Significantly, when a new College charter was granted in 1687, twenty-nine additional members were noted. The College did insist, however, on some sort of doctorate for honorary Fellows, and the king blackballed four existing Fellows for political offenses.

Although the Royal College of Physicians maintained its hauteur towards the rest of the medical world after the issuance of its new charter, the Annals suggest that the physicians were anxious about losing control and patients to surgeons, apothecaries, and irregular medical practitioners. A majority of the Fellows during the last twenty years of the seventeenth century exhibited a sort of professional xenophobia, too, more narrow-minded concerning continentally trained physicians than they had been at mid-century, when half the Fellows were foreign graduates. During the period from 1681 to 1700, thirty-five of the Fellows held their medical degrees from Oxford or Cambridge; only eighteen Fellows had graduated from foreign institutions.[72] In 1694 a College committee proposed double fees for Fellows whose degrees were not from the English universities.

Galen had written that surgery was merely a method of treatment, highlighting a separation of physicians from surgeons in imperial Rome. The medieval descent of doctors from clerics accounted for the absence of clinical and surgical expertise among Renaissance physicians, because an edict issued in 1163 by the Council of Tours prohibited the participation of priests in operations involving the shedding of blood. Pope Innocent III reiterated that ban for clerical practitioners in 1215.[73] Therefore, the actual administration of drugs, the setting of bones, and the performance of operations had to be handled by a surgeon.

By 1435, a Surgeons' Guild developed within the Barber-Surgeons' Company. As a natural progression from shaving and delousing, fifteenth-century barbers also pulled teeth, set broken limbs, and drew blood, the latter procedure acknowledged in their red-and-white striped shop poles. Leaders within the Surgeons' Guild, however, sought emancipation from their tonsorial associates, arguing that their experience in domestic and military medicine warranted the respect only a separate fraternity would bring.[74] Despite this discord, the United Company of Barbers and Surgeons received the right of self-superintendence in its charter, a right reconfirmed by Henry VIII in 1512, which vested supervision in the Master and Governors of the guild. As part of the Henrician reform of medicine, however, surgeons were required to obtain licenses from ecclesiastical authorities. After an initial rush to do so (seventy-two surgeons obtained permits from the Archbishop of Canterbury in 1514), many surgeons practicing in London and its environs ignored the regulations.[75] Barber-surgeons felt they deserved to be regarded as more than common trades-men, but one doctor made typical comments in 1566; he accused surgeons of using "blynde experience" rather than science in their treatments and insisted that no surgical cure should be undertaken "without the phisitions aduyse."[76] Surgeons, however, had to apprentice for years before receiving admittance to the company and normally had bedside training superior to philosophers of medicine. With further preparation and another examination, one might be-come a Master of Anatomy and Surgery with a permanent license to practice, such as Thomas Vicary, Henry VIII's serjeant-surgeon and one of the Masters of the Company. Moreover, anatomical lessons for physicians were given at the Surgeon's Hall; Vicary was the first lecturer there, and he was followed by continentally trained John Caius, one of the most eminent scholar-physicians in the sixteenth century. In the words of one medical historian, "it was the Company of Barber-Surgeons who were responsible for raising the level not only of surgery but in some measure of all medicine as well."[77]

English medical school alumni by comparison still acquired degrees based almost exclusively on book learning, without having participated in any ana-tomical dissections. Many surgeons had the hands-on experience with disease and wounds necessary to a successful convalescence. William Clowes, a royal serjeant-surgeon to Elizabeth I and chief surgeon at St. Bartholomew's Hospi-tal, learned practical techniques on the field of battle; he found that "fingers are the best of instruments and that scabbards make good splints."[78] He read the most recent and advanced imported texts, putting into practice the newest techniques for treating wounds, ligating arteries in amputations, and locating imbedded bullet fragments. Likewise Thomas Gale, another Elizabethan surgi-cal appointee, combined battlefield knowledge, political savvy, and book learn-ing in remarkable ways. He dedicated his writings in 1563 on gunshot wounds to the Earl of Leicester, sponsored the translation of Galen's *Methodus medendi* into English in 1566 because so few surgeons understood Latin, and generally helped to propagate recent continental advances in anatomical study. Gale also made an official visit to metropolitan hospitals, reporting on the woeful condition of over three hundred patients. No wonder patients habitually con-sulted surgeons for all their medical needs.

The feats of surgeons like Clowes and Gale forced the College of Physicians to acknowledge its tardiness in providing for the surgical expertise of its Fel-lows and to sponsor public talks about surgery. John Stow reported the found-ing of a twice-weekly lecture series in 1582 at the College in Knightriders Street; it began two years later under the sponsorship of "the honorable Baron, John Lord Lumley, and the learned Richard Caldwall, doctor in physic." Lumley endowed the project with £40 annually at the instigation of Dr. Caldwall, a former President of the College. Stow noted that the highly respected Richard

Forster was to be the public reader "during his life." Medical comrades in and out of the College acclaimed Forster, an Oxford M.D. and protégé of Elizabeth's favorite, the Earl of Leicester, for his mathematical prowess. Even surgeons found him a worthy reader of the surgery lecture, and it was the reader who had the responsibility of commenting on the anatomical passages presented and demonstrating his commentary on the cadaver.[79]

Despite the efforts of the College to evince a more modern ethos than traditional Galenism implied, surgeons were still coupled in the minds of those who needed relief from sundry maladies with the skills and bedside manner that we would compare with the modern general practitioner or primary care physician. Though most familiar with the popularly understood tenets of Galen, patients actively sought a wider range of medical assessment and interpretive schemes. Ronald Sawyer has argued that despite the proliferation of different types of healers, licensed and otherwise, patients shrewdly selected whom and what they regarded as most appropriate for their cases and conditions.[80] They often chose surgeons because of their versatility. Famed diarist Samuel Pepys found in surgeon Thomas Hollier the ideal general practitioner, and he turned to Hollier for pills, plasters, lithotomy, and phlebotomy. Hollier treated Pepys for painful urination, constipation, hemorrhoids, and "cut [him] for the stone."[81] Surgeons like Hollier also virtually monopolized the treatment of venereal disease.

Physicians were vulnerable to scrutiny on another level, too. While many elite doctors fled London during plague epidemics in 1625 and 1638 and the great scourge of 1665, surgeons stayed to tend to the dying. One wry contemporary chided the Fellows' desertion of London in 1603: "Never let any man ask one what became of our Physitions in this Massacre, they hid their Synodicall heads as well as the prowdest."[82] Furthermore, like William Clowes, military surgeons who accumulated invaluable seasoning during wartime brought an important stimulus to the medical profession on their return to civil society. Richard Wiseman, Charles II's faithful surgeon and a veteran of the battlefield, demonstrated that practical experience could dovetail with erudition. His prudent and insightful books, *Several Chirugicall Treatises* and *Charisma Basilicon*, the latter on Charles touching his subjects for scrofula or the "King's Evil," cemented his prominence as the "Sydenham of surgery."[83]

The increase in the number of London hospitals, stimulated by Edward VI's donation of Bridewell palace and land around the Savoy, was also crucial to the development of surgical skills and training.[84] When the young king established the royal hospitals, London boasted about 100,000 souls, but by 1600 that number had doubled, meaning the hospitals handled around 4,000 people per year. In 1640 over 350,000 lived in the capital, many beyond the limits of the Corporation of the City as well as beyond the limits of the London hospitals' ability to serve them. Sectarian differences at mid-century prevented consistent action to deal with the dearth of medical centers, but Charles II inaugurated Chelsea Hospital in 1682, followed by the establishment of Greenwich Hospital between 1692 and the 1720s. All these institutions offered surgeons opportunities for advancement. Though still paid less than a physician, a surgeon could expect to see that wage gap shrink as his prowess grew. Many surgeons publicly imputed the preeminence of physicians and ridiculed their therapies. Daniel Turner, a surgeon to Queen Anne, derided the use of quicksilver by the illustrious Dr. Hans Sloane. During an autopsy Turner reported that he found a half-pound of mercury in the intestines of a man treated by Sloane.[85]

1.6. Cupping (Kopster) by Cornelius Dusart, 1695. Reproduced by permission of the Wellcome Library, London.

With celebrity, however, came hubris. As early as Tudor times, legislation chastised surgeons for "minding only their own lucres."[86] Waxing famous, surgeons chafed under their affiliation with lowly barbers and sought to separate themselves from the taint of the shop. They did so by charging stiffer premiums than barber-surgeons and lesser practitioners. Charles Bernard became one of the wealthiest surgeons in late Stuart England, inhabiting a new social milieu for a tradesman.[87] Successful phlebotomists could earn £1,000 a year and even a run-of-the-mill surgeon could get rich treating syphilis with mercury; some claimed they could prevent venereal disease with secret nostrums.[88] Ordinary people, even the rising middle class, eventually could no longer afford these princes of medicine and turned to more humble and numerous healers for general health advice. The apothecaries, who concocted the remedies prescribed by physicians, constituted the third leg of the regulated medical tripod in early modern England.

Until 1617 the apothecaries were part of the Grocers' Company, when Dr. Mayerne and royal apothecary Gideon de Laune, both French Huguenots, used their influence at court and a fiat from James I to detach the apothecaries from the grocers and into a separate guild, as in France.[89] The College of Physicians supported the split, as its Fellows assumed, with encouragement from the Crown, that the new society would be more subordinate to College authority over drugs in the capital. Time proved that assumption absurd, as the pugnacious apothecaries straightaway demonstrated the same determination to contend in the medical marketplace with the physicians as they had to rid themselves of the grocers.[90] Moreover, as the apothecaries rose in status as a medical force, they did so without losing what had long been their greatest strength, their abundance. During the seventeenth century, the number of metropolitan apothecaries increased roughly eight-fold, and while some respected College Fellows like Richard Blackmore, John Radcliffe, and Hans Sloane championed the work of apothecaries, that number only exacerbated the alarm of most London physicians.[91]

Like the surgeons, the apothecaries boasted of a more personal care for patients and argued their right to prescribe since no one knew medicaments better than they. Many of them also insinuated in circulars that they were better suited to diagnose illness than physicians trained in outmoded approaches. After apothecary Nicholas Culpeper translated the *Pharmacopoeia Londinensis* into English, knowledge of a doctor's Latin was unnecessary in making medicines. While not able to flaunt the prestige that they thought physicians had, London apothecaries grew rich in the thriving city, and some achieved fortunes. Gideon de Laune was among the affluent inhabitants of the capital, owning a mansion, two shops, and ten tenements. He made thousands of pounds from his recipe for a purgative nostrum and was pressed to lend the Crown funds in 1626.[92] Another apothecary success story was Robert Talbor from Essex, popularizer of quinine, whose "secret remedy" garnered him 3000 crowns and a life pension from Louis XIV for curing the dauphin. Talbor also won the thanks

1.7. The Apothecary's Shop opened, c. 1650, a broadside sold by Nathaniel Brook. Reproduced by permission of the Bodleian Library, Oxford University.

of Charles II, a knighthood, and appointment in 1672 as "Physician to the Person," quite an advancement for a "debauched apothecary's apprentice."[93] Furthermore, in 1678 Charles ordered the College of Physicians not to interfere with Talbor's practice as a feverologist (See Fig. 1.7.).

By the last half of the seventeenth century, many London apothecaries enjoyed financial success, evidenced by the rapidity with which the Apothecaries' Hall was rebuilt after the Great Fire of 1666. While plans for a new College of Physicians languished, a sumptuous meetinghouse for the Society of Apothecaries rose quickly from the ashes. One writer in the reign of Queen Anne estimated that perhaps ten apothecaries boasted incomes of £2,000 per annum, and John Radcliffe's apothecary, Mr. Dandridge, was reputed to have amassed £50,000 from his great partner's prescriptions.[94] With wealth came weight; in London as well as in the provinces, apothecaries assumed civic responsibilities, and a few even won seats in Parliament.[95]

Perhaps to augment their solemn importance within medicine, the apothecaries of London always wore black. Their shops, however, offered a colorful collection of merchandise and usually featured a skull atop a tattered folio written in a classical language. More important to their customers than these props were the herbs sold there as well as powders, pills, electuaries, dentifrices, pomades, and love charms. Popular ingredients found in early seventeenth-century apothecary stores included moss, smoked horse testicles, May dew and henbane; later in the century more exotic ingredients like nutmeg, Jesuits' Bark (cinchona), and spiders abounded, reflecting the importation of cures from overseas territories.[96] Though apothecaries opened for business throughout London, Camomile Street became a prime location for those dispensing herbal tea. Dr. Robert Pitt expressed the disgust of his colleagues when he decried apothecary "shops of medicine [that] fill the town . . . and no alley or passage [is] without the painted pot. . . ."[97]

It would be a mistake to envision the apothecaries as a powerless group hawking their quaint medicines out of whimsical stores, inferior in every way to their medical "betters." In fact, the Society of Apothecaries had shown itself to be a hardy competitor for control of the London medical market. Their alliance with the College of Physicians began to deteriorate almost as soon as the ink had dried on the Society's charter of incorporation. During the reign of Charles I, the Fellows indicted unlicensed practitioners in the city, including many apothecaries; they complained to Parliament that the druggists had become "so bold" in their defiance of the College's right to judge the practice of London medicine that they threatened "general damage" to the vitality and health of the metropolis.[98] The war of words continued during the Puritan Revolution, but the College relaxed its statutory membership requirements and muted its antagonism towards the apothecaries to parry the thrusts of its anti-monopolist critics. Easing the College ordinances, however, satisfied no one.[99]

After the Restoration, the Society of Apothecaries opposed a new charter for the College, tendering lists of demands that confirmed the apothecaries' confidence they should be seen as legitimate, autonomous practitioners and not just as junior partners to physicians. Their objections to the charter were taken seriously by Parliament, and they went on to engage in a brisk pamphlet war with the doctors. One of the tracts published by a physician, Jonathan Goddard's *Discourse Setting Forth the Unhappy Condition of the Practice of Physick* (1670), bluntly admitted that, because their educations cost so much, physicians deserved "to get as great estates as are gotten in any profession or way of trading." Unfortunately, he added, since the apothecaries began cutting into their professional terrain, physicians enjoyed less prosperity than they had thirty or forty years earlier.[100] Besides money, most apothecaries doubtlessly wanted some of the privileges of physicians when they petitioned the House of Commons in 1694 to be relieved, as members of the College already were, of all parish duties. The Royal College of Physicians was thus rightfully concerned about loss of its members' prerogative and income to both surgeons and apothecaries.[101]

In addition to surgeons and apothecaries impinging on their clientele, the College Fellows worried about the number of "irregular" practitioners in London, unlicensed male and female empirics who violated the magisterial canon of medical ethics and worked cheaply among the poor (See Fig. 1.6.). Among their particular targets were wise women, legatees of folk medicine conventions without the credentials needed to practice professionally. Although women could gain admittance to the Barber-Surgeons' Company by apprenticeship or by patrimony, few did so; moreover, of the 850 surgical licenses issued by the archbishops of Canterbury between 1580 and 1775, only seven went to women.[102] Despite the low numbers of documented distaff surgeons, females rendered a substantial component of the health care services in the Tudor-Stuart era, good deeds for which they were repeatedly punished. The names of myriad wise women materialize from its unpublished Annals that prove the active, if unappreciated involvement of London women in medicine. Articulating the opinion of the Fellows, James Primrose, a licentiate of the College, lambasted "women that meddle in physick and surgery" in a 1638 Latin tome, *Popular Errours . . . of the People in Physick.* He groused that while matrons were skilled at making beds and cooking broth, they always wanted to do more, ignorantly insisting that some treatment they had read or heard about might be efficacious.[103] Thomas Hobbes, however, voiced the opinion of many who disdained authorized doctors when he said that he "would rather have the advice or take physic from an experienced old woman."[104]

Traditionally trained doctors, surgeons, and apothecaries viewed the proliferation of charlatans as the regrettable and inevitable product of experimental medicine. If people believed that anyone could discern the symptoms of a particular malady, and that a specific remedy would always alleviate it, then anyone could dispense those cures on any street corner. Culpeper himself happily commented that "all the nation are already physicians," envisioning an informed lay public enlightened enough to practice mainly preventive medicine and to cure uncomplicated maladies. Using that premise, face-to-face meetings between doctors and patients became unnecessary; advertisements in newspapers and handbills enabled anyone to attract customers to alternative medicine and to make some easy money. In January 1688 the College sent a letter to all bishops about mountebanks and their unlawful practice, but the Fellows denied that they sought a monopoly on health care. Regardless, the College beadle was instructed to record the names of empirics and to bring the culprits before the College's Board of Censors for inspection. The Fellows reiterated that the College was simply exercising the trust placed in it by the monarchy, though they did not always concur with their sovereign's judgment. In 1693 the Fellows refused to grant a license to Cornelius Tilborg, prosecuted him for practicing without their approval, and fined him £50. Despite an earlier association with Charles II and the College's disdain, Tilborg was granted a license by William III to sell orvietan, an antidote against poison, from a stage in any city or town.[105]

The Royal College could still punish transgressions within the medical community, as is demonstrated by its investigation of the celebrated man-midwife, Hugh Chamberlen. The last in a long line of Huguenot accoucheurs, Chamberlen had been one of Charles II's physicians-in-ordinary and had written on the efficacy of Jesuits' Bark, quinine from Peru, for recurrent fevers. In early 1689 he was charged by the College with malpractice in the case of Phoebe Wilmer. Chamberlen had dosed her, six months pregnant, with a farrago of vomitories and purgatives besides bleeding her eight ounces on three separate occasions. Phoebe Wilmer miscarried and died. The College found Chamberlen guilty of malpractice and fined him £10, which he paid. It is possible that the Fellows actually wanted to punish Chamberlen for a different infraction of establishment prerogatives. Like his father and grandfather before him, Hugh Chamberlen had recently petitioned the Lord Chancellor for a patent relating to midwifery. The College counterproposed that it would assume control from the bishops, who ordinarily approved midwives for their moral qualification rather than for their technical skills. Though the plans of one midwife during the reign of James II to set up a birthing school as part of a foundling hospital were not carried to fruition, in December 1689, the College did permit the licensing of a midwife after examination. At any rate, the Fellows harbored no permanent hard feelings towards Hugh Chamberlen; he became a member of the College five years later.[106]

Guarding the mysteries of the profession was another totem the College resolved to maintain. John Radcliffe, a curmudgeonly but successful royal doctor and member of the College, was fined by his colleagues for not writing up his cases in Latin. The 40 shilling penalty did not deter him from putting prescriptions into English, for he believed that medicine ought to be intelligible to the unwell. Unbowed when the College dismissed him, he became London's wealthiest physician and left his fortune to build the famous Radcliffe Camera at Oxford University.[107] But the College remained pricklish about its prerogatives, always citing the statutes of three Parliaments to support its medical monopoly. When in December 1692 a letter arrived from the Lords of the Admiralty asking the College to nominate three or four physicians from whom the Lords might choose one to take care of the sick and wounded in the fleet at Portsmouth, the College retorted that it should be able to nominate the one fellow. The College nominated the only medical member of the Kit-Kat Club, Dr. Samuel Garth, but hedged its hauteur with the caveat that no other Fellows could be spared at that time.[108]

Despite the attempts of the College to draw a legal line between its Fellows and unorthodox practitioners, those irregulars can sometimes be hard to distinguish from bona fide medical personnel. Though labelled quacksalvers by the elite, unorthodox healers used many of the same diagnostic tools employed by university-educated physicians. Certain wise men and women, so-called "piss-prophets," touted their skill at uroscopy, making diagnoses by inspecting a patient's urine. One advertising quack, "the Famous High German, Turkish and Imperial Physician" claimed to "cast all sorts of human urine."[109] But Galenic medicine had sanctioned uroscopy for centuries, and classically trained doctors examined their patients' urine, an analysis they called "water-casting." Paracelsus, it will be recalled, had that flask around his neck, at the ready when urine-gazing was called for. As Roy Porter pointed out, medicine practiced in the marketplace by an unorthodox fringe was hardly alternative medicine; in fact, "their notions of health and disease, and therapeutic orientation were remarkably convergent."[110]

What did make the so-called quacks different from the medical establishment was their personal and price accessibility. Consider the availability of William Salmon, who claimed to have cured a long list of ailments: nose bleeds, ague, insanity, dropsy, and consumption.[111] Though he practiced from his house outside the gates of St. Bartholomew's Hospital, he also demonstrated his gifts at such venues as the Cock in Wapping, the Black Boy in Barnaby Street, and the Bear in Moor Fields. Salmon's self-promoting career typifies the larger, cacophonous medical scene in early modern England, which issued from the determination of Englishmen and women to seek relief from pain and infirmity. Medicine had become "beyond comparison the most pamphlet-ridden" of the early modern professions.[112] Divided by philosophical and territorial strife, motivated by conscience and cupidity, all manner of practitioners sought expression for their iatric opinions and theories in the mushrooming world of print. Printers, publishers, and booksellers in turn came to specialize in medical works, making health care literature a genre unto itself and creating a public demand for ever more information, discussion, and advice about sickness and well-being.

Chapter 2

London Publishers and Booksellers in the Seventeenth-Century Medical Marketplace

As we have discovered, the English medical world of the sixteenth and seventeenth centuries was a fractious and fractured one. Theoretical disputes and jurisdictional struggles characterized the contest for supremacy in medicine: university-educated doctors squabbled among themselves about scientific ideology while the Royal College of Physicians in London continued to declare its precedence over organized surgeons and apothecaries through its exclusive licensing power. Even as the credentialed medical corps fought among itself, irregular practitioners, wise women, itinerant mountebanks, and quacksalvers asserted their rights to participate in the vibrant medical marketplace. Competition for the patient's money, already robust, escalated after 1660, and by the end of the Stuart era the medical establishment turned upside down. Continentally trained supporters of experimental and clinical medicine eventually supplanted the more theoretically oriented Galenists in the College of Physicians; at the same time the College failed in its attempt to maintain legal control over the medical community. The expense of using elite doctors exacerbated the decline of those doctors, as English patients sought cheap cures for their ailments and methods of maintaining good health in the future. Roy Porter has conceded that the free market system encouraged empirics with the public demanding "whatever systems, therapies and drugs were on offer."[1]

Booksellers and printers financed, created, and disseminated popular health manuals to a new body of readers.[2] They gathered up the odd assortments of recipes, translated and interpreted terms for a lay audience, and rearranged existing texts to respond to different needs. According to historian William Eamon, "printers became the mediators between folk, popular, and learned cultures," making both recipes and philosophical traditions part of the public domain.[3] For the first time, the widespread availability of books for the erudite and the average made it possible for placebound readers to compare different texts and form new combinations of ideas and systems. Intellectuals and scientists like Copernicus would have been deprived of the vast majority of their source materials if printing with movable type had not been available; Tycho Brahe and Isaac Newton assimilated much by reading on their own, a process of learning that had significant consequences for their work.[4] Less celebrated folk benefitted, too. Formerly cut off from learned culture, literate lay people could now participate in and influence society to a greater degree, simply because, armed with the knowledge that books gave them, they knew how to do things heretofore mysterious.[5] Medicine fell within that new intelligence previously taboo to all but the designated lettered community. Even before Francis Bacon sparked a rush for functional information when he insisted early in the seventeenth century that God invited inquiry into the secrets of nature including the human body and the character of disease, an iatric upheaval was under way.

Among those who capitalized first on the medical marketplace were compilers and printers of astrological almanacs. Tied to Galenic physiology, astrological lore imagined that celestial configurations affected bodily functions; by the fifteenth century astrological medicine was accessible to the vernacular readership in the form of almanacs. Using these almanacs, people could determine if their diseases were acute, governed by the moon, or chronic, governed by the sun, based upon astrological techniques of prognosis. Melancholy, for instance, was regarded as a classic astrological disease, attributed by even expert medical opinion to Saturn's effect on malnourished humors. Stars caused humoral imbalance, but preventive rituals and worshipful living could mitigate menacing celestial influences. Medical horoscopes charted the precise time a patient experienced symptoms and determined the planetary situations that caused the illness. Not surprisingly, given its affinity with Galenism, astrological therapy usually included very specific forms of bloodletting and purging, the rules for which formed an indispensable part of most almanacs. Between 1498 and 1560, at least thirty-five almanac-makers published consistently in England; thirty more have unknown authors.[6] In 1537, *Prognostications*, the first almanac by an Englishman, Andrew Boorde, appeared. Boorde's *The Dyetary*, dedicated to the Duke of Norfolk and published a decade after the almanac, is a self-help book of simples based on medical information gathered traveling on the continent. Though not a degreed physician, Boorde also penned *The Pryncyples of Astronomye*, in which he cast himself as astrological doctor, "for astronomy doth elucidate physic."[7]

After 1600 astrological medicine underwent a decline in esteem, although almanac-maker Richard Forster was president of the Royal College of Physicians in the early seventeenth century. In the unsettled years of Civil War and Interregnum, however, interest in the celestial arts took a dramatic upward turn. Both Royalists and Parliamentarians exploited the propaganda value of astrological predictions, and many physicians continued to follow celestial precepts after the return of the Stuarts. Sir Francis Prujean, knighted by Charles II, was another president of the College who supported astrological medicine.[8] Even the great William Harvey prescribed a mixture to be taken "every new and full moon."[9] Richard Saunders and Joseph Blagrave rekindled the public's attention in the 1670s to the importance of planetary rhythms to health in two influential post-Restoration publications: *Astrological Judgment and the Practice of Physick* and *The Astrological Practice of Physick*. Saunders' book systematically explained astrological therapeutics in prosaic terms, using horoscopical methods to scrutinize urine, sputa, and other excreta. Blagrave reminded his readers to be sure that their physicians should synchronize medical therapies with the stars; if not, the purges that doctors unseasonably administered could act as vomits and vice-versa.[10]

Herbals also contained a great deal of astrological culture.[11] Eleanour Sinclair Rohde counted nearly one hundred separate editions of printed English herbals for the Tudor-Stuart era, beginning in 1495 with Bartholomaeus Anglicus' book on herbs, the first English book to contain a botanical illustration and a product of the prolific press of Wynken de Worde, successor to the printing legacy of the man who introduced printing into England, William Caxton.[12] Andrew Boorde's popular *The Breviary of Helthe*, a 1547 paean to sensible living as a way of preserving vitality, incorporated an herbal and called for seasonal bleeding to coincide with the heavens. In *The Breviary*, Boorde made explicit to his "gentyll readers" his reasons for publishing in English:

> olde auncient and authentic actours or doctours of phiciske in their bokes, doth write many obscure terms, giving also to many and divers infirmities darke and hard names, difficile to understande, some and most of all being Greke words, some and few being Araby wordes, some being latin words, and some being barbarous words. Therefore I have translated all such obscure words and names into English, that every man openly and apartly may understand them.

Publication of *The Breviary* was accompanied, not inadvertently, by the simultaneous printing of Boorde's *Astronamye*.[13]

Among England's early herbalists, William Turner and John Gerard emphasized the astrological virtues of medicinal plants which emanated from sympathies that abided between plants and stars. The Paracelsian doctrine of signatures complemented this tenet of the alchemical tradition: each plant bore a physical similarity to the celestial influence which dominated it or to the organ connected with the disease that plant could cure. The yellow flowers of sulphur-wort, an herb of Mercury, might be used to cure jaundice; betony root, appropriated to the planet Jupiter and shaped like a human foot, alleviated gout.[14] William Turner, called the Father of English botany, developed his expertise in plants on the continent and took an M.D. in Italy. He drafted part of his famous herbal while traveling, waiting to publish it until he returned home; a Protestant refugee from Antwerp, Steven Mierdman, printed the first part in London in 1551. Turner defended his decision to write the book in English from those who worried that "every man without any study . . . of physick will presume to practice . . . ," by reminding critics that informed patients could be certain that what their apothecaries made up for them was good medicine.[15]

William Bullein's book of simples, *The Bulwarke of Defense against All Sickness*, is an early English herbal, written by one of Henry VIII's physicians and first published in 1562 by John Kyngstone, printer to the University of Cambridge; a subsequent issue was put out by Thomas Marshe in 1579. Bullein generally excluded astrological allusion from his interpretation of disease. When discussing heroic medicine in his earlier *Government of Health*, however, Bullein included a picture of the so-called "zodiacal man," an anthropomorphic adaptation of celestial influences on health, and referred his readers to an almanac for current planetary tidings (See Fig. 2.1.). He insinuated how conventional the formalized rules of astrological medicine had become when he recommended springtime as best for taking a purge: "the apt days and signs are commonly known in the English almanacs."[16]

Surgeon John Gerard composed his famous *Herball, or the General History of Plants* in 1597 (See Fig. 2.2.). Dedicated to Elizabethan statesman Lord Burghley and containing over 1800 illustrations, Gerard's herbal displays faith in the efficacy of plants to cure ills of the body and spirit: peony seeds banish nightmares, marjoram consoles those "who are given to over-much sighing," while just "the smell of basil is good for the heart."[17] Along with supervising Burghley's gardens in the Strand and at Theobalds in Hertfordshire, Gerard kept a garden of his own with over a thousand different herbs near Fetter Lane, gathering mallow, woodruff, and betony in the nearby meadows; he received plants from his many overseas friends and passed cuttings along to fellow gardeners. James I named him King's Herbarist. John Parkinson, James I's apothecary and herbalist mentioned in the Society of Apothecaries' charter, authored *Paradisi in Sole, Paradisus Terrestris* in 1629; it contained directions on how to create a beautiful, "virtuous" garden practical for the sick. He called peonies useful for epilepsy, gentian beneficial to the liver, and canterbury bells excellent for a gargle.[18] Friendly with Thomas Johnson, editor of Gerard's herbal, Parkinson drew together in 1640 a collection of materia medica for *Theatrum Botanicum*, including curious plants, unicorn horn, and powdered mummy.[19]

Alchemists, whose influence permeated Elizabethan court circles, furthered the appeal of Paracelsian-style chemical therapy by resorting to the press, particularly through the publication of small handbooks in the vernacular. As early as 1540, a medical book by the medieval scholar Roger Bacon reappeared with substantial portions translated into English.[20] Francis Cox's *Treatise of the Making and Use of Divers Pills, Unguents, Emplasters, and Distilled Waters* surfaced in 1575 and earned him the enmity of the Galenists in the College of Physicians. An entry in the College Annals described Cox as "an English writer, a very obscure man, absolutely unknown and certainly of no merit."[21]

The same year that Cox's pamphlet appeared, John Hester synthesized several iatrochemical works in his *The True and Perfect Order to Distill Oils Out of All Manner of Spices, Seeds, Roots and Gums*, published by Richard Day. What distinguished Hester's publication was the author's stature as a leading London chemical physician, friend of Walter Raleigh, and self-described "practitioner in the art of distillation."[22] Over the next decade, Hester translated a number of Paracelsian works, including *Key to Philosophy* with a section specifically attributed to the master himself. Important late sixteenth-century books about

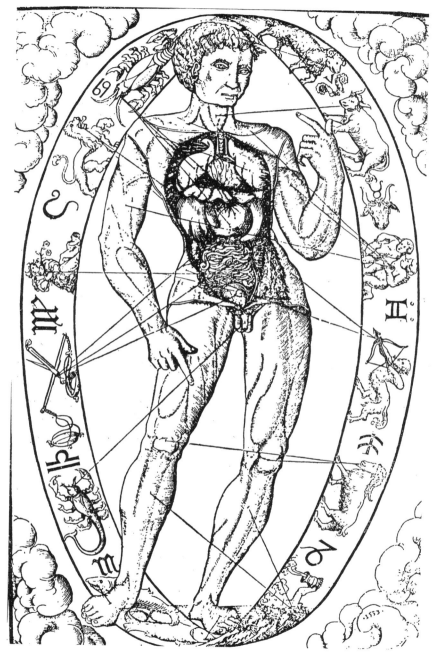

2.1. "Zodiac Man" in William Bullein, A *Newe Booke Entitled The Government of Health* (London: John Day, 1558), fol. xxxiir.

2.2. Title page by John Payne in John Gerard, *Herball* (London, 1633).

natural magic published in English include George Ripley's *Compound of Alchemy* (1591) and *The Mirror of Alchemy* (1597), the latter a collection of venerable pieces representative of alchemical literature. Through these efforts, the works of Paracelsus and others extolling the virtues of medical alchemy became familiar to both laymen and physicians, disseminated widely enough to present practical chemistry as a popular pursuit.

Galenist or Paracelsian, astrological, alchemical, or botanical, remedies for curing ailments and maintaining well-being anchored sixteenth-and seventeenth-century therapeutics, contributing to the contest among different medical groups in England and invigorating the medical marketplace. Information about differing panaceas and therapies spread to doctors and the literate public in a cascade of vernacular medical texts.[23] Unprecedented public discussion and debate in homes, taverns, and other public venues accompanied the reproduction of these tomes, prompting additional production of medical material and more dialogue, a "public sphere" about health topics. Our modern conception of what is meant by the public sphere rests largely on the work of a well-known study by Jürgen Habermas, *The Social Transformation of the Public Sphere*, first published in German in 1962. Habermas characterized the advent of the public sphere as a phenomenon of the eighteenth century, linked with the rise of the middle class and its values of equality and freedom. Governed by reason and exhilarated by the self-confidence that it could understand political processes, the middle class challenged those in power. The opinions they formed, in fact the very nature of public opinion, posed a challenge to authority.[24]

Some scholars have challenged Habermas' time frame in England, pushing the start-up date for the public sphere long before the end of the Stuarts.[25] But more than Habermas' chronology can be impeached: so can the restrictive vision of a single, political variety of public interest. There can be many public spheres, each apprised by germane communication of some sort, but primarily by print, and each a threat in its own way to its authoritative leaders. Just as print stimulated talk about spiritual matters during the century before the outbreak of the Civil War and led to religious nonconformity, so did medical publishing spur competing views on how best to treat disease and to promote well-being. The parallel goes further: if "a nascent public sphere in religion" can be traced to printed debates over rival convictions about the organization of English Protestantism, then surely an incipient public sphere in medicine derived from the publication of differing theoretical and organizational views about sickness and health.[26] A culture of medicine surely existed in Tudor-Stuart England that extended far beyond those teaching, learning, or practicing medicine. Moreover, just as the rise in household theology, a feature of Puritan religiosity, elevated lay management of and instruction in godliness while simultaneously diminishing the authority of clerics, so did responsibility for the physical vitality of family and friends extend increasingly to amateur healers and away from physicians.

Notwithstanding the difficulty calculating general literacy (as reading, un-like writing, consigns few records), probably half of England's population was literate by 1700.[27] Despite something of an educational revolution during the late Tudor–early Stuart decades, the poor remained largely illiterate; neverthe-less, the need to become literate was clearly perceived. Moreover, increasingly confident groups such as the gentry, yeomen, and merchants deduced that ac-quiring useful enlightenment was confirmation of their status and significance. They urged authors and printing houses alike that edifying knowledge, includ-ing medical knowledge, be disseminated to them.[28] They bought books about iatric theory and therapeutics, as well as books of practical advice and rem-edies; those who could not afford the purchase price borrowed from those who could, and those who could not read well enough were read to by whoever was able.[29]

Besides almanacs and primers of health recipes, translations of famous medi-cal authors and plague books dominate any trendy book list of the Tudor and Stuart era. Around 1485, London printer William de Machlinia put out in quarto *A Litil boke for the Pestilence* by Danish bishop Bengt Knutsson, "the most expert doctour in phisicke." New works by Knutsson about plague issued forth from de Machlinia's presses in 1488 and 1490.[30] Merton Abbey canon Thomas Paynell's *A Moche Profitable Treatise against the Pestilence* emanated from the press of Thomas Berthelet in 1534. Likewise, when Thomas Dawson printed J. Stockwood's translation of Theodore Beza's *Short, Learned and Pithie Treatize of the Plague* in 1580, he covered both best-selling bases: the vernacu-lar rendition of writing on pestilence. Simon Kellwaye authored *Defensative against the Plague* in 1593, published by John Windet, later in his career printer to the city of London.

Health data came from official sources, too, further stimulating the need to comprehend more about medicine. The government of Queen Elizabeth is-sued orders in 1588 to be followed "in such townes, villages, and other places, as are or maybe he hereafter infected with the plague."[31] The directive in-cluded "advise set down . . . by the best learned in physicke." In plague years from 1593 to 1626 and in every year thereafter, citizens had the weekly bills of mortality, reproduced for the first time by John Wolfe, London City Printer. Gabriel Harvey edited the bills, although none has been preserved. Wolfe held the right to print the weekly bills until 1603, when he was succeeded as city printer by John Windet. In 1611 the commission to publish, but not the city office, passed to William Stansby. The plague was so bad in July 1625 that the bill, printed by Stansby, sold as "readily as a ballad."[32] (See Fig. 1.3.)

What followed from the expressed determination of Englishmen and women to know more about their own health was a bounty of iatric publications, rang-ing from expensive illustrated albums to one-page broadsides and cheap oc-tavo chapbooks.[33] While some cultural historians have found class polarization in the printing of works for humble readers, Tessa Watt believes that social cohesion resulted as a shared culture "radiated outward to local communities from certain focal points." Divisions between patrician and plebeian, as well as between city and country print, cannot be discerned in early modern England. She also argues that, at least until the Civil War and probably until the eighteenth century, buyers of inexpensive literature came from the middling ranks and gentry; lines separating segments of the reading public tended to be very indistinct, and whatever segmentation did exist was minimal and unthreatening.[34]

A few famous doctors, however, grasped what trouble publishing might cause their profession. Many physicians felt that only Latin texts protected the integrity of medicine and the exclusivity of medical knowledge. Salisbury physician John Securis, pupil of a staunch Galenist at the University of Paris, scornfully speculated in 1566 that "if Englyshs bookes could make men cunnying physitions, then pouchemakers, threshers, ploughmen and coblers mought be physitions."[35] Books in the vernacular abetted the unscrupulous to prey on the public, and entrusted the unskilled to cure themselves; if Securis was correct, then anyone could practice medicine. The distinguished physician John Caius frankly scorned the medical judgment of the masses, whereas Galenist James Primrose, grandson of James I's surgeon, feared that sick people would employ treatments and recipes not designed specifically for them or that they would ignore well-known astrological prohibitions. Lamentably, several of Primrose's published Latin recommendations could have benefitted everyone, particularly his admonition to change the linen of the unwell and his denial that gold boiled in broth cured consumption.[36] University-trained medicos additionally thought that natural philosophy, a subject impossible to probe in a vulgar tongue, was the bedrock of their study, "the true foundation of physick."[37] Objections by physicians to medical publishing in the vernacular displayed real apprehension for the ultimate public value of professional care; English-language books undercut a degreed doctor's practice, cheapened his investment in his own education, and diminished his potential earnings. Dr. Caius also had money in mind when he brooded that the books in English which he authored suffered from a lack of foreign buyers.[38]

Despite these recurrent reservations, it seems as though everyone wanted to write about medicine. Learned doctors might disparage the folk remedies of wise women and the oral tradition from which they derived, but Galenists themselves enthusiastically employed herbal medicines and wrote voluminously about the healing power of plants.[39] Though targeted by their enemies as captives of a pagan past, Galenists did not exclusively write in Latin. As Andrew Wear has reminded us, classical medicine had been increasingly translated into English from the Middle Ages. Of course, these were commercial manuscripts either bespoke by customers or made speculatively for booksellers. The introduction of printing led to fundamental changes in the economics of book production, requiring financial outlay in presses and type. Happily, publishers as early as Caxton could justify those investments in a new vernacular market in England, untapped by continental bookmen, since the English language was virtually unknown outside Britain. Supplying that unique market had nothing to do with medical preference and everything to do with profit. During Tudor times the vast majority of medical books published in England were written in English; by the beginning of the seventeenth century, more than 150 different medical works in the vernacular (in nearly 400 editions) had been published in England, dwarfing the number of Latin tomes. Of the 238 medical books put out between 1640 and 1660, 207 were in English.[40]

The Tudor humanist and diplomat Sir Thomas Elyot ranks among the first champions of writing about medicine in English. His *Castel of Helth,* written in 1534, published in London by the king's printer, Thomas Berthelet, and dedicated to Henry VIII's chief minister, Thomas Cromwell, aimed at making medical learning available to his countrymen. Elyot studied the works of Galen, probably with Linacre, but he was not a medical doctor. In fact, Elyot slighted universities as nonessential for a knowledge of medicine. Undeterred, Elyot put out his treatise on prescriptions for various ailments with an account of his own disorders. That *The Castel of Helth* was written by a layman in the vernacular aroused indignation among accredited physicians in the medical fraternity, compelling Elyot to rebut their reproach in the 1541 printing of his book: "let them remember that the Greeks wrote in Greeke, that Romaines in Latin, Avicenna and the other in Arabicke, which were their owne proper and maternall tongues."[41]

Followers of Paracelsus in England embraced publishing medical intelligence with even more enthusiasm than Galenists because they decried the elitism of physicians and the corner on health care enjoyed by them. To Paracelsians, comparing the hegemony of doctors over medicine to the dominion wielded by the Roman Catholic Church over the Bible made sense. Famed herbalist and radical sectary Nicholas Culpeper expressed this conviction when he inscribed that "there are not such slaves to the doctors as the poor English are; most of them profess themselves Protestants, but their practices have been like those of Papists, to hide the grounds of physick from the vulgar."[42] Of course, emancipating those wretched serfs from medical servitude through published wisdom effected twin rewards: informed, independent patients and enhanced popular reputation for the author. Even fringe doctors found that producing tomes about Hermetic medicine and the occult tended to demystify the arcana of healing and to bring fame to the scholar-printer.[43]

The result of all this activity was the making of a huge range of medical books from elite to popular: textbooks on theory and practice, surgical texts, complicated philosophically based regimens, herbals for apothecaries and wives, plague treatises, suggestions for respite at mineral springs and spas, and modest household recipe books with lists of ingredients and directions for usage. Distinctions between lay and medical readerships blurred; amateurs and professionals both read works which were likely intended for the other. Publishers, both foreign and domestic, benefitted from this bonanza and supplied myriad medical titles for increasing customer demand.[44] Initially, the English government encouraged a good supply of books, and in 1484 a proviso added by the king's council specifically exempted anyone in the book trade from an act limiting the activities of foreign merchants in England. Some continental publishers, like Francis Birckman of Cologne, had books reproduced for the English market in France and kept a shop in London for the sale of printed imports; among these imports were medical tomes.[45]

However, print was an industry the authorities hoped to control, as is evident from later decrees against illicit publishing and illegal importation of certain books. The exemptive proviso of 1484 was repealed in 1534, meaning that aliens could no longer sell books printed or bound abroad and that customers had to buy foreign-published books through the agency of an English seller. The repeal of the proviso pleased native businessmen in the book trade and calibrated policy to the transformed needs of state after the break with Rome. In 1538 a proclamation of Henry VIII forbade "naughty printed books" as well as the conveying of English books from abroad except under "his Majesty's special license."[46] Particularly mindful of the possible political consequences that publishing books in the vernacular might precipitate, Henry's Privy Council insisted upon examining any book in the English tongue, a task that soon became daunting for busy state administrators. A later order in 1546 required all English-language publications to be presented to the mayors of the towns in which the printers lived.

The mayors of provincial towns might manage to scrutinize the handful of materials produced in their communities, but for larger cities the obligation was onerous; for London it would be impossible. Looking for another authority to take on the job of censoring English books, the Privy Council of Edward VI in 1549 shifted the duty to three specific officials: Secretaries of State William Petre and Thomas Smith, or to William Cecil, then Protector Somerset's private secretary. Another two more directives followed in quick succession: one in 1551 reiterating the ban on English-language print, this time without the signature of the king or six of his councillors; another in 1553 from Mary I proscribing all forms of print unless "they have in writing her Grace's special license in writing."[47] Clearly, the Crown needed a more consistent and satisfactory policy of press control, a need that dovetailed with the intent of publishing investors to protect their enterprise.

Therefore, the emergence of the London Company of Stationers, a union of printers, booksellers, bookbinders, and a few paper merchants, as the instrument of controlling the output of the press probably resulted from a combination of governmental necessity, businessmen's demands, and the Company's ambition. Chartered in 1557 by the Marian regime as a vehicle for carrying out royal policy, the London Stationers, in return for the responsibility of policing the book trade, obtained a monopoly of printing in England except for two university presses in Oxford and Cambridge.[48] The Stationers' charter, which specifically restricted printing to freemen of the Company or those licensed under royal Letters Patent, empowered its officers to search for offending books, to punish transgressors with three months imprisonment, and to split the fine of five pounds with the Crown. The charter unquestionably guaranteed the overwhelming hegemony of London in the book business for generations, although it did not create harmony within the Stationers' Company itself. At the outset, printers exercised power on the Court of Assistants, but gradually dominion of the guild drifted to the booksellers, causing friction among the liverymen.[49]

The administration of Elizabeth I, dissatisfied with the language of the charter, complained in its 1559 injunctions of continued abuses by covetous businessmen interested only in gain and contemptuous of public peace. Accordingly, licensing would be required by specific officials in church and state offices with the printers of scurrilous works held accountable in all circumstances. A Court of Star Chamber decree in 1566 reinforced all previous interdictions on unlicensed domestic and foreign books, while another in 1586 insisted on perusal by the Archbishop of Canterbury or the Bishop of London before a book's publication and further clarified the Stationers' privileges and copyrights while exempting the Queen's Printer and judicially approved books of Common Law from the system.[50] Unusual circumstances engendered an occasional prodding of the Company directors to be more vigilant. In 1599 the Archbishop of Canterbury summoned the Master and Wardens of the guild to clamp down on satires, plays, and histories, all notorious genres.

The governing body of the Stationers, the Court of Assistants, concerned about the malapportionment of its members' profits, started to regulate the assignment of printing to poorer liverymen.[51] It also wanted to crack down on the literary pirates who printed titles that other men had recorded in the Company's register, the Hall Book. James I formalized these arrangements, vesting patent rights in the Company. The Court of Assistants divided the rights into shares of the English Stock, as it came to be known, held according to rank in the Company; included in the Stock were steady-selling almanacs, primers, prayer books, catechisms, and psalms. Thus the Stationers' Company had become a willing agent for the Crown with clear commercial benefits for its 500 or so members.[52]

With the collapse of Parliamentary and public support for the policies of the early Stuart kings, additional lines of press censorship fortified the government's bastions against printed criticism.[53] In 1637 a Star Chamber dictum supplemented the Tudor enactments by requiring that all licensed books be entered into the Company register after having been sanctioned according to category by prescribed individuals: the Chief Justices would approve law books, the Secretaries of State books on English history, the Earl Marshal books on heraldry and arms, while all other books including medicine were to display authorization by the Archbishop of Canterbury, the Bishop of London, or their appointees. Books published previously were not to be reissued without obtaining a new license, thereby combatting piratical printing.[54] After the Long Parliament abolished the Star Chamber in 1641, its decrees lost force, necessitating new provisions about the press. Troublesome to the Stationers, the anti-monopolist House of Commons sympathized with attacks on privileges like those enjoyed by shareholders in the English Stock.[55] Significantly, the Lords and Commons in their 1643 Order repeated the Caroline licensing and registering constraints on publishing, but included for the first time a specific classification for certifying books on physic and surgery; those tomes must gain the endorsement of the President and four seniors of the College of Physicians. During the following year, a bill denounced mercury women selling Royalist pamphlets and imposed whippings at the House of Correction at Bridewell for those who did not desist.[56]

Despite these vexing restrictions, the English book trade as a whole flourished and estimates of the number of separate titles produced in England between 1600 and 1700 approach 100,000, a considerable national output.[57] During those decades, London printers and sellers thoroughly dominated the industry. In order to retain the copyright (a word not used until the eighteenth century) to a piece to be published, any stationer by custom had to record the name of the work in person in the Clerks' books kept at the Company Hall; the object of the entry was to indicate ownership by the publisher of the work, the "copy," pending completion of the licensing process. An original registration fee of fourpence (twopence for trifles like ballads) rose to sixpence by 1581, though higher payments to the clerk were recorded. For instance, though John Day was licensed to print a book of physic, Conrad Gesner's *The Treasury of Evonymus*, and paid his entrance fee in 1565, he owed more to the guild based on the size and estimated value of the copy. The Hall Book archived ownership of titles from the very founding of the Company and endured as the definitive reference for customary rights. Well over nine thousand new copies were entered between 1576 and 1640, half of which bore the obligatory licenses.[58] Once obtained, the "right to copy" could be transferred from one stationer to another.

Enterprising printers could use the registration system to their financial advantage, entering editions well in advance of their issuance. Authorization to one stationer blocked any other from putting out that item; no statute of limitations seems to have been in effect. If there was no competition for a copy, the entrance might hold indefinitely, but if the copy was in demand the holder might be challenged. Particularly troublesome was the "blocking" entrance an ambitious printer might make in the clerk's ledger, registering a sweeping series title for anticipated books. Moreover, special arrangements between the clerk and a stationer, called caveats, denied rival printers the ability to register anything on an entire topic. Many medical works fell into the most cutthroat category and no printer's experience more sharply illustrates the dog-eat-dog world of popular iatric publishing than that of mid-seventeenth century stationer Peter Cole, producer of Nicholas Culpeper's oeuvre.

Born around 1613 in Barfold, Suffolk, to clothier Edward Cole, young Peter apprenticed to London Stationer John Bellamy in October 1629 and took his freedom on 11 January 1637. Initially a bookseller, Cole established a business at the Sign of the Glove that he maintained for five years; Cole opened a new enterprise, reflecting his added if unsanctioned specialty, at the sign of the Printing Press near the Royal Exchange in 1643.[59] He sold books from that store for the next twenty-two years, but printed and lived in Leadenhall at another property, also marked by a sign of a Printing Press. An active participant in the City's political life during the Civil War, Peter Cole marketed many of the petitions circulated by Puritan leaders, such as Lord Mayor Isaac Penington, and soon became the favorite publisher of the Independents, those Congregationalists who rejected both episcopacy and the Scottish Presbyterian model. Cole's selections during the Cromwellian era were often theological in character, such as the sermons of moderate Congregationalist minister Jeremiah Burroughs, which Cole generically entered in 1646 though he had not yet received any of them from Burroughs; this entry obstructed another printer from issuing them thirteen years later.[60] Regardless, Cole worked lawfully within a literary system that until the Copyright Act of 1710 gave legal dominance to booksellers and not to authors or publishers.[61] (See Fig. 2.3.)

Peter Cole is best remembered as the publisher of Nicholas Culpeper's medical treatises. A Leveller, Culpeper penned books in the 1650s reflecting the anti-establishment doctrines of Paracelsus and making health care information accessible to the lay reader. Included in Culpeper's output was *A Physical*

2.3. Bookseller's shop. From Johann Comenius, *Orbis Sensualium Pictus* (London, 1664).

Directory (1650) and *A Directory for Midwives* (1651), both printed by Cole. Although unauthorized by the infuriated Fellows, Culpeper translated into English and Cole propagated the Royal College of Physician's *London Pharmacopoeia*, making a doctor's Latin unnecessary for concocting 1,960 medicaments previously encrypted in that esoteric language. Cole published sixty-four of the 158 separate editions of Culpeper's works published between 1649 and 1700.[62] Culpeper foresaw an educated populace well-enough advised to practice a largely preventive medicine and to cure simple ailments. Compelled to leave Cambridge University early because of a restricted patrimony, Culpeper apprenticed himself to three London apothecaries, and by 1640 he had his own shop in Spitalfields.

Aroused by the poverty of his customers, Culpeper supplied them with low-cost plant medicines. The dominion of the College Fellows, it seemed to Culpeper, put basic medical treatment beyond the reach of the indigent. He fumed that in Italy all physicians, whatever their reputation, had to minister to everyone, rich or poor, and that their fees were strictly limited to the equivalent of about twenty cents.[63] A desire to communicate better with his clients, whom he saw at a rate of about forty per day, prompted his decision to publish an herbal in 1649, the same year that his translation of the *London Pharmacopoeia* first materialized. Culpeper admired the herbals of Gerard and Parkinson, but they were available only in Latin and contained, he felt, too many imported drugs. Written in English and based in astrology, his *Complete Herbal* used the common names of plants; moreover, Culpeper often told his readers where in the nearby countryside they could collect the appropriate vegetation. He never recommended more than one plant medicine if only one was needed.[64] Despite his association with Paracelsianism, Culpeper did not ignore traditional Galenic medicine altogether; he coauthored treatises on blood-letting, cupping and scarifying, and the ailments that could be cured using those techniques. Forced by illness to give up his practice and often confined to his bed, Culpeper had the time to provide English readers with numerous medical texts in translation.

Peter Cole certainly encouraged Culpeper's productivity, likely with financial backing from the Society of Apothecaries, christening the series he assembled *The Rationall Physician's Library* and providing an amanuensis named William Reeves to take the sick man's dictation.[65] Culpeper's business associate and publisher for over twenty years, Cole generally embraced the same militant iatric views and paid liberally to reproduce them. He allegedly spent over £5,000, partly his own money and partly from the estates of thirteen orphans, registering the claims and preparing for press thirteen of Culpeper's medical books.[66] Sometimes in collaboration with his brother Edward, Cole produced original works like *Health for the Rich and Poor* and translations of works by Lazare Riviere and Jean Riolan, all of which enjoyed enormous sales.[67] After Culpeper's death in 1654 at age thirty-eight, Cole handled seventeen manuscripts painstakingly prepared by Culpeper for publication; Culpeper's widow invited Cole to produce seventy-nine more, such as multiple editions of the pharmacopoeia, anatomies, herbals, and *The Art of Chirurgery*.[68] Trying to expand the marketability of these works to the broadest medical audience, Cole advertised Culpeper's titles in his other publications and refuted the idea, furthered by practicing alchemists, that Culpeper was exclusively Paracelsian in outlook. In an anonymous 1656 pamphlet entitled *Mr. Culpeper's Ghost*, Cole wrote that Culpeper had mellowed toward Galenism during his final illness.[69]

Peter Cole indubitably regarded himself as the sole owner of all rights to Culpeper's work and wanted to protect his investment. However, Nathaniel Brook or Brookes, a rival bookseller in Bunhill and former friend of Culpeper's, expropriated some of the manuscripts Culpeper's widow intended for Peter Cole, including *Culpeper's Last Legacy* (1655) and *Art's Masterpiece: The Beautifying Part of Physick* (1660). Alice Culpeper denounced Brook, calling the manuscripts that he printed "forgeries and gallimaufries." *Culpeper's Last Legacy* contained a fictitious preface; another title with Brook's imprint, *The Expert Doctors Dispensary* (1657), was indeed spurious, the work of Peter Morellus translated by John Winand.[70] Mrs. Culpeper defended her husband's books published by Cole, mustering nine witnesses to verify their authenticity, but Brook was undeterred by her anger or attestants. He released sixteen pieces bearing Culpeper's name, perhaps constructed from notes remaining after the herbalist's death.[71]

Additional controversy surrounds *Mr. Culpeper's Treatise of Aurum Potabile* (1656), a universal cordial of drinkable gold favored by chemical physicians.[72] Culpeper's amanuensis reported that the herbalist intended to leave his widow a "competent estate" made possible by this alchemical medicine. Historian Graeme Tobyn attributes an anonymous pamphlet which ridiculed aurum potabile, entitled *Culpeper Revived from the Grave*, to Nathaniel Brook, angry then at both Alice Culpeper, "a poor silly woman . . . not much unlike the (whore) of Babylon," and Peter Cole.[73] F.N.L. Poynter agrees, pointing out that Cole expressly came under attack in the booklet for supposedly printing works in Culpeper's name that the herbalist had never written: "the specious pretences . . . cast over this illegitimate libel to the injuries of the dead . . . by the Stationer not far from Leaden Hall."[74] Poynter propounds that Brook clearly had not read the *Treatise* and was unaware that it would not be issued by Culpeper's usual publisher, Peter Cole.

Cole fired back in *Mr. Culpeper's Ghost* (1656), his own essay, which he bundled together and sold with *Medicaments for the Poor* and *Health for the Rich and Poor by Diet*. A flattering letter signed by Cole introduces the departed yet still charitable Culpeper speaking from the Elysian Fields, warning his readers that if the Commonwealth ends and the authority of the College of Physicians returns with the monarchy, all medical books written for ordinary men and women will likely be condemned and burned. Using Culpeper's spectral voice, Cole certifies as genuine both the dissertation on aurum potabile and the translation of Riviere, "the best rules of physick in a Galenical way that are."[75]

Peter Cole was surely financially damaged by Brook's deeds and tried unsuccessfully to obtain an exemption from the licensing provisions of the post-Restoration Press Act, which required copies of all books published and a legal deposit made.[76] Perhaps because of the ignominy that Mrs. Culpeper's denunciation of the "counterfeits" engendered or because Cole had reported his rival to the authorities for other transgressions, Brook, along with printers Thomas Brewster and Simon Dover, was tried in 1664 at the Old Bailey and convicted for publishing seditious books. In the following year Peter Cole hanged himself.[77] Adrian Johns contends that Cole "committed suicide as a bankrupt," but Cole's will, not cited by Johns, conclusively contradicts him. Moreover, F.N.L. Poynter confirms that Cole had "grown rich by publishing (Nicholas) Culpeper's translations."[78] Despite the monetary precariousness of the book trade, at the time of his death Cole was a wealthy man with diverse ventures and holdings. He had pervaded the medical market with Culpeper's useful works, choosing his titles astutely to appeal to all sorts of practitioners and clergymen faced with iatric responsibilities. He had discerned the clamor for medical self-help among midwives, gentry women, and amateur healers. Peter Cole was no destitute fool, and his will attests to solid business acumen and financial planning.[79] By any measure of the time, Cole was a prosperous man of property, unruffled by a lack of assets, who probably killed himself because he was already dying. In his last testament, Cole described himself as "being indisposed in body but of perfect mind and memory, and not knowing whether I may grow worse."[80] Since suicides were considered felons, however, half of Cole's estate devolved to the Crown.[81]

Though Cole waxed successful publishing Culpeper's popular works, other medical bookmen found it rough going, ruined in the world of print. Several printers of medical literature ran afoul of the law for other publishing transgressions.[82] John Streater, a soldier and pamphleteer who succeeded to Cole's copies, made his name during the Interregnum, when he proffered term limits of "one year, not more, rather less," as a means of assuring a natural circulation of interest; he went further, warning against "the danger of trusting the arms of a Common-wealth in the hands of a single person."[83] Incurring the enmity of Oliver Cromwell, Streater nonetheless escaped lengthy incarceration and turned to translating and printing works of mysticism with Giles Calvert, including the entire oeuvre of Jakob Böhme, an ecumenical Lutheran mystic who strongly influenced English religious thought.[84] Given the controversy he courted in the Interregnum, it is not surprising to find Streater in trouble after the Restoration. An entreaty in 1660 against booksellers from journeymen printers to the Archbishop of Canterbury referred to Streater as "a notorious intruder to mischievous printing;" he became a bankrupt.[85]

Streater had a stake in the publishing of vernacular medicine, a clear example of his desire to further the ideals of the Commonwealth, and with his allies produced an outpouring of Paracelsian and lay medical books in English.[86] Like the circle of men around Samuel Hartlib, Streater believed his efforts showed affection for the common man and respect for the common good. An unlikely exemption from the Press Act allowed him to expand his business and by 1668 Streater had the second largest private printing house in London. Despite his success in medical publishing, he turned his attention to law books, got embroiled in a titanic struggle over copy rights with the Stationers' Company, and in 1687 died in debtors' prison, penniless and forgotten.[87]

The career of Cornishman Moses Pitt similarly demonstrates the precariousness of the trade. One of the most important booksellers in the later seventeenth century, Pitt published approximately 160 works, more than a third of which attest to his interest in science and medicine.[88] He produced and distributed translations of foreign tomes such as *Alex von Suchten on the Secrets of Antimony* (1670), *Chirurgical Works of Paul Barbette* (1672), and Raymund Mindererus's *Complete Treatise of Chirurgery* (1674). His two shops, the White Hart in Little Britain and the Angel against the Little North Door of St. Paul's, situated him at the center of the London bookselling business. Pitt spent a good deal on the Angel's lease and even more refurbishing the shop, but he was in fine fiscal fettle by the mid-1670s. Unfortunately, Pitt's commercial dynamism led him to undertake a number of projects, including the extravagant *English Atlas* and John Wallis's *De mechanica motu*, that carried high financial risk.[89] Simultaneously, Pitt's appointment as the executor of a relative's estate enticed him into property speculation in Westminster that diverted his attention and resources on a grand scale from his original business, which he claimed housed stock worth £10,000.[90]

Much of that stock incurred water damage by adjacent construction activity over which Pitt had no control, and the *Atlas* likewise bogged down under enormous costs, subscriber shortfalls, and disagreements with his partners in the enterprise. As troublesome lawsuits encumbered his Westminster holdings, Pitt delegated responsibility for running his affairs to a printer-cousin and divested himself of the bookshops' stock via auctions in 1685. He transferred his assets and created a structure of false debts, a common financial strategy in London, but the cousin manipulated Pitt's wealth for his own parlous ventures and lost the lot. In 1689 bailiffs seized and imprisoned Pitt under a statute of bankruptcy obtained by the cousin; he was still in jail in 1696 but, "unlucky in his timing and (mistaken) in judgment," died the following year at age fifty-two in St. Paul's Bennets Wharf parish, "a low key area in the City."[91]

Several more printers of medical literature ran afoul of the law for other publishing transgressions, including Ann Brewster (widow of Edward), Thomas Burrell, Curtis Langley (and his wife Jane), Benjamin Harris, Joseph Hindmarsh, and Thomas Guy, who made enough money as a publisher and investor to found Guy's Hospital, which opened in 1726.[92] Bookseller Richard Bentley, who handled both Latin and vernacular medical works from his shop on Russell Street, left a legacy of troubled copyrights. Though never even a member of the Stationers' Company, he took on many *ad hoc* partners in book production, notably Joseph Hindmarsh and Thomas Sawbridge, and acquired a share in a block of scientific and medical titles.[93] During the 1680s and 1690s, Bentley advertised extensively in the *Term Catalogues* and on spare pages of the books he published. Catering to well-heeled customers, Bentley produced the tenth edition of *The Queen's Closet Opened* in 1696 and *The Art of Restoring Health* in 1697. By the time of his death later in 1697, Bentley's name appeared on the title page of 250 distinct works and a further 200 reissues, a flourishing business to leave to his family. Although Bentley's wife, Katherine, likely intended to continue his printing house, she assigned away her husband's copyrights after only eighteen months; the convoluted nature of the provenance of these negotiable properties highlights the complex nature of ownership and the difficulty of copyright enforcement after the lapsing of the Printing Act.[94]

Nonetheless, because demand for books proceeded apace, London publishing continued to expand in the last half of the seventeenth century. By 1660 about sixty printers worked in the metropolis, assisted by 160 apprentices and many journeymen; a disproportionate number of them were Dissenters.[95] The government of Charles II, fearful of a completely self-regulating press dominated by religious renegades, instituted a Licensing Act in 1662 which created a new officer, Surveyor of the Imprimery and Printing Presses, charged with suppressing unlicensed printing; Roger L'Estrange obtained the post of Surveyor in 1663.[96] Simultaneously, while endorsing the privileges recorded in the Hall Book and the Company's right to search, the ordinance shifted the balance of power and regulatory responsibility to Parliament and away from the Stationers' Company by limiting to twenty the individuals permitted to keep a printing house. Summoned to the Hall for a head count in May 1663, several printers voiced their dismay and anger at the numerical limitation on presses; some, again unsuccessfully, called for separate incorporation. Furthermore, the Company charter was held in abeyance by quo warranto in 1663 because the king believed that the Stationers were not sufficiently earnest as censors of inflammatory literature and may have even fostered the publication of some scurrilous material.[97] The Licensing Act remained sporadically in force until Parliament allowed it to lapse, first in 1679 and finally in 1694, but it was usually invoked to stifle political literature, especially the Jacobite opposition press after the "Glorious Revolution." Books and pamphlets dealing with medical matters were rarely seized, however, perhaps because no connection was made between their contents and institutional subversion. Nonetheless, book historian John Feather finds significance for the Company and its medical publishing members in the declining number of Hall Book entries from 1678 onwards, due to the lack of legal sanctions and the absence of consensus about the role of the Stationers. He notes that even with James II's revival of the 1662 Act, "the political system of which it was a product had vanished forever."[98]

Residue from Civil War–era criticism of the corrupt, avaricious, and monopolistic practices of Stationers had lingered throughout the reigns of the Stuart brothers. The case of prominent printer and bookseller George Sawbridge the Elder revitalized that commentary. A London Stationer, Sawbridge succeeded his father-in-law, Edward Brewster, as Treasurer of the English Stock in 1647 and held that post for thirty-two years; Sawbridge became Master of the Stationers in 1675. From his shop at the Bible on Ludgate Hill and his house on Clerkenwell Green, Sawbridge sold medical books, particularly the posthumous works and translations of Nicholas Culpeper, including a 1679 edition of the *London Pharmacopoeia*. He partnered with other printers throughout his career, and after the Restoration, Sawbridge formed the King's Printing House with Samuel Mearne, Richard Roycroft, and others, holding shares in the chief publications of his day.

In 1668, as an executor of the estate of Cambridge University printer John Field, Sawbridge deliberately camouflaged his purchase of Field's printing materials and the leasehold of the printing house, still with thirty-four years to run. He paid John Hayes, whose appointment as new University printer Sawbridge had arranged, to pose as the owner of Field's business, though Hayes was really only Sawbridge's agent. By Company statute Sawbridge could not have simultaneously held his post as Treasurer and University printer; he should have reported the profits on his Cambridge business to the English Stock account. In January 1679 Sawbridge's secret connection to Hayes was exposed, and he did not run for another term as Treasurer two months later. The Company, astounded by Sawbridge's deception, revised its rules so that subsequent Treasurers had to give up their bookselling businesses and furnish £1000 in securities through guarantors outside the guild, but the damage had been done to the Stock's prestige and the Company's honor.[99]

Physician-philosopher John Locke, among others, argued that the Stationers made profits from other people's work and gouged consumers with overpriced books. An anonymous petition to Parliament in 1694 decried any monopoly, specifically one like that held by the Stationers, as detrimental to the national interest.[100] Dozens of publishers, printers, and booksellers were summoned to one Parliamentary House or the other in the last Stuart decades to answer charges relating to privilege or contempt; some of them were connected to medicine. When the Printing Act was not renewed in 1695, the book trade appeared very different from what it had been in the first months after the Restoration. New practices, including the removal of licensing privileges from the Stationers' Company, had distanced the industry from the traditional center of power in the guild, which lost additional clout with the relative commercial decline of the English Stock.[101] The book business at the dawn of the eighteenth century was more entrepreneurial than ever before, changed by partisan politics and the demands of a consuming public in ways that paralleled developments in the medical world.

Chapter 3

"Every Man His Own Doctor": Medical Publishers and Booksellers in Early Modern England

In no small part, the triumph of the English medical entrepreneur was due to the publication of popular books of home remedies, herbals, and wellness regimes which purported to demystify diagnosis and cure.[1] Just as the publication of the Bible in the vernacular eventually made ministers redundant, by selling printed matter that enabled every man to become his own doctor, which the title of one publication proposed, London bookmen undermined the legal monopoly of the traditional medical establishment and assured the success of its challengers.[2] Printers whose offerings invariably impugned the authority of the king and his party might be expected to lead the charge against other traditional entities, such as the physicians' monopoly on iatric discourse; booksellers whose shelves groaned under the weight of nonconformist tracts might be assumed to be in the vanguard of medical heterodoxy.[3] However, while the political and religious ideals of several key publishers appear to dovetail with Tudor-Stuart medical populism, their inventories hint at a more financially opportunistic, politically inconsistent agenda. According to mathematician and Royal Society Fellow John Collins, the booksellers of London "would print any book if he be sure to sell eight or an hundred copies for ready money."[4]

Drawing upon *The English Short-Title Catalogues* from 1475 to 1700 and *The Term Catalogues*, the latter a compendium of English advertised publications from 1668 to 1711, I have identified well over 200 printers and sellers who handled medical books in early modern London.[5] A few of these publishers, nomenclature then used interchangeably with printers and sellers of books, put out dozens of medical titles, clearly signalling a specialty within the trade. Available biographical information about these publishers and sellers enables us to ascertain their political inclinations and religious preferences and to judge if, as some historians have supposed, their "religious non-conformity and political radicalism . . . went hand in hand with . . . medical sectarianism."[6] Moreover, clues abound as to the audience, professional or amateur healer, intended for these publications. The size of the paper and the typeface employed, the price of the item, the language used in the text, even the location of the bookseller afford useful information to the historian about targeted audiences. That information is not apodictical, however, as historians have ascertained that the wealthy read chapbooks, that books circulated through many hands, and that all readers shared information with their friends and neighbors. Patrons reciting aloud from printed matter to other patrons occurred constantly in London's public venues.[7] Nonetheless, we should be able to determine if the publishers of medical literature, which by its very existence contested exclusive expertise, meant to thwart the professional establishment or if they were simply trying to profit from opportunities with the book-buying public.

Works on larger sheets (folios) cost more than those on multiply folded paper, octavos and twelves, which were often unstitched and pocket-sized. Those pieces written in Latin foresaw a smaller, elite audience and sold at a higher price than works in the vernacular. Historian Andrew Wear, however, notes that a publication in Latin would reach a large pool of continental learned readers.[8] The kind of typeface used also signified the audience for whom a piece was written: Roman type for the better-educated, black-letter or gothic font for the lower class and the marginally literate. A mixing of types demonstrated a certain visual sophistication on the part of the printer as he emphasized certain words and passages for the reader.[9] England was somewhat late converting to Roman, and black-letter remained the norm for proclamations and ordinances until after the Stuart Restoration. Kevin Sharpe points out that typography could be ideological, concealing and revealing meanings not evident in ordinary readings of words.[10] Regardless of what a typeset piece looked like, however, print was public and it publicized, reaching even the illiterate with its information. For our purposes, published material altered and reflected medical practices in the early modern era. Let us examine some of these published medical pieces and their connection to iatric as well as partisan politics.

Little original work in anatomy came out of Britain in the sixteenth century. Orthodox Christian doctrine proscribed the cutting up of corpses, just as it forbade cremation; entombment of whole bodies conformed to belief in the resurrection of the dead to face the Last Judgment. Dissections were therefore rare, usually performed on those whose souls were assumed to be damned anyway, but unfortunately making anatomical knowledge static and little-related to the true structure of the body. A number of Latin texts combining surgery with anatomy were available for study in Britain and the manuscripts of some continental authors were translated into English, but the first anatomical text, a thirteen-page translation by Peter Treveris of Hieronymus Brunschwig's *Noble Experyence of the Vertuous Handwarke of Surgeri*, did not appear until 1525.[11] (See Fig. 3.1.) The first work on anatomy published by an English author in England was David Edwardes' *De indiciis et praecognitionibus*, produced by Robert Redman in 1532. It also gives the first printed reference to anatomical dissection in England. Though the piece is brief, a mere fifteen pages in which the abdominal viscera are described, Edwardes, an M.D. from Cambridge who performed private dissections, reported that he intended to write a complete book on anatomy.[12]

Only nine anatomical texts in twenty-seven editions were published in England between 1500 and 1600, four by native authors.[13] One of them is

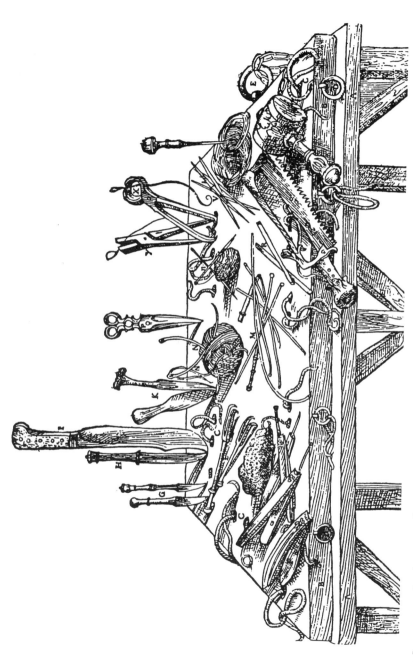

3.1. Instruments for dissection from Hieronymus Brunschwig, *Buch der Cirurgia* (Strasbourg, 1497), reprinted in Henry E. G. Sigerist, *The Book of Cirurgia by Hieronymus Brunschwig* (Milan: R. Lier, 1923).

Thomas Vicary's *Profitable Treatise of the Anatomie of Mans Body*, with the author blazoned on the title page as serjeant surgeon to the Henry VIII, Edward VI, Mary I, and Elizabeth I, as well as surgeon at St. Bartholomew's. Henry Bamforde imprinted the tome in 1577, after the death of Vicary. Despite the absence of significant English contributions to the subject of anatomy in the sixteenth century, the formal dissections held at the Barber-Surgeons' Hall and the anatomical lectures at the Royal College of Physicians, approved by Queen Elizabeth in 1565, encouraged further study. After Lord Lumley in 1582 established the surgical instructorships that bear his name, anatomical teaching at the College received considerable impetus, especially since the Lumleian lectures contained a provision for actual dissection as well as oration. The illustrious William Harvey held the Lumleian post from 1615 until 1656.[14]

Helkiah Crooke, doctor in physick, wrote *Mikrokosmographia or A Description of the Body of Man* and William Jaggard published it in 1615, but the author acknowledged it was a collection of the works of others. Even the two bodies pictured on the title page are lifted from other sources, the veined man from a zodiacal chart on phlebotomy and the woman from an almanac. Although Crooke described himself as "Physitian to His Maiestie, and his Highnesse Professor in Anatomy and Chyrurgery," the Fellows in the College of Physicians did not approve of his book. According to the annals for 1615, the College President "informed the wife of Jaggard the printer" that Dr. Crooke's book on anatomy was "completely condemned" and that if another edition were published, "he would burn it wherever he might find it."[15] One wonders why the President chastised Jane Jaggard when her husband was then running the business in the Barbican. At any rate, the Jaggard press generated two more issues of Crooke's anatomy, and a second edition, printed by Thomas and Richard Cotes for Michael Sparke, came out in 1631.[16] Evidently the College's imprimatur was not crucial to the success of a medical tome, nor did its absence hurt Crooke's career; in 1632 he became the first medical governor of Bethlehem hospital.

In 1616 Jaggard promoted Alexander Read's *Somatographia anthropine or Description of the Body of Man*, an abridgement of Crooke, "set forth either to pleasure or to profite those who are addicted to this study," using Crooke's woodcuts.[17] William Jaggard's father was a barber-surgeon, perhaps explaining his interest in medical publishing. Jaggard asked Read to write the summary, according to his preface "to the courteous reader," so that "being portable (it) may bee carried without trouble to the places appointed for dissection." As printer of the larger volume and a canny capitalist, Jaggard hoped to find an additional audience among those who "are not able to buy or find time to peruse the other." As they had with Crooke's anatomy, the printing Cotes and selling Sparke succeeded Jaggard as marketers of Read's work. In 1634 they made available at the sign of the Blew Bible Read's book on surgery, replete "with the use of three and fifty instruments."

Another publisher of anatomic literature during the reign of the first Stuart kings was Francis Constable, bookseller and printer of Read's *Manuall of the Anatomy or Dissection of the Body of Man*, published in 1634. Besides enumerating the body's parts, the manual purported to show what was usually available only to those who attended "publick anatomicall exercises."[18] Constable had several sites where he dispensed books and pamphlets, including the Crane in St. Paul's Churchyard, under St. Martin's Church near Ludgate, at the Goat in Kings Street, and at his shop in Westminster Hall. In 1637 Constable, better known as a publisher of plays, promulgated Read's *Treatise of All the Muscles*, apparently in conjunction with a public lecture being given by the author "this next Shrove-tide" in the theatre at the Barber-Surgeons' Company.

Textual and illustrative plagiarism was all too common before the establishment of clear ownership of intellectual property, but one particular case may have been tinged by political motivation. In 1648 William Molins wrote a practical account of the muscles, *Myotomia or the Anatomical Administration of All the Muscles of the Humane Body*, based on his knowledge of dissection and "published for the general good of all practitioners in the said art."[19] Molins (or Molines) was the scion of a surgical family associated with Oliver Cromwell despite its royalist leanings.[20] Molins's father Edward was "surgeon for the stone" at St. Bartholomew's and St. Thomas' hospitals. He lost those posts because of his outspoken political views and service to Charles I. While he was away from London with the king's army in the Civil War, the House of Commons ordered his dismissal and nominated a successor. But because of his surgical reputation and in spite of his politics, in 1655 Molins was called to treat Cromwell's gallstones. As a royalist, Molins thought he ought to refuse any reward for curing a regicide, but the Lord Protector asked him to accept £1000 in the name of King Charles.[21] The Molins family could be trusted.

John Field reproduced William Molins's work for Edward Husbands, printer with Field to the House of Commons and a bookseller on Fleet Street. Field was also Cromwell's printer and in 1655 acquired from him the authorization to print for Cambridge University. Even more lucrative than these assignments was Cromwell's order that the copyright of the Bible be registered at Stationers' Hall to Field and Henry Hills. Field printed several editions in different sizes, but he may not have won the entitlement because of his talent with a font. According to Plomer, Field's Bibles "were noted for the number and variety of misprints, the general badness of printing, and their excessive price."[22] Those injured by Field's monopoly focused their objections on his inferior standards and hired William Kilburne to point out the *Dangerous Errors in Several Late Printed Bibles* (1659), errors that might imperil one's soul. Field was the subject of another attack in *The London Printers Lamentation*, but he simply concentrated his attention on new offices on Silver Street in Cambridge.

John Browne later appropriated Molins' work, word for word, as his own.[23] His *Compleat Treatise of the Muscles* came out in 1681, published by Thomas

3.2. Title-page woodcut for Andreas Vesalius, *De humani corporis fabrica* (Basel, 1543).

Newcombe for the author and adorned with forty copper plates. Like the text, the title and illustrations were copied from another work, the 1632 Frankfurt edition of Guilio Casserio's *Tabulae anatomicae*. K. F. Russell calls it "well-illustrated and pretentious."[24] To compound the transgression, Browne, "sworn Chirurgeon in Ordinary" to Charles II, financed its publication by subscription, listing the names of subscribers and what they advanced in a proposal circulated in August of the previous year. Browne asks for a ten shilling deposit with ten more shillings due upon delivery of the book; the tome will be well bound with gilt on the back. Atop the list of subscribers is Prince Rupert, giving £5, the Archbishop of Canterbury, many peers of the realm, various divines, and a handful of doctors. However, Browne brooded that the money he had gathered would not cover the cost of designing, engraving, and printing, requiring more assistance from the public. Not wishing "so useful a work to receive any discouragement," nor wanting to eliminate such frills as the picture of himself by Robert White, the most esteemed portrait engraver of the day, Browne expanded the opportunity to own his book to "every ingenious person."[25] Newcombe, Browne's printer, hardly needed to worry about the risk of producing the *Treatise*. Though he had been associated with Commonwealth literature, by the Caroline years Newcombe was a Common Councillor of the City, held a sixth part in the King's Printing House, produced the Oxford and London *Gazettes*, and owned one of the largest businesses in London.[26]

James Yonge, a surgeon-apothecary who served as mayor of Plymouth in 1694, added the final fillip to this saga of the copying of colleagues' work done by medical men. In 1685 he put out a blistering attack on Browne called *Medicaster medicatus*, exposing the plagiarism involved, and two years later he expanded the offensive by refuting the "diverse mistakes and vulgar errors in chirurgery and anatomy . . . of some great pretenders."[27] Yonge, a friend of College of Physician leaders like Hans Sloane and Walter Charlton, also blasted Browne's *Adenochoiradelogia*, or "an anatomick-chirurgical treatise of glandules and strumaes," printed in 1684 by Thomas Newcombe for Samuel Lowndes, the third part of which is an adulatory account of Charles II touching for the King's Evil, *Charisma Basilicon*.[28] In spite of the review, Browne's book sold well (five English, two German, and four Latin editions), but so did Yonge's denunciation, which was reprinted in 1687 and 1692. As with most of the medical controversies of the day, the professional and personal battles between doctors were fought in print.

Given all the authorial chicanery and plagiarism in English scientific circles, original work deserves particular praise. Harvey's *De motu cordis et sanguinis*, published in 1628, has been called by K. F. Russell "the greatest single contribution to anatomy and medicine in any century." Russell applauds Harvey's devising "simple, clear-cut and conclusive" experiments that could easily be replicated. Yet, even Harvey felt free to copy two plates of the veins from the anatomy of Caspar Bauhin; Bauhin in turn based his illustrations on pictures in the work of Girolamo Fabrici, the discoverer of the valves of the veins and the professor at Padua with whom Harvey had studied.[29] Since Harvey wanted his findings readily available to the European market, he had the book first issued in Frankfurt; it went through edition after edition and along with Harvey's other great work, *De generatione*, established his celebrity. *Anatomical Exercises . . . concerning the Motion of the Heart and Blood,* the English version, came forth from the presses of Francis Leach for Richard Lowndes in 1653. James Young printed the English edition of *De generatione* as *Anatomical Exercitations* in 1653 for Octavian Pulleyn, who was among the more prominent seventeenth-century London publishers of anatomical literature and the recipient of 131 of his father's copyrights. The controversy Harvey's findings engendered actually aroused more anatomical research and provoked the anticirculationists, some of whom flourished in Britain as late as 1700 and publish rebuttals.[30]

Likewise innovative and authentic in his research, Thomas Willis was a boon to mid-Stuart medical publishing, providing printers with plenty of material for new books. Willis's *Cerebri anatome* made a triple debut in London in 1664, appearing from the presses of James Flesher (Fletcher) and Thomas Roycroft, to be sold at the Bell in St. Paul's Churchyard by successful partners in the trade John Martyn and James Allestry, booksellers to the Royal Society, whose shop "was the resort of the wealthy and the learned."[31] Martyn and Allestry always looked for the most important ventures to bolster, including John Ray's *Catalogus plantarum* and Robert Hooke's *Micrographia*; they published over thirty scientific books and the *Philosophical Transactions of the Royal Society*. Their reputation rested on their scientific inventory at the Bell, which introduced new ideas to enthusiasts of Restoration scholarship.[32] Willis's observations surely qualified as a major publishing event. His multipart *Remaining Medical Works* (1681) contained the first appearance in English of his *Anatomy of the Brain*, translated by Samuel Pordage. Among a quartet of publishers for whom the collection was printed is S. Martyn, surely related to John.[33] In 1689 Thomas Basset repackaged the Willis oeuvre as *The London Practice of Physick*.

William Croone, M.D. by royal mandate in 1662, gave anatomy lectures at the Barber-Surgeons' Hall, succeeding Charles Scarburgh in that position. A zealous promoter of the Royal Society, which he served as its first registrar, Croone read many papers to the Fellows, including "A Discourse on the Conformation of a Chick in the Egg before Incubation."[34] Despite an extensive practice in London and the requisite doctorate, Croone did not obtain membership in the Royal College of Physicians until 1675, after waiting twelve years for admission. Croone wrote *De ratione motus musculorum*, a thirty-four page treatise printed in 1664 by John Hayes and sold by Samuel Thompson at the Sign of the Bishop. Hayes, one of the eleven pressmen who drew up a petition in 1660 for the incorporation of printers into a body distinct from the Company of Stationers, and Thompson were both ruined in the Fire of 1666. Ensuing editions of Croone's work were incorporated into the much larger tomes of Thomas Willis. The indispensable publications of Harvey, Willis, and Croone subsequently spurred excitement about anatomical studies, a fact not lost on London bookmen.

Another stimulus to the study of anatomy was the emphasis put on teaching and collaborative research. After the Civil War, renewed interest in intellectual and social reform drew aspiring intellectuals from all sides of the political spectrum to the capital. The College of Physicians, the Barber-Surgeons' Company, and the Society of Apothecaries all took on educational and scientific functions while maintaining their concern with professional matters. Members of the College embarked on anatomical research projects, many inspired by addresses and public meetings, first at Amen Corner of Paternoster Row, and at Warwick Lane after the Great Fire and rebuilding of the collegiate premises. Francis Glisson's monograph on the liver originated in a designated study of rickets by a College committee; he dedicated *Anatomia Hepatis* to his colleagues.[35] Likewise, Thomas Wharton's systematic study of the glands commenced with the encouragement of the College President and evolved during discussions at the College's anatomical lectures; he, too, expressed gratitude to the Fellows.[36]

Gresham College, an educational institution in London established in the 1570s through the largesse of the founder of the Royal Exchange, Sir Thomas Gresham, was better suited to provide for lay education in science. Seven lecturers staffed Gresham, including a professor of physic who was usually a Fellow of the College of Physicians; Matthew Gwinne held that appointment first from 1598 to 1607. Many of the faculty focused on the practical applications of their disciplines, like the use of mathematics for merchants and seamen, and there was a Puritan flavor to Gresham's professorate, as professors in the Elizabeth and Jacobean eras were required to be unmarried scholars. Gresham teachers Henry Briggs, Samuel Foster, and Henry Gellibrand published their popular lectures in astronomy and geometry to considerable acclaim; even Gellibrand's servant, William Beale, got into print with an almanac in 1631 which supplanted Catholic saints with Protestant martyrs.[37] Politics intervened by the late 1630s, and as some of Gresham's more competent scholars vacated the college, the institution took on the appearance of "an almshouse for eccentric old bachelors."[38] Nonetheless, the anatomy lectures of Padua M.D. Thomas Winston, professor of physic from 1615 to 1642, were important enough to be published after his death, and Jonathan Goddard's iatro-chemical experiments while on the Gresham faculty led to his invention of the volatile apoplexy drops that bear his name.[39]

Anatomical instruction given at the Barber-Surgeons' Hall also enjoyed considerable popularity. By 1700, however, the barber-surgeons had much more difficulty obtaining the bodies of executed criminals, so private anatomy schools sprang up in London. Students turned to St. Thomas's and St. Bartholomew's hospitals, where surgical apprenticeships could be entered into for less than the seven years required by the Company. Many surgeons advertised courses of anatomy in the London newspapers, and as the demand for legally dissectable cadavers outdistanced supply, they sometimes fought over corpses with the beadles of the Barber-Surgeons Company at the foot of the scaffold.[40] Therefore, despite the occasional successes of the London vocational organizations, the most important medical and scientific activities seemed to transpiring outside those institutions.

Throughout the fractious seventeenth century, physicians and scientists debated the conceptual and professional issues condensed around the foundations and practice of medicine. Some of them imagined a larger role for the government in health care. One of the first books to fasten on the idea of a national medical service was Robert Burton's *Anatomy of Melancholy*, published in 1621.[41] Burton envisioned an ideal kingdom that supported hospitals freed from capricious and sometimes corrupt philanthropists, one where medical students of all stripes might rely on the public treasury for their education. Likewise, following the continental example of intellectuals establishing formal academies, English sages in the 1640s hoped to revive Francis Bacon's utopian concept of a state-patronized brotherhood of learned men—a universal college—and create an idealized "Solomon's House," in which the new science could be discussed.[42] In 1645 at the instigation of Theodore Haak, a former pupil of Henry Briggs, a politically heterogenous group that included academically qualified physicians like Glisson and Goddard, as well as mathematicians such as John Wallis and John Wilkins, began to meet regularly, sometimes after Samuel Foster's lectures at Gresham and on other occasions at Goddard's lodgings.

Simultaneous with the meetings of the 1645 group arose the so-called Invisible College associated with Robert Boyle, his correspondents, especially saltpeter entrepreneur Benjamin Worsley, and their mutual obsession with practical chemistry and technological innovation.[43] Dating from the summer of 1646, the letter-writers in this geographically challenged fraternity pledged themselves to social action and more partisan political involvement despite the miles that separated them. There is evidence that Boyle's sister, Lady Katherine Ranelagh, exerted as much influence as any of the males in the group and that her home in Pall Mall served as a meeting place for its associates. Moreover, her numerous acquaintances, especially Irish Protestants in exile and Presbyterian Parliamentarians, provided new associates for Boyle and his circle. Boyle's band took on a medical cast when, in 1647, Worsley procured an appointment as Surgeon-General to the army in Ireland and the Dutch brothers Gerard and Arnold Boate, both doctors in conflict with College of Physicians and Baconian enthusiasts, joined the clique.

In the midst of all the activity associated with the 1645 Group and the Invisible College, reformer Samuel Hartlib tried to resurrect the idea of a Universal College using the model of the Parisian Office of Address. He hoped that native and foreign inventors and innovators of products useful to mankind and conducive to good health could be enticed to continue their work in England under state sponsorship. A key confidant of Hartlib's was Nicholas

Culpeper, who voiced initial pessimism that the state would patronize such an agency. Nonetheless, Culpeper lobbied the Independent Members of Parliament, and other associates pulled what strings they could. In 1647 Parliament voted £300 to Hartlib for the Office of Address, but despite his apparent successes with legislative and executive leaders, the convoluted financing of Hartlib's "Colledge of Noble Mechaniques and Ingenious Artificers" proved its undoing. Though stymied with his plans for state involvement in the promotion of medicine, the sciences, and technology, Hartlib turned to private initiative as a way to further public good.[44]

The opinionated tenor of the times colored medical philosophy and vice versa, all of which found its way into print. Among the factors which stimulated the growth of medical publishing at mid-century was the collapse of both censorship and medical licensing. In general, the Puritan-Parliamentary coalition expressed an ideological commitment to medical reform and health literature published in the vernacular. English Puritans believed in a revival of learning, an antidote to the corrupt medical philosophy of the "heathens" that was perfectly consistent with an anticipated political utopia.[45] Parliamentarians agreed that a new medical age was imminent, one that augured both the greater sovereignty of citizens and practical health care. They applauded the efforts of Nicholas Culpeper to lift the veil of linguistic secrecy from medical arcana and destroy the monopoly of the College of Physicians. Culpeper specifically referred to the inevitable triumph of "the liberty of the subject," once that subject had access to facts that better informed his medical choices.[46] Those facts included London deaths, found in the newspaper *Perfect Occurrences*, whose creator, Parliamentary propagandist Henry Walker, led the way in regularly printing the Bills of Mortality. Royalists, who appreciated the reflected hierarchy of an organization like the College of Physicians and the licensing control it had exercised over the profession, warned of calamity should the College's authority collapse. Academic physicians like Harvey, Willis, and Glisson continued to publish in Latin.

But just as publishers of medical books showed themselves to be pragmatists in the marketplace, so, too, did many of the writers of medical works display a surprising flexibility in iatric philosophy that defies easy categorization. The Fellows of the Royal Society offer an ideal case in point. The foundation in 1663 of the Royal Society of London for Improving of Natural Knowledge illustrates yet another "location" outside the professional medical organizations where intellectual affairs took place.[47] Its origins are obscured by conflicting record-keeping, but 1658 or 1659 seems a reasonable birthdate for the nucleus of what became the Royal Society. Early participants included a group of scholars from Oxford meeting at Gresham College as well as a few London physicians and mathematicians. Eventually, the cluster that formed around the Oxford Club included diverse members from the College of Physicians, the Gresham College faculty, the 1645 Group, and Hartlib's Agency. Half of its founding members tended towards puritanism and had collaborated with the parliamentary regime; half embraced Anglicanism and had been intransigent opponents. No wonder the Royal Society, eager to avoid contentious questions, manifest from the outset an "extremely mixed religious and political constitution."[48] The Society employed its own printers, Samuel Smith and Benjamin Walford, prominent London publishers who also issued the works of Robert Boyle.

Some of the more famous intellectuals associated with science and medicine grappled openly with the political implications of the iatric science they practiced and with the medical implications of their politics, trying to meld the two philosophical positions into one coherent pattern of activity. Consider the publishing activity of a trio of titans: Boyle, Thomas Sydenham, and John Locke. None of them had conventional medical credentials: only Sydenham obtained an M.D. (from Cambridge), but then not until he had been licensed by the Royal College of Physicians for thirteen years.[49] They were connected by bonds of mutual friendship and intellectual respect that transcended their political and medical philosophies; all found, after some exploration, a sort of middle medical ground.

Robert Boyle, fourteenth child of the first Earl of Cork, straddled the English political harbor like a colossus. Though not a doctor, Boyle weighed in on the merits of chemical medicine in *The Skeptical Chymist*, published in 1661 by John Crooke, London bookseller and the King's Printer in Dublin.[50] Despite his own love of the laboratory and leadership in bringing Helmontian chemistry to England, Boyle tacitly supported the claims of elites and castigated the methods of many iatrochemists.[51] He criticized what he saw as the insolent overextension of a few experiments by "vulgar chymists" into a grand system: "I fear that the too confident opinion of the doctrine I question has made divers practitioners of physick, make wrong estimates of medicines."[52] Boyle objected to these unknown experimenters creating a new philosophy out of simple notions, of subjecting the entire universe to mere laboratory techniques, but he also disdained "manual operators" who lacked philosophical principles all together. Just as the learned physicians in the College remonstrated uneducated irregulars, so did Boyle chide ignoble technicians for lowering the status of chemistry to ordinary pharmacy and besmirching the reputation of adepts like himself. As historian Michael Hunter has recently suggested, Boyle maintained a medical pluralism.[53]

The influence of the *Skeptical Chymist* can be seen in the work of other critics of obscure empiricists, like that of Boyle's friend George Castle, a physician and Fellow of the Royal Society. In 1667 booksellers Henry and Timothy Twyford published Castle's *The Chymical Galenist*, a specific attack on the anti-Galenic diatribe of Commonwealth journalist Marchamont Nedham, *Medela medicinae*, but which extended his arguments to the full-scale feud between chemical doctors and the College of Physicians. Like Boyle, he found the "conjuring, unintelligible words of the chymists" offensive; the words he lists as obnoxious are all associated with Paracelsian or Helmontian medicine.[54] At the same time, Boyle eagerly anticipated new and powerful medicines that might come forth from traditional alchemy, while chastizing narrow Galenism. Advocates of chemical therapy thought he was their friend, not the College Fellows; Nedham cited Boyle repeatedly in *Medela medicinae* as a reformer with iconoclastic views.[55] As an adept and a hypochondriac, Boyle hoped that the Philosophers' Stone would prove itself a universal medicine. He himself inquired into an economical remedy for rickets, experimented with incalescent mercury, and exchanged recipes for potable gold with fellow chrysopoets.[56] Despite his search for physiological and pathological truth, however, a squeamish Boyle could not bring himself to carry out dissections.

Thomas Sydenham, a Puritan, dedicated his first book to Robert Boyle in 1666.[57] Sydenham's mother was killed in Dorset by a royalist in 1644; he was created Bachelor of Medicine in 1648 without studying for the degree, then went to study at Montpellier in 1659. Andrew Cunningham has argued that "Sydenham's medicine was the produce of a person highly politicized, and in a particular way; . . . his attempt to reform medicine was a contribution of politics by other means."[58] Sydenham's partisan attitudes closely resembled Cromwell's, but even with the fall of the Commonwealth, Sydenham never gave up on his political ideas and tried to exemplify the principles of the Commonwealth in his medical practice. In Cunningham's words: "His medicine was now to be the focus and expression of his politics."[59]

In particular, Sydenham fought for an understanding that symptoms of disease were complex phenomena that must be closely studied and understood before treatment could be prescribed. He professed that the body had its own powerful means of dealing with disease and that "recuperative energy which belongs to every organized being ought not to be interfered with." Physicians should assist nature in the healing process, not intrude by prescribing quack cures, and even if he cannot know the ultimate cause of any illness, the physician must still try to bring his patient relief. Sydenham managed to offend both Galenists and empiricists, although his therapeutics presuppose his avowed practical method of clinical observation.[60] Though licensed in 1663 by the College of Physicians after passing three of its exams, Sydenham never applied to the Fellowship; he also never belonged to the Royal Society. Walter Kettilby, a publisher of learned literature, handled some of Sydenham's books. Despite this low profile, Sydenham influenced John Locke more than anyone else.

According to one biographer of Locke, the great philosopher's political precepts were "deeply governed by his way of thinking as a physician."[61] Historian Peter Laslett agrees, noting that "empirical medicine, rather than philosophy, seems to be the model . . ." for Locke's comments on politics; "Locke the doctor rather than Locke the epistemologist is the man we should have in mind when we read his work on government."[62] Though Locke is better known for his connection to the "Glorious Revolution" than for his physic, it is Lockean thought that buttressed the American Declaration of Independence and resonates in Parliamentary-based governments today. Beginning in 1652, John Locke

matriculated in medicine at Christ Church College, Oxford, taking the prescribed courses in Galen and Hippocrates, but also attending the lectures of
the anti-Galenic Thomas Willis. Curiously, he said he "pitched upon the study
of medicine" to keep "as far as might be from any public conerns."[63] After a
chance meeting with Anthony Ashley Cooper, Chancellor of the Exchequer,
who had come to take the waters near Oxford, Locke left the university in
1667 without having obtained a medical degree. He became the medical operator in London to Lord Ashley, later Earl of Shaftesbury, and successfully
removed an internal abscess from his patron in 1668. The operation made
Locke famous and changed the course of his career; enjoying a political,
intellectual, and social life in the Restoration capital, Locke became a philosopher.

In that philosophy, however, one can find medical references at every turn,
used as examples in his own working out of problems and for the reader of his
published material to comprehend. For instance, Locke attributed "the well
management of public or private affairs" to "various and unknown humours . .
. ," and just as experience informs us "whether rhubarb will purge or quinquina
cure an ague," it likewise instructs about those public or private affairs.[64] Something of a medical agnostic, he penned the unpublished "De arte medica," a
treatise on the art of physic in 1669; three of his pieces appeared in the *Philosophical Transactions* of the Royal Society and he probably provided some of the
research data used by Boyle. Locke finally obtained a Bachelor of Medicine
degree from Oxford in 1675, after which, despite an academic appointment
there, he left for France. Charles II expressly expelled Locke from his post at
Christ Church in 1684.[65]

Locke met Sydenham sometime in 1667. Scholar Patrick Romanell has found
shifts in Sydenham's thought—a more critical approach to medicine—trace-
able to his friendship with Locke. Conversely, through his reading of Sydenham's
clinical notes on smallpox, Locke came to articulate in a medical context "the
very doctrine that was to characterize his whole philosophy."[66] Romanell asserts that Locke learned from Sydenham how to appreciate the empirical method
in the concrete and that theory should not affect medical practice. Sydenham's
utilitarian motto, "whatever is useful is good," became the hallmark of Lockean
philosophy.[67] The symbiotic affinity of Sydenham and Locke affected both of
their work and animated new ways of thinking about medicine and its relationship to the broader world.

Personal antipathy, sometimes based in politics or philosophy and sometimes in clashing personalities, also fired up the medical publishing scene. When
William Lilly, the self-styled "English Merlin" and writer of medical almanacs
during the mid-seventeenth century, found out that his principal rival in the
prognostication business, George Wharton, embraced royalism, he declared
himself a Parliamentarian. Though previously apolitical, Lilly may have been
motivated in his intense opposition to Wharton because they shared the same
publisher, John Partridge.[68] Perhaps Lilly's politics made him laughable to

Caroline bureaucrat Samuel Pepys, who recorded that he and some friends chortled over Lilly's prophecies in his 1667 almanac.[69] Henry Stubbe, a Warwickshire physician, wrote against the dangers to established scholars, the church, and universities posed by the new philosophy behind medicine. His own milieu included friendship with Stuart tutor and supporter of monarchical authority Thomas Hobbes, and he had royalist patrons, like Thomas Willis and Alexander Frazier. Moreover, Stubbe had served Charles II directly as king's physician in Jamaica until the mid-1660s. Conceivably these personal connections caused him to impugn John Wallis, a cryptologist for the Parliamentary party who had been rewarded by Cromwell with a sequestrated living. A confidant of Robert Boyle, the acknowledged leader of the Invisible College, Wallis participated in and reported on the planning of the Invisible College and the Royal Society, an institution to which Stubbe, an anti-apothecary essayist, strenuously objected in *Legends no Histories* (1670).[70] Stubbe, who had to pay to have his own works published because he believed his enemies blocked his works from reaching print, may also have envied Wallis for getting his books put out by Oxford's most illustrious bookman, Richard Davis, the nonpartisan investor also behind William Harvey's publications.[71]

The great Harvey had professional headaches of his own, caused by a bevy of personal and political foes who tried to discredit his reputation among contemporaries. Though Harvey had supported the creation of the Society of Apothecaries, in May 1632 he presented the Privy Council a detailed set of proposals on behalf of the College for the better supervision of druggists. The Fellows expressed concern that apothecaries gave patients drugs without a physician's prescription and cited the wrongful administration of mercury sublimate, mithridatum, and lac sulphuris in deaths reported to them. Later that year the guild filed a complaint against all collegiate physicians and Harvey in particular, accusing him of causing the death of a patient at St. Bartholomew's Hospital. The College investigated the charge, but even though Harvey was cleared of any wrongdoing, the episode caused him and the institution some embarrassment.[72]

Ironically, one specific antagonist soured on Harvey because of an unsuccessful attempt to join the College of Physicians, though Harvey himself had faced several years waiting before the College decreed in 1607 that he could practice in London. James Primrose (Primerose), a Franco-Scot who had both a Montpellier degree and court backing, could not secure candidacy to the Fellowship in 1629, the very year Harvey basked in the limelight of his lectures at the College. Stymied by the rules of admission and resentful of Harvey's celebrity, Primrose vehemently attacked him the following year in print as both a medical apostate and an official of the College. *Exercitationes in librum De motus cordis* was published in Leiden by John Maire, who also issued Harvey's *De motu*. Oddly, the Fellows maintained a conspicuous silence in the face of Primrose's vituperation, even abstaining from comment when a foreign supporter of Harvey's defended his discovery of circulation.[73]

Another prominent rival of Harvey's was John Clarke, an M.D. from Cambridge who occupied the post of second physician at St. Bartholomew's Hospital. Harvey, chief physician to the hospital, was so often at court tending to the king's health that the secondary position had to be created; evidently Clarke did the lion's share of ministering to the sick there. Whatever hard feelings that situation might have engendered were exacerbated by the politics of the Civil War. Harvey followed the court on its movements around the country, while Clarke, a Parliamentarian, remained in the capital organizing medical aid for the Parliamentary army. For his services, the House of Commons tried unsuccessfully to supplant Harvey at St. Bartholomew's with Clarke's son-in-law. Moreover, Clarke's increasing prestige in London resulting from the war led to his election as President of the College of Physicians in 1645. Meanwhile, Harvey was denied a request to visit the imprisoned Charles I in 1648 and was even required to get Parliamentary permission in 1650 to attend a patient in London. Despite Harvey's devotion to the College, he refused to attend meetings of the Fellows during Clarke's term of office and did not resume his duties at St. Bartholomew's.[74]

Disparagement of Harvey's standing as an anatomical physician continued after his death. Some Helmontians stubbornly deprecated the importance of anatomy altogether, perhaps irritated that a learned man like Harvey had made such a breakthrough discovery. Marchamont Nedham, who became a practicing physician after the Stuart restoration, wrote in *Medela medicinae* that the study of anatomy was useless, complaining that physicians like Harvey slighted chemistry in their pursuit of anatomical information.[75] The aforementioned Henry Stubbe set out in 1670 to examine whether or not Harvey was "the first inventor of the circulation of the blood." He argued that if one examined certain passages in the ancients—Hippocrates, Plato, and Aristotle—the foundation of Harvey's "discovery" could be discerned in their work. In fact, as Stubbe insisted in *Plus Ultra Reduced to a Non Plus*, some modern anatomists clearly beat Harvey to the finish line. At the end of the sixteenth century, Andreas Caesalpinus of Tuscany anticipated Harvey, not only discovering "this motion of the blood (even through the lungs) but giving it the name of *circulatio sanguinis*." According to Stubbe, Harvey merely took "up this opinion from my author."[76] Luckily, some of Harvey's formerly reticent friends began to speak out in his defense, acclaimed medical men like Francis Glisson, Thomas Willis, and Richard Lower, who carried on his investigatory tradition. Moreover, his two major works, *De motu cordis* and *De generatione*, exercised great influence and were widely read even beyond medical circles.

Hence, Harvey's career encapsulated the various medico-political controversies of his age. As an applicant to the College Fellowship, he ran into the kinds of roadblocks critics complained kept too few physicians among London's burgeoning populace. As an officer of the College, Harvey locked horns with the apothecaries over questions of medical jurisdiction and precedence, and as a Stuart royal physician he faced the wrath of the Puritan-Parliamentary party, which facilitated the attempt by his enemies to tarnish Harvey's eminence. As an English medical celebrity, Harvey endured denigration of his achievements while alive, detractions which continued long after his death. Politics of all sorts played a part in the establishment of Harvey's reputation: his connection with Charles I first helped, then hurt his career, but when Charles II reclaimed the throne, the Harveian legend finally took shape.[77]

Another level of political bickering, apart from that generated between ambitious royalists and parliamentarians, separated the traditional doctors in the College from the government of the City of London. As an extra-municipal corporation, the College failed to establish a dominant position among the civic institutions of the capital, giving way to the Barber-Surgeons' Company and the Grocers' Company. Exempt from community responsibilities which other associations fulfilled, like serving on the Common Council or the Court of Aldermen, the College never enjoyed more than indifferent relations with City authorities and was little consulted in times of public health emergencies. Many complained that, in addition to abdicating its obligations to the collective well-being of London, the genteel physicians of the College, purportedly accompanying their aristocratic patients, deserted the metropolis at the first appearance of epidemics. No wonder Londoners relied on surgeons, apothecaries, and mountebanks during plague years, consuming large quantities of panaceas concocted by quacks.[78]

Although questions of turf still pertained after the Stuart restoration, the arguments that found their way into print had to do with the new philosophy of medicine associated with the "virtuosi," or rivals of the College Fellows, versus the traditional ways of "physic" practiced by men sensitive to change. As Harold Cook has argued, these medical debates encompassed more than physiology or healing techniques; they spurned the natural philosophy upon which learned medicine was based. The virtuosi promoted natural history rather than philosophy and plumped for quicker curative discoveries, challenging the university-trained doctors' belief that therapeutic medicine alone would not suffice. Learned physicians saw the virtuosi as philistines and allies of medical quacks.[79]

Henry Stubbe spoke for traditional medicine in his books attacking the proponents of the new philosophy and the Royal Society which housed them. Some historians have suggested that Stubbe was hired as a penman by the College Fellows to defend the traditional medical preparation and authority of the "ancients" against the "moderns."[80] However, his discounting Harvey's discovery of circulation shows that royalists were not monolithic in their medical opinions or steadfast in their allegiances. Some who have studied Stubbe have emphasized the influence on him of Hobbesian thought—not Hobbes the monarchist, however, but Hobbes the social contract theorist. They suggest that Stubbe actually articulated the dangers of materialism and capitalism abiding in the Royal Society while promoting broad-minded fellowship.[81]

Among the handful of bookmen who dominated the printing and selling of medical works during the later Stuart era, Samuel Smith, a Tory publisher, must rank at the top. Alone or with the name of his partner, Benjamin Walford, Smith's name was attached to nearly fifty medical publications from the mid 1680s to 1707. He and Walford, who was a prominent auctioneer, functioned as the official printers for the Royal Society, dedicated to the promotion of experimental learning, and were noted for their association with foreign books. Their shop was located at the Prince's Arms in St. Paul's Churchyard, the most favored location for bookstores before and after the Great Fire.[82] That situated them close to the College of Physicians in nearby Warwick Lane. At first Smith created folio and quarto-sized, deluxe editions in Latin, works that were clearly aimed at the preferred community of university-trained physicians, but by the early 1690s several translated versions of medical works appeared with Smith's imprint, and by 1700 the overwhelming majority of his titles were smaller-sized editions, written in English for the layman.[83] Smith and Walford segued into publishing books and pamphlets that may have sabotaged the control of the College of Physicians; however, a few of the authors of their self-help manuals, like Dr. George Bate, were themselves Fellows of the College.[84] In short, Samuel Smith's conservative politics did not invariably govern his medical book business.

Second only to Smith in the number of medical works published during the later Stuarts was Walter Kettilby. Kettilby ordinarily specialized in religious titles, but he set his imprint on and sold many Latin medical works in folio from his shop at the Bishop's Head in St. Paul's Churchyard. In 1675 he distributed a vindication of the College of Physicians and in 1686 an attack on a pamphlet condemning the College. Nonetheless, a number of the titles in Kettilby's later inventory implies greater publishing pragmatism. For example, he published several pieces by Thomas Sydenham, the practical English physician concerned with the classification of symptoms. Although regarded today as the "English Hippocrates," Sydenham studied under French physicians at Montpellier; he was little favored by his professional colleagues or by the Stuarts because of his military service for Parliament in the Civil War. Despite his extensive London practice, the College admitted him only as a licentiate, never as a fellow, probably because Sydenham disdained interference in the natural healing process.[85] Besides Sydenham's titles, Kettilby furnished an "Englished" version of Frenchman Nicholas Lemery's *Universal Pharmacopoeia* in 1700 and three editions of Lemery's *A Course in Chymistry*, translated from the French. Incidentally, the Lemery translator was Walter Harris, M.D., Fellow of the College, Charles II and William III's physician-in-ordinary, and something of a pragmatist himself.[86]

Daniel Brown was one of the most prolific publishers of works that directly and perhaps deliberately jeopardized medical orthodoxy. Among the titles that Brown handled were books on apoplexy, gout, bones, and snakebite. He allied with Sir John Colbatch, author of more than a dozen books on7health and a vigorous pamphleteer on behalf of "experimental philosophy."[88] Brown presented most of Colbatch's tracts in octavo or twelves, indicating that the edition was likely meant for the reading public and not for professional medicos. Brown also produced a number of foreign texts, translated into English, at moderate prices, usually two to three shillings. His shop was just outside Temple Bar, the western limits of the City, suggesting distance from the medical establishment. Brown's list seemed to pose an undeviating threat to metropolitan physicians, however, even though his inventory mingled in some Latin texts, a few by Colbatch himself.

A fourth medical publisher worth noting is Henry Bonwicke. Many of his titles promoted self-diagnosis or at least promulgated medical awareness. From his first imprints in Everard Maynwaring's books on pain (1678–82) to his 1707 production of a second edition of John Pechey's herbal, Bonwicke featured inexpensive, English-language health manuals. He made several books by Thomas Sydenham available, but, like Brown, he carried Latin medical texts, and like the more conservative Kettilby, his shop was in St. Paul's Churchyard. Right behind Bonwicke in the number of medical tomes is Thomas Basset, a seller often identified with legal tomes and maps; Plomer said that Basset was "chiefly remembered for the Catalogue of Law Books which he published in 1673."[88] Nonetheless, Basset published medical works by Maynwaring, Thomas Cocke's *Kitchen Physick,* and *Treatise of the Eyes* by William Read, an itinerant quack who claimed to be an oculist and was knighted by Queen Anne. Basset's Fleet Street shop also carried several Latin texts. Additionally, Basset released *The Art of Restoring Health* by M. Flamand and *The London Practice of Physick* by Thomas Willis, another Fellow of the College with a lucrative London practice and a leading proponent of clinical observation. Like other late seventeenth-century authors and publishers, Basset hoped to appeal to all sides of the medical debate.

Recognizing the potential market for a periodical devoted solely to medicine, Basset edited and published the first such journal, *Medicina Curiosa,* the premier issue of which appeared on 17 June 1684. Historian F.N.L. Poynter avowed that as "a periodical devoted exclusively to medicine, . . . *Medicina Curiosa* has no rival."[89] Its entire title was *Medicina Curiosa, or a Variety of New Communications in Physick, Chirurgery, and Anatomy, from the Ingenious of Many Parts of Europe and from Other Parts of the World,* no doubt intended to pique the interest of all constituents in the substantial audience for a medical gazette. In the preface to the first issue, Basset explained the mission of his periodical:

> I thought it might not be an unacceptable labour for me, if I undertook constantly to give Accounts both of what is printed by direction of publick societies . . . and likewise what is contain'd in the Books of Physick daily set forth by

particular men. I design to be pretty short in the Accounts of the Theory, and larger upon the practical part.[90]

In *Medicina Curiosa* Basset resolved to provide readers with a summary of existing medical publications rather than a vehicle for original works. Moreover, Basset's pledge to limit the recondite interpretations of medical theory while concentrating on practical aspects of medicine indicates that he likely meant to cater to non-traditional healers and the laity. Aware that his publication might incite the wrath of the College Fellows, Basset demurred that he "might be guilty of a Culpepperism, as to advise all Persons to be their own Physicians." He merely intended to provide "when the best methods have effected little some satisfaction to sick men's minds to pursue a Book of Physick." Further defusing potential controversy, Basset promised to defer in all his advice to the sick to the College, "whom the World will own for Great and meet Judges in matters belonging to their Art."

Only two issues of *Medicina Curiosa* ultimately appeared, no doubt diminishing an historical acknowledgment of its significance.[91] The content of those two issues, however, explains the medical contest over beliefs and bailiwick in laymen's terms. In the first issue, fifty-six pages in length, Basset assembled pieces on medicine, surgery, and anatomy from authors in London, Leiden, and Rome. An aural theme dominates this edition, with several selections concerning hearing. Basset himself wrote the opening entry, translated from a French scientific journal, describing the work of Louis XIV's doctor Joseph du Verney on the anatomy of the ear. Basset commented in a second essay that the Gallic physician used both Galenic and chemical methods treating ear disorders, bleeding, purging, and injecting the patient with various decoctions. A third entry summarizes two new ways to improve hearing and describes a sort of stethoscope. Another piece in the first edition contains the case studies of an unidentified surgeon, notably one on the death of a man bitten by a rabid cat. From Basset's description, it is clear that the surgeon accelerated the poor man's demise, cauterizing the puncture wound and prescribing ferocious emetics. Other articles in the eclectic first issue instructively recount the way urine passes into the bladder and an anatomy book review.

The second issue of *Medicina Curiosa* came out on 23 October 1684. Like the first number, its contents embraced extracts from books translated by Basset along with his editorial commentary, and clustered around a specific subject: fever. He assimilated a number of possible treatments for febrile patients, including mercury, cinchona, and wine, as well as treatments recommended by various French authorities, including the maverick practitioner Nicholas de Blegny.[92] Basset also reported on the gloomy statistics in the General Bill of Christenings and Burials with its disproportionate tally of births to deaths, nearly 6,000 more of the latter than the former. He noted that most of those deaths were attributed to consumption, fevers, and smallpox.[93] Basset clearly intended to publish a third issue of the periodical, alluding to its next appearance at the end of Number 2. Though no other issues were forthcoming, Basset remained active in publishing long after his journal's demise; he put out John Locke's *Essay Concerning Human Understanding* in 1690.

Consider next in our list of politically unpredictable medical printers Robert Clavell, a known Tory but publisher of *Every Man His Own Doctor* and *Physick for Families*. Clavell, at the Cross Keys in Little Britain, sold everything from arcane Latin books on hysteria and hypochondria to *The Sick Christian's Companion*. It was he who compiled the *Catalogue of All Books Printed in England since 1666*, the basis for *The Term Catalogues*.[94] Other prominent Tory publishers of medical titles were the husband and wife team of Henry and Joanna Brome, who put out several works by Ambrose Paré and advertised pills against all diseases, and Benjamin Tooke, responsible for two editions of Richard Wiseman's surgical writings. George Sawbridge and his wife Hannah, who succeeded him in their printing business at the Bible on Ludgate Hill, published divers works by medical iconoclast Nicholas Culpeper, most notably *Medicaments for the Poor* in 1669 and a 1679 edition in octavo of *Pharmacopoeia Londinensis or the London Dispensatory*. But Sawbridge was no renegade himself. Besides being treasurer to the Company of Stationers, he became a partner after the Restoration in the King's Printing House, holding shares in some of the most lucrative publications of the day.

Prominent Whig publisher Awnsham Churchill and his brother John printed medical handbooks in the vernacular encompassing several anatomy texts, treatises on muscles and blood, and works by Culpeper, including *A Directory for Midwives* and *The English Physician*. In 1702 the Churchills generated an inexpensive version of the *London Pharmacopoeia* in twelves. Yet their inventory contained a diatribe against Dr. Colbatch as well as Latin aphorisms by Martin Lister, Fellow of the College and court physician for William III and Queen Anne. Though the Churchills' partisanship surely dovetailed with John Locke, whose works they published, their business practices and those of their colleagues drove him to distraction. In 1704 Locke complained in a letter to a friend that "books seem to be pestilent things, and infect all that trade in them . . . with something very perverse and brutal. Printers, binders, sellers, and others that make a trade and gain out of them have . . . a corruption of mind . . . not conformed to the good of society. . . ."[95]

Though he moved to the Bell in St. Paul's Churchyard and into partnership with James Allestry after the Fire, John Martyn continued to run another Bell just outside Temple Bar. From there he handled many books which dealt directly with the medical establishment, such as Jonathan Goddard's pamphlet (1670) on the troubles besetting the practice of physick and the College's official version of the *London Pharmacopoeia* (1677). Despite this shop's relative distance from the elite medical community, the bulk of Martyn's iatric titles were Latin works aimed at the College Fellows. On the other hand, the publications of Martyn's contemporary, George Conyers, merit attention, particularly the cheap, practical manuals that were the focus of his business. From his shop in Little Britain, he printed and sold "pocket companions" for tuppence, booklets that explained various diseases, taught blood-letting, and asserted the medicinal value of eating fish. Last but by no means least, Dorman Newman, whose shop was part of a knot of Whiggish booksellers on the Poultry, published treatises on gout, muscles, and good health in English, but two in Latin. He also printed and stocked *Medela Medicorum . . . an Enquiry into Reasons of the Contempt of Physicians* (1678) in twelves by the nearly anonymous S. W.

At least one of the periodicals that Newman printed, *Mercurius Reformatus*, contained dozens of advertisements for the medical publications that Newman and others disseminated.[96] (See Fig. 7.1.) Dr. James Welwood, author of the Williamite journal of opinion, implicitly encouraged the anti-establishment effect of these works despite his own active membership in the Royal College of Physicians. He embodies the ambiguity of the medical debate in London. Though himself the product of a traditional Galenic curriculum at the University of Reims, as a physician-in-ordinary to the Dual Monarchs and superintendent of the surgeons in the fleet, Welwood supported the medical reform program for the military envisioned by the king, a program which advocated a more systematized approach to battlefield wounds. Such systemization, associated more with surgeons and clinically trained doctors, clashed with the principles of most English physicians prepared in medicine at Oxford and Cambridge. Civilian doctors may have had the luxury of individualizing patient diagnosis and delegating actual treatment to a surgeon or apothecary, but military medicine combined surgery and treatment directed toward the rapid recovery of a sizeable clientele. The government's medical reforms favored empirical theories and pharmaceutical specifics. Welwood's newspaper touted such irregular products as liquid snuff for headaches, a massage oil for lunatics, and a licorice extract for colds, none of them his own concoctions; in fact, Welwood never published any medical work, treatise, or recipes of his own.[97]

Besides these aforementioned printers and sellers of numerous books about medicine, there were dozens of other London bookmen from all sides of the political and religious spectrum who made some medical material available to the reading public. Although their individual outputs did not exceed a dozen medical titles, collectively they produced some of the most influential volumes. Within any list of popular medical selections should be a quartet of octavos marketed by Andrew Bell: two editions of Francois Mauriceau's book about childbirth, translated by famed English accoucheur Hugh Chamberlen; a description of simple medicines translated from the French; and a dissertation on Bath waters by William Oliver. Among the few medical items in John Harris' merchandise at his shop in the Poultry was "The Treasury of Druggs Unlock'd" by Joseph James Berlie. Jacobite Bookseller Joseph Hindmarsh vended apothecary Robert Talbor's "The English Remedy," a supposedly secret cure for agues that was really Jesuits' Bark or cinchona, renamed for a new commercial cycle and no longer a secret. Many stores stocked recipe books like Thomas Fuller's *Pharmacopoeia Extemporanea, Dr. Willis' Receipts for the Cure of All Distempers,* or the Countess of Kent's *Manual of Secrets in Physick and Chirurgery.* Titles concerning the use of antimony and tincture of coral, the curse of the French pox, and the long-lasting effects of sea disease and "looseness" were common-place in London bookshops.

Uncommon was Charles Allen's book, *Operator for the Teeth,* the first den-tal book in English; it was published first in York in 1685, but sold in London by William Whitwood, whom bookman John Dunton quipped was a "rolling printer," as much for his engravings and to his constant changes of address.[98] Whitwood's frequent moves, though usually all around Duck Lane, could not have enhanced the sales of Allen's book. Dentistry belonged to the realm of surgery, "a difficult part," according to the author.[99] Allen offered suggestions on how to restore teeth in young or old, what to do about toothache, and how to preserve teeth and gums from all accidents. He included a section of the use of the "polican," the "instrument wherewith they are drawn on all occasions," as well as a discussion on the circulation of the blood as opined by Galen, Richard Lower, and Thomas Willis. William Salmon, an empiric often the object of professional ridicule, included dental sections in his *Ars Chirurgica,* a seven-volume compendium published in 1698 by John Dawks and sold by a number of book dealers. Twelve plates precede the main text and depict eight dental instruments. Seven of the eight are copies of German surgeon Johann Scultetus', and the eighth instrument is a "pelican" or "polychon." (See Fig. 3.3.) Evidently, Salmon did not practice dentistry, but his book contains a good deal of information about teeth and their treatment, including graphic descriptions of extractions, artificial teeth, and whitening with sulfuric acid. Salmon warns patients that "all sweet things, as sugar, honey, (which have in them a radical acid), raisons, figs sweetmeats and confections, rot and totally spoil the teeth." He remarked that most confectioners have rotten teeth, "for the very fumes of sugar destroy them."[100]

Taking all this information to heart, ordinary Londoners, understandably concerned about health matters, diagnosed and prescribed for themselves. Samuel Pepys composed rules for his own physical well-being that he proposed to live by: 1) to keep warm; 2) to "strain as little as ever I can backwards . . . ;" 3) "either by physic forward or by clyster backward, or both ways, to get an easy and plentiful going to stool and breaking of wind;" 4) to take precautions "when I begin to become costive and bound, and by all means to keep my body loose. . . ."[101] Bookstore aficionados like Pepys customarily availed themselves of printed advice about health.

Can we presume anything about the intentions of the publishers of such medical materials? Probably not, other than their goal of making money by selling books with plenty of appeal. Although a few of the bookmen who printed and sold medical tracts specialized in chapbooks and cheap literature, others were just as likely to concentrate on more expensive science books or plays or music. Most of the larger publishers, regardless of religio-political associations, were absolutely catholic in their lists.[102] Bookmen put out Galenic classics and shelved them alongside Paracelsian and Helmontian attacks on the Galenists.

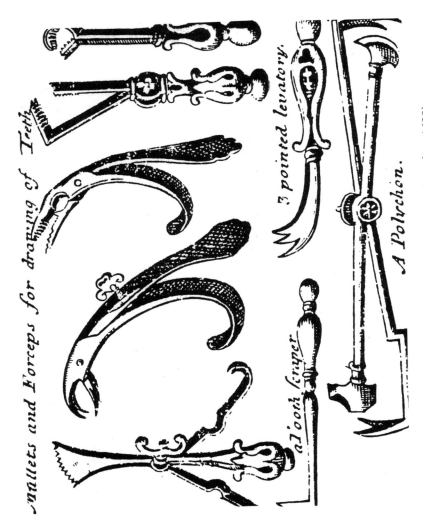

mallets and Forceps for drawing of Teeth

3 pointed levatory.

a Tooth scraper

A Polychon.

3.3. Dental instruments. In William Salmon, *Ars Chirurgica* (London, 1698).

The same publishers produced the works of contemporary medical men and women diametrically opposed in beliefs and status, in fact, their support of these printed debates energized the philosophical and personal controversies which in turn vitalized the marketplace for medical literature. No hard and fast generalizations about the political preferences of pressmen and women can be maintained. In short, even notorious Whig printers did not exclusively spawn anti-establishment medical books nor did more conservative publishers invariably embrace the notion of a medical hierarchy and proselytize for the College of Physicians. Those publishers whose lists abound with iconoclastic titles which challenged the medical establishment hedged their bets with the occasional conciliatory or esoteric book aimed at the professional; booksellers who carried Latin texts also stocked the latest popular manuals. These printers and sellers may have been part of, or even instigators of a restyling of the medical world, but there is little concrete evidence that anything other than the profit motive spurred them to action.

Chapter 4

PROFIT OR PRINCIPLE? RELIGION, PUBLISHING, AND MEDICINE

Setting off a lively discussion among historians that shows no signs of abating, sociologist Robert K. Merton consigned his name in the 1930s to a theory that associated Puritan thought with the flowering of English science. Attempting to explain the growth of interest in Tudor-Stuart science and technology, Merton sought to identify a causal hypothesis and found that religion, specifically Puritanism, "provided major . . . support in that historical time and place."[1] A generation later, expanding the Merton thesis to include medicine, Allen Debus linked the acceptance of Paracelsianism in England with the "Puritan Revolution" of the 1640s. Debus contended that prior to that time, practical-minded doctors distrusted even useful Paracelsian remedies, because they associated those remedies with mystical alchemy and occultism. Whatever compromise among the College Fellows led to the 1618 *London Pharmacopoeia* contained only a very small Paracelsian component, since Galenists absolutely rejected the "speculative chemical cosmology and medicine of the Paracelsians."[2]

Medical historian Charles Webster, however, has located the impetus for iatric remodeling well before 1640, even as early as the last quarter of the sixteenth century. He disagrees with Debus that before the Civil War the impact of Paracelsian reform was imperceptible, and he demonstrates substantial immersion in chemical pharmacology among Elizabethan doctors and scholars. They collected the works of Paracelsus and thoroughly assimilated his ideas by 1600; even Shakespeare commented on the polarization of medical practitioners into Galenic and Paracelsian camps.[3] While Webster conforms to the premise that Protestantism facilitated Paracelsianism, albeit earlier than the Civil War, he posits the additional explanation that foreign travel, sometimes spurred by religious exile, exposed English medical students to empiricism at iconoclastic continental academies.[4]

Other scholars, nonetheless, have found reasons to concur with the historical judgment that God-fearing reform dominated the religio-iatric connection in the mid-seventeenth century when fratricidal warfare cemented the alliance between radical Protestantism and chemical medicine. Hugh Trevor-Roper concluded that the Puritan Revolution undermined whatever medical compromise had been achieved in the College of Physicians between Anglican Galenists and Puritan Paracelsians.[5] Nevertheless, revisionist Peter Elmer has challenged the nexus between Puritanism and science or medicine altogether, arguing that the radicalism of the Puritans has been exaggerated and that deep divisions within puritanism "invalidate the concept of a homogeneous movement" for innovation within the medical professions. Moreover, Elmer points out that Anglican physicians "before, during and after the revolution" promoted the new medicine with as much enthusiasm as their sectarian counterparts.[6] Most recently, Andrew Wear has cautioned against stressing differences between Catholics and Protestants as they relate to medicine. He asserts that partisan, nationalistic historiography has disregarded the implicit theological similarities of all Christians in the sixteenth and seventeenth centuries and slighted the culture of Latin-based university studies they usually shared. Furthermore, Wear takes issue with the assumption that early Protestants uniformly opposed traditional medical authority, a viewpoint echoed by William Birken. Birken, specifically repudiating "what might be called the Webster-Rattansi thesis," has found that "Puritans could be found in nearly every medical current, progressive and conservative."[7] Let us turn to an examination of the link between religion and medical publishing during a turbulent epoch of ecclesiastical and governmental change.

Religion and medicine have intertwined from time immemorial, and like its ancient spiritual counterparts, Christianity offered both an explanation for illness and a cure. In the Christian canon, God visited disease upon individuals and whole communities as evidence of His power and as punishment for human failings; prayer and repentance were the remedies for such reproof. Weekly public fasts, consisting of abstinence, sermons, and supplications, not only complemented but empowered medical treatments. During the plague epidemics of 1625 and 1636, over half of the works published about the disease were of a strictly religious and devotional nature, offering spiritual consolation rather than physical antidotes.[8] Moreover, disciples beheld Christ as the Great Physician, a healer of the sick who could even raise the dead; in the Eucharist Christ's body was also medication for any ailment. Medieval doctors had usually also been priests, but until the sixteenth century no conflict disturbed the relationship between Christianity and the secular medicine of Hippocrates and Galen applied by clerical healers. Even after the professional segregation of clergymen from the practice of medicine in 1555 by the London College of Physicians, believers accepted the precept that body and soul coupled until death. That moment of transition when the soul migrated to the next world was directed by the church. At the hour of a patient's death, those imperious English doctors who had barred clerics from medical practice got their comeuppance, customarily excluded from the dying person's bedside in favor of priests and ministers. But despite the attempted detachment of medical personnel from religious and vice versa, ambiguity persisted over the actual borders of the physical and spiritual realms. It should come as no surprise that clerics had difficulty divesting themselves of medical metaphor in their sermons.[9]

Religion and medicine particularly blended on the pages of late medieval almanacs, kalendars, and prognostications, among the most popular books in the English language. By Tudor times, almanacs had become "necessary annual books of reference," giving conjunctions and oppositions of sun and moon, dates of eclipses, and movable feasts. They were often attached to kalendars, prayer books marking the saints commemorated on each day of the year. Intended for students and physicians, almanacs shrank to octavo size to fit pockets and even appeared as sheets to be fastened to the wall. They contained useful information about phlebotomy, purging, bathing, zodiacal references, and general medicine; the accompanying kalendar marked the proper days for medical treatment with black and red crosses. Separate from them was the prognostication, which contained information gleaned from the almanac and heralded the future. Generally gloomy, printed prognostications sold for one pence and predicted famine, plague, war, and death; the earliest ones in England were imports from the continent.[10] Certain pressmen specialized in this sort of literature: Richard Pynson, Robert Wyer, John Redman, Richard Grafton, and Thomas Marshe dominate the first half of the sixteenth century, while the Elizabethan era records the names of Richard Watkins and James Roberts, who only printed the works of Englishmen, as the dominant publishers.[11]

Though one might assume almanacs and other such books would be produced by lesser craftsmen, the printing houses of those who issued these books turned out works of remarkable magnitude. Richard Pynson, a Norman by birth, maintained a high standard of workmanship at his shop near Temple Bar and became printer to Henry VIII; Robert Wyer published the influential tomes of Christine de Pisan and Andrew Boorde, a Carthusian monk who accepted the Henrician schism. John Redman, who succeeded to Pynson's business, printed the Magna Carta in 1525, no modest undertaking. Thomas Marshe had a shop in Fleet Street, but his enterprise pales in comparison to Grocer Richard Grafton's. Grafton printed the Bible in English in 1537, and although his fortunes took a tumble with Thomas Cromwell's, he regained royal favor. As printer to Edward VI, Grafton produced the first Book of Common Prayer in 1549 and Acts of Parliament for the Edwardian reign. Out of favor again during the monarchy of Mary I, Grafton retired from printing and turned to recounting the history of recent times. Though he squabbled with rival chronicler John Stow, Grafton remains best known for his annals of England. Lastly in our litany of important printers are Richard Watkins and James Roberts, partners in a twenty-one-year patent for almanacs and prognostications given them by Elizabeth I. Watkins also printed Gabriel Frende's famous almanacs, and Roberts put out editions of The Merchant of Venice and Midsummer Night's Dream. When James I ascended the throne in 1603, he gave the right to print almanacs to the Stationers' Company.[12]

Before and after the break with Rome, the Church officially deemed oracles as violators of God's laws. Nonetheless, friar Andrew Boorde wrote an almanac and prognostication, the first Englishman to do so. Additionally, he acknowledged in his preface that soothsaying was against the laws of the realm.[13] Boorde also authored a health primer which advised that the sick should embrace

Christ's passion and death in order to mitigate their own illnesses. At the same time, he emphasized the need for patients to obey their doctor's orders and avoid the sin of self-destruction: "He doth kill himself who does not observe the commandment of his phisicion."[14] Anthony Askham, who like many almanac writers combined the roles of physician and priest, issued two works during the reign of Mary I, published by William Powell, which correlated eclipses, diseases, and weather. He foresaw many "cold sicknesses both of dry humoures and waterishe," as well as lots of stomach aches.[15] The prophecies of the mythical Mother Ursula Sontheil Shipton of York, a sixteenth-century Yorkshire woman who supposedly foretold the deaths of Thomas Cardinal Wolsey and Lord Henry Percy, were not published until the seventeenth century. In 1644 Richard Harper at the Bible and Harp in Smithfield printed *Nine Notable Prophesies,* including Mother Shipton's dire predictions, later interpreted as such, for Civil War and Fire. Samuel Pepys in his diary for 1666 referred to statements by his friends that her prophecies had come true.[16] Author-publisher Richard Head embellished the fantasy further with his 1667 production of Shipton's "biography," complete with portraits of her as the devil's daughter and a hideous old crone. Such divinations were wildly popular and very lucrative to publishers like Harper and Head.[17]

Richard Napier of Buckinghamshire offers a splendid example of what it meant to be an astrologer-clergyman-doctor. Although he had no university degree of any sort, Napier was ordained in 1590 and admitted to the rectory of Great Linford, a post he held for forty-four years. A disciple of the notorious astrologer Simon Forman and, like Forman, a physician, Napier claimed to be in contant communication with the archangel of healing, Raphael. This heavenly credential evidently mattered more than a medical diploma to the archdeacon of Buckingham, who provided Napier with a license to practice in 1604. John Aubrey relates the story of a female patient of Napier's, Lady Honywood, cured of an ague by his efficacious spells, who was cursed by her minister for making use of diabolical help to feel better. He ordered her to burn the spell or face damnation, but when she did as commanded, her distemper returned. The woman employed Napier's incantation again and recovered, only to be condemned a second time by the parson. Her death followed shortly the final discarding of Napier's spell. Napier instructed other ministers in astrological medicine as well as his nephew and namesake, and left most of his income to the poor.[18]

Protestant clergymen who wrote diaries often expressed religious sentiments and beliefs about illness. Ralph Josselin, vicar of Earls Colne in Essex from 1641 to his death in 1683, accepted that sickness was either a divine purge, as in the story of Job, or a punishment for sin. In either case, affliction could be interpreted as a blessing from God, since it led a Christian back to the right pathway, morally strengthened by suffering. Illness taught believers piety, patience, and endurance. Moreover, in Josselin's creed, a loving God provided all the natural remedies required for those well-deserved torments. When he was stung by a bee, he found its sting soothed by daubing it with honey, further proof of divine benevolence.[19]

Many ministers acted as healers; indeed, medical practice proved to be especially meaningful to Dissenters. As William Birken has noted, many Puritan families had no trouble reconciling their religiosity with the medical profession. Medicine was an almost ideal Dissenter profession, proof against the unwarranted authority of English bishops.[20] Their religious learning gave them an instinctive justification for pursuing medical knowledge, and their congregations provided a reliable core of patients. Clerics and gentlewomen often dispensed free medical services, acting as samaritans asking only for spiritual gain for their charity. Christian concern for the health of the poor motivated many who questioned the efficacy of the medical status quo. The new medicine involved nothing less than religious duty and, for many who shared this way of thinking, sectarian medical wisdom was concomitant to a spiritual rebirth with the gift of grace.[21]

Certain physicians deliberately consolidated religion and medicine in their practices and in their written works. Thomas Browne's *Religio Medici*, arguably the most important spiritual book by an English physician, sought to distance its author from the widely held conviction that doctors had no religion, "the general scandal of the profession." Published in its first authorized English edition in 1642 by Andrew Crooke, Browne's "partly skeptical, partly credulous work" brought him public notice and admiration for the depths of his devout thought. Crooke, one of the leading publishers of the day and Master of the Stationers' Company, went on to produce corrected versions of the Norwich practitioner's classic.[22] Deeply reflective, Browne asserted the right to be guided by his own reason where scriptures or church teaching provided no precise counsel. In Rome that audacity got his book listed on the *Index Expurgatorius*, but undeterred Englishmen demanded and received multiple editions of *Religio Medici*. In 1664 Browne was elected an Honorary Fellow of the College of Physicians and knighted seven years later by Charles II.[23]

Browne was not alone in his sanctity; even the seasoned Elizabethan surgeon William Clowes had interjected a prayerful supplication to "the heavenly Physician" to bless his labors and make him effective as a doctor.[24] For Dr. Robert Burton, author of the celebrated *Anatomy of Melancholy* (1621), religion and medicine invariably coalesced. Since Satan personally and directly visited sinful man with sickness, "we must use prayer and physick both together, and so no doubt but our prayers will be available and our physick take effect."[25] And the disciples of William Harvey discerned a theological significance in his investigations. Walter Charlton, in a 1652 tract against atheism, referred to Harvey as "that incomparable indagator of Nature's Arcana," who always found the variety of nature inspiring and serendipitous. Five years later, in a tract on the soul's immortality, Charlton repeated his appreciation for Harvey's doctrine of the circulation of the blood, "the common medium cement or glew" that united body and soul.[26] For Robert Boyle, anatomy in general and the circulation in particular proved the existence and attributes of the divine being; Harvey's demonstration of anatomical truths showed God's providence and goodness.

Most writers commenting on the social responsibilities of medicine favored Paracelsian iatrochemistry, seeking a complete break from ancient procedures. Disciples of Paracelsus, cognizant of his association with Protestant mysticism and alchemy, argued that divinely inspired experimentation coupled with the benevolent observation of patients offered new and fruitful opportunities for healing.[27] They hoped to create a total and harmonious relationship between man and the universe, reversing the effects of the Fall, and prolonging man's lifespan. They could also improve their capacity to compete with the organized sections of the medical profession. No wonder Paracelsianism had great appeal, mental and emotional, for unlicensed "chemical practitioners." By following Paracelsus, these men and women could become refine the traditional procedures, infuse them with novelties, and give them an intellectual basis.

Historian Andrew Wear, however, insists that Protestants did not always seek to undermine the authority of learned doctors or their traditional Galenism. Instead, he argues that the Reformation "produced new doctrines which could be used to justify physicians' claims to a monopoly of practice."[28] Unlike Martin Luther, who emphasized the atheistic base of classical learning and demanded remodeling of university curricula, John Calvin construed ancient knowledge and the authority of the medical establishment as divinely inspired. William Perkins, a Calvinist divine in early Jacobean England, echoed that approval of the enlightened heritage which university-educated medicos had mastered and denounced the public's fascination with empirics. Perkins condemned magical remedies and the cunning men and women who used charms and spells to heal. In fact, it would be "better for a man to die of his sicknesse, then to seeke recovery by such wicked persons."[29] In 1603 Perkins' contemporary Henry Holland, a Puritan minister and medical practitioner, similarly upheld the notion that it was the learned physician who was God-given; he quoted from the Bible to "honour the physician with that honour that is due unto him for the Lord hath created him."[30] Even Wear acknowledges, notwithstanding, that the post-Reformation ideal of Christian charity damaged the public's respect for learned physicians who charged their patients excessively.[31]

The collapse of the early Stuart medical compromise, which had promoted peaceful coexistence between home-grown physicians and those educated in continental curricula, came with full force, inspired in large part by the impact of evangelical medicine in England and facilitated by the recurring terror of pestilence.[32] If Paracelsianism had made something of an impact on England by the early Stuart years, the affiliation of its Puritan proponents with those of Jan Baptista van Helmont did even more to revitalize the medical world. When van Helmont's collected works, published posthumously and edited by his son, reached England in 1648, a comprehensive religious reinterpretation emerged of what a medical vocation meant. Pious practitioners thereafter felt divinely incited to recover the remedies made available by God to Man in Nature. Puritan doctors beheld themselves as God's chosen people, part of the new Covenant; they judged their Galenic rivals in the College as ungodly, medically redundant, and irreligious. Hence, the contest between the old and new medicine went well beyond the boundaries of iatric philosophy. As Helmontian physician George Thomson asserted, this new medicine had been "ordained by special providence of God, for the comfort and relief of distressed Man."[33]

Repeated cycles of plague intensified the need for a religious rationale and worshipful approach to what the Bible taught was one of the trio of shocks (war, famine, and pestilence) inflicted by God to punish his people. The Puritan minister William Gouge wrote about the divine purpose of pestilence in his influential 1631 book, *Gods Three Arrows: A Plaister for the Plague*.[34] Major plague epidemics devastated urban communities at regular intervals throughout the Tudor-Stuart era, but none rivaled the scourge of 1665, when more than 80,000 Londoners died, almost 20 percent of the city's population. Unlike the earlier pandemics, the pestilence of 1665 brought to a head the controversy over remedies between Galenists and an impassioned group of Paracelsian-Helmontian physicians. Printed salvos emanating from the medical rivals drew the public into the debate and a vigorous pamphlet war ensued.

As for the College Fellows, their concerns about maintaining orthodox medicine and professional authority paralleled in many ways the fortunes of the Church of England and the King who was its head. The College's authority as a regulatory body depended on the monarchy which had endowed the institution with its legitimacy through incorporation. But Englishmen looked upon government differently in the Stuart century than they had when the Tudors ruled. As respect for sovereigns declined, so did the legitimacy of the organizations those sovereigns had created.[35] The obverse is also true. Chipping away for various reasons at the right of the collegiate doctors to oversee medical practice in London, Puritans, Paracelsians, and Presbyterians articulated disdain for the whole idea of hierarchy. The learned physicians appeared in the minds of critics analogous to bishops, both groups exercising authority to keep honest underlings in line. Moreover, these medical antagonists bristled even more when bishops licensed physicians, surgeons, and midwives, an episcopal privilege rooted in medieval canon law and Henrician-era legislation. A law of 1511 required that bishops consider the expert advice of professional men before certifying any medical personnel, but, even with the setting up the College of Physicians a few years later, the "right to practice was still dependent upon episcopal license."[36] Anti-episcopalians and their anti-College equivalents could be easily recast by circumstance as republicans, sabotaging even the monarchy itself. As James I crisply noted: "No bishops, no king."[37]

Disdain for episcopacy was rooted in the virulent and widespread anti-Catholicism which colored all aspects of life in early modern England. Hatred of popery rubbed off on the College of Physicians, not only because of the bishop-like paternalism the Fellows manifested, but because the founding and expansion of the College's prerogatives was associated with Catholicism. Although the College officially received its charter from Henry VIII in 1518, it was Henry's chief minister, Cardinal Wolsey, who arranged for the charter and for its confirmation by Parliament in 1523. At the time of the medical incorporation, Wolsey also served as papal legate, and the king had recently been awarded the Defender of the Faith designation by a grateful Roman Catholic pontiff for writing against Martin Luther's theses.

In spite of the College's genesis as a patriarchal institution, the Fellows carefully masked their sectarian allegiance. Though most remained adherents of the older faith, they kept quiet in the chaotic years following Henry VIII's divorce, the dissolution of the monasteries, and the fall of Thomas Cromwell. Several early Fellows served as royal physicians to Protestant and Catholic alike, loyal to learned physic over any particular religious outlook. That caution paid off in 1588 when the Crown revived the College's lapsed juridical powers. As Harold Cook has remarked, the members of the College survived Tudor religious storms by bending in the winds. That suppleness displayed itself in the seventeenth century as well, when several court doctors segued from Stuart to Cromwell and back again. While the faith of the Fellows had meaningful consequences in their private lives, the College itself as a corporate body did not epitomize any particular point of view.[38]

Nonetheless, critics of the Church of England targeted the College as a dangerous, reactionary fragment of the crypto-Catholic, hierarchical menace. The College President sat on a cushion, holding a silver caduceus, while the ranks of the organization addressed him as "your excellency."[39] Even as the religious diversity of the Fellows grew to embrace a wide array of beliefs, the College stayed through the 1630s on the conservative side of English society. During the tumultuous 1640s, the Fellows recognized what they needed to do to preserve their institution, and once again they conformed to political reality. The College started to petition Parliament about its business, not the Privy Council, and in 1642 elected as its President a Puritan, Othowell Meverall. John Clarke, a strong Parliamentarian, followed Meverall in 1645. The execution of Charles I pushed the Fellows into a more truculent posture: outright Catholics, suspected recusants, and right-wing Anglicans occupied major College offices; they shifted again in 1655, electing as president a Cromwellian champion, Edward Alston.[40] The flexibility that had saved the College in the sixteenth century came across in the mid-seventeenth as weak desperation, offering the best opportunity for its critics to attack.[41] And when they did go on the assault, the Fellows' adversaries framed their attacks in religiously charged language.

During the Interregnum of Oliver Cromwell, religious Nonconformists made clear their position on medicine and medical activity: they strenuously objected to elite doctors with their preference for esoteric Latin and to the arbitrary licensing monopoly enjoyed by the Fellows of the College. Utopian critics and religious militants championed wholesale reorganization of the medical services, calling for the state to take charge of such improvements. Some Commonwealth reformers even proposed, in contravention to the customary policies of the College of Physicians, that ministers should practice medicine. The Leveller William Walwyn, for instance, viewed caring for the sick as an act of Christian piety and articulated that position in *The Compassionate Samaritan*. Since medical care was a charitable manifestation of true piety, he thought that doctors should be state-salaried and receive no private fees.[42]

The Puritan physicians who embraced Paracelsian-Helmontianism had an articulate spokesman during the Commonwealth in Samuel Hartlib, an emigré to England during the reign of James I who maintained a signficant correspondence with like-minded theorists on the continent. Hartlib called for general revision of medical training while vigorously promoting the religious transformation of society as a whole. His adherents, the so-called Hartlib Circle, wrote numerous books and pamphlets calling for utopian reform; their quest received the blessing of a number of wealthy patrons close to the Cromwellian government. Hartlib intended nothing short of training the "good commonwealth man," whose moral rectitude embraced social progress through science and technology. This devout hunt for knowledge, medical knowledge included, cut a swath through ignorance to salvation.[43]

Inspired also by a hatred of monopolies, the Puritan party recognized that it had something else in common with irregular practitioners besides the new medicine and attacked the control exercised by the College of Physicians over the profession in the capital. The animosity of Dissenting Protestants to the Fellows may have had come in part from perceptions of class differentiation. In his study of the Dissenting Academies, David Reid has determined that the bulk of seventeenth-century Dissenters came from the middling sort: low-level shopkeepers, traders, hosiers, clergymen, and lawyers.[44] They may have assumed, incorrectly as it turned out, that because of their juristic dominance over medicine the members of the College of Physicians descended from wealth.[45] Moreover, since even affluent non-Anglicans were barred from Oxford and Cambridge universities before the Restoration, Dissenters would have been particularly resentful of the Galenic doctors who graduated from either Oxbridge institution. Ironically, official requirements for licensing did not prohibit Dissenters from practicing; both the College and lenient provincial bishops were willing to grant licenses to them.[46]

Intrinsically suspicious of classical authorities, George Starkey used Helmontian medicine, which by the Civil War had eclipsed that of Paracelsus, to completely denigrate Galenism and repudiated any possible theoretical truce with the obsolete physicians in the College. Starkey charged that the Fellows were motivated by vocational imperialism and personal avarice. His 1657 publication, printed by the widow of the official City Printer, *Natures Explication and Helmont's Vindication*, exhibits his sway as iatrochemistry's most active pamphleteer.[47] Puritan Noah Biggs, referred to by a medical rival in 1653 as "Helmont's parrot," demanded "reformation of the universities and the whole landscape of physic [so that] the *terra incognita* of chymistrie" might be discovered.[48] Religious radicals found the traditional humanistic curriculum worthless for preparing medical students to handle the realities of everyday life; they found time spent on the mastery of ancient languages, abstract logic, and the cultivation of elegant prose wasteful. Basic religious education, instruction in the vernacular, and natural philosophy topped the exemplary Puritan course of study. Reformers, who promoted the public use of more critical, rational habits of thought, hoped to combine the pursuit of scientific knowledge with the simultaneous quest for virtue.[49]

Samuel Hartlib and his medical associates sought unsuccessfully during the Commonwealth to establish a protective society for unlicensed doctors, a College of Graduate Physicians, in opposition to the College of Physicians. Hartlib, whose charity to destitute scholars was so profuse that he impoverished himself, was friend to divers Fellows of the Royal Society, seen by many in the College as a rival organization far more amenable to the experimental medicine of the empirics. In 1665 the Restoration Society of Chemical Physicians was established, but in an atmosphere less congenial to the charitable social attitudes of medico-religious reformers, that assembly quickly disintegrated.[50] Of course, even royalist-Anglicans could embrace Helmontianism and engage in College-bashing. George Thomson, who fought in Prince Rupert's successful campaign and was captured in 1644, took his medical degree at the University of Leiden, where he came under the spell of the new medicine. In 1665, joining the chorus of Helmontians, Edward Thomas published Thomson's *Galeno-Pale*, an attack on Galenists within the College; Grub Street printer Robert Wood, known for political pamphleteering, reproduced *Galeno-Pale* for bookseller Thomas. Predicting correctly that his "cowardly" adversaries would flee the City in the event of contagion, Thomson dedicated the pamphlet to Gilbert Sheldon, the recently appointed Archbishop of Canterbury, himself an advocate of chemical medicine.[51]

Writing about medicine at all, let alone publishing recipes and remedies in the vernacular, undermined the secretive traditions of the orthodox medical community. One extraordinary family, the Chamberlens, famed for the invention of the obstetrical forceps, did much throughout the century to subvert those traditions.[52] Starting as early as the first decade of James I's reign, the Huguenot Chamberlens emerged as among the most effective adversaries of the College with influential supporters among courtiers and nobility. Tracking their activities is complicated by the clan's habit of christening many of its sons, even brothers, with the same first name: Peters and Hughs, all medicos, abound on the family tree. Surgeon Peter Chamberlen the younger (d. 1626) began the tradition of confrontation with the College. Despite the impression given by the Fellows that they were protecting patients from incompetent practitioners, Peter the younger had impressive medical credentials. A member of the Barber-Surgeons' Company and surgeon to James I's queen Anne, he had obtained a license in 1600 to practice midwifery from the bishop of London, but his use of the obstetrical forceps angered the Fellows. Fortunately, the king's Privy Councillor, William Herbert, Earl of Pembroke, and prominent Protestant pastor-physician William Delaune, Chamberlen's father-in-law, could be relied on to plead his case. After several unpleasant encounters with the College, Chamberlen tried unsuccessfully to join it in 1610, but his efforts to organize London's midwives into an association soured his relationship with the Fellows. He asserted forcefully in January 1617 before a special committee that none of the College Fellows could deal with a difficult parturition better than an obstetric surgeon, and that he and his brother were the only two experts in these matters. Rebuffed by the offended committee members, Peter the younger failed in his plan to create a midwives' corporation, but that dream was revived in 1643 by his son, Peter Chamberlen III (d. 1683).[53] Another legacy for Peter III was his father's Christian repugnance for what he regarded as the supercilious and dogmatic medical elite.

Peter the younger's brother, Peter Chamberlen the elder (d. 1631), functioned as a tenacious and ambitious unlicensed practitioner who bedeviled the College by not sticking to his surgical specialty. Peter the elder, accoucheur to Queen Anne, had powerful friends who could parry the assaults of elite doctors hoping to prosecute him. On four occasions between 1607 and 1620, he was found guilty of practicing medicine illegally, practicing it badly, or both. In 1609 the Fellows indicted him for giving a certain medicine and fined him forty shillings. During Harvey's first term as College censor, Peter the elder was summoned to defend his "complex, ill and illicit practice."[54] He was condemned for malpractice in 1612 and a warrant was issued for his apprehension and incarceration in Newgate prison, but the Lord Mayor and the Archbishop of Canterbury interceded for him at the queen's insistence and obtained his release after a few days.[55]

Peter Chamberlen III, a Baptist and Fifth Monarchist during the Interregnum, continued his father's promotion of incorporated of midwives; he also championed public baths for better health. An M.D. from Padua, he found means, through his continental training, to personally help the poor: free medical aid. He published voluminously in English, defiling the restricted nature of responsible medicine by expressing contempt for keeping iatric secrets that might help sick people get well. Though Peter III had his degree incorporated at both Oxford and Cambridge, the College of Physicians had only reluctantly admitted him in 1628 with the warning that, despite his populist sentiments, he needed "to alter his style of clothing from that more like the dress worn by the very gay young men at court: that he would not be admitted until he accustomed himself to the decent habits of the Fellows and wore quiet garments."[56] Given that attitude toward Chamberlen, it is not surprising that when the College was asked in 1647 to comment on Chamberlen's advocacy before Parliament of the salubrious effects of hydro-therapeutics, the Fellows equivocated. Peter III grumbled that he was motivated solely by the spirit of God and that the College was made up of men opposed to his Puritan ideals.[57] He was eventually expelled from the institution in 1659, ostensibly for poor attendance. To a man, the four generations of Chamberlens validated their hopes for iatric reform in their spiritual code.

Less is known about the connection between medical iconoclasm and religious principle after the Stuart Restoration and the reestablishment of traditional monarchy with its noble hierarchy and elite prerogatives. How did Nonconformist supporters of the new medicine react then? For one thing, they had to deal with one of the more galling protocols reinstituted with kingship: the royal touch for the "King's Evil." The English name given to scrofula, the Evil was a disease of early life often characterized by slowly suppurating abscesses and fistulous passages. The most common form of tuberculosis in preindustrial Europe, it could be cured, many thought, only by the sacred touch of a divinely chosen potentate. Kings and queens of England dating back to Edward the Confessor in the eleventh century touched, thereby bolstering their legitimacy and popularity as magical "doctors."[58] Probably due to infected milk, scrofula caused a significant number of deaths that were recorded throughout England in the sixteenth and seventeenth centuries. Monarchs recognized the potency of touching ceremonies and publicized them in broadsides and pamphlets put out by the royal printer. Henry VII, the first Tudor and king before the break with Rome, developed specific rituals for curing the Evil; those customs still resonated two hundred years later in a twelve-page booklet published in 1686 by a Catholic printer to fortify the legitimacy of James II, his co-religionist. Both Stuart King Charleses proclaimed the time and place for their touching observances in ways calculated to emphasize their special healing gifts from God.[59]

During the reign of Queen Mary I, the royal thaumaturgy occurred on Good Friday, but observances could also be held on Easter Sunday, Pentecost, and the Feast of Michaelmas; elaborate liturgical elements included a reading of two passages from the Gospels: the verse from St. Mark referred to mysteries performed by the Apostles, and the words from St. John were often used in blessings or exorcisms. A church official brought the scrofulous person directly to the seated sovereign, who laid hands on the sick and made the Sign of the Cross over the "patient's" sores. Making the hallowed gesture, Queen Mary actually caressed the raw wounds several times.[60] After completing the first touching, she then brushed the person's sores with a gold coin or amulet (usually pre-pierced and threaded onto a ribbon), which was then hung around the sufferer's neck. Around the edge of the Marian coin ran the words: "This was the Lord's doing, and it is marvellous in our eyes." In the minds of the English, these coins, called "angels" because they depicted the figure of St. Michael, became instruments of the monarch's sacerdotal power. A Venetian witness recorded that Mary made each patient promise never to part with the gold piece "except in case of extreme need."[61]

The monarch's healing force could prevent illness, too. At the same Good Friday service, to the right of the high altar, the queen blessed containers of rings, some expressly obtained by her for this purpose and others provided by their owners, marked with their names for later retrieval. Mary prayed and passed her hands over the receptacles, separating and fingering the gold and silver bands, which were then distributed. Her subjects cherished these cramp-rings, as they were known, regarding them as talismans containing the power intrinsic to the touch of an anointed monarch. Mary's sanctified rings were uncommonly coveted, not only in England but in foreign courts as well, especially in Scotland.

In 1558 Elizabeth I assumed the mantle of an English monarch and the supernatural powers that went with it. Despite ridicule from some freethinking foreign religious reformers who thought kingly "healing" superstitious and silly, she perpetuated the royal touch for curing scrofula, carefully preserving "the traditional ceremonial, merely cutting out from the liturgy a prayer that mentioned the Virgin and the saints, and probably translating into English the Latin ritual of the previous ages."[62] She even made the Sign of the Cross over the affected parts of the sick. Catholics rejected Elizabeth's powers on the grounds that she was an excommunicated heretic, but her healings were cited as proof that the Papal Bull of Excommunication had failed to take effect. Puritans thought the practice irrational and absurd. In response to their challenge, official preachers defended the ancient privilege of the English monarchy against unbelievers. Elizabeth's chaplain, William Tooker, penned the first book in praise of the royal marvel, and at the end of her reign, one of the queen's surgeons, William Clowes, provided an apologia for the wonder-working virtue of English rulers.[63] Though she maintained the touching rubrics, at the beginning of her reign Elizabeth quietly ceased to distribute cramp-rings on Good Friday, essentially halting that ancient rite. Despite her own health concerns and mindful of royal prestige, the queen retained the ceremony that brought her into direct contact with her suffering subjects and jettisoned the one that did not.[64]

Though interested in practical matters of health and science, James I manifested skepticism about some elements of English conventions. He scoffed at the miraculous formality of touching for the King's Evil, nearly dealing it a mortal blow. Despite James' written support for the divine right of kings, his Calvinism made him reluctant to participate in superstitious liturgy, and he asked to be excused from the rite.[65] His advisers convinced him of the practical need to touch and he complied, albeit with some changes in the traditional agenda, such as deleting the Sign of the Cross performed by the king over the afflicted subjects, and restyling of the "angels," which no longer bore the picture of a crucifix on them or the word "miracle." Miracles surely existed, wrote Francis Bacon, James's erudite Lord Chancellor, but they had to be authenticated as such.[66] James sporadically performed the office on progresses throughout the realm, as in 1617 when he touched several hundred scrofulous subjects en route to Lincoln and another several dozen in the minster itself.[67] Fittingly, Oliver Cromwell disdained touching for the King's Evil and the supernatural privileges of royalty in general. During the years of the Commonwealth and Protectorate, there was no miraculous princely healing by anyone in Great Britain.

Charles II, a stranger to most of the country, astutely revived the royal touching ceremony, thrilling his subjects and reminding skeptics of the ineffable privilege of a king. Presumably, he assumed that he had the marvelous ability to heal from the moment of his father's death, as his subjects indubitably believed. Preachers, writers, even physicians and scientists touted the amazing potency of the royal gift. Some even thought that the king, the nation's first physician, could cure diseases like the French pox, scurvy, rickets, and goiters.[68] Charles performed the hereditary spectacle in exile, touching scrofulous followers ferried to the temporary court in the Low Countries by enterprising merchants. Since the Stuart purse was empty, Charles distributed silver touchpieces instead of gold, but the passionate feeling imparted by the ritual was the same. Popular belief in the supernatural remedy for the King's Evil, a remedy denied its victims for so long, furnished Charles Stuart with a weapon of wonder (See Fig. 4.1.).

Richard Wiseman, Charles's surgeon on the continent, witnessed the touching of multitudes of believers and reported that inexplicable cures resulted from the Stuart touch, enhancing Charles's mystique throughout Britain. While only just recognized as sovereign by Parliament and still at Breda, Charles presided over a somber healing liturgy. Only a few days after arriving in England, he touched six hundred persons in one sitting; he subsequently touched throngs for the King's Evil every Friday in the Banqueting House at Whitehall. Wiseman kept meticulous track in the King's Register of Healing of the numbers attending these solemnities. From May 1660 to September 1664 the king touched twenty-three thousand persons; thousands more came to see him in subsequent years, perhaps as many as one hundred thousand, seemingly "half the nation," during his twenty-five-year reign.[69] The first edition of Wiseman's narrative by royalist booksellers Richard Royston and Benjamin Tooke in 1676 helped to boost Charles II's reputation during tenuous times; a second edition by the same publishers in 1686 did the same for James II.

Naturally, recognition that the king and his party were clearly in charge mitigated hostility towards him and what he stood for. Known critics of the dynasty suddenly muted their objections to Stuart social policy. Even Dr. Peter Chamberlen joined in the acclaim for Charles II. Furthermore, Chamberlen asserted the right, unsuccessfully, to be appointed as the king's physician-in-ordinary since he had ministered to Charles I. Chamberlen's *Humble Petition*, a proposal for public baths and bath-stoves originally published in 1648, was reprinted in 1662, touting him as "first physician to the royal progeny and to His Most Sacred Majesty." One of Peter's many sons, Hugh, did serve in 1682 as physician to the king.[70]

Another Interregnum-era critic of elite medicine who later revised his views was William Walwyn. Styling himself physician and scientist, Walwyn had

London Printet for Dorman Newman at the kings Armes in the Poultry &:   F. H. van. Hove Sculp:

4.1. Charles II touching for the King's Evil, by F. H. van Hove. Broadside printed for Dorman Newman, 1679. Reproduced by permission of the Wellcome Library, London.

disparaged the potions used by university-educated doctors in his 1654 pamphlet, *Spirits Moderated*, and had offered instead soothing health beverages of his own concoction. Although he persevered to popularize self-diagnosis after the Restoration and published additional recipes in *Physick for Families* (1669), Walwyn subsequently came to defend the common practice of physicians to keep their formulas and remedies secret.[71]

But despite these individual modulations, the dissemination of medical literature and the debates that accompanied iatric publication proceeded apace after 1660. Philosophical divergence in the post-Restoration medical contest often came cloaked in religious language. Marchamont Nedham, a former propagandist for Oliver Cromwell, returned from exile and started badgering the College Fellows, calling them a benighted, Latinate, and Jesuitical body of old-fashioned Galenists. Some scholars have contended that the return of the Stuarts was the ruin of Puritan reformers' dreams for better, more enterprising medical service in England.[72] Others have supposed that after 1660 "religious non-conformity and political radicalism [remained] hand in hand with medical sectarianism."[73] Contemporaries like Henry Stubbe, a staunch defender of the College of Physicians, thought so: he made a case for seeing the proponents of chemical medicine as a threat to the Crown, Church, and College.[74] The evidence, however, presents a more complicated reality for Restoration medicine.

Although challenges to the institutional preeminence of the College of Physicians did not end with the return of the Stuarts and the reimposition of hierarchy, some of these challenges emanated from beyond Nonconformist circles. In April 1664, the House of Commons refused to ratify the College's new royal charter, reflecting broad sentiment against the Fellows. Though the College officers worked closely with the Crown and Parliament to have the institution's legal powers over London medicine reinstated, they were unable to overcome opposition mounted by the Society of Apothecaries and the Barber-Surgeons' Company. Moreover, with the plague of 1665 and the fire of 1666 multiplying these intellectual and institutional hazards, the fragile nature of the College's public authority lingered. Despite the lack of Parliamentary validation, the Fellows reasserted their rights to license qualified practitioners and to punish the unlicensed, based on the charter given them by King Charles I. A new charter, not even submitted to Parliament for ratification, was eventually presented to the College in 1687 by James II.[75]

Misgivings about the medical establishment surfaced even in Charles II's court. In 1665 Thomas O'Dowde, a groom of the bedchamber and self-described chemical practitioner, wrote a pamphlet called *The Poor Man's Physician*. In it, O'Dowde announced the inauguration of the Society of Chemical Physicians, strongly condemned the Galenic orientation of the Fellows of the Royal College, and emphasized the probity of practical medicine over elitist theory.[76] In later handbill, O'Dowde touted his own chemical cures for plague and bemoaned the repressive regulation by the Fellows of inventive scientists like himself. His patients, mentioned by name in the broadside, consisted of several men well placed at court, many of them in the circle of James, Duke of York.[77] Moreover, like the anti-Galenist George Thomson, O'Dowde dedicated his publication to Archbishop Gilbert Sheldon, hardly a friend to Dissenters.[78]

Therefore, despite the reestablishment in 1660 of traditional status and historic jurisdictions such as the licensing prerogatives of bishops, condemnation in print of university-educated physicians and the circulation of medical information and prescriptions in the vernacular persisted.[79] But the consistency of personal convictions among bookmen, even spiritual convictions, appears to have mattered less in the burgeoning medical marketplace during the reigns of the Stuart brothers. While it is true that "Grub Street" publishers, simply by plying their trade, bridged common and learned cultures, the assumption that Dissenting printers exclusively issued materials which challenged established physicians is erroneous. All sides to the continuing religio-political struggles sought financial advantage regardless of where that profit might be found.[80] Specific evidence for this ostensible pragmatism can be found in the medical texts and self-help manuals that proliferated in the last decades of the seventeenth century. Nonconformist publishers often printed and sold books in Latin unquestionably intended for university-educated doctors, despite the philosophical preference of those publishers for the more empirical medicine and less elitist attitudes of surgeons, apothecaries, and other irregulars.

Of course, some religious dissidents after the Restoration still strongly supported making every man his own doctor, the title of John Archer's well-known work, published in 1671 by London printer Peter Lillicrap.[81] For instance, Anabaptist John Darby, undeterred by his arrest in 1664 for printing a satire about King Charles's mistress and again in 1667 for criticizing the state's persecution of the godly, put out William Penn's controversial Sandy Foundation Shaken in 1668 from his shop in Bartholomew Close.[82] The following year Darby produced an English-language version of The Complete Chymical Dispensatory. The Chymical Dispensatory purported to show how minerals, animals, and vegetative materials could be used in physick by "merchants, druggists, chirurgions, apothecaries, and such ingenious persons as study physick or philosophy."[83] Another of Darby's imprints was on an English translation (by Hugh Chamberlen) of François Mauriceau's Diseases of Women with Child and in Child-Bed; the book promised "fit remedies" for mother and newborn alike.[84] Likewise, Master Stationer Thomas Parkhurst, a Presbyterian cited for the unlicensed printing of A Friendly Debate between a Conformist and a Non-Conformist, distributed Thomas Nevett's Treatise of Consumptions, a malady cured through a "new and extraordinary method by specific medicines."[85] The Harrison family of printers, publishers of Quaker literature who got into trouble occasionally with the authorities, also generated popular medical works.[86]

Despite the supposed philosophical preference of Nonconformist publishers for the more empirical medicine and the less elitist attitudes of surgeons, apothecaries, and other irregulars, entrepreneurs like Daniel Brown often printed and vended expensive books in Latin that were unquestionably aimed at university-educated doctors. Nonconformist booksellers whose shops were in proximity to the College of Physicians stacked their shelves with folios full of esoteric arguments honoring the Fellows; even those whose enterprises were at some distance from Warwick Lane carried rare medical and scientific texts.[87] At the same time, pressmen with Church of England affiliations, who might be expected to support the privileges and prerogatives of the Fellows at the College of Physicians, printed and sold the works of Paracelsian and Helmontian medical challengers trained in a continental curriculum inimical to what was still being taught at Oxford and Cambridge. Some Anglican pressmen even published the works of revolutionary quacks in cheap pamphlets aimed at the broadest possible readership and seemingly most detrimental to hierarchical medical authority.[88] Walter Kettilby was described by fellow London printer John Dunton as "the most eminent episcopal" bookman of his time.[89] As noted earlier, however, he published several pieces by Puritan Thomas Sydenham.

Dunton characterized bookseller Henry Bonwicke, the son of an Anglican minister, as "zealous for the church."[90] Bonwicke's shop in St. Paul's Churchyard dealt chiefly in works of divinity, but he also became one of the most prolific medical publishers in London during the last quarter of the seventeenth century. Many of his titles promoted self-diagnosis or promulgated medical awareness. Among Bonwicke's titles, all in English and all in octavo, are herbals and books on practical physick by John Pechey, anatomies and dictionaries of diseases translated from the French, and books on pain and surgery by medical populist Everard Maynwaring. Many of these works went into second and third editions. After Bonwicke's death, his wife Rebecca carried on the business.[91]

Publisher Joseph Hindmarsh was devoted to High Church ideals and faithful to the concept of the divine right of kings, especially his beloved Stuart princes; his presses in Cornhill stamped out anti-presbyterian, pro-episcopal tirades.[92] Yet, despite Hindmarsh's preference for ancient customs and the order created by rank, his printing house manufactured popular, inexpensive books about medicine, including an English version of *The Doctors Physician or Dialogues concerning Health* by Nicolas Fremont d'Ablancourt, a practical conversation about various ailments and remedies. Hindmarsh also dispensed one of the most influential pieces of medical iconoclasm: apothecary Robert Talbor's *The English Remedy*, a paean to cinchona or quinine, known then as Jesuits' bark, a favorite of empirics and of Charles II.[93] After the Glorious Revolution, Hindmarsh published at the Jacobite end of Grub Street, still loyal to his hereditary sovereign.

Is there anything besides the desire for profit that accounts for such practical-mindedness in English medical publishing after the Restoration? Perhaps a growing popular secularization explains some of the shift from a widespread acceptance of purely spiritual explanations for and responses to disease. For instance, the supernatural element in published plague literature diminished after the Restoration to only one-third of the total output—still significant, but down considerably from what was produced by the previous generation. Monthly fasts replaced weekly ones, signifying a decline in public religious expressions of concern for pestilence.[94] People after 1660 wanted to read about the scientific causes of pestilence and prevent it, for prayer did not seem to be as efficacious as they had been taught by their parents' generation. Medical and scientific handbooks tended to undermine the old healing methods and folk remedies, reflecting general disenchantment with superstition and secrecy among the literate.

Regal rites for the King's Evil lost their import with the accession of William and Mary after the Revolution of 1688. Given the number of people claiming to be able to cure scrofula, the cachet of the royal touch likely fizzled earlier. Credence was given to the avowal of the "Irish stroker," Valentine Greatrakes, that he could cure scrofula; others made similar claims. Both the Duke of Monmouth, Charles II's bastard son, and his half-sister, Mary Fanshawe, alleged their ability to heal lymphatic diseases.[95] William of Orange had a pragmatic view of medicine, eschewing magic and miracles, and as king refused to touch. Educated in the tenets of Calvinism, he saw only superstition in the healing ritual, not a role for himself as the first physician of the nation. His deferential Stuart queen, Anglican by upbringing and conscious of the popularity of touching when performed by her uncle and father, did not perform the ceremony either. In abandoning the royal ritual, which seemed ludicrous to the practical Dutchman, the dual monarchs contributed to a lessened sense of awe and allegiance on the part of their subjects, a topic of much discussion after the revolution. The end of the Stuart lineage, Queen Anne revived the protocol during her reign, performing it for the last time shortly before her death in 1714. Anne's finale, actually a coda, signals the permanent discontinuation of the royal observance; no English sovereign from that day onward has touched the sick or distributed medical amulets.[96]

Widespread confidence in the dependability of science brought a restyling of medical explanations from interpreting divine dramatics to more secular practices and earthly meanings. Even the devil disappeared from discussions of medical evils, victim of the drive to "naturalize the supernatural."[97] Perhaps the diversity of the religious affiliations held by participants in the various disputes over medical knowledge after the Restoration subverted the constancy with which those tenets were held. Religious orientation "seems to have been at the bottom of these arguments only some of the time rather than always."[98] Although supernatural theories went out prior to the arrival of more effective techniques, physicians came to understand, as they had not before, that medical problems were open to human investigation and that diseases might be prevented by something other than prayers and incantations. Scientists disproved many of the "magical" concepts embraced by medical men of the Tudor-Stuart era like the doctrine of signatures and healing by sympathy; botanist John Ray, among others, completely rejected the doctrine of signatures, and several rationalists including Reginald Scot repudiated the hocus-pocus of weapon-salve.[99] Whatever the cause, the science and practice of medicine had gradually disengaged from spiritual matters.

Chapter 5

"A Way to Get Wealth": Women, Print, and Medicine

By virtue of custom and statute, females in England were prohibited from equal membership in the world of medicine until the nineteenth century. Among the more frequent explanations given for this situation is an exclusionary bias against women resulting from the association of medicine and science with ancient patriarchy and with the ascetic clerical hierarchy of the later Middle Ages.[1] Yet, despite the gender system produced by traditions and institutions, women did manage to engage in the masculine culture of Western science and medicine by employing a variety of imaginative strategies which enabled them to achieve some measure of vocational satisfaction and purpose through innovation.[2] Included in the tactics they used were defying outright license requirements and organizational dominion, functioning in a secondary capacity as research assistants and laboratory helpers, and acting as "angels," endorsing and sometimes financing scientific experimentation and medical empiricism. Women also published and sold medical literature as participants in the marketplace for iatric information. To a great extent, women played a subversive role in medicine and science, barred as they were from these disciplines' orthodoxy, by espousing and encouraging empiricism and experimentation. This chapter investigates the eclectic character of female influence on English medicine, encompassing the insurgent impact they had through print. Against the odds and in the most substantial sense, women in early modern England were dynamic practitioners, patrons, and publicists of medicine.

In early modern England virtually all of the normal avenues to instruction about established medicine or science were closed to females. Women were banned from Oxford and Cambridge, universities still dominated by clergy and gentleman. As the natural sciences gained prestige, Englishmen questioned whether women were capable of abstract thought and exiled them from the public realm of scholarship.[3] Even the masculine ethos of natural history worked against women. Plant taxonomies defined female flower parts as inferior to the male; Carolus Linnaeus' naming of "mammals" also emerged from the deep cultural roots of gender politics. Furthermore, fellowship of like-minded professionals in the medical colleges, scientific societies, and livery companies associated with health care was denied to females.[4] One needed a medical degree to be considered even for honorary membership in the Royal College of Physicians, thereby blocking women from that prestigious association. And, when in 1727 the unmarried daughter of a deceased freeman of the Apothecaries' Society surprised the company by applying for patrimonial admission, the company decided that her technical qualifications were inadequate and paid generously for her admission to another company.[5]

Except during the Interregnum, Church authorities controlled midwifery, one medical field initially permitted to women. In seventeenth-century England, bishops licensed only those midwives who could produce a certificate from the parish churchwardens testifying to her orthodox faith and reputable character.[6] There was greater concern for the moral rather than the medical prowess of midwives in the event they had to baptize infants at birth. Wise women who did employ their talents in violation of the law sometimes faced persecution on charges of witchcraft, as did their female customers. Despite these roadblocks to the distaff practice of medicine, the hauteur of male doctors, as well as their exorbitant fees, insufficient numbers, and fondness for heroic medicine, necessitated the existence of providers of remedies, even if they were women, who would make house calls and charge their clients less. Wise women, midwives, and other female "irregulars," like their iconoclastic male counterparts, practiced medicine in England throughout the early modern era by circumventing the legitimate medical community.

On a more elemental level, the practice of midwifery undercut the bastion of traditional medicine. Because childbirth was a natural process, not one involving disease or necessitating much intervention, and because the presence of a physician during labor was deemed inappropriate, midwives performed a needed function for all childbearing women. Stuart royal midwives like Anne Dennis and Margaret Mercer received generous warrants for their essential services to the nation. Some even feared the power of the midwife. Paranoid Whigs thought that Mrs. Labadie, Mary of Modena's accoucheuse, was influential enough to be a political conspirator in the suppositious birth of James II's heir. There were complaints, however, that midwives lacked medical training and were little more than poisonous crones. Jacob Rüff's sixteenth-century textbook, *The Expert Midwife*, was translated into English in 1637, and herbalist Nicholas Culpeper wrote a *Directory for Midwives* in 1651, so that women might be better able to deal with the complexities of "conception, bearing, and suckling of children."[7]

But if midwifery needed supervision, why couldn't women administer other women? Oversight of Quaker midwives was one of the responsibilities of the Women's Meetings; on more than one occasion a Meeting ordered a midwife deficient in medical knowledge to hire an assistant or let the buyer beware.[8] Elizabeth Cellier, a renowned Catholic midwife implicated in the spurious Popish Plot, also provided female leadership on the issue. Noting the conflict between physicians and midwives and citing grim statistics of dead mothers and babies, she petitioned James II for professional examination of midwives and for the founding of a royal hospital to be maintained by a self-governing corporation of 1000 skilled, dues-paying midwives.[9] Her ideas were never implemented, perhaps because her religious affiliation worked against her once the Catholic king had been toppled.

In the seventeenth century, men began to act as obstetricians when the financial rewards became apparent, further undermining well-defined medical roles. These practitioners were called "man-midwives," demonstrating the clear understanding that obstetrical expertise had belonged earliest to the women's sphere of medicine.[10] Several generations of Chamberlen males worked as accoucheurs, and a family-invented forceps gave them dubious notoriety in the medical world (See Fig. 5.1.). Peter Chamberlen the younger fruitlessly petitioned James I that some order for the instruction and monitoring of midwives be enacted; the College of Physicians responded that such incorporation was neither necessary nor convenient. In 1672 Hugh Chamberlen translated François Mauriceau's illustrated treatise on diseases in pregnancy, calling it "very necessary for chyrurgeons and midwives," but not everyone agreed men should be midwives.[11] The following year, another edition of the translated Mauriceau text appeared as *The Accomplisht Midwife*, printed by John Darby and sold by Benjamin Billingsley. In 1671 Jane Sharp, active for forty years in childbirthing and proud of her own polyglot research into the subject, authored *The Midwives Book*, an argument for the natural prerogatives of women to deliver healthy babies. She addressed her fellow midwives as "sisters," and published her book to keep midwifery in women's control; it is full of jokes at men's expense.[12] Elizabeth Nihell, who studied midwifery at the Hotel-Dieu in Paris, dismissed men-midwives as a French fad and denied the incompetency of her circle.[13] (See Fig. 5.2.)

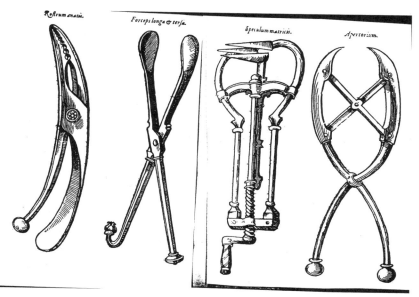

5.1. Obstetrical instruments (pincers, forceps, speculum, and apertorium). From Jacob Rueff, *De conceptu et generatione hominis* (Frankfurt, 1587).

5.2. Birthing chair. From Rueff, *De conceptu et generatione hominis* (Frankfurt, 1587).

English wives and mothers constitute an unlikely category of medical renegades, but their "practice" of learned physic was certainly without formal authorization. In fact, class distinctions notwithstanding, women were expected to provide for the well-being of their families with salutary home remedies. For instance, Lady Grace Mildmay, who married into a Puritan aristocratic Northamptonshire family, had been educated at home in "phisicke and surgerie," and often read William Turner's popular herbal. Lady Mildmay kept a journal from 1570 to 1617, which tells of a variety of medical activities, the recurrence of which attests to its centrality in her identity. She surmised that healing was a component of her religious duty: "It is good sometimes to be alone and meditate, but it is also good to call on one's neighbors to comfort their souls and bodies."[14] Countless ladies bountiful also dispensed free medical advice and remedies to the parish poor; a trio of Elizabeths offers evidence. One celebrated patrician practitioner was Elizabeth Grey, Countess of Kent, the originator of "Kent's powder," a much-favored mixture of steel filings, ground pearl, and sugared spices for a condition known as the green sickness.[15] Elizabeth Walker, a rector's wife in late seventeenth-century Essex, studied the theory and practice of medicine and amassed an impressive medical library, so that she might be proficient enough to help those who needed her.[16] At a lower social level Elizabeth Ray, the smithy's wife at Black Notley, developed a reputation for botanical competence and herbal therapies.[17] Herb women came from an even more plebeian caste, but they were respected, nonetheless, as everyday purveyors of medical lore.

Given the scarcity of qualified M.D.'s, especially in rural areas, some physicians inadvertently contributed to their own decline by providing helpful hints to "petticoat doctresses."[18] *The Family Physitian* by George Hartman was written to be "useful for families and serviceable for country people."[19] Dozens of similar titles appeared in Stuart Britain, some written by women, a tacit acknowledgment of the importance of the amateur care-giver to the nation's health. Most wives' pharmaceutics remained unpublished, treasured legacies for their daughters to use in their households, but Lady Margaret Hoby's diary of her record of attendance at births, sicknesses, and recoveries was printed, as were the notes of Scotswoman Lady Grisell Baillie.[20] London stationers distributed several editions of Hannah Woolley's ambitious recipe book, *The Accomplish'd Ladies Delight in Preserving, Physick, Beautifying and Cookery*, first published in 1675 by Benjamin Harris.[21]

Threatened by all these "irregular" practices, the Royal College of Physicians got tough on unlicensed practitioners, and prosecutions for unsanctioned activity escalated through the seventeenth century. Approximately fifteen percent of all the "irregulars" pursued by the College were women.[22] The names of myriad wise women emerge from the unpublished Annals of the College meetings to prove the active involvement of London women in medicine. In 1605 the Fellows indicted Anna Dickson for killing a gentlewoman with vomitories and charged Thomasina Scarlet with illegal treatment; Dickson admitted giving a jaundiced customer oxyacantha or barberry.[23] Both women were fined £5 and sent to prison, as was Catherine Clark, who conceded that she urged senna on her clients with swollen feet and ulcers. Similarly, Joan Thumwood acknowledged that she practiced medicine illegally, but explained that she attended only women and children. Although the College ordered Thumwood's husband to post her bail, the Fellows did not always punish the accused.[24] Susanna Gloriana, whose patient died after taking a recommended purgative, was simply admonished not to practice in the future because the Fellows noted that she was young, poor, pregnant, and had a baby not yet weaned. At the other end of the mercy spectrum, eighty year-old Alice Stanford received a mere rebuke for her illegal practice when she confessed that it was her only means of support and "after her son stood surety for her under £20 penalty."[25]

Credentialed London surgeons were kept busy in the seventeenth century with syphilis or the French pox, but the College called in dozens of law-breaking wise women who specialized in treating the pox. The Annals describe Mrs. Bryers as "an aged quack with a long face," who used sudorifics, ointments, plasters, and potions on her patients. Jane Waterworth wielded a French pox purgative made from senna and wild saffron. Both were punished, as was Anna Croney, who hawked dangerous drugs in Covent Garden. The Fellows issued a certificate proclaiming her lack of medical skill. Sometimes, of course, other women impeded the distaff practice of physic. Thomasina Scarlet sought to escape punishment after admitting giving purgatives to more than one hundred people by implicating an abortionist, Mrs. Sharde of Turnbull Street. In turn, Mrs. Sharde, along with providing her own confession, incriminated the surgeon who taught her about abortifacients and another abortionist, Anna

Baker.[26] On every level imaginable until the Victorian Age, circumstances hindered women from the practice of lawful medicine.

Some found a way. At the top of the social pyramid, Queen Elizabeth I and Queen Anne legitimately figured in a health-related practice, touching for the King's Evil. The Tudor and Stuart kings, as we saw in chapter 4, touched tens of thousands of diseased subjects; Elizabeth and Anne emphasized their Englishness by doing so.[27] Another queen of England, though neither hereditary nor native-born, Henrietta Maria contributed to the apparent flowering of female interest in medicinal and pharmaceutical matters. As Charles I's consort, Henrietta Maria inhabited what has been called "the cross-disciplinary or pre-disciplinary culture of the Renaissance."[28] Her entourage included Dr. Theodore Mayerne; mathematician John Pell; John Evelyn, who earnestly investigated botany and nutrition; and the highly respected apostle of the new science, Kenhelm Digby, Henrietta Maria's chamberlain. Not surprisingly, her bookish circle of associates—patrician ladies and learned men—relished discussions about medical science. In 1655 Nathaniel Brook put out *The Queen's Closet Opened*, containing "secrets in physick (and) chirurgery," recipes "honoured with her own practice, when she pleased to descend to these more private recreations."[29] Clearly, Brook expected to make money from the publication, especially in the atmosphere of growing disquiet after the beheading in 1649 of Charles I and the exile of his family. Also in 1649, Nicholas Culpeper's original edition of the translated London *Pharmacopoeia* came out, stimulating public demand for more do-it-yourself prescriptions. What better way to combine both sentiments—regret over the king's execution and interest in medical "receipts"—than via the dowager queen's book of remedies?

Aristocratic women in early modern England led the way in dispensing medical advice and care, believing in themselves as much as in *noblesse oblige*. Katherine Boyle Jones, Lady Ranelagh, centered a group of intellectuals in London from 1640 to 1660. Some of the same men in Henrietta Maria's clique, plus Samuel Hartlib, John Milton, and René Descartes, contributed to a scriptorium run by Hartlib, using Lady Ranelagh's address as its headquarters. Correspondents referred to *The Queen's Closet Opened* and to *Natura Exenterata or Nature Unbowelled*, a tome on medical and household science from the pen of Alethea Talbot, Countess of Arundel and Surrey.[30] In another mode, Margaret Clifford had medical knowledge, and as her daughter Anne recorded she "was a lover of the study and practice of alchemy, by which she found out excellent medicines, that did much good to many."[31] The family "Great Picture" shows a library containing John Gerard's *Herball*, perhaps the source of treatments for relations and household members.[32]

Other genteel women reached out beyond their domiciles. After an assault on Nottingham Castle held by Parliament, Puritan Lucy Hutchinson, the well-educated wife of the governor, dealt with casualties from both sides of the battle lines brought to her when no other surgeon was available.[33] Lady Anne Halkett treated over sixty royalist soldiers injured at the battle of Dunbar, whom she encountered while traveling from Dunfermline in 1651. Acting as their physician and surgeon, she ministered to them at her lodging in Kinrose and later tended the sick at another residence, meriting eventual acknowledgment from Charles II for her medical services.[34] These ladies gained their knowledge through experience, by conversation with learned men, and by studying books. Some affluent women, however, sought official endorsement of their medical know-how. Elizabeth Strudwicke of Kirdford, the wife of a wealthy man, obtained a license to practice surgery in 1673 from the Bishop of Chichester, but this was unusual for females who did not make a living from medicine.[35]

One of the biggest handicaps for women hoping to practice some sort of medicine was the difficulty in acquiring a good and recognized education. The medical faculties at Oxford and Cambridge did not encourage distaff study; females were barred from both lay and ecclesiastical institutions where the healing arts were taught. Henry VIII's reforms required the licensing by bishops of all medical practitioners, except for Oxbridge graduates, but some confusion and equivocation resulted when the Barber-Surgeons' Company was simultaneously charged with supervising its members. Latin language requirements for surgeons fluctuated from time to time according to the guild's statutes, further obscuring entry into the Company ranks; expectations that a candidate could read and write Latin were repealed in 1557, restored in 1629, and were still in effect as late as 1727. The Latin prerequisite would have excluded all but a handful of leisured women, blessed with the opportunity to receive private instruction in the classics but unlikely to seek their living as surgeons.[36]

Those females who sought a working surgeon's license came generally from families of traders, craftsmen, clergy, and medical men. Typical of them are Eleanor Woodhouse of Shoreditch, the wife of a vintner who sought a surgical license in 1613 from the Archbishop of Canterbury, and Alice Blower, a clothier's spouse seeking the same document in 1620. A few years later, Mrs. Isobell Davis of Gravel Lane near Aldgate was episcopally licensed as a surgeon, specializing in the treatment of women and therefore no threat to her male competitors.[37] Jane Pernell of Southwark, who had two husbands in medicine and specialized in treating the King's Evil, obtained a license from Archbishop Sancroft in 1685 after offering a painstaking deposition of the cases she treated. Though the residents of the parishes where she practiced were generally poor, her patients came from a broad spectrum: the offspring of titled gentry, merchants including a book-seller, and servants.[38] Elizabeth Francis was authorized by the Bishop of London to practice surgery and obstetrics in 1689; two physicians, including one from the plentiful Chamberlen clan, championed Mrs. Francis for practice. These women of acknowledged competence and preparation could bequeath their knowledge to a new generation of surgeonesses by means of apprenticeship; surely, more than these few whom we can enumerate did so as well.[39] Among females of the middling sort who slipped through the medical regulatory net altogether were a few women like Mrs.

Susanna Holder, the sister of Christopher Wren, who treated Charles II's injured hand "to the great grief of all the (male) surgeons." Parallels to man-midwives, "shee-surgeons" performed outside the conventional borders of healing, designated as unlike the majority in the field.[40]

Less refined females just as stubbornly persisted promulgating their medical talents. Sara Jinner sturdily defended women in her series of almanacs for the mid-seventeenth century. An *Alamanack or Prognostication* bearing Jinner's name appeared before and after the Stuart restoration, but she was decidedly republican in her politics. Her almanacs are anti-authoritarian and include medical notes, apparently the first to be written by a woman for women. She unnerved at least one misogynist who wrote *The Womans Almanack* in 1659, a satire which attacks Jinner in particular and women in general.[41] Mary Holden, a midwife and astrologer, put out two almanacs around the time of the Glorious Revolution similarly aimed at a female audience. She also sold a toothache cure, mentioned in her almanacs, "because I see such great cruelty in them that cure by plucking out of teeth, and braking of jaw-bones in young children, that they never have any teeth in their places."[42] A third distaff almanac-writer, Dorothy Partridge, probably composed *The Woman's Almanack for 1694, adapted to the Capacity of the Female Sex.* Later almanacs issued under her name may be spurious, a deception of publisher Benjamin Harris to manipulate the female market.[43]

Some craft guilds, such as we shall find with the Stationers' Company, permitted the widows of members to carry on the work of their deceased husbands.[44] According to the court records of the Barber-Surgeons for 1613, relicts of their liverymen could keep shop and bind apprentices, provided they paid quarterly dues, but while some barbers' widows carried on their husbands' trade, the widows of surgeons did not. The evidence unearthed by Doreen Evenden points to systematic exclusion of surgeons' relicts from the guild's rights and privileges; indeed, company policy indicated that members regarded women as unacceptable supervisors of apprentices and inadequate partners in their husband's practice.[45] Surgeons, of course, were not alone in their dismissal of the possibility that females might be more than competent amateurs in health care, relegated to the lower caste jobs of nurse and midwife, which were thought to be innately female skills.

Early modern colloquies of status and rationality remained elite and patriarchal, forestalling the inevitable participation of females in university-level science. Just as a lack of Latin training kept a woman from learned medicine, the absence of science on her résumé would have diminished the possibility of working in the laboratory. If a woman science lecturer had existed, she would have complicated the strains in an already class-conscious culture which justified a correlation between reason and social status.[46] Even noblewomen found the door to amateur scientific societies opened barely a crack. Margaret Cavendish, Duchess of Newcastle, visited the Royal Society in 1667 after prolonged debate among its membership.[47] After a lifetime trying to win the respect of the male scientific community, she was permitted to watch various experiments performed by famed scientists Robert Boyle and Robert Hooke for her edification, albeit she could not join the coterie. The duchess failed to gain entry, not because of her autodidactic opinions, but because she seemed brazen and common. According to diarist Samuel Pepys, who observed the gathering in question, the duchess's "dress was so antique and her deportment so ordinary, that I do not like her at all, nor did I hear her say anything that was worth hearing."[48] No wonder the duchess, a former maid of honor to Henrietta Maria, spoke out vigorously and candidly for more and better education for women.[49]

But as Englishwomen doggedly persevered in their attempts to glean more knowledge about medicine and science and to discuss what they learned, entrepreneurs began to recognize a reading market. The dedication of *The Surgion's Directorie for Young Practitoners . . . and Gentlewomen*, a 1651 reprint of Thomas Vicary's *The Englishman's Treasure*, summons "vertuous ladies" to the art of medicine for the general good. Following on its heels, Leonard Sowerby wrote *The Ladies Dispensatory* in 1652; it contained herbal and other medical advice.[50] Even more popular was the oft-reprinted *The English House-Wife* by Gervase Markham, first published in 1615. Acknowledging that the housewife had responsibility for the preservation of her family's well-being, Markham offered "ordinary rules and medicines" for her edification and advice on broken bones, burns, and the sewing up of wounds: "if it be fit to be stitched, stitch it up." Additionally, Markham suggested the use of quicksilver for venereal disease, evidently also the province of the medically astute English gentlewomen.[51]

The Athenian Mercury, a twice-weekly periodical published in London by John Dunton from 1690 to 1697, went even further in its approbation of the distaff mind and commended itself to the female scientist manqué. Using a question-and-answer format in its "Ladies Day" section, the journal was soon so overwhelmed with letters of inquiry that Dunton begged his readers to refrain from submitting more. Some querists sent in bones and other objects for examination by experts. An Athenian Society evolved from the *Mercury*, and as dozens more publications, written by men, targeted the erudite female, the "scientific lady" became quite stylish, making real contributions by women possible.[52] Scientific primers for women followed, such as Jasper Charlton's *Ladies Astronomy and Chronology* and Charles Leadbetter's *Astronomy*, dedicated to Catherine Edwin, a woman of "great learning and skill in the mathematical sciences, especially in the celestial one."[53] Finally, by the mid-eighteenth century, three science journals edited by women for women appeared: *The Female Spectator* (1744–46), *Epistles for the Ladies* (1749–50), and *The Lady's Museum* (1760–61).[54]

Moreover, bright women were often indispensable assistants to their scientist fathers, husbands, or brothers, and their collaborative work was often innovative. Lady Ranelagh, previously mentioned sister of Robert Boyle, participated fully in the so-called Invisible College, the aim of which was chemical and mechanical experimentation. Male members of the Invisible College later formed the founding nucleus of the Royal Society, but in the 1640s they met at Lady Ranelagh's London home in Pall Mall. She and her illustrious brother lived together the last three decades of their lives, and Boyle built the Golden Phoenix laboratories on the back of her house. Both siblings happily experimented with distillation and chemistry there over the years, dying within a few months of each other in 1692.[55] Bathsua Makin, sister of mathematician Robert Pell and tutor of Charles I's daughter Elizabeth, became an influential scholar and pedagogue in the mid-seventeenth century. She espoused science and mathematics as subjects more relevant to women than either the conventional feminine skills or the traditional masculine preserve of the classics. Makin also insisted that a wife "could not look well to the ways of her household, except she understood physic and chirurgery."[56] Mary Trye was an anti-Galenic chemical physician who took over the practice of her father, Dr. Thomas O'Dowde, and challenged the male medical establishment in her book, *Medicatrix or the Woman Physician*.[57]

As patrons of medical and scientific endeavors, all classes of English women played a vital, if vicarious role in the evolution of British science and medicine by encouraging empiricism and experimentation, hence impairing the professional monopolies of men. The royals had the most patronage at their disposal, and through their sometimes generous intercession, queens and princesses affected the direction of English medicine and science. The tradition of regal advocacy began with Henry VII's mother, Margaret Beaufort, Countess of Richmond, who made benefactions to English academies and virtually founded St. John's College, Cambridge. The first English publication for midwives, a translation of Eucharius Rösslin's *The Birth of Mankind*, was presented in 1532 for her approval to Katherine of Aragon, Henry VIII's initial queen and sponsor of humanist erudition.[58] Queen Katherine's sincere penchant for learning made intellectual interests including science fashionable for women in the highest ranks of society. As one patroness died, another took her place. Katherine's daughter, Mary I, the first Queen of England in her own right, provided modest grants to Oxford University and Trinity College, Cambridge during her reign; her will specified £1,000 for poor scholars at both universities.[59] At the command of Queen Elizabeth I, Sir Francis Walsingham petitioned the College of Physicians on behalf of Margaret Kennix that "she be able to administer her small talent and craft" in medicine. The Fellows politely declined.[60]

During the reign of Elizabeth's successor, James I, as a component of the wholesale roundup of medical women, the College questioned a Mrs. Bryers, who claimed to be a "royal physician" to James I's queen and was recorded as such in the Annals.[61] Mary II urged publication of the observations made by famed German scientific midwife Justine Siegemundin; her sister, Queen Anne, though hardly an intellectual herself, generously supported the work of the Royal Society, especially under the presidency of Isaac Newton, whom she knighted in 1705. Anne ordered her foreign ministers and governors "to contribute all they can . . . towards promoting the designs" of the Royal Society.[62] Additionally, she had her physician extraordinary, Dr. John Arbuthnot, instruct the Society to oversee the Royal Observatory at Greenwich, her solution to the ongoing squabbles among the virtuosi that had stymied scientific cooperation and delayed publication of major works. The queen's intercession succeeded, resulting in official printing of John Flamsteed's star catalogue and Edmund Halley's *Historia coelestis* in 1712.[63] Besides interjecting her presence into the Royal Society, Anne may have inadvertently sabotaged the efforts of the Royal College of Physicians to root out quackery in London when she patronized the unlicensed oculists Sir William Read, whom she also knighted, and Roger Grant. Read advertised in *The Tatler* that he could also cure hairlips, cataracts, and cancer. Incidentally, Lady Read took over her husband's work when he died in 1715.[64] (See Fig. 5.3.)

Likewise, aristocratic and gentry women financed a wide range of medical and scientific work, a portion of which was accomplished through charity. All hospitals looked for alms. Lady Elizabeth Speke, the wife of a sixteenth-century Somerset knight, gave money to leper houses in the West country; Lincolnshire women donated generously to hospitals and almshouses there. Ladies of the Marian court subscribed towards new bedding and equipment for the restored Savoy Hospital, as did their Elizabethan successors.[65] Puritan women, such as Lady Ranelagh, her sister-in-law Lady Margaret Clotworthy, and Lady Mary Vere, were extremely active in matters of patronage.[66] Flourishing urban elites and local gentry had unique philanthropic impact in Tudor Devon, none more so than Ibote Reigny, foundress of an almshouse at Eggesford. Joyce Flamank bequeathed one pence to every poor man and woman in the chapel-hospitals of two Cornish parishes.[67]

Besides their direct participation in medical matters, women in the book business facilitated the changes occurring in health care by publishing, printing, and selling iatric literature. This indirect medical activity by presswomen has been heretofore neglected, yet given the prospects for enterprising females in the world of print their influence as medical publishers should not surprise. Publishing gave opportunity to females unlike most other crafts. Throughout Britain, but mainly in London, a noteworthy number of females, married and unmarried, ran their own bookselling establishments and played a major part in the popularization of reading. As a result of acceptance into the trade by the Stationers' Company of the widows and daughters of its members, dozens of women printed and sold books, pamphlets or mercuries, and newspapers in the City during the Tudor-Stuart and early Georgian years, many running larger publishing houses which employed subordinates.[68] During the Stuart century, Jane Bell and Mary Roberts printed almanacs and calendars for the Stationers, a tacit acknowledgment of the recognition women enjoyed in the guild.

Entry for females into the book business usually came through marriage and family. During the first century of the Stationers' Company, nearly four dozen women are listed in the guild archives, most of them widows of printers who carried on their husbands' work. Consider the Allde wives, booksellers Marga-

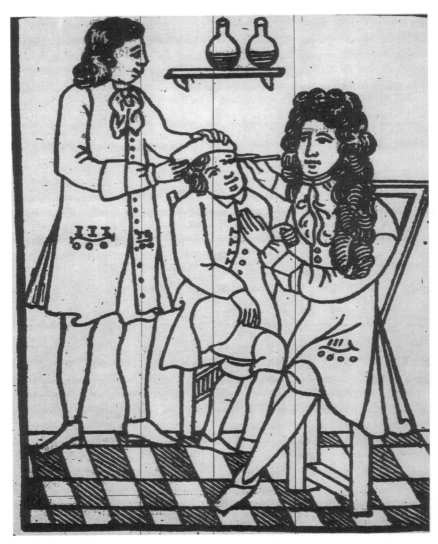

5.3. Sir William Read operating. Reprinted in John Ashton, *Social Life in the Reign of Queen Anne* (London: Chatto, 1904), 324.

ret and Elizabeth. After John Allde's death in 1584, his relict Margaret continued in the trade at the Long Shop in the Poultry, first in conjunction with her
son Edward, and then alone after 1589, when he moved his premises to the
Gilded Cup in Cripplegate; Margaret Allde took apprentices from 1593 to
1600. Her daughter-in-law, Elizabeth Allde, likewise maintained Edward Allde's
business after his death in 1628; moreover, her son by a previous marriage
helped run the Gilded Cup and her daughter married a stationer, Richard
Oulton, to whom Elizabeth Allde made over all her copyrights.[69] Elizabethan
era print-wives Joan Orwin and Frances Simson both showed an amazing occupational attraction by marrying three consecutive bookmen: Mrs. Orwin
had already buried husbands John Kingston and George Robinson when she
married Thomas Orwin; Mrs. Simson later wed Richard Rede and Georege
Elde.[70]

Other early lady printers made their mark in the trade and participated in
activities commemorated by the Company of Stationers. Jane Yetsweirt inherited a patent in 1595 for printing law books from her husband Charles, Clerk
of the Signet. In 1583 bookseller Joane Jugge "presented" Gabriel Simson to
the Association for admittance to the freedom of the guild, as did Jane Yardley
several apprentices in 1604; Joan Broome, a bookseller for ten years at the
Great North Door of St. Paul's Church following her husband's death in 1591,
exercised her rights by entering three comedies in the register at Stationers'
Hall from the pen of John Lyly, performed by the Children of Paul's; and Joane
Newbery registered books at the Hall and took apprentices in her business at
the Ball in St. Paul's Churchyard after John Newbery's death in 1603.

Occasionally, one glimpses what may be deliberate interaction within this
sorority of bookwomen. In 1637 widow Joane Greene, who had shops in Cambridge and London, signed over to London bookseller Anne Boler, relict of
James Boler, all her interest in several publications. The prolific printer Ellen
Cotes often did jobs for busy publisher Anna Seile in the 1660s. Not yet
grounded in a "shared sense of gender identity," the community of women
printworkers reflected "overlapping relationships" to the new print environment; as literary scholar Paula McDowell has noted, for female entrepreneurs
in the book business, "gender was not necessarily the first category of identity."[71] Family clearly was such a prime category. Joyce Macham, relect and
executrix of Samuel Macham, maintained the shop at the sign of Time in St.
Paul's Churchyard for eleven years after her husband's death in 1615. She arranged for residuals from certain copyrights (two shillings per ream of any of
the works) to be paid her son until he attained his freedom as a stationer, after
which the complete rights were to be reassigned to him.[72]

Book trade families became increasingly common in the last half of the
seventeenth century as the whole household pitched in to make the business
thrive. Intermarriage between book trade families was frequent, for sensible
business reasons and because of the apprentice system, which introduced ambitious young men into domiciles likely to have marriageable daughters ac-

quainted with the craft. For instance, Benjamin Allport, a London bookseller in the 1680s, married Dorothy Dawks, daughter and sister of prominent printers with whom he collaborated; at Allport's death she wed another pressman, William Bowyer.[73] Women in early modern England did not typically work with their husbands in a harmonious domestic setting, but changing conditions in the literary world coincided with the emergence of distaff printers and sellers. Some wives became full partners in the book business; many ran stalls to sell the products of their husbands' presses. Still others traded as personal agents while their spouses were away or tended the family shop with their unmarried daughters. Such endeavors accent the striking rise in female learning in London.

It is difficult to state apodictically how many women were in the book trade in early modern England. By the sixteenth century, women were well established in all facets of the business—printing, publishing, and bookselling—and over sixty women are listed in the seventeenth-century records of the Stationers' Company.[74] Approximately four percent of the booksellers and printers in England active from the Restoration to the reign of George I were women; more than 58 percent of these were printers' widows and 6 percent were daughters of freemen. Historian Hannah Barker, by including distaff shop owners, printers, hawkers, and distribution agents throughout England, calculates the number of bookwomen at 10 percent. While warning of the dangers of misleading records, Maureen Bell counts 320 women connected with the London trade between 1557 and 1700, and about 50 more in the provinces.[75] Whereas women were usually barred by custom from the brotherhood of city livery companies, London Stationers' relicts had the right to take apprentices and hold shares in the English Stock, a monopoly on psalms, psalters, almanacs, and primers held jointly by members of the Company; some females, up to ten percent in the eighteenth century, even attained the designation "master printer" in the guild's lists.[76] And when they died, printwomen without heirs often left their property to the guild.[77] However, the majority of printers' mates, even the most active ones, cannot be easily differentiated until their husbands' deaths, since the "existence of a man effectively blots out any record of activity by the woman."[78] As the sly saying goes: "anonymous was a woman," a truism for the book trade where the slightly more daring females disclosed themselves with initials. At any rate, recognizing a printer's gender at a time when so many in the business shielded their identities on political grounds can be difficult.

The Stationers set conditions that affected the ease with which a widow continued her spouse's printing business. The business had to have been fully licensed and active at the time of the printer's demise, and even a properly licensed widow forfeited her rights and her shares of English stock if she wed someone other than a freeman stationer.[79] Moreover, women were implicitly excluded from Company offices reserved for its most successful men and almost never wore the livery, the hallmark of its fraternal solidarity; moreover, the guild never became a route for women to obtain civic enfranchisement. Though they rarely obtained the "freedom" of a prestigious mystery, more females could be found in the minor companies and in trades of intermediate status, certainly retailing and shopkeeping. And, of course, many London booksellers were not members of any guild at all, further hiding their identities.[80]

When needing to face the circumstances of business ownership thrust upon them by the death of a stationer spouse or father, women sometimes reorganized their operations. Elizabeth Purslowe, widow of George, ran his business for fourteen years after his death in 1632, but used her own initials on the books she printed.[81] A few less intrepid relics scaled back their ventures, perhaps eliminating the printing side of an enterprise to keep a typefoundry going; others took extra help, filling their own former positions as second-in-command within the establishment. Sons and daughters in the trade could be promoted to partnership or, lacking natural children, business women might elevate an apprentice, sort of a surrogate offspring anyway, to partnership. Jackin Vautrollier, an unaffiliated pressman's widow forbidden to print by the Stationers' Company, solved her business problem by marrying her husband's much younger apprentice in 1588, less than a year after Thomas Vautrollier died.[82] Whatever strategy they employed, women in printing trade households, widowed or not, played significant roles in the family business and usually took charge when conditions warranted. Evidently husbands generally recognized their spouses' capacity for competent management and business partners, since most men in the livery companies named their wives sole or joint executrix of their wills.[83] Reflecting a widespread decline in the rate of remarriage, most widows in the book trade tended not to remarry, doubtless cognizant that their independent status as "femmes soles" under the law would be compromised if they wed, though there were some exceptions to this custom.[84]

Probably meriting the distinction "first English woman printer," Elizabeth Pickering, widow and sole executrix of bookman Robert Redman, reproduced the second issuance of Thomas Moulton's *This is the Myrror our Glasse of Helth* in 1541.[85] According to the preamble, Moulton, a Dominican, said he was motivated to pen this part-medical, part-astrological tome out of compassion "for pore people . . . destroyed by default of help." Pickering was no shrinking violet. In the colophon to Moulton's book is recorded: "Imprinted by me Elysabeth late wyfe unto Robert Redman."[86] Evidence exists that Elizabeth began printing at the sign of the George near St. Dunstan's church even before her husband's demise, as her married initials, E.R., can be found on books put out by Redman in 1539, including *The Treasure of Poor Men*.[87] Reverting to her maiden name after Redman's death in 1540, Pickering also produced an anonymous volume in octavo that same year about urine: "all the coloures that urynes be of, with medycines annexed to every uryne and to every urine his urynall much profitable for every man to knowe." After two years running the business on her own, Elizabeth married Ralph Cholmondeley, a man not in the Stationers' Company, and passed the printing house to William Middleton.[88]

Printers exerted powerful influence, helping to shape cultural, social, and medical change. Women worked side by side with men to choose what would be printed, to set type, to operate the press, and to illustrate and proofread the text. Another among the earliest distaff publishers of medical material is the aforementioned Joan Broome. In 1591 she published an edition of one of the most important surgical treatises of the Elizabethan era, William Clowes' *A Prooved Practice for All Young Chirurgians*. Clowes, sergeant surgeon to Her Majesty, criticized the battlefield medicine he observed while assigned to the army with the Earl of Leicester in the Low Countries and charged incompetent military doctors with slaying more English soldiers than the enemy.[89]

Anne Griffin, widow of Edward Griffin, carried on the business after his death in 1621 with her son and printed Thomas Bedford's *True and Certain Relation of a Strange Birth* in 1635 to be sold by Anne Bowler in London and William Russell in Plymouth. A woodcut of conjoined twins, born in Plymouth and interred there, is on the verso of the title. She also printed the 1637 edition of Markham's *English Housewife* and his *Cheap and Good Husbandry* for bookseller John Harrison. In 1643 Griffin, described as forty-eight years old, gave a deposition against Archbishop Laud, who had threatened her for printing an anti-popish diatribe six years earlier. Griffin's son also left an able widow to take over the family business and manage it for twenty-one years: Sarah Griffin. For prominent publishers Henry and Timothy Twyford, Sarah Griffin printed George Castle's *The Chemical Galenist*, an important salvo in the medical wars. During their respective careers at the shop near the Old Bailey, the two Mrs. Griffins took a total of sixteen apprentices.[90]

Ellen Cotes, widow of the official printer to the City of London, had a large establishment at her headquarters at the Barbican. Surveyed in 1668, she reported employing three presses, two apprentices, and nine pressmen.[91] In 1665 Mrs. Cotes published an important seven-hundred-page illustrated volume containing the translated works of French surgeon Ambrose Paré and some selected tracts of Dutch anatomist Adriaan van de Spiegel. Richard Cotes had printed a 1649 discrete edition of the Spiegel; the title page of that anatomy, *Aggeiologia, or a Description of the Vessells in the Body of Man*, touted figures that were "the largest and fairest that ever were published with any English book." Mary Clark, widow of Ellen Cotes's frequent collaborator Andrew Clark, printed the same combined Paré-Spiegel tome in 1678, eight years after Mrs. Cotes's death, indicating that one distaff printer without heirs amiably handed the rights off to another with a large clan in the trade; Mary Clark continued at the business in Aldersgate Street until 1696.[92]

At least twenty female publishers in late Stuart London produced dozens of medical tomes of consequence, adding to the clamor for change in health care. Medical titles and recipe books constituted roughly five percent of the books published by distaff printers from a sampling of the last half of the seventeenth century.[93] While that amount may seem modest, some women made it their trade specialty, and works attributed to presses run by these women were among

London's most significant and familiar. Some bookshops carried medical books as a trademark feature, but the gender of the printer or seller does not appear to have any express bearing on the kinds of books printed or sold. The few women who operated their own businesses followed whatever pattern of publishing their husbands had pursued without any apparent change in agenda, at least in the medical realm.[94]

Although several Fellows in the College of Physicians themselves wrote books about their particular remedies, many still subscribed to the notion that any public disclosure of the contents of medications and their prescribed usage for certain ailments was irresponsible to the profession and dangerous to society; their objections, however, were drowned in a "torrent of vernacular literature."[95] Chemical physicians, surgeons, and apothecaries, the principal challengers to the monopoly of elite Galenist doctors, had no such qualms about disseminating useful information to laymen, especially in a vibrant medical marketplace. They wrote their books in English as did the writers, many of them women, of best-selling cookery books that often contained sections on household treatments and self-medication. For instance, prolific publisher Gertrude Dawson issued at least seven of the earliest editions of the Countess of Kent's sought-after *A Choice Manual of Rare and Select Secrets in Physick and Chyrurgery*, which encompassed a variety of wellness recipes aimed at females responsible for extended households. Bookseller Margaret Shears, the widow of a stationer with five shops and businesswoman in her own right for thirty years, is named as the specific distributor for one edition.[96]

In addition, women booksellers and stationers often sold nostrums in their shops, creating "the most important distribution network for proprietary medicines" in the late seventeenth century.[97] True to her Puritan, anti-establishment creed, entrepreneur Hannah Allen peddled elixirs from the family bookstore off Lombard Street in the early 1660s while her second husband, Livewell Chapman, was incarcerated for libelous printing. Others sold remedies just to make ends meet. Mrs. Stampe, a bookseller at the Queen's Head in Westminster Hall in the 1660s, openly advertised in *The Newes* (December 17, 1663) that she dealt in patent medicines, and widow Sarah Howkins in the 1690s vended panaceas from her store in Lombard Street.[98] Publisher John Dunton commended Benjamin Billingsley's wife for maintaining the family bookselling business during her husband's lengthy bouts of madness; Mrs. Billingsley kept things together by selling for ten shillings a powder purported to cure stones in the bladder and kidneys.[99]

Among the more conspicuous distaff publishers of medical works in London who added their own contributions to the publishing commotion were Susannah Miller, Hannah Sawbridge, Mary Kettilby, and Rebecca Bonwicke. Miss Miller, daughter of bookman William Miller, inherited what his contemporary John Dunton reported was "the largest collection of stitched books of any man in the world."[100] She took over the business at the Acorn in St. Paul's Churchyard after her father's death in 1696. Under his colophon, she published a new edition in octavo of Jane Sharp's famous *Mid-Wife's Book* and brought out an eleventh edition of the Countess of Kent's *Choice Manual* in affordable twelves, both medical books by women, for women, published and sold by a woman.[101] Hannah Sawbridge, relict of George Sawbridge, continued the family business for seven years at the Bible on Ludgate Hill after her husband's death in 1681; fifty-two imprints are attributed to her. She also negotiated restitution with the Stationers' Company for improprieties committed by her deceased mate while Treasurer of the English Stock. Sawbridge had bilked the Company out of royalties due it when he camouflaged his ownership of the print shop that handled Cambridge University's business, but Hannah Sawbridge paid the Stationers £158 in 1683 to settle the matter.[102] A savvy entrepreneur who emphasized medical tracts, Mrs. Sawbridge printed and sold Culpeper's various anti-establishment guides, his translated pharmacopoeia, and his directory for midwives.[103] She supervised the development in 1684 of a new edition of another of Gervase Markham's popular self-help books, *A Way to Get Wealth: The Office of a Good Housewife in Physick*.[104] During the following year she oversaw the printing of a second edition of *The True Preserver and Restorer of Health* by advice-giver George Hartman. The result of her skillful management of the family business was an enormous legacy for her children.[105]

Walter Kettilby published nearly two dozen medical titles during the quarter-century his book business headquartered at the Bishop's Head in St. Paul's Churchyard. He published several pieces by Thomas Sydenham, the practical English physician who endorsed "old women's experience [rather than] learned men's theories."[106] At the turn of the century, Walter Kettilby's wife Mary took over the business and added to the deluge of health-related tomes by creating *A Collection of Above Three Hundred Receipts in Cookery, Physick and Surgery; for the Use of All Good Wives, Tender Mothers, and Careful Nurses*. In her preface, Mrs. Kettilby, like her spouse a defender of hierarchy, voiced the hope that the College physicians would not "misconstrue this . . . as an invasion of their province or a disrespect to their persons."[107] Like the Kettilbys, Henry Bonwicke was a prolific publisher of medical literature, but his stock inclined toward the medical challengers and, after his death in 1706, his relict Rebecca carried on the business, producing new editions of *The Compleat Surgeon* by Daniel Le Clerc and John Pechey's *The Compleat Herbal*, both deplored by the College Fellows.

Some females not known for a medical publishing specialty nonetheless produced influential books in the field. Joan Dover, whose imprint is found in *Physical Nosonomy* (1665) by William Drage, was the widow of Simon Dover, tried and convicted in February 1664 of publishing a piece critical of the Stuarts. After his death two months later, Mrs. Dover had to scrape up his fine of 100 marks and probably realized a profit from Drage's popular medical work.[108] Printer Martha Harrison, sometimes herself in trouble for publishing seditious material, put out a few medical and astrological manuals around the time of the Restoration. Elizabeth Calvert printed and sold an expensive folio edition of

Renodaeus' *Dispensatory*, "containing the whole body of Physick, discovering the Natures and Properties, and Vertues of Vegetals," from her shop at the Black Spread Eagle.[109] Jane Bell, printer of calendars and almanacs for the Stationers, published John Partridge's *Treasury of Hidden Secrets*, commonly called *The Good Huswives Closet*, a compendium of "necessary physick helps . . . and the names of diseases." Printer's widow Mary Clark, with over 100 of her own imprints, reproduced a folio edition of *The Works of Ambrose Paré* in 1678. Perhaps because her shop was located near the College of Physicians, Margaret Bennet during the reign of William III produced several expensive Latin works probably aimed at the Fellows, while her contemporary, Elizabeth Whitlock, implicitly supported their rivals (and her neighbors) in the Barber-Surgeons' Company when she made and sold Daniel Turner's *Vindication of the Noble Art of Chirurgery*.[110]

Anne Baldwin, spouse of the well-known Whig publisher Richard Baldwin, printed a few scientific and medical tomes. Despite the proximity of her store to the College of Physicians, she published *The Honour of the Gout* by Philander Misiatrus in 1700. Its format, in twelves, signalled a broadly intended audience, notwithstanding gout was still commonly thought of as a rich man's disease. Elizabeth Harris, whom Dunton described as "the beautiful relict of my worthy friend, Mr. John Harris," released *Ettmullerus Abridg'd or a Compleat System of the Theory and Practice of Physick* by Michael Ettmullerus in 1702.[111] When Elizabeth Blackwell's printer husband, Alexander, was thrown into debtor's prison near the end of the Augustan age for financial problems in his business, she designed, engraved, and published *A Curious Herbal*; the subscriptions she solicited for it released her husband from jail.[112] Clearly, there was money to be made by female printers in medical publishing.

The contributions made to their trade by females as printers and sellers and to the readers of early modern England were many and meaningful. Yet, like their male counterparts, these women resist easy categorization, and their motives, other than earnings, remain obscured by the contrasting things they published.[113] Employing Marx's concept of class, Paula McDowell argues that a variety of differences hindered these bookwomen from understanding themselves as a group.[114] Although there are some exceptions, most distaff publishers continued their family businesses with no demonstrable ideological change in the sorts of books produced and sold. As dispensers of news, mercuries, and partisan broadsheets, women publishers—like their fathers, husbands, and sons—helped advance the process of political polarization.[115] Their religious editions, regardless of doctrinal affiliation, furthered the popularization of personal meditation and spiritual inquiry, albeit making a very secular profit. The contributions of female printers to controversies in medicine and their lucrative promotion of common health remedies, although heretofore overlooked, surely promoted change in the medical marketplace, though not necessarily verifying a theoretical or jurisdictional predilection of presswomen.[116]

After the middle of the eighteenth century, while the number of actors in the print world surged, fewer women prevailed in the creative facets of book publishing. Some historians have theorized that as a business was capitalized and industrialized it was completely taken over by men; a few point to new laws that protected the investments of major publishers and squeezed out the lesser press. Still others are not sure why women were "unable to respond as effectively as men to the new opportunities within their trade" or even that there was any substantial break in female work patterns.[117] For instance, Margaret Hunt has discovered that 6.7 percent of stationery businesses and 4.4 percent of bookstores insured with Royal Exchange Assurance between 1775 and 1787 were owned by women, not much of a decrease in their trade activity.[118] However, Henry Plomer records only about fifty women in the trade in England from 1726 to 1775 in his *Dictionary* for that period, and the individual printers indexed in Maxted's *London Book Trades, 1775–1800* include less than 2.5 percent women. D. F. McKenzie numbers only two dozen women to whom apprentices were bound between 1725 and 1800, a marked decline in female leadership and mentoring.[119] By the census of 1841, only 161 females were identified as printers in England and Wales, compared to 15,582 men.[120] Whatever the reasons and whenever the time, as women lost their central role in the making and distributing of printed texts, they also surrendered their access to the press as a powerful political tool.[121]

Chapter 6

LOCATION, LOCATION, LOCATION: BOOKSHOPS IN LONDON AND MEDICAL CONTROVERSY

"Our streets are filled up with blue Boars, black Swans, and red Lions; not to mention flying Pigs and Hogs in Armour, and with man other creatures more extraordinary than any in the Desarts of Africk." So wrote Joseph Addison in the *Spectator* about the bewildering signs of late Stuart London.[1] Until street numbers were inaugurated in the eighteenth century, pictorial signs marked inns, taverns, shops, houses, and even rooms inside larger edifices. Besides being important as a means of identification, signs in Tudor-Stuart England often served as personal trademarks, but there was some inevitable duplication of symbols, so members of the same trade customarily avoided use of similar emblems within neighborhoods. That kind of implicit business cooperation, even in a nascent trade like printing, exemplifies the understanding of London entrepreneurs who had staked out new enterprises, literally and figuratively, at the intersection of medicine and publishing.

Booksellers as a class produced more kinds of signs and signboards than any other group of traders. The most common signs for bookshops sort into four types: birds and animals, religious objects and themes, heads of famous people, and miscellaneous devices like arrows or anchors not immediately associated with the book trade.[2] No allusions in this pattern of signage identify booksellers who handled medical tomes. Despite their sometimes obstructive nuisance, signs persisted until the aftermath of a tragedy in 1718 when a billboard-sized plank in Bride Lane crashed to the ground killing four people.[3] Public agitation over the dangers of large, hanging placards led to the proclamation in 1762 of law requiring the numbering of individual houses and businesses.

The first location associated with the book trade was London Bridge, where the making and selling of manuscript books transpired. The "Mistery of Stationers," organized in 1403 and awarded a royal charter in 1557, was the book craft guild. The company included textwriters, manuscript artists or limners, parchment sellers, bookbinders, and, ultimately, printers and booksellers. Between 1395 and 1540, over seventy stationers' names appear in the Bridge House records, the archive related to the running of London Bridge and the management of its assets. As shop tenants, the stationers operated out of property rented to them by the Bridge or as recipients of special commissions from

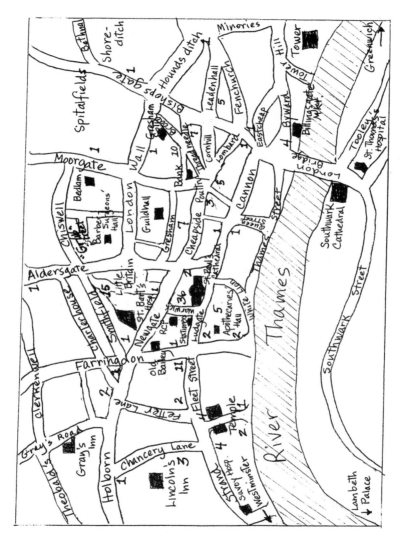

6.1. Map of central London in the late seventeenth century showing locations of groups of book-sellers and printers.

the Bridge Wardens for making and repairing books. For instance, service books in the Chapel on the Bridge needed constant repair, requiring the talents of bookbinders; account books of the Clerk of the Bridge also needed binding. Moreover, the Clerk of the Works bought parchment, vellum, and paper from dealers in residence on the Bridge.[4] Sales of more costly books on and around London Bridge began to dwindle as the environs became "a rather low shopping area," and by the seventeenth century, sellers of less expensive printed items supplanted up-scale emporia.[5]

The original Stationers sold books from temporary stalls, becoming fixed to a site by camping against the wall of a building under the protective overhang of its upper stories. These impermanent structures gave way by 1600 to low sheds built more strongly as the business prospered.[6] By mid-seventeenth century many bookshops were in substantial houses, with cellars for storage, spacious ground floor rooms for sales, and upstairs residence for the owner or his tenants. It was not uncommon to find bookstores in structures with frontages of thirty feet, equal depth, four levels and garrets above. Mimicking their humble pedigree, booksellers sometimes set up auxiliary displays on retractable porches in front of their shops, employing projecting, hinged "stall-boards" on which merchandise could be shown under a projecting, hinged canopy.[7] Unlike residents of other metropolises, Londoners of different stations lived in close proximity, their communities circumscribed by street, ward, and parish. Joseph Addison reported that though the city was "an aggregate of several nations," ways of life defined one's locality: "The inhabitants of St. James's, notwithstanding they live under the same laws, and speak the same language, are a distinct people from those of the Temple on one side, and those of Smithfield on the other, by several climates and degrees, in their ways of thinking and conversing together."[8]

Prior to the Great Fire of London in 1666, Paul's Cross Churchyard and vicinity had become the center of the book trade, with nearly every frontage in the Cross Yard occupied by bookshops. Given the concentration of literacy in the sector, it may have been historically inevitable that the Cross Yard became the focus of the world of print. After all, the cathedral district held a large ecclesiastical administration before and after the Reformation; like all cathedrals in capital cities, St. Paul's had attracted stationers prior to the advent of printing. Bills were posted in the nave of the old basilica invariably beginning with the word *sisquis*, or "if anyone"; later this Latin opening was adopted for ecclesiastical matters only.[9] So integral did St. Paul's Churchyard become to the Tudor-Stuart booktrade that Daniel Defoe could scoff at any stationer locating elsewhere, "the same thing as for a country shop-keeper not to set up in or near the market-place."[10]

As early as 1543, Reyner Wolfe set up the initial printing house in the Cross Yard and sold books from a large property rented from the Bishop of London. His enterprise flourished, and by the time of his death in 1573, Wolfe's holdings stretched along 120 feet of "the best bookselling frontage in England."[11] Even before the sixteenth century, however, Paternoster Row, the narrow street north of the churchyard, burgeoned with renters marketing books and other print materials, becoming in time a particularly well-defined craft quarter. This venue provided a nucleus for the brotherhood of Stationers where fraternal bonds could be formed among artisans and shopkeepers in the book business. Records indicate that many of the Paternoster Row printers and sellers held prominent posts in the guild and in the City.[12] St. Paul's Churchyard identified the whole precinct, encompassing the immured expanse within the gates of the cathedral grounds and streets to the south.

Peter Blayney has meticulously reassembled the location of individual bookshops in that precinct before the Fire. Among his findings is the repeated use over the years of a property for the same purpose but under a different hallmark. For example, Humphrey Toy held a seventy-year lease from the College of the Petty Canons for a shop at the sign of the Helmet that faced south on the Churchyard opposite the great north door. He, Thomas Chard, his former apprentice, and Nathaniel Fosbrooke, another stationer who followed them in 1606, found the frontage opposite the cathedral portal particularly desirable. Right next door to the Helmet was Arthur Johnson's White Horse, another bookshop with a long lineage, likely in business under that sign from 1604 to 1665. Just across Canon Lane from the White Horse was Thomas Adams's White Lion, later the Three Kings, and later still The Prince's Arms. And adjacent to that site was The Bishop's Head, the business of William Ponsby; Ponsby was succeeded by his former apprentice, Edward Blount, by William Lownes and his son-in-law, George Latham.[13] The Bishop's Head counts as the fourth bookshop of an eventual seventeen in a row along the north side of the Cross Yard to Paul's Gate; more could be found from there to St. Paul's School and bookselling bays lined the cathedral wall.

One of the largest and best known of the Cross Yard bookshops bore the sign of The Judith until 1547, The Holy Ghost between 1548 and 1613, and The Three Pigeons from 1614 until around 1684. In its incarnation as The Three Pigeons, four different stationers occupied the premises: William Barrett, who added two white birds to the sign for the Holy Ghost and changed the shop's name for good, John Parker, Humphrey Robinson, and John Baker II. All carried a variety of books, although the smaller formats predominated. Parker was the publisher of Francis Roys' *Diseases of the Time Attended by their Remedies*, printed for him in 1622 by William Stansby, a man of considerable standing in the trade and Parker's colleague in the livery. But Parker was the real star of Stationers' Company, serving as Warden for three years and Master from 1647 until his death the following year. Robinson, one of the most successful booksellers of the mid-seventeenth century, succeeded Parker at the Three Pigeons and eventually as Master of the Stationers' Company, rebuilding the structure after the Great Fire. Baker, who often partnered with Edward Brewster, leased the shop from Robinson's heirs from 1670 to 1684.[14] All in all, the site and its proprietors exemplify the vitality of the London book business and the stability of its locations.

The Stationers' Company headquartered its activity at St. Paul's Church-yard until acquiring a site on the east side of Milk Street off Ludgate Hill in 1606; the Hall, erected in 1611, burned in the Great Fire and was rebuilt by 1673.[15] Many printers and sellers launched their shops in proximity to Statio-ners' Hall. Elizabethan-era writer and critic Thomas Nashe called the precinct "the Exchange of all authors" and Bishop of Salisbury John Earle, a perceptive social commentator, went further: St. Paul's was "the great Exchange of all discourse, the general Mint of all famous lies."[16] Anyone wanting to compose, translate, or edit a text in his time went there to do business. But between 1640 and 1650 a building boom west of the cathedral created new residential and commercial communities which attracted stationers and shifted the book trade to the New Jewry and Anchor Alley. Though in a decrepit state, the cathedral crossing flowed with boisterous traffic, a main thoroughfare for gossips and peddlers, and booths smothered the church facade. Noisy commercial deals were struck in the nave, causing Cavalier poet-priest Richard Flecknoe to la-ment that "the buyers and sellers have drov'n out the Temple."[17] The Statio-ners' church, Saint Faith's, occupied the crypt of the building, and booksellers rented warehouse space elsewhere in the basement. Consequently, booksellers suffered more than most in the Great Fire of 1666, losing, besides their shops and houses, whatever inventories they stored at the cathedral.[18]

The status of the area declined somewhat after the fire, but the trade's con-centration by St. Paul's persisted; some thirty bookshops still used the Church-yard as their address in 1700. The first City club met nearby at the Castle Tavern on Paternoster Row, with booksellers among its most prominent mem-bers. The Castle provided a conclave for authors, booksellers, and printers in-tent on making deals for the production and distribution of books. In St. Paul's Churchyard itself, Child's Coffeehouse became a favored haunt of physicians, scientists, and Fellows of the Royal Society. Joseph Addison and Richard Steele chatted at Child's, habitually mentioning it by name in *The Spectator*, Addison calling those assembled there "the fraternity of Spectators" and extolling the "love of society" that such establishments engendered.[19] Not all of the caf-feine-facilitated conversations there were pleasant. In 1710 the Royal Society obtained supervisory power over the formerly independent Royal Observatory, and John Flamsteed, the Astronomer Royal, met with Dr. John Arbuthnot and James Hodgson, Master of the Royal School of Mathematics, on behalf of the Fellows to discuss publication of his catalogue of planetary tables, but Flamsteed's rival and former assistant Edmund Halley, now secretary of the Royal Society, had already made many alterations to Flamsteed's list without his consent. Even more humiliating, Halley had taken a copy of Flamsteed's manuscript to Child's Coffeehouse and pointed out all its errors to his friends.[20] Auctions disposing of entire libraries occurred at coffeehouses near the cathedral, like Child's and the Chapter on Paternoster Row, the latter noted for its plentiful supply of books, where authors fraternized with the publishers who promised to make their names famous. The Chapter was home to the Congers, an association of booksellers who met to divide expensive publishing ventures into shares and thereby reduce individual risk. Renowned for housing entire runs of London newspapers, the Chapter kept a library of recent publications maintained by its bookselling clientele.[21]

Even before the conflagration of 1666, however, there were many more options for commercially ingenious printers and sellers. Unlike those along the Seine in Paris, London bookshops did not accumulate along the banks of the Thames, because there was no riverside promenade. Instead, stores abounded on major thoroughfares and near bridges, gates, and public buildings. Due to its proximity to the courts, Westminster Hall itself was lined with stalls of booksellers and law stationers,, though some thought this was a lamentable situation. The proclivity to build bookshops near approaches to the city applied long before the Fire. St. Mildred's Church on the eastern end of Cheapside stood on the very edge of the Wallbrook, one of the many streams that flowed across the city from the northern heights. Nearby the aged parish church stood a row of diverse shops, the one closest to it a printing house known in the trade as the "Long Shop in the Poultry," an alley of chicken-sellers. The annals for the "Long Shop under St. Mildred's Church wall" begin in 1523 and continue for over a century, held by a succession of men whose changing techniques and equipment, like those occupants of The Three Pigeons, typify the evolving trade in England.

Richard Banckes, the first known occupant, printed curious books about drunkenness, a known problem in the neighborhood; he also produced an important work on navigation in 1528, various herbals, and Thomas Moulton's popular book on medicine, *Mirror or Glasse of Helthe*.[22] He was succeeded by Richard Kele around 1542, who put out an English primer, Christmas carols, and Chaucer in folio, but despite this activity, Kele was imprisoned. By 1559 the premises were inhabited by Kele's apprentice, John Allde, who carried on an even busier business than his predecessors. Allde had as many as eight apprentices working for him concurrently; he needed the help to produce a plethora of ballads and broadsides, as well as weightier tomes like law books and sermons. His son Edward issued books from the "Long Shop" until 1588, after which he imprinted works "at the sign of the Gilded Cup." But the shop continued to function, like the Three Pigeons, as a a durable site in the world of print. John Allde's widow identified the shop as hers in early seventeenth century broadsides and pamphlets before selling it to a bookseller Henry Rockett; his relict sold the place in 1611 to stationer John Smyth on behalf of the Company. Though the records waste away after that, the lengthy tenancy of the "Long Shop" by bookmen was probably destroyed only by the flames of 1666.[23]

Reconstruction after the Fire transformed the city streets, gave birth to new enterprises at old addresses, and produced knots of bookshops in other parts of town. North of St. Paul's, Duck Lane and Little Britain, less exclusive than the Churchyard, enjoyed a surge in business in the later seventeenth century as international book dealers plied their trade. Secondhand booksellers and newspapermen continued to live and work in Little Britain until well into the eighteenth century, though its cachet as a book paradise had declined by then. Book auctions took place periodically in Covent Garden piazza, where Samuel Pepys browsed for secondhand volumes to add to his growing collection. Moorfields attained a notoriety among London environs as a locale where the lowest ranks of the trade gathered. Always a zone of dubious reputation and bawdyhouses, Moorfields further declined as a stable neighborhood after 1668 when violent rioters, including numbers of apprentices, attacked the brothels there. The Stationers' Company did not recognize bookshops and printers clustered there, so infamous was the district's character. Robert Hooke, who kept tabs on all of his bookmen contacts in St. Paul's and Little Britain, hardly ever recorded the identity of Moorfields book dealers. Moreover, Hooke expressed something akin to shock when he found books by his patron Robert Boyle "exposed in Moorfields on the railes."[24]

Refashioning burnt-out stretches of the city continued unabated for years. A main concourse that was developed after the Fire from Cheapside to Cornhill contained twenty bookshops. The richest London stationer and a Member of Parliament, Thomas Guy, lived at the junction of Cornhill and Lombard Street. In the remodeled Poultry, home to a bevy of printers and sellers, fabricative commotion was ever present as the road was widened into a veritable High Street. Several major streets including Lombard, Threadneedle, Princes, and Walbrook converged at the east end of the Poultry, making a hub for the City.[25] St. Mildred's, the parish church at Scalding Alley and the Poultry, was redone by Sir Christopher Wren. Simultaneously, just a few lanes away, workers remade St. Christopher le Stocks under Wren's supervision. City Surveyors oversaw private rebuilding and recorded descriptions of street-fronting properties. The sector became decidedly mixed in its usage, containing a variety of shops, coffeehouses, garden courts, personal dwellings, and the Poultry compter or sheriff's jail, down a passageway just east of the Grocers' Hall court. In the 1680s the Grocers' Hall itself served as the residence of London's Lord Mayor. Poultry property owners with multiple holdings included several livery companies, physicians, lawyers, and real estate speculators who leased offices to businessmen, many of them booksellers.

The London book trade replicated the topography and occupational character of the city. I have plotted the "addresses" of scores of printers and sellers associated with medical literature after the Restoration (See Fig. 6.1.). The largest numbers of bookshops carrying any iatric titles could be found around St. Paul's, in Little Britain, on Cornhill, on Fleet Street, and in the Poultry. There were approximate partisan neighborhoods in late seventeenth-century London. Tories typically operated their bookshops closer to the cathedral and in Little Britain, while Whiggish printers often ensconced themselves in enterprises away from St. Paul's. This general observation does not always hold true, nor do the settings of London bookstores offer conclusive proof about the medical politics of their proprietors. They do not offer, posits Adrian Johns, any consistent information about the political or religious orientation of the stationer. He wisely cautions that "one should not assume, let alone romanticize, connections between commerce and radicalism."[26]

The dozens of booksellers around St. Paul's were close to the Royal College of Physicians, but they were equally convenient to Stationers' Hall, site of their livery company. The several bookshops in Little Britain which handled medical texts were as accessible to physicians at St. Bartholomew's Hospital as they were to the Barber-Surgeons' Hall, locus of an association that sometimes defied the College. Fewer book businesses stocking medical items circled the Apothecaries' Hall near Blackfriars, yet by the end of the seventeenth century their society provided the greatest challenge to establishment doctors. In 1714, guide-book writer John Macky observed that ancient books in all languages might be found in Little Britain and Paternoster Row, divinity and classics were available on the north side of the cathedral, law and history bookshops bunched around Temple Bar and next to the Inns of Court, French booksellers lined the Strand, and near the Royal Exchange works on mercantile affairs filled printshops.[27] A diverse and extensive trade in second-hand books blossomed throughout the metropolis with its own specialist markets and sales procedures.

Some members of the Stationers' Company also sold "pictures," the word being applied indiscriminately to painted and printed images. By the Stuart era, some shops came to feature prints, the best located around Covent Garden where leading engravers conveniently lived. But map and chart sellers scattered their shops throughout London in shops that astutely acknowledged geographical and economic niches in the market. Peter Stent printed maps and pictures while handling an array of engraved prints and books for twenty-three years from his shop at the Whitehorse in Gilt-spur Street near Newgate in the western part of town. His advertisements are the first by an English printseller and help reconstruct his stock of plates.[28] John Seller sold charts and mathematical works to the eastern suburbs at the Hermitage stairs on the Thames, though he also set up stalls in Westminster Hall; his son, however, opened a shop at the west end of St. Paul's Churchyard near the traditional center of the booktrade. Staking out the lower monetary end of the market, John Cluer, at the Printing Warehouse in Bow Churchyard, produced woodcuts for six pence that were within the reach of everyman.[29]

Jacob Tonson, founder of the Kit-Kat Club and publisher of the *London Gazette*, exemplifies the diverse enterprises many booksellers ran, and in Tonson's case he was aided in his undertakings by the Whiggish Kit-Kats. Club members took out subscriptions to buy Tonson's books, a form of patronage that embraced the promotion and distribution of a work as well as its commission. In the later Stuart decades, the number of subscription volumes rose rapidly, and many costly iatric manuals were marketed in this way. With down payments secured and promises made to purchase a book before its publication, production and distribution costs were covered before the project went to press. All participants in the subscription process seemed to benefit, certainly the author, who would be guaranteed publication and, with a well-managed effort, possible financial independence. A substantial proportion of subscription editions included a list of patrons, a fitting way to advertise a subscriber's largesse and good taste. Besides reduced risk, the publisher anticipated additional sales that the list of distinguished subscribers encouraged.[30] Through their subscriptions, the Kit-Kats helped make Tonson "chief merchant of the Muses" and the dominant bookseller of his day; in gratitude he hung their portraits in his house. With the financial support and patronage network of his friends, Tonson acquired the copyrights to Shakespeare and Milton, published Dryden, and commissioned a number of portraits and panoramas, including one of Dryden to accompany his works and a view of Blenheim Palace available as a separate sheet.[31] Besides the strategy of subscriptions to reduce risk, Tonson combined with several printsellers to jointly own the expensive copper plates used to produce pictures for his publications. In short, the trade had many different trademarks.

Tonson, of course, occupied an upper rung of the book business; most of his compatriots in the industry did not. By the Stuart Restoration, dozens of book vendors labored throughout London, and by 1700 bookseller John Dunton estimated that 150 entrepreneurs traded in books there.[32] The gross profit margin in the retail book trade throughout the seventeenth century hovered around fifteen percent, less the cost of binding and transport. Campaigners against usury contended that ten percent was a normal and reasonable return on investment, but merchants looked for more. Pre–Civil War members of the Stationers' Company could count on the additional income of dividends from the English Stock, about 12.5 percent before 1640.[33] Dunton was hardly sanguine about his occupation, however, lamenting while in hiding from his creditors that

> were I to begin the Trade of Bookselling once again, I'd never give myself the Trouble to keep open Shop. Unless a Man can haggle half an Hour for a Farthing, be Dishonest, and tell Lies, he may starve behind his Shop-Board, for want of Subsistence.[34]

The same caveats applied to running printing houses. Both types of enterprises were ensconced in buildings of several floors that were formerly dwellings. The workshop or selling space was on the ground level, above which lived the master printer, his family, with journeymen, apprentices, and servants housed aloft, a domestic physical placement in reverse order to importance; in this arrangement, workplace and lodgings were kept discrete.[35] The printing plant needed to have a solid, level floor, with firm walls and a ceiling strong enough for presses to be braced to it by stout beams. Each press occupied about seven feet by seven feet of floor space and required installation by a northern window that cast enough light on the workers in the winter without scorching them in summer. An apprentice assigned by the Company to the printer acted as protégé and dogsbody. While apprentices learned their trade in his "chapel," as print shops were customarily called, the owner could employ them in his flourishing businesses and supervise the development of their good work habits.[36]

Simple printing firms were of necessity self-contained. With growth, larger businesses used more than a single press, periodically casting type, making ink and buying paper, and employing many specialists to compose and correct, and at least two men to press the finished product. Typefounding by printers remained the normal practice for leading businesses throughout the Tudor years. Experts have speculated about productivity: one authority calculates that seventeenth-century pressmen usually labored twelve-hour days beginning at six A.M. and produced 2,500 impressions or 1,250 sheets in that time; another figures a staggering 3,000 sheets by two experienced men in fourteen-hour days.[37] For high quality works, production fell well below 1,000 sheets per day. By contrast, smaller shops had a single press, set used type bought from typefounders, and enlisted wives and daughters to compare the original text with proofs. By the middle of the sixteenth century, tools and methods had been developed that did not greatly alter for 300 years. In 1683, Joseph Moxon, printer and typefounder at the sign of the Atlas in Cornhill, provided the first detailed account of typefounding in the second volume of *Mechanick Exercises on the Whole Art of Printing,* a remarkable piece of contemporary testimony issued in parts.[38] Moxon's foundry was outfitted with a large assortment of Dutch and Irish fonts, although Henry Plomer dismisses as poor the quality of his work as a printer.[39] Printing offices often stored their valuable type in cases on the shop floor, although it was not uncommon in England for cases containing type to be housed in separate rooms, a distinction from continental layouts.[40] Additional equipment crowded into the setting included wooden frames holding the fonts, "chases" or metal frames that locked in the type, leather-covered balls on sticks for applying ink, and the press itself, a significant investment and formidable piece of machinery. All this, plus room in which to hang wet pages made for very cramped working quarters.

The press itself needed to be carefully devised, an artifact of commerce. Joseph Moxon recommended a design by Amsterdam globe maker and cartographer Willem Jansen Blaeu that spoke to him of mathematical science and precision, "a machine invented upon mature consideration of mechanick powers, deducted from geometrick principles."[41] That Blaeu had worked with Tycho Brahe and incorporated some of Brahe's unpublished observations onto his globes duly impressed Moxon; so did Blaeu's nine new presses, named for the Muses. The object of Moxon's esteem featured a few different parts, imperceptible modifications to the layman, that facilitated efficient work, but Moxon appreciated equally the philosophical need for harmony of movement around the press and applauded the nuances of Blaeu's configuration.[42] Unfortunately, most presses in use in England were less awe-inspiring than Blaeu's, breaking down repeatedly and requiring perpetual attention if they were to keep working. Moreover, wooden presses demanded great strength and coordination on the part of pressmen, dubbed "horses" for their physical stamina.

Just as pressmen needed light and space for their work, so did compositors. Usually relegated to the least frequented part of the chamber and near the fire so that recently used wet type could dry, compositors arranged characters for printing, plucking type from their cases and sliding them into an iron composing stick which held about nine lines. When the stick was full, he or she emptied the stick into a wooden frame called a galley, and when complete, the galley would be laid on an iron frame or the chase, fixed with wedges, and carried to the pressroom.[43] The compositor needed to display sufficient agility, recollection, and artistic sense to finish off an octavo page in an hour, as quick work was crucial to the printing house's bottom line. At the same time, the compositor exercised considerable discretion, interpreting the writer's intent while maintaining the reputation of his master. As a back stop, operating out of a "little closet" adjoining the compositors' room, the corrector caught errors and removed them. Correctors, even temporarily hired readers, could also alter the text, and Moxon described how the master had someone "well skill'd in true and quick reading" read the copy to him before a final proofing by the corrector.[44] If any errors cropped up after that, the corrector could be held accountable and fined for them, so a test run of one copy might be done to assure that all the changes had been properly implemented. No one wanted to waste precious paper on mistakes that would have to be rectified at the printer's expense.

Living and labor conditions in print shops were not ideal. As early as 1585, mindful of the toxic environment in which printers worked, an unknown Member of Parliament asked for "a visitation as the phisitions do visit the poticary shoppes for ill druges so prynters shoppes were surveyd for those kinds of drugges and poyson with which our youth is poysoned."[45] Historian Michael Harris has underscored the human cost of the printing process, linking work with specific physical illnesses. Lead, combined in type with antimony, copper, arsenic, and tin, can produce plumbism or "printers' colic," an antecedent to tuberculosis.[46] Lead poisoning was suspected by the mid-eighteenth century as a cause of nervousness and paralysis, but compositors still commonly held disintegrating type between their teeth as they arranged lettering and ate their meals on the job in the midst of lead-saturated dust. Typesetters regularly succumbed to phthisis or consumption; they worked in small confines, usually within unventilated domestic housing, breathing in stale printers' ink with the dust.[47]

Moreover, suicide was not unknown in the trade. Richard Smyth, a book collector familiar with the publishing business, recorded the known suicides of three metropolitan printers in his famous *Obituary*, listing of deaths over a fifty-year span, including that of Peter Cole, Nicholas Culpeper's printer. Printing in later generations continued to drive its tradesmen to desperation and self-destruction. Historian Thomas Oliver remarked that the mortality among Victorian-era printers from alcoholism doubled in a decade, while deaths from suicide tripled during the same period; he commented that printers "are somewhat addicted to suicide."[48]

They also may have been addicted, like their bookselling counterparts, to coffee. Introduced during the Interregnum, coffeehouses became central to the political culture of England after 1660. Adrian Johns reminds us that, like printing houses and bookshops, they fomented "a heady mixture of the heights of truth and the depths of deception."[49] Found in close proximity to bookstores, the coffeehouses gave their customers a bargain: a savings of "two pence a week in *Gazettes* . . . news and coffee for the same charge" as they sat at tables or in snugs rather like an English public house today. Books and pamphlets could be borrowed there by those who could not afford the full purchase price. Given these services, the "middling sort" and even those lower on the economic scale had access to print culture. By stimulating debate on subjects like science, philosophy, and medicine, the coffeehouses added to the "paper-fuel," propelling even impecunious readers to the bookshops nearby. Bookmen offered personal credit to their customers who became intrigued by a pamphlet or a tome at a coffeehouse; some stationers even owned coffeehouses or shared their premises with one for added convenience.[50] However, the practice of coffeehouses buying one copy of a work and lending it gratis to regular patrons eventually rankled those in the trade with no coffee connection, and London booksellers complained in 1742 of what had become a "scandalous and low custom."[51]

Since houses and apartment buildings in Tudor-Stuart London had no numbers, a man had his mail or any other correspondence delivered to his coffeehouse. Discussion clubs met at coffeehouses, such as the Rota Club to which Samuel Pepys belonged and which gathered during the waning days of the Interregnum at Miles' Coffeehouse in New Palace Yard, Westminster. Pepys inscribed in his diary the vigorous debates over the political theories of James Harrington that took place among club members in January 1660. Lively conversations that buzzed in places like Miles' originated in printed information provided by the coffeehouses. After the Restoration more than 500 licensed coffeehouses in London provided newspapers, usually buying four copies of each leading paper for the use of their customers. By 1700, there may have been 1000 establishments, meaning half the men in London visited a coffeehouse every day.[52] Runners were dispatched to the coffee houses to relate major events of the day, such as victory in battle or political upheaval. Open from 6 A.M. to 10 P.M., coffeehouses provided space for reading and writing. Customers paid a penny for admission, and might be charged more for the use of pen, ink, and paper for the season.

The coffeehouses themselves, "nurseries of sedition," became a problem for authorities intent on managing the press. Bookmen had their favorite establishments, as did political factions, and various other business activities ensued there, such as miscellaneous auctions, the buying and selling of copyrights, and the insuring of shipping and foreign trade. Somewhat like an indoor commons, coffeehouses offered the opportunity to tattle while carrying on business. Apothecaries reportedly found physicians "keeping office hours" in a coffeehouse, further demystifying medicine. During the various crises of government in the later Stuart age, coffeehouses were the preeminent meeting places for men of letters to engage in partisan discussions. Political and religious moderates, as well as the more fervent Whigs who would not endorse popular sovereignty, staunchly defended coffeehouses, the concept of the public sphere, and meaningful citizen discourse.

Though the Whigs had brought him to England via the Glorious Revolution, King William saw little advantage after his accession to open debate, particularly in coffeehouses or in the press. Whiggish literature would be read aloud and tacked up on the walls of the informal Whig clubs in coffeehouses like The Grecian in the Strand, referred to as "the Athenaeum of its day" and a choice of medical men, and the St. James in Westminster, another favorite of Addison and Steele; it was said that no Tory would allow himself to be seen at the St. James. Though they might be afraid of workmen and other susceptible groups habituating such gathering spots, the Tories had their establishments, too, like the Cocoa Tree Chocolate House in Pall Mall or Garraway's Coffeehouse in Cornhill, where Dr. Arbuthnot rendezvoused with Flamsteed about celestial matters on the physician's political turf.[53] While the government as late as 1675 tried fruitlessly to shut down these hives of dangerous gossip out of fear of treason and sedition, Roger L'Estrange, the king's own censor and a Tory journalist himself, was known as "the soul of all coffee houses, and the delight of those that love to dung and read at the same time."[54] Though some coffeehouses had distinct sections reserved for combating zealots, social contacts between Whigs and Tories became sporadic by the end of the Stuart dynasty as each formed their own clubs in separate coffeehouses.

For the most part, regardless of the vagaries of politics—in fact incited by them—business went on as usual for printers and for their merchandising partners in the trade. Mindful of Dunton's advice to "take a convenient shop in a convenient place," bookshop owners provided public access to printed matter for a price, preferably in a building fronting a major thoroughfare.[55] Like printing houses, bookshops were generally the homes of their proprietors. Thanks to a survey conducted in 1670 by William Leybourn for the Stationers' Company, we know a great deal about the functional arrangement of a typical bookshop: brick-paved cellar with storage space for coal and beer, the showroom on the ground floor with a yard out back, kitchen on the second story, with bedrooms on the third floor or in the attic. Since most city shops were rented rather than owned freehold, bookmen made additional income by subleasing rooms to other dwellers.[56] With all the competition for business and the need to make those monthly rent payments, keepers of bookshops tried to lure customers to their specific locations. They routinely touted merchandise available at their stores in dozens of newspapers, pamphlets, and books printed and disseminated throughout the capital. Announcements of this sort generally cost about a shilling for eight lines.[57] Once tempted by an ad to go to a shop, people could stay and read on the premises before choosing something to buy.

But what do we really know about literacy rates, readers, and the material they actually read? Though all the figures point to an increase in literacy from the Tudor era on, the growth was, according to David Cressy, "irregular and halting, rather than steady and progressive." A surge in literacy charted during the reign of Elizabeth leveled off in the Stuart century. Cressy insists that "early promoters of literacy exaggerated their case," that being able to read "was by no means a necessity in early modern England." Moreover, he argues that "traditionalists had never conceded that Bible literacy was essential to religious devotion."[58] But Puritans alleged that people languished for lack of knowledge, and they proselytized for literacy. Reverend Richard Baxter, a fecund religious writer and renowned bibliophile, counseled parents to "let children be taught to read . . . or you shall deprive them of a singular help to their instruction and salvation."[59] Apart from the spiritual, reading had practical benefits, enabling the literate to avoid embarrassing and costly disadvantage in business and to their personal reputations. In the later Stuart decades, male literacy was "occupationally specific," consolidated among the gentry, professionals, government officials, retail merchants, and skilled tradesmen; illiteracy among London tradesmen declined to seven percent by the end of the seventeenth century. Relatively high rates of literacy, defined as the ability to sign one's name, have been found among "middling women" in London, 62.5 percent after 1680.[60]

The topic of reading has undergone radical revision in recent years; no longer "unproblematic and obvious," the scholarship of reading has become a field of intense debate.[61] Attempts to derive information about past readership size from bibliographic evidence in short-title catalogues founder in the maddening gaps within the historical record. The exact size of most editions before 1800 remains unknown, as few shop ledgers have survived to inform us about printing runs, and, since estimates of publication output are meaningful only if the nature of the market is understood, gauging the size and makeup of English readership continues to require caution when projecting from the partial evidence that remains.[62] It is even harder to judge whether books were considered luxuries or necessities of life to Londoners. Surely, people did expect to own a range of domestic goods including books; moreover, reading books was one of the non-material pleasures of life treasured by individuals.[63]

Less concerned with these academic subtleties, Tudor-Stuart entrepreneurs developed real and sophisticated expertise at arousing extensive public interest in books and other goods available at their emporia. Book stores were among the best outlets to frequent in the city, and well-heeled readers went from shop to shop looking for new titles; retailers openly courted potential repeat customers as browsing developed into an urbane diversion. Tudor-Stuart bookshops were not purely retail establishments; the early trade relationship was markedly personal, requiring close, congenial involvement by buyer and seller. Shopkeepers served a numerically small clientele, perhaps as few as thirty people per shop.[64] Pepys regularly frequented the shop of John Cade at the Globe in Cornhill, where he purchased books, maps, prints, and stationery. So familiar a customer did Pepys become that Cade permitted him run of the warehouse. More than merchant and patron, Cade and Pepys were candid with one another about political matters. During the anxious times of the second Anglo-Dutch war, Cade reported to Pepys that "the Queene-Mother," Henrietta Maria, had negotiated some sort of accord with France, which "as a Presbyterian" Cade did not like, fearing "that it will be a means to introduce Popery."[65]

Booksellers traveled abroad to buy their wares, handling a variety of retail goods as well as serving as bankers and property developers.[66] They came to observe the genteel conventions of the clients they wooed, knowing that politeness was both prudent and profitable. They overheard refined conversations and brought such civilities to the art of business. Accordingly, bookmen had standing and influence. In Jacobean London, seventy-three of 140 aldermen were in the domestic distributive trades like bookselling, although printing was regarded as "mechanical" and a somewhat lesser occupation.[67] Discretion and confidentiality, especially concerning the more desirable elements of society, came to be valued as wise principles for the aspiring book entrepreneur to live by. So averse was he to bring attention to a light-fingered man of the cloth who pilfered his stock, Stationer Thomas Sawbridge tactfully declined to prosecute William Clewer, the notorious shoplifting vicar of Croyden. Thieves of lesser caste were not so fortunate; William Bond was transported for stealing books.[68] By behaving well and assiduously cultivating book aficionados, print merchants could weather the fates and succeed.

Even the mass destruction of their stores and stocks could not deter the resolute men and women of the London book trade. For instance, despite the losses they sustained in the Fire, bookmen John Martyn and James Allestry recovered, and by 1669 reestablished their shop in the Churchyard, where regular buyers included one of their stable of authors, Robert Hooke, as well as Sir Christopher Wren, Dr. Thomas Gale, the Master of St. Paul's School, and Abraham Hill, patron of the arts and Treasurer of the Royal Society. Martyn particularly enjoyed warm friendships with his customers, discussing new publications, sipping brew at nearby Man's Coffeehouse, or inviting them to his home in Bow Lane. Moreover, the Bell became a center for the exchange of letters among bibliophiles.[69]

According to Plomer, Humphrey Moseley and Henry Herringman were the most important booksellers of the last half of the seventeenth century. Moseley catered to a well-heeled clientele at the Prince's Arms in St. Paul's Churchyard, becoming the chief publisher of finer literature, including John Milton's poems and the works of John Donne. Among the medical titles he had printed was John Bulwer's *Pathomyotomia or a Dissection of the Significative Muscles of the Affections of the Minde* (1649). Bulwer encouraged observing head movements in order to perceive the voluntary or impetuous motions of the mind. Herringman, mainly a publisher of plays and lighter fare, also backed iatric works, including Walter Charlton's *Natural History of Nuitrition, Life and Voluntary Motion* (1659). His shop at the Blue Anchor in the lower walk of the New Exchange became "the chief literary lounging place in London." Pepys recurrently referred to it and Edward Arber deemed Herringman the first whole-sale publisher in London.[70] Herringman held a share in the King's Printing House and eventually concentrated on large publishing ventures like the works of Chaucer and Shakespeare, turning over the retail business at the Blue Anchor in 1684 to Francis Saunders and Joseph Knight, who relished the chance to rub shoulders with "the nobility and gentry of the first rank in England."[71]

It made economic sense for book traders to fasten much of their attention on the upscale side of the market, producing short print runs which depended for sales on the dedication of well-informed book buyers. Ornately bound folios with attractive woodcut illustrations were costly, and appealed to the prosperous. Pepys liked to have his unbound purchases covered alike, so better to display his growing collection, and occasionally he hired bookbinder William Richardson to stitch the pages and "gild the backs of all my books to make them handsome."[72] In May 1667, Richardson brought Pepys a costly Bible in quires from Cade's shop for him to buy, but Pepys decided against the expense since "it is like to be so big, that I shall not use it." The Bible in question was produced by John Ogilby, publisher of some of the finest books issued in Pepys' time. To facilitate sales of these extravagant tomes, Ogilby established a lottery, the prizes all his own works. Pepys had "won" two Ogilby volumes in February 1666, but ended up spending more than he intended on binding and vowed to reduce his book buying habits.[73]

Fortunately, bookmen did not have to rely solely on Pepys, inveterate buyer though he was. Access to books became status symbols to London's sophisticates and arrivistes. During the Elizabethan period, fashion dictated that elite social groups spend nine months of the year in the capital. John Stow noted that with such a plentiful number of gentlemen and their entourages in residence for so long, "retailers and artificers . . . find a ready and quick market."[74] As many as 5,000 gentry families resided in the London environs during the later Stuart era, and book ownership was considered an important index of wealth in their household inventories as well as in the households of the city's professionals and merchants. Pepys, Rev. Baxter, Dr. Richard Mead, Royal Society President Martin Folkes, barrister John Bridges, and others boasted of collections of thousands of books and left abundant library legacies.[75] Less imposing, but no less significant, is the incidence of book ownership among Londoners of all stripes. Drawing upon probate inventories between 1675 and 1725, Lorna Weatherill has calculated that approximately 31 percent of those who bequeathed property owned books and that the level of ownership rose to 56 percent by the end of the period. The higher the value of the whole inventory, the more likely the individual owned books, topping out at 46 percent for inventories over £500. If analyzed by occupation, merchants, mercers, and shopkeepers displayed the greatest measure of book ownership.[76] However, according to another historian, relying on probate inventories for evidence about book ownership is problematical, given the majority of citizens omitted from the historical record.[77]

In addition to the capital's permanent residents, seasonal visitors, business-men, and Members of Parliament swelled the numbers of probable moneyed book buyers.[78] Therefore, the book industry in the metropolitan region en-joyed a sizable and affluent clientele; moreover, because bookshops were viewed as "polite" businesses, seventeenth-century London book stores appealed to both sexes. In fact, Weatherill's study of probate inventories turned up surpris-ingly robust ratios of book ownership women to men in the same trades, par-ticularly among those in sales and service jobs.[79] Whereas in rural areas, women made do with what few tomes they could find, in the metropolis buying and borrowing books was an opportunity for excellent women to go out, see, and be seen.[80] At the same time, many booksellers employed an alternative marketing strategy to appeal to a less discerning clientele more likely to buy affordable, simplified editions of expensive books or serialized, unbound literature. Fur-thermore, newspaper publishers still relied on street hawkers and peddlers to aid in the advertising and distribution of periodicals and chapbooks to who-ever passed by.[81] Chapmen carried the humblest literature in heavy packs as they traveled about selling reading matter, trinkets, household goods, and toys. In the sixteenth century, this printed matter included traditional stories and moral tales, but by the Stuart era jokes and riddle books could be found in the chapman's knapsack along with severely abbreviated novels. Badly printed but cheap, these small volumes were popular with all classes of people. However, just as stationers ultimately manifested disenchantment with the book-lend-ing practices of coffeehouses, they developed hostility towards the itinerant book salesmen whom they had employed to distribute material. Some strains in these opposing merchandising schemes resulted, as respectable businessmen with permanent bookselling establishments and upwardly mobile aspirations hoped to divorce themselves from common chapmen. By the 1680s, London shopkeepers, including some bookmen, openly agitated against street vendors, forming a pressure group against nuisances and riff-raff who detracted from the business of traditional tradesmen in regular locations.[82]

Urban bookmen had stationery, paper, sealing wax, various inks, and quill pens on hand for purchase, although they stocked fewer of these wares than a typical provincial bookseller. Others offered their customers complex math-ematical instruments, globes, and eye spectacles; some even acted as agents for insurance firms.[83] London book emporia carried games, plays, and other de-lights for customers to consider, including a variety of cards that presaged mod-ern comic books and collectibles; many of them reveal a decided partisan bias. By the end of the Stuart dynasty, stationers had risen above the echelon of mere shopkeepers, at least in their own minds. In the last half of the seven-teenth century, leading booksellers could make a fortune, as did Thomas Guy, the wealthy founder of Guy's Hospital. Besides the prestige attached to their capital and their enterprise, retail booksellers became the nucleus of the writ-ing community, employing printers and commissioning authors. Bookstores of publishers, like the aforementioned John Martyn, became magnets for poets and playwrights, who stopped by to engage in literary conversation and stimulate interest in their works.[84] Bookshops throughout the city also served as distribution points for the newspapers, pamphlets, and broadsides that residents of the capital wanted. Much of the very latest stock was unbound, scattered about the store in loose sheets which could be sewn together at the store or sutured privately if a reader decided to make them a permanent part of his library. Smaller publications, printed in octavos or twelves and usually unstitched, cost less and appealed to a lower economic stratum, but one with some disposable income.

Like paper size, the kind of typeface used by a printer indicated what the potential audience was for a piece. Roman type was associated with better-educated Englishmen, while the black letter font remained the type of the lower class and the marginally literate. Black letter persisted as the typeface for ballads, broadsides, and jest books, particularly for depiction of English words. In a glossary appended to Edmund Coote's Elizabethan era textbook, *The English Schoolmaster*, "Directions for the Unskilful" explains that different type identifies the languages in which they are set: roman for Latin and other learned parlances; italic for French words that had come into English; and "those with the English letter are meerley English or some from other vulgar tongue."[85] Paradoxically, black letter concurrently endured as the print of the Crown; statutes, proclamations, and plague bills employed black letter, reinforcing its association with authoritarian controls.[86] Seventeenth-century printers often used a mixture of typeface—with italic tossed in for good measure—for decoration and emphasis, signifying that the material was intended for a sophisticated reader. A few printed chiefly on folio sheets with mixed types, the distinguishing trait of an elite retailer.

Bookshops figured prominently in the philosophical and jurisdictional debates that both fed and fed on the medical marketplace. Although the Royal College of Physicians tried to regulate the profession and practice of medicine in the capital, Londoners bought hackneyed herbals as well as quack remedies of all kinds at their favorite retail sites. The shop of one prominent post-Restoration stationer, Dorman Newman, provides us with a splendid case study of the ways in which bookmen affected the iatric struggle raging in the capital. Newman implicitly supported the medical challengers by publishing and selling books from his shop in the Poultry aimed at making every man his own doctor. An anti-institutional chapbook, *Medela Medicorum, or an Enquiry into the Reasons and Grounds of the Contempt of Physicians and Their Noble Art, with Proposals to Reduce Them to Their Wonted Repute*, emanated from Newman's presses in 1678. As early as 1676, he produced Thomas Cocke's *Kitchen-Physick, or Advice to the Poor*, containing rules and directions on preventing sickness and curing diseases by diet; a short supplement descanted on "stoving and bathing." In 1684 *The Art of Physick Made Plain and Easie* by the Frenchman Nicholas LaFramboisière could be bought at Newman's store in the Poultry, along with a copy of Everard Maynwaring's *Method and Means of Enjoying Health*,

Vigour, and Long Life, adaptable for every person regardless of age, customs and valetudinary states. Timothy Byfield's 1685 enchiridion on consumption promised a new method of home cure. Of course, there were legitimate reasons to question traditional theories of medical treatment, and many continentally trained doctors and scientists did just that.

In addition to the impact that the publications they carried had on medical self-treatment, bookstore owners handled nostrums advertised in handbills and newspapers, making bookshops the chief retail outlets for proprietary medicines in early modern England. In the Jacobean era, William Besse sold the London Triacle at his shop in the Poultry for 2s.8d. a pound or 2d. an ounce; he guaranteed it as "the enemy of all infectious diseases."[87] While many booksellers sold medical concoctions on site, a few may even have been actually involved with the manufacture of nostrums.[88] In the course of time, some of them became better known as patent medicine peddlers than printers or chapmen. Bookmen often bought out the proprietor's rights and became the sole vendor of a remedy. As Mary Fissell has noted, this commercialization of domestic medicine had contradictory consequences on the connection between doctors and their patients, blurring the differences between professional and lay healing while simultaneously limiting choices for the poor.[89] A sick person could purchase an "over-the-counter" remedy at a bookshop without seeing any sort of doctor, let alone the maker of the medication. Patients tried prescribed drugs, patent medicines, and home panaceas in whatever combinations they wished, their choices expanded by the health care market. But with the sweeping acceptance of a cure, its cost and that of its ingredients escalated beyond the reach of the average laborer.[90]

One such notable late seventeenth-century remedy was John Colbatch's "Vulnerary Powder," granules to stop wounds from bleeding. Hailing from Worcester, Colbatch, a correspondent of Thomas Sydenham, moved to London after the Glorious Revolution and began to circulate news of his medical breakthrough among the capital's health care community. Claiming to have found his remedy by experimenting in his laboratory on animals, Colbatch directed that the powder be dissolved in water (or urine if water was unavailable) and applied to the surface of the wound. The lips of the wound were then to be stitched together and the patient given a dose in wine of "Tincture of the Sulphur of Venus," another Colbatch invention. He avowed painless cures even in the body cavity in a matter of days by following these instructions.[91] London surgeons took notice of Colbatch's testimony and with his approval arranged for a public trial of his medicines on a dog, a scientific test of interest to the Fellows of the Royal Society.

William Cowper witnessed the demonstration and wrote his observations for the *Philosophical Transactions*.[92] He reported that the abdomen of a large canine was pierced, its intestines removed and sliced, then put back into the surgical opening. After an application of Colbatch's powder, the dog healed without any ill symptoms or the usual dressings. After a few days, satisfied with the animal's recovery, surgeons amputated the dog's leg; once again the animal survived. The investigation moved to human subjects under the supervision of one of the Master-Surgeons of St. Bartholomew's, but this time the outcome was not so auspicious. Surgeons spread the powder on the bleeding stumps of two patients at the hospital who had required amputation. Their blood would not be stanched by the remedy, however, and conventional bandages had to be applied. Worse yet, the patients "suffered extravagant pains" and were left with large scars and a horrid appearance."[93]

Despite Cowper's gruesome report, Colbatch denied that his remedy had a fair trial and suggested that the surgeons had financial reasons for adulterating the demonstration and impugning his invention. He got another chance to substantiate its efficacy on soldiers in 1694, but unhappily some of his patients died in the presence of the Colonel of the Coldstream Guards, Lord Cutts. Colbatch saw more enemies behind this failure and suggested that his very life was at risk from jealous army surgeons. Yet again, Colbatch persevered and treated several wounded men in Holland during the next summer's campaign, losing only one in the field.[94] Unlike many empirics, Colbatch had not advertised his invention in London, but with questions about the safety of his medicines whirling about him, he published a book in thrifty twelves about his surgical innovation, *Novum Lumen Chirurgicum or the New Light on Chirurgery* (1695).

Daniel Brown, Colbatch's publisher, profited from the pugnacious debate over the Vulnerary Powder, which once begun would have been difficult to stop. Counter-attacks from various surgeons called Colbatch's character into question as well as his fascinating if erratic remedy. But the publicity that the chemical styptic engendered proved invaluable to the sale of Colbatch's books. Moreover, anticipating an escalation in demand for Colbatch's medications, in 1696 Brown bought the rights to both the powder and tincture at considerable cost, being "better able to dispose of them for the public good of mankind," according to Colbatch.[95] Brown advertised that although Colbatch's hemostatic cures used to sell for a guinea a bottle, he made them available at his shop at the Black Swan and Bible without Temple-Bar in smaller quantities (that would "cure at least ten considerable wounds") for half a guinea. Colbatch himself, "bound in an obligation of two thousand pounds," would inspect the preparation of all the medicines to be sold.[96] Through Brown's network of distributors in the city and beyond, Colbatch's remedies achieved great notoriety; Brown stimulated the market for the astringent powder and tincture with Colbatch's books, the sales of which were in turn spurred by widespread dissension over the remedies.

Colbatch was not Daniel Brown's only resourceful client, though he did dominate the list of iatric books, mostly in the mid-price range, published by Brown. Colbatch penned pieces on gout (1697) and snakebite (1698); his *Four Treatises on Physick and Surgery* went through three editions in a year. As usual, ripostes followed, one written by Richard Boulton, a quondam pen for the

College.[97] He got into another dispute over medical alkalies which many physicians, including Sydenham and Walter Harris, believed in for a variety of ailments, but which Colbatch repudiated in favor of acids. One of his antagonists, William Coward, fired back in *Alkali Vindication* (1698), and the furor only furthered Colbatch's renown.[98] Brown commissioned many additional remedies by issuing books written by their creators, or "authors" in the parlance of the times. He could then stock the medications they had formulated for his bookshop customers to buy. Brown became the effective agent for experimental and controversial medicos such as William Cole, Edward Tyson, and John Spinke, putting out their books and vending their remedies. His stable of writers methodically reinforced one another's products in print; Dr. Cole produced a volume on apoplexy for Brown which Colbatch endorsed in his book.[99]

Like Daniel Brown's, Dorman Newman's bookshop had a veritable pharmacy of extraordinary medicaments for its consumers to sample, including the amazing "Liquid Snuff of Padua, prepared for the Queen by Her Majesty's Sworn Servant." In *The Weekly Remarks* of 22 April 1691, Newman announced his exclusive metropolitan monopoly of Dr. Patrick Anderson's authentic "Scotch Pills," and cautioned its customers to take heed of "dangerous counterfeits since the unfortunate death of Mrs. Katherine Anderson," daughter-executrix of the inventor. Bookseller Ebenezer Tracy distributed his patent medicines at Newman's, including Balsam de Chili, a cure for "Most Diseases in Human Bodies," despite the fact that Tracy claimed in his own pamphlets "the true balsam is sold at the Three Bibles on London Bridge at 1s per ounce; and no where else."[100] Additionally, Newman was the sole dealer of "Bateman's true Spirit of Scurvy-grass, golden or plain;" Daffy's Elixir-Salutia; and "that well-known and often experienced medicine, Fletcher's Powder, which radically cures all diseases in men, women, and children, where recovery is possible with ease, speed, and safety." The chemist John Rudolph Glaubor developed two vendibles to be had at Newman's: a book on his medical and alchemical secrets, including the making of saltpeter, translated into English by Christopher Packe, the "phylachymico-medicus;" and "Spirit of Salt of the World," a nostrum with myriad functions. For only one shilling, Newman's buyers could employ the commodity as a medicine, a dietary supplement, and in the mechanic arts. Its amazing properties served both the "necessaries and recreations of life," valuable in brewing, preserving wine, baking, making sauces, dyeing cloth, and against distemper and scurvy. Directions for usage came with each bottle.

Of course, the best advice for living well and happily included temperance. Dorman Newman featured Thomas Tryon's discourse on long life and happiness, a treatise on "meats, drinks, air, exercise, &c., with special directions on how to use each of them to the best advantage of the body and mind." Tryon, identified as a student of physic, included information on herbs with examples and demonstrations "made easie and familiar to the meanest capacities." Tryon believed that for the general good, ordinary families should have such knowledge communicated to them and not be held captive to expensive health caregivers in the city. Judging by the number of health manuals and medicines associated with irregular practitioners that lined the aisles of his mercantile, Dorman Newman tacitly agreed with that philosophy, putting him at odds with London's medical organization.

Resembling activity in today's book superstores, on-site reading grew into a fashionable pastime, as patrons could peruse reading matter before buying it. Once again, Dorman Newman was on the cutting edge of modernity, providing stools for his customers' convenience; presumably, the publicity generated by reading in the shop compensated him for whatever nuisance the service might cause.[101] Nevertheless, by making on-site reading privileges too generous, Newman risked loss of sales, and so he would have pushed for eventual purchase of the material. He likely succeeded in getting his customers to buy his wares, for thanks to the publishing revolution, they lived in an unprecedented culture of print. For the medical world, bookshops symbolized the challenge to established authority and health care, stocking on their shelves and in their warehouses the manuals, recipe books, and drugs that made Everyman his own doctor.

Chapter 7

Medical Advertising: Publishing the Proprietary

Published advertising arose in England in the late Elizabethan era, when other means of investment supplanted declining literary patronage. Books were among the earliest things to be advertised, a catalogue being distributed by Andrew Maunsell in 1595.[1] Paid commercial ads in newspapers, promoting products or services, first appeared sparingly in the 1620s; book notices appeared in periodicals by 1646 and medical advertisements commenced in November 1652, when Theophilus Buckworth of Mile End Green exalted his "famous lozenges or pectorals" for consumption, catarrhs, and all other contagious diseases in the weekly paper *Mercurius Politicus*.[2] In 1653 the *Perfect Diurnall* had about half a dozen messages (sometimes called *sisquis*) priced at one shilling each.

Even more ambitious was Marchamont Nedham, an ally of Oliver Cromwell and the recipient of the lone license to print awarded from 1655 until after the Lord Protector's death. Under government supervision, Nedham published two official papers, *Mercurius Politicus* and *Publick Intelligencer,* the latter a weekly pamphlet begun in 1657 and containing only advertisements. His list of charges for a four-week ad package escalated according to the value of the goods or services advised; physicians were charged ten shillings for offering such "advice." Usually their ads contained graphic lists of diseases to be cured and faddish remedies including coffee, which was available in Bartholomew Lane. Termed

> a wholsom and physical drink, (coffee) closes the orifice of the stomach, fortifies the heat within, helpeth digestion, quickeneth the spirits, maketh the heart lightsom, is good against eyesores, coughs or colds, rhumes, consumptions, headach, dropsie, gout, scurvy, King's Evil, and many others. . . .[3]

After the Stuart Restoration, Surveyor of the Press Roger L'Estrange enjoyed a monopoly of printing newspapers and advertising matter by the grant of his appointment in 1663. His *Intelligencer* and the *Newes* featured advertisements for doctors and medicines; out of 166 ads in the first twenty-four issues of these two papers, fifty-two were medical. During the pestilence of 1665, the *Newes* rallied readers with a notice on 15 June that plague prevention and remedies could be effected "with many cheap medicines set down by the Colledge of Physitians, by the Kings Majesties special command, and sold by his majesties printer in Blackfriars, London."[4]

In its first years, the *London Gazette* intentionally eschewed advertisements, setting up separate printings for mercantile communiqués and public announcements.[5] Nonetheless, advertisements for lost property, missing persons, and land for sale soon surfaced in the *Gazette* proper, and gradually the volume and variety of its advertisements expanded.[6] Papers in 1650 generally charged advertisers three pence for fifty words or less and sixpence for a longer piece, perhaps double for bold type; by 1657 the advertising rates for the *Publick Advertiser* rose to two shillings sixpence.

Throughout the Tudor-Stuart period, London ripened into a bustling sales entrepôt where the demand for business information was tremendous. Along with financial news, prices, and exchange rates, announcements in recurrent publications helped to provide a portion of that information. Thomas Bromhall, Clerk and Register of the Passes, capitalized on his knowledge of London trade and began publishing the *Mercury* in 1667. Fully one-third of the notices that appeared in his initial issues dealt with medical products. Moreover, Bromhall contracted with John Piercy, servant to the Queen Dowager, to publish his advertisements for plague antidotes and other medicines every week at 2s. 6d. each; Piercy's remedies sold at thirteen London and six provincial outlets.[7] In 1679 Benjamin Harris put out an unlicensed paper, the *Domestick Intelligence*, that elucidated the virtues of his own medicine, an "admirable and effectual water for the griping of the guts," stocked at his shop along with others advertised; Harris's paper was probably read by more the of middling and poorer sort in the capital than the *London Gazette*.[8]

With the founding of John Houghton's first industry paper, *A Collection of Letters for the Improvement of Husbandry and Trade* (1681–83), periodicals mutated into veritable shoppers' guides. Houghton, an apothecary by training who became a Fellow of the Royal Society, built an eclectic business as an agent, broker, and vendor of chocolate, sago, and "German Spaw water."[9] Since ads could provide most of a publisher's profit margin, why not eliminate the news altogether? In Queen Anne's reign, biweekly advertising sheets were doled out gratis in London and the provinces; one such report, the *Generous Advertiser*, mainly a proponent of books and medicines, claimed to have dispensed 4,000 free copies of each issue. Hoping to quell Whiggish criticism of its policies, the Tory government by an Act of Parliament in 1712 made advertisements in weekly periodicals subject to taxation of a shilling each and exacted a halfpenny levy on each printed half-sheet.[10] Since advertisements furnished the greater part of a periodical's income, the tax on ads hit Grub Street particularly hard. One casualty was Richard Steele and Joseph Addison's *The Spectator*, the most representative periodical of the Augustan Age and among the first issued daily. While *The Spectator* carried ads that had "crystallized into the forms with which we are now familiar," the number and length of notices dramatically declined after imposition of the assessment.[11]

Advertisements were the province of the publisher, the person with the main financial interest in production, forming an important element in the equation of profit and loss.[12] Customers ordinarily took their advertisements directly to the printing house, but they sometimes submitted them at affiliated coffeehouses and bookshops.[13] Ads in periodicals for iatric personnel and commodities tended to be rather bland and brief, but that advocacy alone yielded popular approval. A handful of quack ads used woodcuts to attract attention, but medical notices were seldom illustrated except for the occasional pointing index finger. Instead, primitive items relied on theatrical text to lure clients, but their usual placement at the end of the final column of news certainly diminished their impact. A few lines in small print was typical and some ads employed ever smaller fonts to cram in as much material at the end of the blurb as possible. Ads about health matters in newspapers repeatedly touted other forms of printed material such as books and brochures. Advertisements for "patent medicines" constituted one of the most common categories of promotions found in all manner of English newspapers and journals of opinion. The term patent medicine originated in the Statute of Monopolies, enacted in 1624, whereby Letters Patent granted the sole right of manufacture of a new substance for fourteen years. A patent for a medicine of undisclosed ingredients could be applied for by any person, but most aspiring medicos failed to obtain a patent; only eighteen were issued for branded medicines between 1650 and 1750.[14] Perhaps this lack of protection for trademarked remedies made defending them in advertisements necessary. Assiduous championing of "secret" medications, however, impressed the public more than any patent.[15]

Dr. James Welwood, author of the periodical *Mercurius Reformatus* (1689–91) and a staunch supporter of William III, was a Fellow of the Royal College of Physicians of London, an officer in that institution. The College, as we have seen, routinely prosecuted mountebanks and quacksalvers who championed their secret remedies, cure-alls and specifics, throughout the city. Yet, Dr. Welwood's own newspaper contained many ads for fabulous remedies from the laboratories of unlicensed empirics, such as one for "Extract of Liquoras," which was vouched for as an antidote for colds, coughs, and consumption.[16]

> It is exceedingly good . . . if taken in the morning fasting, half an hour before dinner, and before supper, in the bigness of a nutmeg at each time, letting it dissolve gently in the mouth and abstaining as much from drinking (especially cold or small drink) till the cure is perfected. It may be taken at any other time, and the oftner the better; being so safe and pleasant, that it may freely be given to a child of any age. This extract is (for convenience of carrying it in the pocket) made up into rolls, and sold for one shilling the roll by [bookseller] Dorman Newman.[17]

Equally extraordinary was Fletcher's Powder, "that well-known and often experienced medicine which radically cures all diseases in men, women, and children where recovery is possible with ease, speed, and safety."[18]

Nameless entrepreneurs inserted many of the medical notifications in London's newspapers, like the gentlewoman at the Golden-Ball in Castle Street, whose excellent plaster "safely and without pain dissolveth and taketh away all wens and moles on the face or any other part of the body." She wanted no reward for her secret, unlike a mountebank, until the convalescence was perfected.[19] The same gentlewoman hawked "a cephalick water for bathing the temples and snuffing up the nose to comfort the brain and remedy the gripes."[20] An unknown but "experienced operator" in the Strand undertook to ease the pain of toothache "without drawing them," but rather by "bleeding in the mouth three or four ounces at a time;" he also claimed in his ad in *The Spectator* to "cup without an engine, without fire, scarcely to be felt." No name was attached to the "incomparable powder for cleaning the teeth" which also cured "worms at the roots of the teeth," but it could be obtained at various shops in London, according to a notice in *The Spectator*. Some establishments carried certain kinds of remedies from unidentified formulators specifically appropriate to their clientele. For instance, Mr. Osborn's Toyshop on Fleet Street boasted in another *Spectator* ad that it was the sole distributor for "an admirable confect, which assuredly cures stuttering or stammering in children."[21]

Most medicos, however, had no qualms about using their names to sell panaceas. Thomas Kirleus, recognized as a collegiate physician and doctor to Charles II, trumpeted his multipurpose drinks and pills for ulcers, scabs and "scurfs in the face," the King's Evil, leprosy, and venereal disease, which had "cured above 500 persons in this city, many after fluxing." The purgative cost three shillings for a quart to drink or only one shilling for a box of two purges-worth of tablets. Not only would the remedy get rid of those troublesome scurfs, but it could also expunge gout and the stone. Dr. Kirleus gave "his opinion for nothing, and his medicine for little" from his location in the Plow-Yard of Gray's Inn Lane.[22] An apothecary at the Unicorn in Southwark named R. Stoughton, who advertised extensively and verbosely in London newspapers, lobbied those afflicted with smallpox and measles to consult him for treatment, since "not three in twenty" had died in his hands.[23]

Glaubor's aforementioned Spirit of Salt of the World, promoted exhaustively in print, challenges simple characterization. Its multifarious functions encompassed medicine, diet, and fashion: it was promoted as good for scurvy, preserving beer and wine, and as a base for kitchen sauces. If Glaubor's medicinal or nutritional uses did not compel you to buy, you could always dye your clothes with it. Directions for usage were provided with each bottle, priced at only one shilling and available at Dorman Newman's bookshop. However, medicinal ads in periodicals ordinarily claimed relief from specific maladies, a therapeutic approach closely associated with empirics. The ailment for which Bateman's True Spirit of Scurvy-Grass, both golden and plain, worked wonders is evident, but should not be confused with Parker's Spirit of Scurvy-Grass. Readers of John Houghton's *Collection for the Improvement of Husbandry and Trade* were warned that Parker's wares could be discerned by its "bright, lovely green," whereas all other spirits were "white and languid."[24] Liquid snuff was publicized in print for headaches and epilepsy; newspaper ads extolled the virtues of an incomparable pain water for twixt their King and two Princes, who only were able *to crush this Cockatrice in the Shell,,* gave her the Means and Power to appear at this Day, with formidable Navies in the Ocean.

In fine, it was *Charles* II. and the late K. *James,* that may juftly be charged with being the Caufe of the Greatnefs of the *French* King by Sea : And albeit nothing could be more inconfiftent with, or repugnant to the true Interest of the *Englifh* Nation ; yet all interefts whatever, and Honour it felf, behoov'd to yield to *the Motives,* and *Ends* of that unhappy Friendfhip In the Reign of *the Firft,*we were obliged to make War upon a *Neighbouring Proteftant State,* in conjunction with the *French,* meerly to teach the latter the Art of Fighting at Sea ; and by weakening both our felves and the former, to ftrengthen the common Enemy. The *French* were not very careful to hide this their Defign, and gave evident Proof whereto their Alliance with *England* tended, feeing upon our Engagement with the *Dutch,* the *French* Squadron ftood by idle Spectators of the Combat , and one of their Captains, who had either more Honour than the reft,or was lefs acquainted with the Intrigue , for his venturing to give a Broad fide upon the *Dutch,* was difgraced at his return to *France.*

To enumerate all the Methods taken by the late two Kings of *England,* to render their infeparable Ally, the *French* King, great at Sea, is both a needlefs and a melancholy Task ; All *Europe* have

Subjects , that was but an opportunity, to vindicate their Liberties by their Arms.

• ADVERTISEMENTS.

In Plow-Yard *in* Grays-Inn-Lane, *lives Doctor* Thomas Kirleus *a Collegiate Phyfician, and Sworn Phyfician to* Charles II. *until his Death : Who with a Drink and Pill, hindring no Bufinefs, cures all Ulcers, Scabs, Scurfs in the Face, or elfewbere ;* Kings-Evil, Leprofie, *and Venereal Difeafe, 'expecting nothing if he Cures not. Of the laft he hath Cured above 500 Perfons in this City, many after Fluxing. It quickly and fafely cures it in the beginning, which cannot be done with* Mercury, *without danger of Life. The Drink is 3 s. the Quart ; the Pill 1 s. the Box, which is two Purges. They excel all Purgers in cleanfing all Crudities and Impurities, and fo prevent and cure many Difeafes, and efpecially the Gout and Stone. In all Difeafes he gives his Opinion for nothing, and his Medicines for little.*

There is now Publifh'd in a fmall Volume *The Confeffion of Faith : Together with the Larger and Leffer Catechifms. Compofed by the Reverend Affembly of Divines, then Sitting at* Weftminfter : *Prefented to both Houfes of Parliament: Again Publifhed with the Scriptures at large, and the Emphafis of the Scriptures in a different Character.*

London, *Printed for* Dorman Newman, *at the* King's Arms *in the* Poultrey, 1689.

7.1. Advertisement in *Mercurius Reformatus,* 14 August 1689. Reproduced from the collections of the Library of Congress.

only 6 pence a bottle.[25] A notice in *Mercurius Reformatus* offered a "cure for lunaticks," an oil to be massaged into the head only; it alleviated melancholy as well as madness. A list of people helped by the oil could be obtained from a Mr. C. Adams, at his lodgings at a haberdasher's near the pump in Chancery Lane, but if the remedy failed to work its magic, the same C. Adams offered his house in Fulham as a refuge for "all sorts of distempered persons."[26]

An ad in *The Flying Post* for 5–8 September 1702 heralded hope for those tormented by "griping in the guts." Peter Sayre, who lived in Pye-Corner, informed readers that he made and sold for forty years "an excellent water which cures the griping of the guts and surcharges of the stomach"; the aqua also prevented vexing surfeits. Sayre invoked a frequently used escape clause in medical advertising: the efficacy of his remedy depended on divine approval. Fortunately for business, Sayre's water, "by God's blessing cured thousands of people every year." The price for the liquid corrective was two shillings eight pence per quart with printed directions.

Perhaps no purgative enjoyed more popularity than Patrick Anderson's Scots Pills. The Stuart era presses teemed with claims and counterclaims concerning one of the oldest patent medicines in Britain. Anderson, who practiced in Edinburgh, claimed to be a doctor to Charles I, but while there is doubt whether he had a medical degree, there is no doubt he lacked any royal appointment.[27] Based on a formula Anderson said he obtained in Venice and on sale in England as early as 1630, the pills were a mild aloetic purgative containing colocynth and gamboge. In his 1635 treatise on the pills, *Grana Angelica*, Anderson promised long life for those who swallowed his medicine. He bequeathed the financially valuable right to manufacture and sell the pills to his surviving daughter, Katherine Anderson, who in turn sold the rights in 1686 to an Edinburgh surgeon, Thomas Weir. The following year, Weir obtained Letters Patent for the pills from James II.[28]

As late as 1705, Weir still held the patent, and he published a broadside, complete with a drawing of Patrick Anderson, entitled "Grana Angelica," listing the uses for the pills, insisting that only he had the "secret of composing" them, and reiterating that his shop in Edinburgh was the sole source of the true Scots pills. The picture of Dr. Anderson could be used to verify the seal on the box of genuine pastilles.[29] But with no outlet for the pills in London, imitations made their way to the marketplace, the most competitive of which was the commodity of Isabella Inglish, a former servant in the Weir household. Although the Edinburgh Town Council denounced her purgative as counterfeit in 1690, she continued to make and merchandise True Scots Pills. Mrs. Inglish advertised her medicine in the *London Gazette* and in *The Observator* as

faithfully prepared by Mrs. Inglish from Edinburgh, now living at the Golden Unicorn in the Strand. To prevent counterfeits from Scotland, take note that the true pills have their boxes sealed in black wax with a lyon rampant and three mullets argent, Dr. Anderson's head betwixt I.I. with his name round it and Isabella Inglish underneath with his name on a scroll.[30]

The ad goes on to claim that the pills are particularly efficacious when taken with medicinal waters. Fittingly, Mrs. Inglish herself suffered from competition, "counterfeits from Scotland," and frauds in her own neighborhood. "Beware of counterfeits," she cautioned readers, "especially one Mussen, an ignorant pretender who keeps a china shop . . . and sells a notorious counterfeit instead of the true pill within three doors of me, I. Inglish."[31]

Testimonials for Spooner's Purging Sugar Plums for Children appeared in *The Flying Post* and in *The Female Tatler*. They "sweetened and purified the blood to admiration, killed worms, cured green sickness, . . . and (were) good in all cases where purging is necessary."[32] Spooner evidently went back to the drawing board and improved his nostrum, asserting later that they were "entirely without mercury" and tasted just like a lump of sugar loaf. Less appetizingly, the plums on Christmas Eve 1714 "brought near half a pint of all sorts of worms with the slimy corrupted matter that breeds them from the child of Mr.

Dixon, a taylor in Feathers Court."[33] Initially printed up and marketed by Mr. Bradshaw, the plums became a franchise offering, "guaranteed to produce very great profit," or Bradshaw would refund your investment.[34]

Dr. Salvator Winter, self-described as famed for his "Elixir Vitae" and other miraculous cures, broadcast his return from a Welsh vacation in December 1689 and urged patients to call on him. His purl, or medicated liquor, that "excellent life-preserving remedy," rekindled spirits and repaired "decayed nature." Dr. Winter's elixir even "revived great numbers of people supposed to be dead." He gave meticulous directions on how to find him at his house "at the sign of St. Paul's Head in Kings-Street in St. Giles's in the Fields, near Covent Garden." He added that he placed the newspaper ad "because he was reported to be dead," but certainly not by anyone who knew the reputation of his restorative.[35] Evidently rumors of the deaths of medicos ranged broadly through London, for Dr. Greenfield (better known as Johannes Groeneveldt), "a College Physician," took out an ad in *The Spectator* to refute his demise, "industriously reported" by his rivals in medicine, as "absolutely false, he being now alive and well," and to affirm that he still successfully cut patients for the stone at the "Golden-Wheat-Sheaf in the Old Bayley."[36] Even distaff healers had to quash such pernicious gossip about their passing. Margaret Searl enlightened her clients in 1706 that she still lived in West Smithfield and was not dead; happily, she alone maintained the secrets of curing deafness taught her by her father and husband, both physicians. Someone else must have been claiming to know the method, for Searl had a document printed "to certifie that neither my father or husband ever instructed or communicated this secret to any of their servants or any apprentice whatsoever."[37]

Female humbugs like Searl often boasted of their specialties in newspapers. Mary Norridge bruited in the *Athenian Gazette* that she could cure the stone; the powder she marketed could be identified by the paper it was wrapped in: sealed with her distinctive coat of arms. She also purported to correct deafness, sore eyes, and baldness for fees ranging from one shilling to a half crown.[38] Certain physicians who advertised in newspapers sought to engage readers in holistic medicine, such as the initially anonymous E.M., M.D., author of *A Serious Debate Relating to Health and Sickness*. His booklet sold so well that in a second impression he revealed himself as Everard Maynwaring and added clarifications in a postscript. Another approach to health was proffered by Timothy Rogers; his printed sermons entitled *Practical Discourse on Sickness and Recovery* originated in his own recovery from an illness of two years duration. Temperance provided the key to health, long life, and happiness, according to Thomas Tryon, self-described "student in physick"; his tract argued for moderation in diet and exercise coupled with the use of all sorts of English herbs.

Advertising manifestos in newspapers predictably led to ripostes by rival healers. Roger Grant, the one-eyed "oculist extraordinary" from Wapping, in June 1709 avouched to have cured a young man of blindness from birth, and Richard Steele, writing from White's Chocolate House two months later, devoted a column in *The Tatler* to the episode.[39] The publicity engendered prompted Timothy Childe to write an exposé of Grant, charging that the young man was neither born blind nor rehabilitated by the operation. Seeking refutation of Grant's achievement and hoping to forestall payment to him, Childe reported that the patient asked his minister to certify the cure, which the cleric would not do, thereby shielding his parishioner from the oculist's unethical fees. According to Childe, a forged affidavit from the minister soon surfaced and appeared in advertisements in *The Daily Courant* and other papers on 29 July. On top of this egregious deceit, Childe condemned Grant as an illiterate cobbler and an Anabaptist preacher to boot.[40] Queen Mary II had prudently resisted Grant's tenacious bid to help with her watery eyes as he repeatedly tried to get appointed to court, but her sister Queen Anne actually consulted him for her own "defluxion." Grant thereafter styled himself "Oculist and Operator in Extraordinary to Her Majesty" in newspaper ads.[41]

Printers habitually vaunted other works they developed, including medical tracts, in the back of disparate books they put out. Peter Cole, Nicholas Culpeper's principal publisher and a savvy entrepreneur, mastered this technique when he realized the marketing capability of medical works by the famed herbalist and other writers. Knowing Culpeper's books would sell, Cole charged other printers to run advertisements for their titles in those editions. For instance, in the 1650 edition of the London *Pharmacopoeia*, Cole appended ads for works by Ambrose Paré and Alexander Read, though they were controlled by other booksellers. The following year, in Culpeper's *Directory for Midwives*, Cole incorporated advertisements for two other titles by Culpeper which he printed, beginning a pattern of self-promoting products from the Cole presses in Culpeper books. Furnishing medical information to all segments of the market, Cole systematically publicized Culpeper's Latin *Dispensarium*, the English *Dispensatory*, and the *English Physitian* in both folio (for physicians) and inexpensive octavo (for apothecaries, laymen, and women). In all, Cole inset 206 ads for the Culpeper oeuvre in sixteen books by Culpeper; within those same sixteen books, he lauded an additional 41 medical volumes by others.[42]

The title pages of published works offered another obvious venue for marketing printed matter, and were "advertisements in themselves" in the highly competitive book business.[43] Throughout London booksellers posted surplus title pages of the books they carried in their shops as random promotions and handed out table-of-contents pages to potential buyers. Every Saturday night, the titles of new books to be bound in the coming week were posted by apprentices; in addition, booksellers' catalogues became common forms of advertising by the 1690s, distributed free at coffeehouses.[44]

Besides announcements that appeared in periodicals and other literature, individual handbills advanced medical treatments and remedies for every conceivable ailment. Unlike ads in periodicals, handbills remained untaxed by Parliament. They became popular with advertisers, particularly those on the fringe of iatric practice. The earliest of these handouts may have been created by Master Gervaes around 1535, who was quick to seize upon the advantage printing afforded for promulgating his services; the circular is in the Library of the Royal College of Surgeons, London.[45] Besides recommending marketed cures, the broadsides came to serve as wrappers for the medicine bottles before labels were affixed, explaining recommended dosages and providing other details to the customer.[46] The practical nature of handbill advertising demonstrates why both the celebrated and the obscure utilized them for so long. Just nine days before he died in 1654, Culpeper advertised Aurum Potabile, "drinkable gold," manufactured by Doctors Freeman, Harrington, and himself (See Fig. 7.2.). In the ad, Culpeper insisted that the universal remedy had "cured diverse people of that most horrid, putrid fever which so violently seized on men's bodies to the great admiration of many." After Culpeper's death, Aurum Potabile was sold by Culpeper's widow and administered by a physician in her house "on the East side of Spittle-fields, next door to the Red Lion."[47]

Less celebrated than Culpeper, Sarah Gardiner of Southwark claimed to lessen all sorts of agues with her late husband's secret remedy; if she could not do so, there would be no charge. Likewise, Isabella Inglish complemented her newspapers ads for the True Scots Pills with a broadside listing their virtues and uses, while Mrs. Gill at the Sign of the Blew-Ball put her appellation on a flyer touting twenty years of fashioning remedies for scorbutic humors and rickets.[48] Some healers professed to assuage a wide range of afflictions, while others, who gave their addresses and hours of business but not their names, specialized in particular maladies. Only a smattering cautioned against a drug's side effects: Drops of Comfort, for use against "chollick, gripes, and agues," should not be taken by pregnant women as "it will carry off the conception."[49]

Although these leaflets were more often thrown away than other printed materials and not intended for to be kept for any length of time, the British Library maintains three separate collections of medical flyers, dating roughly from 1660 to 1715 and totalling 512 health care advertisements.[50] Most of the medical handouts consist entirely of text and are without ornamentation, though a few are illustrated and some contain the admonition to pocket the page for future reference or to find the advertiser's location. For instance, Restoration-era John Russell's broadsheet, topped by his portrait and decorated with crude woodcuts, depicted many dramatic surgical operations.[51] An ad for a doctor who expelled kidney stones delineates a hand holding a urine sample and requests that you "bring your urine with you and my bill also to prevent mistakes;" another for venereal disease cures blazons the armorial bearings of the "renowned Dutch operator" and suggests, after giving lengthy instructions on how to get to the back door of his lodgings, that you "keep this bill that you may come in the way as directed and not mistake the house."[52] When Mary Norridge, the gout specialist, moved from the Pewterer's to the Linen-Draper's in the Strand, she informed clients of her change of address in a circular that bore her trademark heraldic crest.[53]

The printers of these items are not normally identified on the page, but were likely the owners of small workshops or corner presses, the term for a

...ertues, Use, and Variety of operations of the true and Phylosophical AURUM POTABILE. Now made and sold by Dr. Freeman, as also by Dr. Harrington, and me Nich. Culpeper, in Spittle-fields, on the East side, next door to the Red Lyon.

Courteous and Friendly Reader,

THis precious Jewel of Aurum Potabile, which Dr. Freeman and my self have attained to the perfection thereof, is now only in the hands of Dr. Freeman and my self, and Dr. Harrington, who hath long and often tried, and known the Vertues, Use, and Manner of operation thereof, to the great comfort of many who had Diseases, which otherwise might have proved inseparable and incurable, as sufficient witnesses can testifie: It cures all Agues, whether Quotidian, Tertian, or Quartan; as also it cured divers people of that most horrid, putrid Feaver, which so violently seized on mens bodies (both before and after Michaelmas, 1653.) to the great admiration of many; and when the parties diseased have been both senceless and speechless, so that neither that, nor any other Medicine or Panacea, though never so gentle, could safely be administred into the body; it hath beyond all hopes by external application on the stomach, revived them from death: It cures the Gout of all sorts so perfectly, Being administred as the Authors shall advise, that I dare undertake it shall never trouble the patient more, if the cause that first brought it, whether it be by Diet, or otherwise, be forborn. It causeth Women subject to Abortion or Miscarriage to go their times, and yet being administred when the time comes, it causeth a speedy and ease delivery. But to what purpose do I go about to nominate Diseases in particular, when it is an Universal Remedy for all Diseases, being administred as the Authors give Directions? for its chief aim is exhilerating the vital Spirits and Heart, which supplies the Microcosm as doth the Sun the Macrocosm; for Joshua knew right well that if he commanded and made the Sun to stand still, that all the Macrocosm must: so of necessity must Man, the Microcosm when his Heart, viz. the Microcosms Sun, is at a stand in his operations. Thus doing, it both binds, and stops fluxes, yet purges: It both Vomits, and staies vomiting: it causes sweat, yet cures preternatural sweating, and performs all its operations as Nature her self would have it, because it only fortifies her in her Center, and it was never yet at any time known, but if Nature be strengthened, and have an Enemy in the Body, but that she will to work to expel him, or correct him.

To conclude, It's an Universal Fortification for all Complexions and Ages, against all sorts and degrees of pestilential and contagious infection, both preventing before their possession, and extirpating of them after it. But why Glauber (in his description of the true properties of that he pretends for true Aurum Potabile) would not have it give any color to the hands, or any thing else, and yet it self a most pure Tincture, neither he, nor I, nor any mortal man can tell.

I shall say no more at present, but refer you to a Treatise that shall shortly be published on this Subject.

Jan. 1. 1653.   NICH. CULPEPER.

7.2. Nicholas Culpeper's ad for aurum potabile, a broadside dated 1 January 1653. From Mr. *Culpeper's Treatise of Aurum Potabile* (London: George Eversden, 1656).

business with one press run by a printer who was also a designer and printseller.[54] He or she may have been assisted by a compositor and a corrector or by an apprentice acting as a general helper, but typically shops which printed ephemera were meager, one-person operations whose technology had remained static since mid-Tudor times. Such workshops conventionally produced flyers and other cheap typographical objects for a large public. A printer, acting as compositor, could fashion about one sheet per day; the daily rate of typographical printing was about 500 sheets, both sides, per press.[55]

Among the pamphlet-printing houses regularly contracted by quacks and fully occupied with unsophisticated material was that of George and Henry Parker. George Parker styled himself an astrologer and physician, eventually turning to printing at the Blue Ball off Fleet Street. His son Henry Parker almost exclusively spawned medical and literary advertisements.[56] Thomas James typeset broadsides throughout his forty-year career at his shop in Mincing Lane, and put his name on single sheets lauding Doctor Blagrave's and Richard Fletcher's scurvy medicines. Bookman John Dunton described James as competent, but better known for being the husband of "that she-state politician," Mrs. Elinor James, the author of over fifty partisan pamphlets.[57] A third printer identifiable from existing broadsides is George Larkin the elder, living in Scalding Alley in the Poultry around 1680. In trouble with the government for printing works that gave offense to the crown, he turned to producing octavo sheets, such as that for Benjamin Shove trumpeting Dr. Trigg's Golden Vatican Pill, available at many bookshops. Dunton regarded him warmly and called him his friend of twenty years; happily, George junior took over the family business around 1706 and later managed to ingratiate himself with King George I. Finally, in 1690 one J. Gardiner, possibly a Roman Catholic, created a handbill for "The Lady Moor's Drops," prepared by Mr. Wells, and sold the concoction at his shop near the Plough Inn in Little Lincoln's Inn Fields.[58]

Mercury women, pamphlet shopkeepers like Elizabeth Nutt and Ann Dodd, were responsible for most of the distribution of newspapers throughout the capital. Hired hawkers and criers—usually older, illiterate females, many of whom were homeless, hungry, and infirm—dispersed those newspapers twice a week throughout town, in the marketplace and in the street, at St. Paul's churchyard, Temple Gate, and City coffeehouses; they also transmitted pamphlets and broadsheets. Publishers like John Dunton appreciated the role of the hawkers, the "messengers of fate" who could make or break a product with their "vigor(ous) declaims against its rivals and enemies."[59] Yet despite their value to the print trade, female hawkers often led desperate and hazardous lives. Paula McDowell reports on "Blind Fanny," "Lame Cassie," and "Irish Nan," as well as septuagenarians and older who cried papers just to get by. The Lord Mayor and Court of Aldermen, doubtless hounded by their constituents, disapproved in 1679 that hawkers around the Royal Exchange were pestering citizens and forbade future crying in the City; the Marshal of London was empowered to set offenders at hard labor.[60] The Act for Licensing Hawkers and Pedlars (1698) prohibited street vendors outside the City from handling any books or unauthorized papers, but they could distribute any lawful handbills including medical broadsides.

Varying in size from four to eight inches in length, in the quality of their print, and in the number of sides, single or double, these circulars publicized iatric merchandise and services. Those that were printed on one side could be plastered to walls at busy intersections, such as the list of miscellaneous cures affixed at "the Sign of the Angell, near the Great Conduit in Cheapside." Posters lauding infallible lozenges, sovereign cordials, incomparable drinks, and royal antidotes against pestilence blanketed London during epidemics.[61] Sheets with additional material continued on the reverse were likely meant to be read in private or aloud in public venues like coffeehouses or pubs to those who could not read for themselves. Humorist Ned Ward wrote in London Spy that you could not enter a coffeehouse without being inundated by advertisements for "May Dew, Golden Elixirs, Popular Pills, Liquid Snuff, Beautifying Waters, Dentifrices, Drops, and Losenges, all as infallible as the Pope." Ward joked that had a friend not otherwise apprised him, he might have thought he was in "the parlour of some eminent mountebank."[62]

Conveniently, the medicines and succor so advertised might be purchased at those same coffeehouses and taverns. At Peel's in Fleet Street, John Hinge dealt with corns and nails each morning, the start of his circuit of half a dozen establishments. More alarmingly, Mr. Wilcox, a former cupper at the Royal Bagnio, set up at the Turk's Head in Newgate Street, ready to "sweat, bathe, shave, or cup after the best manner" either at the coffeehouse or at his patrons' homes. Daniel Defoe reported that the brochure of one mountebank proposed "an excellent electuary against the plague, to be drunk at the Green Dragon Cheapside at six-pence a pint."[63]

Sometimes the hawked material accompanied another kind of publication. Lionel Lockyer, "authorized physician and chemist," put out a twenty-one page brochure in 1667 for his "excellent pills called Pilulae Radiis Solis Extractae," a pill of "all-healing virtue." Though he denied that his recipe contained sulphur of antimony, it probably was an antimonial preparation used as an emetic and diaphoretic in fever cases.[64] Extensively embellished handbills promoted the pills to a different constituency than the one that read the pamphlet. A broadsheet from around 1702 bearing Lockyer's likeness and a sketch of him in his laboratory extols the universality and infallibility of the medicine, describes its usages, and enumerates its satisfied customers; venues where the pills might be purchased are helpfully listed. The sale of Lockyer's Pills, easier to ask for than Pilulae Radiis Solis Extractae, continued for 150 years after the inventor's death. John Archer, author of one of the most important early manuals of medical self-help, Every Man His Own Doctor, published a leaflet to hail his book and to remind its readers of his office address in the Haymarket. He offered a variety of nostrums for sale at that location, including tobacco, sneeze powder, elixirs, cordials, capsules, and purging boluses.[65] Through his primer

7.3. "Mountabanck." From Marcellus Laroon, *Cryes of the City of London* (1687).

and the drugs at his establishment, Archer deliberately encouraged his patrons to keep stocked medicine chests while enabling them to self-diagnose and self-dose without further professional advice.

Salvator Winter, the creator of "Elixir Vitae" who advertised in newspapers for patients, commissioned a handbill to exhort merchants to sell his medicines abroad to such disparate points as "France, Germany, Italy, Virginia, New England, Barbados, Jamaica and many other places." Of course, the advantage that an empiric like Winter commanded from dealing personally with patients was lost when the medico became a faceless entrepreneur behind a product. Later, Winter's son and scion of the family business, alleged in a flyer that Dr. Winter senior had lived to be ninety-nine, probably because he always carried "a bottle [of the elixir] in his pocket, drinking a spoonful four or five times a day and snuffing it up very strongly into his nostrils and bathing his temples."[66]

Many circulars came from immigrant practitioners or female irregulars unlicensed by the College of Physicians and forced to rely on self-aggrandizement to attract patients. Of course, the Fellows generally scorned broadcasting one's medical skills, and their contempt for publicity-seeking unorthodox healers only waxed greater.[67] Foreigners sometimes bragged of their cosmopolitan training and manipulated their ethnicity to advantage, such as the Dutch doctor Gerardts Gonsale, who directed his pitch at Netherlanders living in London with promises of consultations in their native tongue.[68] Women doctors had to flaunt their credentials even more than their male analogues. Calling herself a seventh daughter who could interpret dreams as well as heal, one advertiser claimed she learned her craft from "one of King Charles's and King James's twelve doctors."[69] In the 1690s, Mary Green of Chancery Lane bragged that she had a license to practice medicine from the Archbishop of Canterbury, but to drop more names, she included endorsements from important people cured of constipation and coughing by her when eminent physicians and surgeons had failed.[70] Mary Norridge used her change-of-address handbill as an occasion to list the names of many Londoners who successfully took her powder for the stone and gravel: Alice Fielding had a violent fit due to the stone and stoppage of urine for five days; Grace Allen was unable to micturate for eight days, but passed two huge stones after ingesting two doses of the powder; and though William Tuff could not urinate for five days and nights, one portion of Mrs. Norridge's powder and his urine returned in the space of an hour.[71]

Although clients of irregulars like Mrs. Norridge risked seeing their names in print alongside rather indelicate symptoms, females unfailingly pronounced themselves in notices as ideal for the distaff sick who might prefer privacy from the male medical gaze. Some men were forced to agree. Peter Bartlett, a specialist in ruptures whose bulletin is adorned with a cupid holding a truss, even assured potential lady patients that his mother, who lived at his house, was "skilful in the business to those of her own sex;" Dr. Abraham Souberg likewise recommended his sister, "who lives with me and has been brought up all her life in the knowledge of physick."[72] On the other hand, Stephen Draper, "M.D.

and man-midwife," implored the women patients he solicited "to leave their child-like niceties, and to be no longer ashamed to apply themselves to me, for I will keep your secrets as my own life."[73]

Advertising helped many women make their livings as healers. Elizabeth Maris, explaining that she might have remained unfamiliar to the public without "this printed paper," described herself as "a true German gentlewoman, who . . . with good success remov'd all distempers incident to womenkind"; Sarah Cornelius de Heusde, who professed knowledge assimilated from both her late husband and father, insisted that she could fix a number of gynecological problems as well as the stone, the pox, and freckles; and Willemina van Soeburg, perhaps Dr. Souberg's sister, who could be found at her lodging in Exeter Street, maintained she could heal bruised children as well as their mothers.[74] A gentlewoman in business near the Hay Market promised comeliness to her female patrons: she could smooth complexions, kill "black and white worms" on the face, and get out unwanted hair, "root and branch, leaving the patient . . . as a newborn child.[75] One self-described equal opportunity "doctress" promised not only to fix "glimmering gizzards and quavering kidneys" in both sexes, but to restore "beauty and youth to ladies of fourscore (and) take away cuckolds horns."[76]

Though divulging the secrets of the trade was frowned upon by traditional physicians, a few College Fellows advertised. During the epidemic in 1665, the Lord Mayor and the College published the names and addresses of doctors ready to visit the sick along with their recipes for recuperation. One valiant physician, William Page, related in his own broadside that he had recovered from the plague, "which he had taken while visiting the sick," and was "prepared to take up his duties again."[77] Less community-minded medicos pushed iatric merchandise in handbills, trumpeting their credentials and connections. Hans Sloane, President of both the College of Physicians and the Royal Society, sold an eye salve and Dr. Richard Mead, at the end of his illustrious career physician to George II, concocted a secret powder for the bite of a mad dog. One unidentified "licensed physician," warned that:

> "Physick (from those don't understand),
> Is like Sword in a mad Man's Hand."

However, he was not above advertising like an empiric himself and announced that he could cure "the most inveterate pox, . . . the sooner you apply yourselves to me."[78]

John Pechey, an Oxford graduate, employed handbills to blazon his cures and to offer his medical aptitude to regular patients for two shillings sixpence. The poor he pledged to serve for free. In his advertisements, Pechey cautioned that his medicines were available only from his retail outlet and that clients could identify him by his one-horse calash.[79] He justified his self-promotion as the epitome of public service: for how could one justify concealing medicine "of such great virtue" when so many bad concoctions were being foisted off on the unsuspecting? He referred to his patients as "people of eminence for their rank in the world and their parts," but loathsome quacks Pechey called "cobbling doctors" and cautioned the unwary to avoid their "prepared trash and skill in nonsense."[80] He labelled his critics, who failed to make the distinction between an entrepreneurial physician and a charlatan, as jealous failures.

Another establishment figure, Nehemiah Grew, M.D. from the University of Leiden, Fellow of the Royal Society, and a leading Restoration scientist, dabbled in proprietary medicine. Grew published extensively on floral physiology, including his magnum opus, *The Anatomy of Plants* (1682), dedicated to Robert Boyle. As secretary of Royal Society, he edited its *Philosophical Transactions* and conducted experiments on saliferous vegetation. He patented Epsom Salts, described as excellent for colic, worms, and indigestion.[81] John Radcliffe, a society doctor though a maverick one, peddled a purging drink, Radcliffe's Royal Tincture, a "rectifier of the nerves, head and stomach." One quaff of Radcliffe's purl mixed with beer, ale, or sack, and all "irregularities of the head and stomach," even those caused by "hard drinking or otherwise," would be corrected.[82]

But while Grew and Radcliffe were bona fide physicians, William Read was not, though he certainly had all the right connections. An itinerant tailor who prated that he could eliminate wens, harelips, and cataracts became Queen Anne's oculist-in-ordinary, and she knighted him in 1705 for allegedly curing blind seamen. Inventor of styptic water to be used instead of cauterization, Read flaunted cancer removal as another of his specialties, but in his book, *A Short But Exact Account of All the Diseases Incident to the Eyes*, Read combined conventional Galenic treatment with his own recipes for eye health. In the publication, he corrected the errors of other oculists, especially those whose remedies "heat the brain" and therefore dull the sight; he recommended drinking beer in the morning, to help those with "dry brains," plus the usual bleeding and cupping. Read, termed a "coucher" for his use of a "couch needle" to push coagulated, viscous humors (cataracts) below the axis of vision, prescribed an eyewash of sulphur, turpentine, vivum, and honey of roses. Practicing at the York Buildings in the Strand, Read became very wealthy through advertisements in *The Tatler*; Joseph Addison branded him "the most laborious advertiser of his time." According to Jonathan Swift, Read was able to afford lavish parties where good punch was served in golden vessels.[83] Read's status at court or ostentatious affluence did not protect him from derision in print. *The Oculist* (1705), a typical Augustan age satire in verse, (1705) ridiculed both of Queen Anne's eye specialists, Roger Grant and Read:

> Her majesty sure was in a surprise
> Or else was very short-sighted
> When a tinker was sworn to look after her eyes
> And the mountebank tailor was knighted.[84]

Like many popular practitioners in the capital during the Tudor-Stuart period, Simon Forman and William Salmon tried to bridge the gap between the respectable healers and the notorious. Forman was a late sixteenth-century doctor, astrologer, and alchemist, who utilized both Galenic and Paracelsian rubrics interspersed with sorcery and magical seances, "beyond the established borders [of] . . . accepted classical views."[85] He had no formal medical training, not uncommon among doctors, but he had attended Oxford and worked as a schoolteacher.[86] Although he eventually obtained a Cambridge University license to practice medicine, Forman was hounded with fines and imprisonment by the College of Physicians for two decades, forcing him to move across the Thames into Lambeth. Prosperous in his practice, Forman exemplifies the unaccredited healer who, despite the rhetoric of the authorized physicians, was as financially successful as they were.[87] He likely advertised his therapies, both medical and surgical, and broadcast his locations before and after the move to Lambeth; he certainly intended to solicit business with his pamphlet, *The Groundes of Longitude*, in 1591. Besides arguing that an unknown like himself could determine longitude, the seven-leaf quarto mainly cheers Forman's professional aptitude.[88] Outrageous in his personal life, Forman remained controversial in death. He was implicated in 1613 in the conspiracy to murder Sir Thomas Overbury with poison, even though Forman himself had died two years earlier. Though clearly in the notorious category, Forman's biographer argues nonetheless that most of the time he functioned within the mainstream of iatric therapies pursued in late Elizabethan London.[89]

William Salmon's only training, according to his post-Restoration critics, was as an apprentice to a mountebank whose travels took the youngster to New England. Back in London by 1670, Salmon inaugurated his own career as a medical educator and savvy businessman. He published extensively throughout the last three decades of the seventeenth century; his titles encompassed lofty subjects like the principles of Hermes and Hippocrates (1670); useful compendiums such as the seven-volume *Synopsis medicinae* (1682) and *The Family Dictionary* (1696) on domestic medicine; and a paean to Thomas Sydenham (1695). In 1672 Salmon's publisher, Richard Jones, also generated his *Polygraphice: The Art of Drawing, Engraving, Etching, Limning, Painting, Washing, Varnishing, Colouring and Dyeing*, at the end of which Salmon promoted his own pills at three shillings a box. Though an autodidact, he had a library of over three thousand volumes and two microscopes. He felt sufficiently well informed and influential to sanction the College physicians in their conflict with metropolitan apothecaries over the dispensing of drugs to poor Londoners.[90]

But as an empiric, Salmon also advertised broadly, apprising possible clients of his whereabouts outside the Smithfield gate of St. Bartholomew's Hospital and offering to accommodate patients where convenient. In broadsheets he specified whom he treated, of what, and where: Ambrose Webb at the Three

Compasses in Westbury-Street of a great bleeding at the nose; Joan Ingram near the Bear in Moor Fields of the gout; and the son of William Ogden, near the Black Boy in Barnaby-Street of a long and tedious ague and madness. Controlling melancholy was one of Salmon's supposed fortes and he enthusiastically prescribed his own Elixir Vitae. Moreover, adding to his persona as a quack doctor, Salmon designed a prophetic almanac in 1684, the first of its kind, but in the preface he indicated a penchant for medicine over soothsaying. And Salmon tirelessly promulgated his eponymous pastilles all over England, arranging outlets for their distribution in Worcester, Newbury, Braintree, Ruthin, Lichfield, Stafford, Dorcester, Devizes, Gloucester, and London; Martha Fripp sold Salmon's Pills at Cowes on the Isle of Wight.[91]

It should be apparent that the line which separated legitimate doctors from illegal practitioners blurred due to the activities of both groups. M.D.'s vended special concoctions, consulted the stars, and published narcissistic books little different from the quacks they loathed; conversely, unlicensed practitioners plied many medical techniques similar to their credentialed counterparts. Sometimes the lines converged on a single medical product like the famous anodyne necklace, a so-called sympathetic medicine. George Hartman wrote a book for families in 1690 in which he advised wearing amulets for sickness.[92] Advertisers soon clamored to sell medicinal necklaces, and one of the first, Major John Choke, claimed that his eased teething in infants. About the size of a nutmeg, Choke's talisman also helped soothe the fevers and distempers that often accompanied teething.[93] In his numerous handbills, Choke, whose wife was purported to be the daughter of the famous chemist-physician van Helmont, gave himself a royal coat of arms, attributed his successes to God, and overwhelmed the reader with the names of satisfied customers.[94] After Choke's necklaces sold vigorously at shops all around London, each claiming to be the sole outlet for authentic necklaces, facsimiles flooded the marketplace.

Most of the extant advertising broadsides summon patients with explicit directions to visit the healer's premises or to rendezvous in a handy, if sometimes unseemly location. Peter Maris, husband to the aforementioned Elizabeth, invited patients to see him from eight until twelve in the morning and from two in the afternoon until eight at night at his lodgings in High Holborn between the great and little turnstiles at the Crown and Golden-Ball Inn; an anonymous German doctor's hours in Little Russell Street were from 6 to 10 A.M. and 6 to 10 P.M.[95] Agnodice, a self-described "woman physician," practiced from an inn disconcertingly named the Hand and Urinal. It might be worth the trip to see her, however, since she dispensed Italian washes for blemishes, Spanish rolls for wrinkles, and correctives for the "Scotch disease," a nasty itch.[96] Anne Paverenst, another "German Gentlewoman" recently arrived in England, instructed possible buyers to look for her where a red cloth with "coagulated stones taken out of the bodies of the female sex" could be seen hanging out of the balcony at the King's Arms Tavern in Arundel Street. Perhaps someone advised her that such a bloody flag might be off-putting, because in another notice she announced her availability at the Coffin and Child in Southampton Square, equally macabre for a healer who purported to cure children.[97]

Patients who might wish to avoid the aggravation of such public appointments could have remedies discreetly "delivered in [the] hands of civil gentlewomen and maidens," as one circular promised, or shipped via the penny-post.[98] The proprietor of "The True Spirit of Scurvy-Grass" explained in a broadside that if his customers wrote out clear directions where to send the medicine-filled vessels, the "glasses . . . will be brought as safe as if fetch't by themselves and as cheap as one." Buyers should put sixpence for each container, with a six-pack minimum for a parcel, into letters requesting penny-post delivery, plus a penny to pay the carriage back, "for no body can think the profit great."[99] Such a method of delivery was safe, secure, and anonymous. As Kevin Siena points out in his analysis of advertisements purporting to treat venereal disease, for the privacy of their customers healers routinely sold their medicines and instructions through retail agents, the most common of which were booksellers.[100] Confidentiality was not always a top priority for quack healers, however; one mountebank offering a cure for syphilis named and furnished the address of a patient whom the curious were invited to inspect.[101]

Medical entrepreneurs feared unfair competition and counseled buyers to check for item authenticity. Mrs. Barret's Grand Restorative, good for rheumatism and stinking breath, bore a distinguishing wrapper with three bucks' heads. Elizabeth Russell packaged Dr. Jones's Friendly Pills, "being tincture of the sun that cause all complexions to laugh or smile in the very time of taking," about twenty to a box; the box was then sealed with a lion and cinquefoil to thwart frauds.[102] Flyers sometimes spotlighted strife between entrepreneurs, containing strong language that repudiated assertions coming from rival medicos, while at the same time recommending a superior commodity. Consider the war of words over Daffy's Elixir Salutis. Thomas Daffy, rector at Redmile in Leicestershire, had invented the original elixir; by 1673 it was already a famous medication with a considerable reputation. During Daffy's lifetime, his son Daniel, an apothecary in Nottingham, sold the elixir. After Daniel's death, Katherine Daffy, the rector's daughter, sold the soothing syrup at two dozen sites in London—shoemakers', milliners', perfumers', and coffeehouses—as well as diverse towns outside of the metropolis. She advertised the elixir in the *Post Boy* of 1 January 1708 and *The Spectator* of 17 April 1712, explaining that the ingredients had been shared with their physician kinsman, Anthony Daffy. According to a corresponding broadside, Dr. Daffy "had published it to the benefit of the community and his own great advantage." But Katherine also had the authentic recipe; she vowed in the handbill that she was no imposter nor was her elixir.[103]

Katherine Daffy's right to market the Elixir Salutis was disputed by Elizabeth Daffy, daughter-in-law of Anthony Daffy and wife of Cambridge scholar Elias Daffy. Mrs. Daffy proclaimed herself the proprietress of the popular concoction and zealously guarded the family formula for good health. Her elixir bore insignia attesting to endorsements from two royal doctors. The final salvo, however, had not been fired in the Daffy war. In March 1709, Elizabeth Daffy brought her commercial differences, not with Katherine Daffy, but with John Harrison, to the public in a series of sheets labeled advertisements that mainly consisted of charges and rejoinders over who had the real elixir salutis. Mrs. Daffy denounced Harrison for pretending to be Anthony Daffy's assistant and with concocting a counterfeit tincture. She accused Harrison of squatting at a house in Prujean's Court near the Old Bailey which he claimed in his notices was his. Harrison rebutted that he leased the house lawfully; he disavowed her denigration that his elixir was spurious, relating that he learned how to prepare it on the continent fifteen years earlier. He boasted that many persons of rank had taken the liquid panacea with great satisfaction. At the conclusion of his single-sheet bulletin, Harrison solicited testimonials of affirmation about the tincture and his professionalism, and urged potential clients to avoid any elixir salutis but his.[104]

The explosion of iatric advertising in early modern England reflected an awareness on the part of entrepreneurs that ordinary citizens demanded alternative and affordable forms of health care treatment than those provided by expensive physicians or by their costly counterparts among legitimate surgeons and apothecaries. The purveyors of treatments and medicaments recognized that the printed word could arouse in the minds of countless customers the desire for a particular product and direct those customers to places where they could buy those exact remedies. Advertisements in newspapers and on broadsides delivered sellers of cures to buyers in need of medical relief. In so doing, those printed ads facilitated and intensified the popular movement already begun, away from medical arcana imposed by the elite on the unknowing patient and toward self-diagnosis and informed consumer activism.

Chapter 8

Worth a Thousand Words: Medical Illustrations and Their Effect

In his *New Herbal* of 1543, Leonhart Fuchs asserted that "pictures can communicate information much more clearly than the words of the most eloquent men."[1] Fuchs's conviction applies fittingly to books about medicine in general and to herbals, almanacs, and anatomies in particular. Consider the importance to herbals alone that reliable illustrations provided. Since many ordinary people in early modern England gathered or grew medicinal herbs for the self-treatment of sickness, not to mention the healing botanicals prescribed by their physicians and supplied by apothecaries, correct identification of the curative plants was crucial to amateur and professional alike. However, the primitive style of many medieval illustrations made them useless for plant identification by Tudor times. One sixteenth-century writer complained that important medical plants known to the ancients could no longer even be recognized.[2] Although naturalistic renderings of plants appear in some early manuscripts, the woodcuts which ornamented medieval herbals in England had originally been wielded for textile printing. Woodcutters formed part of the carpenters' guild; their products were simple carvings, not sophisticated floral facsimiles. Occasionally non-union labor contributed to illustrated books, such as the remarkable Bridgettines, nuns closely associated with Caxton and his successors. They furnished early English printers with woodcuts, notably ones associated with Syon Abbey.[3] As a piece of pictorial type, woodcuts print pictures in the same way that fonts print letters of the alphabet; block could be stored, inked, and printed along with type.[4] Relief blocks could also be cut into metal, copper being the most common medium. Not long after Gutenberg's printing of the Bible, relief-printed blocks combined with type had become frequent. Whatever the material utilized or the printing technique, any books with medical repercussions needed more meticulous illustrations.

Understanding the necessity for accurate plant likenesses in herbals, Fuchs himself hired Albrecht Meyer as the botanical artist for his *De historia stirpium* or *Inquiries on Plants*. Fuchs, who had two sets of wood engravings prepared for his herbal, occupied the vanguard of those herbalists who insisted that flora be shown in their natural state. The famed illustrations done by Hans Weiditz for Otto Brunfels's 1530 *Herbarium vivae eicones* or *Herbal of Living Images* offer another early example of effective, modernized pictures that accompanied plant descriptions. Thereafter, other writers found high-quality illustrations indispensable to their herbal texts. Accurate depictions of leaves, flowers, roots, bark, and wood enabled harvesters to pick the right therapeutic plant. Illustrated herbals demonstrated for all to appreciate the popular doctrine of signatures, the theory that the plant's appearance suggested its medicinal application. Exquisite sketches showed those visible characteristics that made a particular herb appropriate for a specific treatment. For instance, lungwort, whose spotted leaves resemble a diseased lung, was recommended for chest ailments. Herbalist William Coles, in *The Art of Simpling,* cited walnuts as bearing "the whole signature of the head," but warned his readers that even if plants display no apparent hallmarks, they still might have use.[5]

In England, the first vernacular book on herbs, William Turner's *A New Herball* (1551), offered careful descriptions of plants along with warnings that unscrupulous apothecaries might be selling deleterious substitutes for beneficial herbs in their shops. One of the most attractive features of this herbal is the number of beautiful woodcuts with which it is illustrated. A few were specially drawn and cut for the author, but most are duplicates of the drawings from a 1545 octavo edition of Fuchs's *De historia stirpium.* Over 400 of Fuchs's blocks were employed in the completion of Turner's herbal, borrowed by Turner's printer at Cologne.[6]

Later generations benefitted from many medicinal plants imported from the New World, and herbalists had to acquaint their readers with these foreign drugs. In 1577 John Frampton translated and published *Joyfull Newes out of the New Founde Worlde,* based on the account of Nicolas Monardes, that captured the excitement of the times and the optimism that exotic remedies could complement indigenous ones. It contained a draft of tobacco, the first printed illustration of that plant to appear in an English book. John Gerard's 1597 *Herball* overflowed with 1,800 configurations of unfamiliar plants like sassafras and sarsaparilla, both sometimes ingested as blood purifiers to treat venereal disease. Gerard also touted imported goldenrod, but reminded his readers that they did not have to spend half a crown an ounce for the dry herb from beyond the sea; since goldenrod flourished in Hampstead, "no man will give half a crown for a hundred weight of it."[7] Gerard's publisher, John Norton—the Queen's Printer in Greek, Latin, and Hebrew—procured the loan of superior woodblocks to illustrate the herbal from a Frankfurt shop, but Gerard added sixteen cuts of his own. Among the latter is the first published representation of the "Virginian" potato.[8]

Gerard made mistakes, however, with the illustrations. A London apothecary, James Garret, called Norton's attention to the errors. According to Matthias de l'Obel, a Flemish physician living in Highgate, Norton asked him to make over a thousand alterations to correct the work. Creator of *Stirpium adversaria nova,* published in London in 1571, de l'Obel had perhaps too lofty a reputation for Gerard to ignore; the flower lobelia is named for him. Nevertheless, with the credibility of his herbal at stake, Gerard ordered that the emendations cease, declaring his herbal to be sufficiently accurate and insulting de l'Obel's mastery of English at the same time. For his part, de l'Obel bitterly alleged that Gerard had stolen parts of his own writings without acknowledgment.[9]

Other English herbals profusely depicted their subject. John Parkinson made a name for himself with a gardening book, *Paradisi in sole paradisus terrestris, or A Garden of Pleasant Flowers*, published in 1629.[10] The woodcut frontispiece to *Paradisi* boasts a lavishly illustrated epitome of Eden, replete with Adam grafting an apple tree and Eve fetching a pineapple. The flowers are out of proportion, much larger than in reality, but the most intriguing oddity on the page is the "vegetable lamb," growing on a stalk and grazing on the vegetation around it. Also known as a "Scythian lamb" and venerated in medieval myth, this creature was deemed both plant and animal, a favorite snack for wolves who appreciated its lobster-like taste. Parkinson also spotlighted the Scythian lamb in his famous herbal, *Theatrum botanicum*, the largest in the English language, published in 1640, when he was seventy-three. He apparently accepted the tales about this strange living plant that grew near Samarkand, "rising from a seede somewhat bigger and rounder than a melon seede."[11] The ornamental title-page of *Theatrum botanicum* stacks levels of figures and scenes: Adam and Solomon occupy center stage with four female incarnations of the known continents, surrounded at the design's corners by specimens of foliage associated with those territories. Parkinson's portrait graces the bottom tier.

The first volume of John Ray's *Historia plantarum* was published in 1686, after the introduction of an enormous number of hitherto unknown plants from Asia and America. He had already prepared a catalogue of English plants, printed for the first time in 1670, but undertaking a universal herbal was remarkable for a man living in a remote Essex village. More remarkable still, his three-volume *Historia plantarum* "stands as the most important English botanical work published" under the later Stuarts, "a mine of information much quarried by Ray's 18th-century Swedish successor, Carl Linnaeus."[12] Though the text was in Latin, selected terms, highlighted in black letter, were in English, signalling the author's hope for a broader audience. Ray wanted his magnum opus to contain illustrations, but booksellers balked at investing further in a second volume after the initial one did not sell well. Despite an effort by Ray's publishers to raise money by subscription to procure engraved plates for all three volumes, Ray reluctantly concurred in the financial decision to exclude illustrations.[13] Ray's assistant, James Petiver, an apothecary, advertised quack nostrums while dabbling in botany and entomology. After Ray's death, Petiver published an extensive catalogue of plants with engraved figures on sixty-seven copper plates, partly as a memorial to his mentor and partly "to advantage himself by the sale of dried specimens of the plants illustrated."[14] The hand-colored folio plates were engraved by Sutton Nicholls, a mediocre London draftsman who frequently did street scenes and portraits of authors ad vivum for printers to add to textual material.[15] (See Fig. 8.1.) Petiver's homage to Ray's work appeared in 1713 through the bookshop of Christopher Bateman.

Almanacs comprise a second category of printed textual material whose medical utility was transformed by pictures. Tudor and Stuart almanacs explained that different parts of the body were affected by the qualities of the planets and the signs of the zodiac. To illustrate exactly what planet governed which parts, a "zodiac man" demonstrated celestial influences. Sixteenth-century engravings also related the four humors to astrological signs, such as blood to Aries; those born under that sign were thought to exhibit sanguine personalities (See Fig. 8.2.). Gabriel Frende provided an unusual anatomical figure in his almanac to demonstrate the best times for a practitioner to bleed, purge, or operate. His zodiac man showed the veins commonly punctured in phlebotomy with a note to the surgeon that "this figure is prefixed, thy hand to guide."[16] The publisher of another almanac, The Infallible Astrologer by Silvester Partridge, a weekly periodical of "prophecies and predictions" printed at Bond's Stables in 1700, trimmed costs by using fifty-year old woodcuts in its first issues. Even when its budget warranted newer cuts for later in the series, the illustrations were in the outmoded style of ballads and chapbooks.[17]

Textual illustrations, however, became more elaborate with the passage of time. During the Tudor-Stuart era, printers employed two methods of reprography, each based on a different principle and the working of a different raw material: relief printing used blocks of wood and intaglio utilized metal plates. Though the squares used in relief printing were cheap and easy to work with, the chief drawback of wood was an inherent structural weakness that could cause distortion. Lacking a middle tone, woodcuts were not always useful in the pathology of medical illustration; they could not be used to render skin diseases or the rough lesions of leprosy.[18] Intaglio printing developed in Germany and Italy among fifteenth-century goldsmiths, augmented by applications of etching and mezzotint to print.[19] Because intaglio made use of metal plates, which were inherently stronger than wood, it could sustain a finer line. These processes greatly enhanced content, especially where exactness was needed, as in maps, geometrical and mechanical diagrams, and medical drawings. Although more expensive than wood, metal plates lasted longer, but illustrations could not be implemented simultaneously with the letterpress. During the sixteenth century large printing offices had their own rolling presses for printing intaglio work with the text, while smaller establishments contracted the job out to specialist printing shops.[20]

Engraved title pages became stylish even before the seventeenth century, and quality books featured sketches, chapter headings, and tail pieces throughout. The magnificently engraved title page of Thomas Linacre's translation of Galen, Methodus Medendi, a folio edition published in Paris in 1530, overflows with spectacles of healing (See Fig. 8.3.). A panel honoring Christ healing a leper centered between the patron saints of physicians, Sts. Cosmas and Damian, crowns a hectic dissection scene.[21] Likewise, the 1597 edition of Gerard's Herball sported an elaborate frontispiece, festooned with gardens, fruits, and vegetables; John Payne executed the multi-faceted line engraving for the title page of the

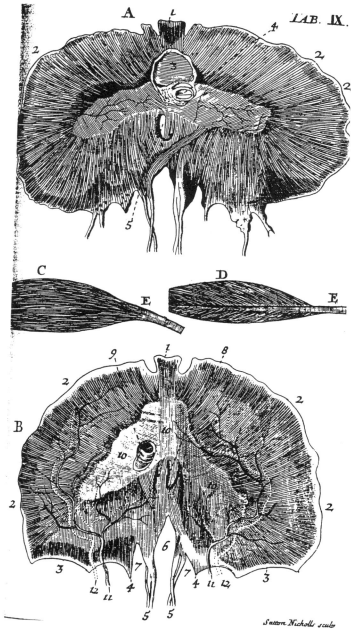

8.1. Diaphragm, drawn by Sutton Nicholls. From William Cheselden, *Anatomy of the Human Body* (London, 1713).

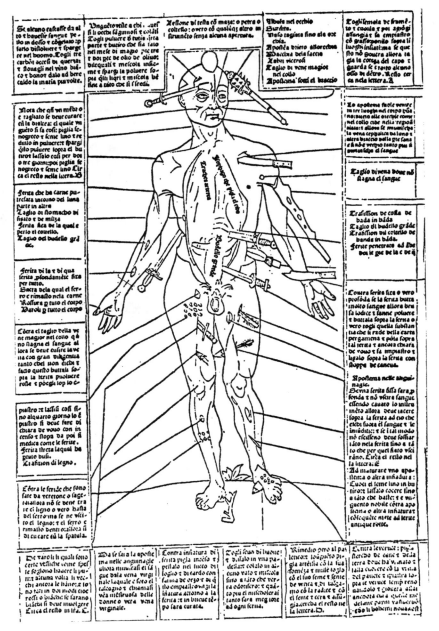

8.2. "Wound Man." From Johannes de Ketham, *Fasciculus medicinae* (Venice, 1493).

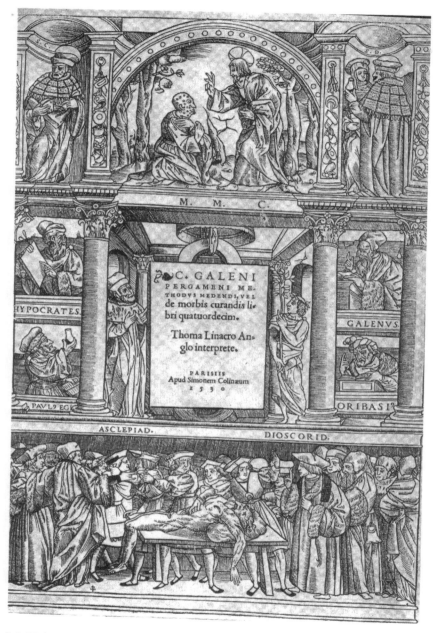

8.3. Title page of Galen, *Methodus medendi*, ed. Thomas Linacre (Paris, 1530).

1633 version, procuring for himself the notice of King Charles.[22] Chemical therapy lent itself less felicitously to illustration, but some of the antidotaries produced by English surgeons contained representations of Paracelsian medicine. In 1639 an elaborately illustrated title page of John Woodall's *The Surgeon's Mate* depicted a portrait of Paracelsus, the first time his likeness was included in a work published in England.[23]

John Evelyn wrote several horticulture books for which Richard Chiswell, his publisher, saved some production costs by using the same frontispiece engraved by P. P. Boncho for Evelyn's *French Gardener* (1658) and reversing the copy for *Kalendarium Hortense: Or the Gard'eners Almanac*.[24] By the end of the seventeenth century, title pages were works of art in themselves. The Dutch edition of George Bate's *Pharmacopoeia Bateana*, first published in 1688 and destined to become one of the most popular medical handbooks of the period, proffers an idealized pharmacy and medical garden on its striking title page (See Fig. 8.4.). The scene, executed by the renowned engraver Jan Luyken, depicts old Latin tomes to be consulted, an active and well-stocked pharmacy patronized by informed and affluent clients, and a garden glimpsed through an open door to connote the knowledge of natural history.[25]

Progress in surgery depended upon a more detailed study of human anatomy, our third category of reproduced iatric works impacted by illustration. Four woodcuts illustrated the earliest anatomical booklet issued in English, Peter Treveris' 1525 translation of Hieronymus Brunschwig, but these were incidental to the text.[26] The printing in 1543 of Andreas Vesalius' *De Humana Corporis Fabrica Libri Septem* marked a major change in medical publishing (See Fig. 3.2.). Besides correcting many of the fundamental errors in Galenic anatomy and kindling a revival in surgical learning, Vesalius inaugurated a didactic and systematic method of observation to accompany exploration of the human body (See Fig. 8.5.). Suitably, he provided his seven-part text with extraordinary anatomical illustrations that established the *Fabrica* as "one of the masterpieces of sixteenth-century printing."[27] Vesalius chose Jan Stephen van Calcar, a Netherlandish draftsman who had been in Titian's studio, to illustrate the *Fabrica*. Carved from pear tree and prepared by Venetian woodcutters renowned for their skill, Calcar's human blueprints can be still effective in teaching anatomy today.[28] Vesalius probably aimed at medical students specifically in his briefer, less expensive *Epitome* (*De humani corporis fabrica librorum epitome*), published simultaneously with the *Fabrica*, which could be purchased with colored anatomical "cut-outs" that, when assembled like accessorized paper dolls, displayed the body from its surface to the innermost parts. Students using the *Epitome* could page backward through the illustrations, uncovering successive layers of flesh until reaching the skeleton, in a clever process that simulated dissection.[29]

Inspired by Fuchs's viewpoint concerning the value of pictures to medical books and commissioned by Henry VIII to produce a version of Vesalius for English surgeons, publisher-engraver Thomas Geminus in 1545 transformed the Calcar woodcuts into copper plates, directly pirated from the illustrations

8.4. *Pharmacopoea Batheana* (Amsterdam, 1698), the Dutch version of George Bate's Latin *Pharmacopoeia Bateana* (London, 1688).

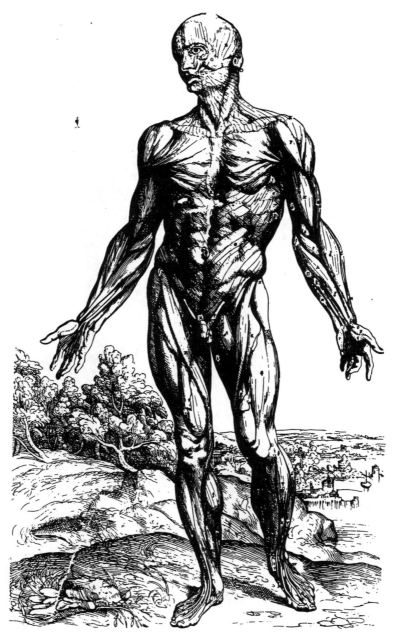

8.5. The third "Muscle Man." From a series of fourteen in Vesalius, *De humani corporis fabrica* (Basel, 1543).

8.6. Title page of *Compendiosa* by Thomas Geminus (London, 1545).

that accompanied Vesalius' anatomical works.[30] He also included the Latin text of the *Epitome* in *Compendiosa Totius Anatomie Delineato*, crediting Vesalius, but the ancient language was not of much value either to surgeons or to the medical-reading public. Vesalius was hardly flattered by the imitation and wrote that Geminus had stolen his own drawings as well as Calcar's, specifically those of the blood vessels.[31] Despite sluggish sales for the first edition, Geminus persisted, next hiring Eton Headmaster Nicholas Udall to redo the content for an English version.[32] Udall just paraphrased a now-uncredited Vesalius, but the redistribution of the illustrations and the notes to them proved invaluable. Geminus' theft of Vesalius' material and business ethics notwithstanding, the replicated Calcar plates have been hailed as the first artistic copper engravings fashioned in England.[33] (See Fig. 8.6.)

Some of the foremost European artists in the Renaissance and Baroque periods drew anatomical illustrations, stimulated as linkage between medicine and the arts intensified. The first illustration of syphilis was the work of Albrecht Dürer, elucidating a 1496 pamphlet by Theodoricus Ulsenius, city physician of Nuremburg. Ulsenius attributed the appearance of the disease to a malignant conjunction of Jupiter and Saturn in 1484, and the picture contains suggested astrological influences hanging over the diseased man. Drawing from dissected corpses became common practice in the sixteenth century; Leonardo da Vinci calculated that he had dissected "more than thirty bodies of men and women of all ages."[34] Anatomical studies specifically for art students spared them the disagreeable ambiance of the dissecting room. Peter Paul Rubens kept an album containing his observations on anatomy drawn from the écorché or skinned cadaver, which Rubens' students later scrutinized as reference.[35] Raphael drew a partly anatomized Crucifixion after expressing dissatisfaction with life studies. He sought to rectify the shortcomings in his technique by comparing the muscles of anatomized bodies with those of the living. In the Sistine Chapel's *Last Judgment*, Michelangelo's figure of St. Bartholomew, who in his martyrdom was skinned alive, afforded a prototype for the anatomized écorché. These continental masters displayed consummate understanding of human anatomy and influenced the depiction of the body in Britain.

But England had its share of artists who served the needs of medicine. Christopher Wren may be better known for his magnificent metropolitan buildings constructed after the Great Fire, but at Oxford and in London he was an intimate of the scientists who changed medicine and a participant in their greatest discoveries. A prodigy in science and mathematics, Wren became an assistant to Dr. Charles Scarburgh even before entering college, designing and demonstrating the anatomical preparations Scarburgh unveiled in his lectures at Surgeon's Hall. In 1657, at age twenty-five, Wren became professor of astronomy at London's Gresham College and befriended Robert Hooke. Wren himself formulated intravenous therapy while only twenty-four, and he was "pleased to celebrate . . . the circulation of the blood," a particular English contribution.[36] More importantly for our purposes, Wren illustrated the anatomical work of Thomas Willis.

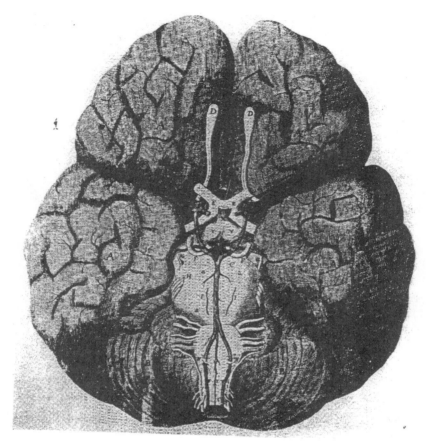

8.7. Drawing of the base of the brain by Christopher Wren. From Thomas Willis, *Cerebri anatome* (London, 1664).

In 1663 Wren assisted Willis in his investigation of the brain at Oxford and drew the pictures for *Cerebri Anatome* (See Fig. 8.7.). Doubling as Willis' dissector, Wren provided two finely engraved illustrations for the text, accurate if stylized depictions of the "circle of Willis," the pressure regulator and safety-valve in the arterial supply to the brain.[37] Historian William Carleton Gibson likens Wren's diverse accomplishments to Leonardo's and calls Wren's conception of the circle "better than Willis's explanation of it."[38] Wren also made drawings of minute bodies enlarged by microscope, magnifying flies, fleas, and lice. As President of the Royal Society, Wren set up a committee on anatomy.

The surgeon William Cheselden, then only twenty-five years of age and already a Fellow of the Royal Society, composed a landmark English illustrated anatomy in 1713, *Anatomy of the Humane Body*, destined to become a standard medical text. Nathaniel Cliff and David Jackson, partners at the Bible and Three Crowns, and William Innys, one of the leading booksellers of the era and publisher of many works by Isaac Newton, commissioned the earliest printing, which was not registered at Stationers' Hall. Twenty-three copper plates, "all done after life" by "sculptor" Sutton Nicholls, contained in the economical octavo first edition showed specific pathological conditions, such as intestinal fistula, in modestly dressed patients. One patient, Margaret White, displays a prolapsed colostomy, the result of Cheselden's operation on a strangulated umbilical hernia; he resected the gangrenous large bowel, the first record of a successful surgery for such a condition.[39] (See Fig. 8.8.) Designed to be slipped into students' pockets, the book bound together a syllabus of lectures following 187 pages of anatomical text. Later editions of the *Anatomy* included additional engravings (there were forty plates in the 1740 version) by Gerard Vander Gucht, who did countless etchings for printers and booksellers, including the eight-volume, 1762 edition of *The Works of Shakespeare*.[40] Thousands of copies of the *Anatomy* were printed before April 1749, when Cheselden sold the copyright for £200 to two prominent London bookseller-publishers with whom he had worked on other medical tomes, Robert Dodsley and Charles Hitch.[41] The property was still sufficiently valuable for shares to have been sold in 1771 and 1778; it stayed in print until 1792.

Cheselden's star had risen rapidly in the surgical profession from humble beginnings as a "bound apprentice" to William Cowper at St. Thomas Hospital, where he eventually captured the post of full surgeon. He developed a reputation as a skilled lithotomist and devised a new operation for removing bladder calculi. Until Cheselden's innovative technique, stones were removed by midline perineal lithotomy, resulting in significant morbidity and mortality; he advocated a "high" operation, a suprapubic incision, which he blazoned in his *Treatise on the High Operation for the Stone*.[42] A rival London surgeon and Cheselden's predecessor as lithotomist at the Westminster Infirmary, John Douglas, objected to Cheselden's claim to having invented the approach and accused him of professional appropriation, but Cheselden explicitly acknowledged Douglas in his remarks, defusing the plagiarism slur.[43]

Although the camera obscura or darkroom had been in use for hundreds of years, its usage in medical illustration remained undocumented until 1733 and the publication of Cheselden's *Osteographia or the Anatomy of the Bones*, the first full and accurate description of the human osseous anatomy (See Fig. 8.9.). Ancestor of the modern photographic device, the camera obscura was probably first employed to view solar eclipses; one could see images projected through a pinhole onto a pristine surface and not damage the eyes.[44] The system presents an inverted picture on the chamber wall facing the perforation, but concave mirrors can correct the inversion. The first such chambers were actually as big as a house, therefore solid and immobile, but by the seventeenth century inventors designed portable models, smaller and handier for the illustrator. Designed by Gerard Vander Gucht, Cheselden's title page shows a coffin-size

8.8. Patient displaying prolapsed colostomy after successful resection surgery by William Cheselden. From Cheselden, *The Anatomy of the Human Body*, 5th edition (London, 1740).

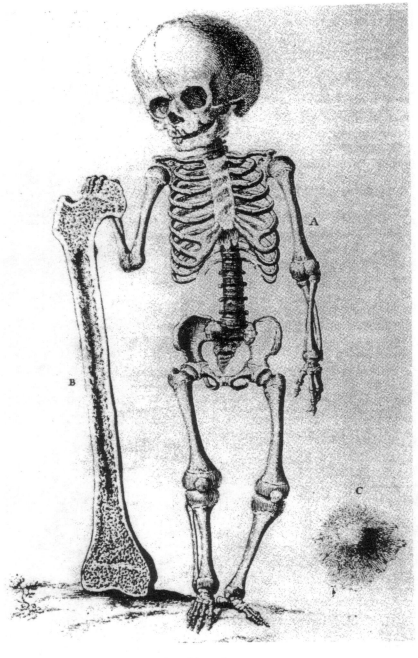

8.9. Child's skeleton. From Cheselden, *Anatomy*.

camera obscura on pedestals. The preface describes its manner of use: a drafts-man sits at the end of the camera and traces the projected image, a skeleton in this case, made bigger or smaller by an "object glass" moved backward and forward. Cheselden solved the problem of inversion by simply hang-ing the skeleton upside down.[45]

Another distinction of the fifty-six illustrations in *Osteographia* is that they were etchings, not engravings. Etching came from wax-coated plates, scratched through the waxy "ground," then immersed in acid, which ate into the exposed metal to produce incised lines. After removal of the ground, the inked plate could be passed through a rolling press like an engraving. This technique, a refinement of the intaglio process, allowed for the correction of errors and the depiction of non-linear features such as the spongy texture of bones.[46] Most of the book's illustrations came from Vander Gucht, but several were from Amsterdam-born Jacobus Shinevoet (or Schijnvoet). Cheselden considered Vander Gucht the superior of the two, admiring his "open free style" and abil-ity to express the different properties of the bones. Vander Gucht also contrib-uted to the decoration of Saint Paul's cupola by Sir James Thornhill, who judged him to be "the best engraver of history that ever was in England."[47]

Plates by engraver Jan Wanderlaer, also realized using a camera obscura, illustrated the 1747 edition of an English plagiarism of Govert Bidloo by Cheselden's mentor, William Cowper. The Wanderlaer pictures were belat-edly brought into Cowper's anatomical atlas to help erase one of the most notorious cases of authorial theft in medical literature.[48] Govert Bidloo, who received an M.D. from the Dutch University of Franaker in 1682, pursued a career as professor of anatomy and surgery at The Hague and Leiden. Acting as royal dentist for William III, he was called to England on occasion to tend the king's loose teeth. Bidloo blamed most dental problems on scurvy, and advised the king to rinse with a mouthwash made of tincture of myrrh and "fair wa-ter."[49] In 1685, after nine years of preparation, Bidloo assembled an anatomical atlas in Latin and Dutch to be published by a Dutch company, created by three investors for the sole purpose of distributing the most splendid medical book ever published (See Fig. 8.10.). One hundred five anatomical drawings by Gérard de Lairesse (called the "Dutch Poussin"), derived from autopsies accomplished by Bidloo and engraved by Abraham Blooteling, illuminated the text. Lairesse's remarkable prints of dissected pregnancies and prematurely born infants dis-play accuracy and compassionate regard for their subjects; Blooteling's master-ful engravings suggest contour and shading like an original pencil drawing.[50] All involved in the project rethought how the body might be shown in a natu-ralistic way with such attention to detail that, to emphasize the appearance of realism, a fly perches on one cadaver. Critics, however, including Bidloo's own teachers at Leiden, groused that while the engravings were aesthetically pleas-ing, their accompanying explanations were worthless, and that Bidloo's ana-tomical knowledge was incomplete, particularly regarding the muscles. The atlas, despite of the hopes of its sponsors, did not sell well.

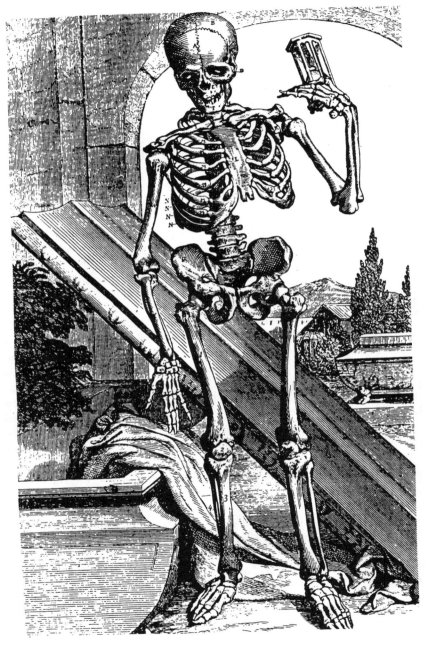

8.10. Skeleton. From Godfried Bidloo, *Anatomia humani corporis* (Amsterdam, 1685).

Nevertheless, in 1698 William Cowper issued a version of Bidloo's atlas under his own name, called *Anatomy of Humane Bodies*, with the Lairesse illustrations and an improved text. The plates were exact copies of the dramatic originals, but Cowper's publishers added superfluous vignettes of putti disemboweling live animals.[51] Furious at the plagiarism if not at the putti, Bidloo turned to the Royal Society in protest, demanding that it rebuke and dismiss Cowper, but in the end the Society gave no judgment.[52] Cowper claimed that his publishers had signed an agreement with Bidloo's for the engravings and for translation of the text. Besides, no international copyrights existed at that time to protect bona fide creative achievement. Cowper issued a pamphlet, *Eucharistia*, replying to the complaints Bidloo made to the Royal Society, but while Cowper feigned an apology in the tract, he actually further insulted Bidloo's work.[53] In spite of the controversy, Bidloo became William III's supervisor of all physicians, surgeons, and apothecaries in Holland, and he managed all Dutch civilian and military hospitals. In 1692, the king extended Bidloo's oversight to the British army. Perhaps because of Bidloo's prominence in medical administration, overt support for Cowper tapered off and Bidloo himself became a member of the Royal Society in 1701.[54]

One wonders why Cowper chose to poach any of the Bidloo-Lairesse plates rather than supply illustrations of his own for the *Anatomy*. The plagiarism episode has almost completely obscured Cowper's own large body of authentic craftsmanship in anatomical expression, mostly done in concert with his long-term collaborator, Antwerp-born engraver Michael Vander Gucht, father of Gerard. Cowper provided his own illustrations for *Myotomia Reformata, or an Anatomical Treatise on the Muscles of Humane Bodies* (1694) and included nine new plates in an appendix to the *Anatomy*, seven of them from his own drawings. *Glandularum Quarundam* (1701), a printed account of Cowper's presentation to the Royal Society on the glands that now bear his name, came from Smith and Walford's presses and contained new drawings by the author.[55] Moreover, Cowper executed the illustrations for books done by his friends, such as Humphrey Ridley's *Anatomy of the Brain* (1695) and supplied both text and plates for James Drake's *Anthropologia Nova* (1707).[56]

In addition, Cowper dissected as well as he designed. A member of the Barber-Surgeons' Company, Cowper presented a paper in 1694 to the Fellows of the Royal Society denying the hemostatic effects of a styptic powder (Vulnerary Posder) developed by John Colbatch.[57] Cowper suggested such medications be tested in experimental cases before being made available to the populace. That same year appeared the initial edition of his anatomical treatise on the muscles, *Myotomia Reformata*, put out in octavo with ten plates.[58] Two years later he reviewed for the Royal Society the process of digestion and "chyfilication," further heightening his reputation as a scientist. The Fellows of the Royal Society responded in 1696 by electing Cowper to membership, the first surgeon chosen for the prestigious association, and as a member he contributed numerous pieces, illustrated by his own plates, in the Society's *Philosophical Transactions*.

Undaunted by the Bidloo unpleasantness, Cowper continued to publish on a variety of subjects. Some scholars rate his 1705 paper on arteriosclerosis "a landmark in the history of surgery."[59] A second edition of Cowper's *Myotomia Reformata*, put out posthumously by publishers Robert Knaplock and William and John Innys in 1724 under the supervision of Dr. Richard Mead, contained sixty-six lavish plates and imaginative decorative initials.[60] At the time of his death at forty-three, Cowper left unfinished a new work on anatomy, specifically dedicated to artists and inspired by Rubens, Raphael, and other great masters. Like many physicians, Cowper prized his close ties with leading experts and his fellowship in the Virtuosi of Saint Luke, an early English art club of which he was a founding member.[61]

Besides illustrations that depicted the textual material in economical almanacs, mid-priced herbals, and expensive medical books, separate delineations of the human body—ephemera called anatomical fugitive sheets—appeared on the print market with resounding commercial success as early as 1538. Four fugitive sheets of domestic origin were issued in Britain in the sixteenth century. One folio page from about 1550 was headed *The Anathomye of the Inwarde Parts of Man, Lyvyely Set Fourthe and Dylegently*, done in letterpress and copper engravings; there was a corresponding sheet for woman. Like many of these single-page paper bodies, the London folios were tinted various shades with superimposed strips of paper that, when raised in sequence, uncovered the body's internal organs.[62] Vesalius endorsed such ingenious flaps on his renderings to show overlying and underlying parts; a German version of the *Epitome* published in 1543, and popular with surgeons and apothecaries, contains woodcuts with flaps. Moreover, to make the spectator of the illustration into a surrogate eyewitness to a dissection, some editions of the *Fabrica* and his *Epitome* were printed with cut-outs so that pieces could be pasted together by the book owner to make a figure with super-imposed flaps. Some copies included figures already assembled and colored by hand.[63] Anatomical fugitive sheets continued to be produced until the end of the seventeenth century and were intended for a surprisingly broad audience. While publishers directed the more elaborate sheets with accompanying Latin passages at physicians and medical students, less intricate ones with super-imposed flaps but no text were meant for the illiterate masses whose learning was founded basically on icons.[64]

In the same category of transitory literature, illustrated broadsides, some published by important printers, spread tidings to the literate and illiterate alike. After the Stuart Restoration revived demonstrations of royal power, pictorial evidence of the sovereign's legitimacy could be advantageous to the government. The ceremony of the "royal touch" vaunted the divine gift of healing, an event immortalized in pictures. A 1679 engraving of Charles II by Frederick van Hove interpreted the traditional ceremony enacted by the monarch as he cured scrofulous subjects afflicted with the "King's Evil," calling attention to a spiritual act that could be perfected only by the rightful sovereign. The timing of the publication of van Hove's vignette may have been aimed at diluting some of the hostility towards the king and his brother resulting from the Popish plot that same year. Even anti-papists grudgingly acknowledged that charismatic acts such as touching bolstered hereditary monarchy. Stationer Dorman Newman printed and sold the van Hove sheet from his shop at the King's Arms in the Poultry.[65]

Towards the end of the Stuart dynasty, new vehicles for picturization emerged: newspapers and magazines. In 1700 newspapers were still relatively scarce; by 1713 the annual total sale was around 2.5 million issues. They were almost entirely devoted to print, save for a few primitive pointing hands in their relentless, repetitive advertisements.[66] Magazines followed, offering a more felicitous venue for illustration. Daniel Defoe put out his *Review* in 1704; Richard Steele founded *The Tatler* in 1709, and the first *Spectator* arrived in March 1711. Hundreds more titles ensued, among them the *Gentleman's Magazine*, containing medical coverage that was simultaneously comprehensive, spirited, and reputable.[67] These periodicals helped form a national print culture and created a stock of cultural clichés, character types, and moral messages, many about medicine. Anti-establishment healers bore the brunt of savage caricature, ridiculed as money-grubbing charlatans, foreign mountebanks, or unscrupulous drug peddlers, but even respectable physicians came in for their share of scorn. As *The Spectator* sneered: "When a nation abounds in Physicians, it grows thin of people."[68]

Some of this visual, public criticism targeted healing women, not all of them for being greedy. The frontispiece of James Primrose's 1651 edition of *Popular Errours . . . of the People in Physick* features a neatly dressed woman being restrained by a guardian angel, allowing the true physician to come to the bedside of a sick patient. Though the charitable woman was well-meaning, the author's explanation of the picture underscores how wrong her remedies were and how right the heavenly protected art of the doctor must be.[69] Less kind and more typically anti-female of the style, in a 1695 etching done by the Dutch artist Cornelius Dusart, androgenous-looking crones masquerade as surgeons, wearing outlandish headgear as they bleed the foot of a protesting patient (see Fig. 1.6.).

Rapacious quacks, male and female, starred in dozens of mezzotints, seizing bacon and other comestibles from poor families in lieu of payment. Itinerant barbers were depicted with harlequins and magicians, a fraternity of mysterious performers. Snakes, monkeys, and bizarre zanies added to the entertainment value of the medicine show, often launched from a temporary platform. Three travelling tradesmen, Glysterpipe Fillpacket ("the Merry Andrew"), Peregrino Mountebanko ("the unborn doctor"), and Timothy Mouth ("the Raree Show-Man"), paraded their wares in vicious cartoons replete with doggerel.[70] Marcellus Laroon assembled an illustrated collection of denizens of the metropolis for his 1687 *Cryes of the City of London*, among them a prancing mountebank dressed in a jester's costume. He bamboozles the unsuspecting with phony testimonials, a monkey in a tutu, and theatrical patter; for good measure he carries a sword with a handle shaped like a parrot.[71] (See fig.7.3.) The picture compilation went through five editions in the next two years and was advertised in the *London Gazette* (28 February 1689) as "newly drawn after life in great variety of actions and dresses, curiously engraven by the best artists." The *Cryes* succeeded both as a document in the social history of London and as a triumph of popular British art devoted to picturing street hawkers.

Cartoons equally jeered establishment doctors as indifferent to their patients' sufferings.[72] Printed burlesques portrayed physicians mouthing recondite jargon, too intent on the Latinate babble they spouted to notice that their patients had died. Those same comic-strip medicos primped and preened in outrageous wardrobes, perukes, and tricorn hats, indiscreetly personifying the self-aggrandizing profession that ignored the health of the nation. Caricature presupposes the recognition of fixed iconographic prototypes in art and flourishes when authoritarian structures break down, as they did in the sixteenth and seventeenth centuries. Ridicule of medicine and its practitioners coincided with the decline of the old medical regime in Stuart England and the emergence of "irregular" practitioners. Droll comic doctors, both lawful and spurious, carried urinals and dead ducks in printed pictures as well as on stage in the theater.[73]

Even expensive books sometimes carried farcical visuals satirizing particular doctors. The frontispiece of the four volume *Works of Thomas Brown* (1707) made fun of Whig doctor Richard Blackmore, poet manqué and Padua M.D. In hyperbolic and hideous verse, Dr. Blackmore had compared William III to King Arthur; in appreciation His Majesty knighted Blackmore and appointed him physician-in-ordinary. The combination of honors and the wretchedness of his poetry made Blackmore the bull's-eye of non-partisan mockery, such as the tableau by metal engraver Elisha Kirkall of Blackmore scribbling another inept poem, "Satyr against Wit," while taunted by an imp.[74] Of course, doctors brought much disdain on themselves when they engaged in inter-professional rivalries. When not the object of popular derision, medical maestros lambasted one another with public charges and countercharges, adding to the chorus of disrespect. M.D.'s belittled the ignorance of surgeons, but Richard Wiseman, England's most admired late Stuart surgeon and chronicler of Charles II's touching for the King's Evil, overlooked the slight and wore his status proudly. He boasted, happily segregating himself from the learned physicians: "I am a Practiser, not an Academick."[75] Occupational segregation, however, did not guarantee professional bliss. Cheselden, besides being the object of a competing surgeon's charges that he had stolen a lithotomy procedure, fell afoul of his own livery company when he offered private tutorials in anatomy, thereby competing with lessons at the Barber-Surgeons' hall. Dissecting the bodies of malefactors at his own house without permission of the Company further alienated his comrades in surgery by challenging their exclusive control of anatomy in London. Ironically, despite this rancor simmering against him within the Barber-Surgeons and the professional jealousy evident among his colleagues,

Cheselden later played a pivotal role and spent considerable money persuading Parliament to detach the surgeons from the barbers, a move that led to the creation of the Royal College of Surgeons.[76]

Of course, surgeons not only quarreled with one another. Daniel Turner, inventor of the skin-soothing Turner's Cerate and a member in 1700 of the Barber-Surgeons' Company, continued the sequence of condescension, taunting the lower ranks of empirics as riffraff "bred up to a Mechanick Employment."[77] Turner vied with those quacks in the medical marketplace, not only as he merchandised his ointment, but as he expounded other eccentric, eye-catching treatments, such as recommending that blood from the tail of a black cat be applied to shingles. In 1711 Turner applied for a discharge from the Barber-Surgeons' fellowship and became a licentiate of the College of Physicians. His habit of disparaging other healers accompanied him to his new vocational circle, and he decried the use by some doctors of mercury as a remedy for venereal cases. Recall that he castigated Hans Sloane, later president of both the College and the Royal Society, for prescribing mercury for an ailing Barton Booth, at whose postmortem Turner found a half-pound of the metal in his intestines.[78] Some irregular practitioners accused regulars of impulsive recourse to hazardous remedies, echoing Turner's dismay at the widespread enthusiasm for quicksilver. Humbugs also insisted that their medicine provided better value for the consumer than that of their credentialed, self-important competitors. The fractious diorama of medicine and its practicing personnel, framed by the foregoing professional disarray, was not an agreeable one. Learned physicians were particularly undermined in the people's regard by the rampant disparagement of their ethics.

Regardless of this occupational discord, contrapuntal canvases flattering to celebrated doctors hang on museum and library walls throughout Britain, portraits of notable men serenely peering out from the medical past.[79] Painted by acclaimed artists, Tudor and early Stuart medicos tender a solemn face to the world, their figures grave of countenance and their clothing that of lugubrious professors. Skulls, symbols of the medical profession as well as reminders of mortality, often haunt the foregrounds of these portraits. Tudor physician John Securis reinforced the earnest demeanor doctors should project to the world:

> The physitian must be of a good disposition of the body: he muste also be had in estimation among the common people, by comely apparel and by sete savours . . . for by such meanes the pacientes are wont to be delited. . . . Hys countenance must be like one that is geven to studye and sadde.[80]

Physician-priest Thomas Linacre lived up to that charge. Though no contemporary portraits of Linacre exist, an extensive iconography of the good doctor spans more than three centuries and includes paintings, drawings, engravings, and sculptures. The most recognizable of the Linacre portraits, in the Royal Collection at Windsor and copied for the Royal College of Physicians in London, had been attributed without critical appraisal since the eighteenth century to Quentin Metsys, who was thought to have painted it around 1520. The Linacre depicted in the Windsor picture embodies the Oxford don that he was. Unfortunately, experts in the late twentieth century refuted the attribution of the portrait to Metsys and disavowed that the sitter is Linacre.[81] (See Fig. 1.2.) Other paintings purporting to be Linacre, many of them copies of the Windsor portrait, convey the same sense of abstemiousness, discretion, and intelligence.[82] The National Gallery in London acquired a portrait believed to be a Linacre image in 1878, but it, too, has been unmasked, catalogued as Netherlandish School and the unknown Dutch sitter entitled "Man with Pansy and Skull."[83] Despite the lack of a verifiable Linacre likeness, the historical impression of this Tudor medical luminary as an archetype of learning and integrity lingers.

Dr. William Butts, Henry VIII's physician, sat for the illustrious artist Hans Holbein the Younger as part of a planned group portrait of the chartering of the Barber-Surgeons' Company. Butts, one of the first physicians to forge a distinguished lay career rather than clerical, was a key figure in the protection and patronage of the new religion at court. The king confided in Butts and another royal doctor, John Chambre, when he was unable to consummate his marriage to Anne of Cleves, and Butts' testimony helped secure an annulment of the unfortunate union with Henry's fourth wife. A near-contemporary copy of Holbein's original portrait, probably executed for a junior branch of the family, hangs in the Isabella Stuart Gardner Museum in Boston. A Holbein portrait of Chambre was transformed around 1620 by limnist Peter Oliver into an admirable miniature, the artistic form for which the English Renaissance is famed. Oliver was the son of Isaac Oliver, in whose studio he began his career. The Chambre original is known to have belonged to Charles I, for whom Peter Oliver produced dozens of miniature copies of the royal collection in Whitehall. Like Butts, Chambre, who signed himself "priest" when he attended the birth of Edward VI and was the head of Oxford's Merton College, is attired somberly, befitting both a cleric and a seventy-seven-year-old physician.[84]

Peter Paul Rubens drew James I's chief medical man, Theodore Turquet de Mayerne, as a bit more flamboyant than Linacre but still exemplifying wisdom and confidence born of study. Corpulent and colorful, Mayerne nonetheless points a finger at the stark skull resting conspicuously on his ample stomach. In a later mezzotint of Mayerne done by Jean Simon, the skull is gone, but the portrait is otherwise executed as Rubens planned.[85] (See Fig. 8.14.) One of only two portraits saved at the Royal College of Physicians from the Great Fire, a three-quarter length canvas of William Harvey by an unknown artist had to be restored due to damage, probably by Walter Bolt, who received fifteen shillings in June 1691 "for mending Dr. Harvies picture."[86] In the painting, Harvey holds a black doctor's hat and wears plum-colored velvet; behind him is a stone pillar with a coat of arms at its base. Wenceslaus Hollar, Charles II's drawing teacher and coronation designer, may have sketched a fur-draped Harvey; in Robert Gaywood's undated etching from the Hollar, the sitter firmly grasps the arm of a straight-backed chair while the winds of change ruffle background draperies. In 1677 William Faithorne, a member of the Goldsmiths' Company and John Payne's pupil, executed a line engraving of rickets specialist Francis Glisson, judge-like in wig and robe, medical brother to venerable clergymen.[87] Less pretentious than the foregoing examples, Mary Beale's oil painting of Thomas Sydenham focuses intently on the sitter's face. Beale, a neighbor of the estimable practitioner and a pupil of famed court painter Sir Peter Lely, installed her subject against a black background and draped his shoulders in plain brown cloth. Only the graceful swirls of Sydenham's lace collar intrude on the austerity of Beale's Puritan subject. Mary Beale charged £5 to paint a subject's head and £10 for a half-length portrait.[88]

Supposedly averse to finery, Thomas Browne, author of *Religio Medico*, sought balance in his deportment and demeanor. His portrait by an unknown artist at the Royal College of Physicians displays that plainness of fashion and ornament; Browne wears a black gown with simple white collar, his hands covered with brown gauntlet gloves. Probably painted about the same time as the Browne portrait, the features of John Clarke, a contemporary of Harvey's at St. Bartholomew's Hospital, were captured by another unknown artist. As a Parliamentarian, Clarke's status rose during the Civil War, and the Fellows elected him President of the College in 1645. During his administration, he brought out a new edition of the *Pharmocopoeia*. Despite the wealth that he accumulated from a lucrative London practice and the addition of properties in Essex, Clarke is also presented decorously, in dark gown and lighter collar against a dark brown background. Similarly unassuming in pose, Charles Scarburgh, a protégé of Harvey's at Merton College, Oxford, sat for his portrait around 1660, before he became first physician to Charles II and a knight. The unknown artist arranged a globe, two prisms, and an open copy of Vesalius on a table next to Scarburgh, testimony to his studies.[89]

Later in the Stuart era, controversial physicians posed for posterity as rock-solid establishment figures, men of means rather than abstinence. Having one's portrait painted lent an air of respectability even to the disreputable. Valentine Greatrakes, the so-called Irish stroker, reputedly exercised miraculous healing gifts as he touched for the King's Evil, a disease usually reserved to the thaumaturgical powers of the monarch. Ague and migraine were other specialties of the stroker that awed even scientists like Astronomer Royal John Flamsteed and physicians like Henry Stubbe, who explained Greatrakes' ability as "miraculous agency."[90] The Wellcome Library in London owns two oil portraits of Greatrakes, the finer one with him sporting a mustache and looking a bit like Charles II, his competitor in touching, and the other showing Greatrakes clean-shaven. Both include a child receiving the wondrous caress of the stroker. The more polished work was painted by William Faithorne, who, besides the aforementioned Glisson engraving, also executed a portrait of another physician, Edmund King.[91] The mustachioed Greatrakes wears a square-collared tunic devoid of ornamentation and stands in front of an open window through which other afflicted supplicants can be seen wending their way to his door. A placard on the wall identifies the healer as

Valentine Greatrakes from Affane, County Waterford. In the other portrait, doubt-less a copy of the first, there is no window, no facial hair, and the sign on the backdrop erroneously dubs Greatrakes "Nathanial."[92]

Some women who claimed health-giving knowledge enhanced their words to the wise with pictures of themselves in books with medicinal and therapeu-tic content. Henrietta Maria, dowager of Charles I, whose *The Queen's Closet Opened* was published in octavo in 1655, produced a practical product designed to help others, drawn from "incomparable secrets in physick, chirurgery, pre-serving, candying, and cookery" that had been presented to her.[93] Though the format of the book was modest, an unflattering portrait of the queen in widow's weeds by Faithorne stared out opposite the title page. Similarly, Lady Alethea Talbot, Countess of Arundel and Surrey, welcomed readers to *Natura Exenterata or Nature Unbowelled*, a bountiful source of "receipts . . . collected by persons of quality."[94] The frontispiece derived from a double portrait of Alethea and her husband, Thomas Howard, painted by Anthony Van Dyck in the 1620s. The engraver copied the manner of the sitter, but depicted Lady Alethea alone, fingering the pearls of medicine instead of navigational instruments as in the original.[97] Portraits of distaff authors displaying serious mien were intended to add weight to their medical books.

Visual paeans to establishment physicians were pervasive. Credentialed doctors who normally thumbed their noses at propriety sought validation and remembrance in formal paintings of themselves, not all of which were stipu-lated for mere private satisfaction. Philanthropic medical men donated their authorized likenesses to the colleges, hospitals, and organizations with which they affiliated. Naturally, they expected their countenances to be exhibited prominently. Church monuments to men in the medical and scientific com-munity bloomed throughout the capital, reminding citizens of their achieve-ments. Reproduced prints of those portraits and memorials circulated like books, making connections between people and ideas accessible to a wider commu-nity; since books were often sold unbound, such prints might be an optional purchase which, for extra charge, printsellers colored and framed.[96] Men who wrote weighty tomes flaunted their portraits as frontispieces for their publica-tions on natural history, philosophy, and medicine; for instance, a full-page portrait of John Gerard graced his *Herball*. Periodicals, those spawned by special-ized institutions and general magazines as well, often offered biographical tales of revered doctors accompanied by their pictures. Perhaps the most unlikely inter-pretation of a doctor's visage embellishes the Bath Oliver biscuit, a cracker named for its creator, William Oliver, who practiced medicine in Bath and promoted its mineral waters during the town's zenith (See Fig. 8.11.). Dr. Oliver, a Cambridge M.D. and Fellow of the Royal Society, bequeathed the recipe for the popular edible along with £100 and ten sacks of good flour to his coachman.[97]

More conventionally, John Radcliffe's oil portrait by Sir Godfrey Kneller depicts the maverick physician in full-bottomed wig and sumptuous garb. A funerary engraving done after Radcliffe's death in 1714 by Michael Burghers

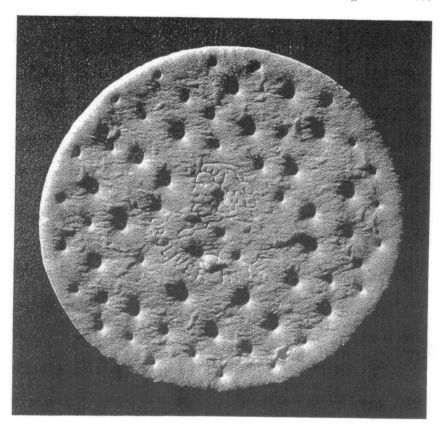

8.11. Bath Oliver biscuit. Photo by Michael Brandon-Jones in Ludmilla Jordanova, *Defining Features: Scientific and Medical Portraits, 1660–2000* (London: Reaktion Books, 2000). Permission to reproduce from Ludmilla Jordanova.

touts the good doctor's legacies to Oxford University, University College, and St. Bartholomew's Hospital.[98] Dr. Radcliffe, a Jacobite, smugly insulted Princess Anne on two occasions and arrogantly dismissed King William's condition with the oft-quoted remark that he would not have his majesty's two legs for all his three kingdoms.[99] Radcliffe blithely violated the College totem by not writing his cases up in Latin; he published a recipe book with six hundred pages of prescriptions and observations. The first edition sold 1,600 copies in six months.[100] Kneller, the most fashionable society portraitist of the Augustan Age, whose own 1670 self-portrait includes an écorché statuette, painted Sir Samuel Garth as a man of the world. Garth, best known as the *Dispensary* poet who mocked the apothecaries, hobnobbed with fellow Whigs at the Kit-Kat Club and wrote minor verse ridiculed by Radcliffe.[101] John Woodward, pam-

phlet polemicist, Gresham College professor of physic, and the object of frequent raillery from rivals at the Royal Society, sat for a portrait that underscored his occupational dignity. At the same time, however, rumors abounded
that he was a sodomite with a fondness for enemas and young boys.[102] Even
discounting those slanders, Woodward constantly flouted the conventional
bounds of good behavior, crudely quarreling with other doctors and duelling
over slights with one of Radcliffe's comrades, Richard Mead.[103]

When Mead was nearly seventy, he himself posed for an oil portrait in the
grand manner by his friend and protégé Allan Ramsay; the portrait depicts him

8.12. Portrait of Richard Mead by Arthur Pond. Reproduced by permission of
the National Portrait Gallery, London.

in a luxurious setting, arrayed in magnificent finery and coiffure. Mead intended it to be a gift to the London Foundling Hospital, which he served as a Governor and in which he took a keen interest.[104] Mead also sat for painter Michael Dahl and for a colleague in the Royal Society, Arthur Pond (See Fig. 8.12.). Pond's etched portrait of Mead in profile conveys obvious classical allusions, evoking antique coins and medals, reinforced by the sitter's inscribed motto, Non sibi sed toti: "Not for himself, but for all."[105] Unfortunately, the demeaning anecdotes about Mead's lecherous sex life, circulated in pamphlets ridiculing the veteran doctor and his susceptibilities, found immortality in the character Kunastrokius, a physician in the novel *Tristram Shandy*.[106] In short, gracious portraits can deceive. Heedless of the consequences to honor and reputation, elite London doctors like Radcliffe, Garth, Woodward, and Mead enjoyed behaving badly, all the while brandishing symbols of their wealth like the College of Physicians' famous gold-headed cane.[107]

Group portraits, such as of the Barber-Surgeons' Company or the Royal Society, ornament the walls of many institutions. Although physicians helped to foster the notion that learned men relished solitary, contemplative lives, the basic premise of many professional associations was that natural philosophy could best be advanced through group activity and collective experiments.[108] Among the more famous depictions of group activity among medical men is Hans Holbein the Younger's 1540 drawing of Henry VIII at the union of the Company of Barbers with the Guild of Surgeons. Commissioned to paint a great inventive canvas and to eternalize the king's interest in medicine, Holbein executed a fanciful sketch of the granting that year of a new charter to the united Company by the king. In it, Henry hands the charter to royal surgeon Thomas Vicary to glamorize the event while apt, if imagined witnesses look on.[109] The king's physicians, Drs. Chambre and Butts, appear in a place of honor immediately on Henry's right, while Thomas Alsop, Henry's best-known apothecary, stands on the king's far right. Tall and handsome, Alsop wears a fur-edged robe and chain, indicative of his stature and riches. A cartouche reads: "To Henry the eighth, the best and greatest King of England . . . Defender of the Faith, and next to Christ, supreme Head of the Church of England and Ireland. . . ."[110] Holbein, however, was unable to complete the final version, succumbing to pestilence in 1543.

Engraver Wenceslaus Hollar created another imaginative gathering for the frontispiece of Thomas Sprat's 1667 *History of the Royal Society*.[111] Hollar's etching, based on a composition by diarist John Evelyn, meant to show the Society in a positive way (See Fig. 8.13.). It depicts Charles II, being crowned by Fame, flanked by Francis Bacon and the Society's first president, who happened to be a friend of Evelyn, Lord William Brouncker, an Oxford M.D. Various instruments and books decorate their surroundings. As befitting a nobleman and physician, Lord Brouncker's face smiled forth from more than just the Hollar scene. Famed artist Peter Lely, known best for his series of frail and fair "beauties" at Charles II's court, painted Brouncker's solo portrait, a treasure maintained at the Royal Society.[112]

8.13. Wenceslas Hollar, frontispiece to Thomas Sprat, *History of the Royal Society* (London, 1667), showing Fame crowning a bust of Charles II, as Lord William Brouncker, the Society's first president, and Francis Bacon look on.

Buildings with medical significance also displayed enough eminence of their own to merit commemoration, and collectors of architectural plates eagerly sought out these prints. In 1708 the Governors of the Royal Hospital for Seamen at Greenwich complained in the *London Gazette* that a recently published print of the Hospital was "notoriously false and much to the discredit of that noble structure." However, a "true and perfect design" of the building would be published soon.[113] In the mid-eighteenth century, at the request of the Fellows, William Stukeley, himself a doctor who had studied under Mead at St. Thomas' Hospital, depicted the attractive inner courtyard of the College of Physicians on Warwick Lane, its third headquarters. The College interiors were not overlooked either; the Long Room, repository of the institution's art collection, was itself the focus of a satirical etching peopled with crotchety, pompous blowhards disputing in a gallery filled with the portraits and busts of their laudable predecessors.[114] (See Fig. 1.5.) Christopher Wren and Robert Hooke, another architect-scientist, designed the new building after the destruction of the College premises on Paternoster Row in the Great Fire; it welcomed its members after completion in 1676 and became a well-known London landmark.[115] Stukeley, incidentally, as befitting a College and Royal Society Fellow, posed for his own portrait in oil by Kneller, sat for an engraving by Elisha Kirkall, and had a medal cast of his profile wreathed in oak leaves.[116]

Given the cultural significance among physicians of having one's likeness left to posterity, they became of necessity familiar with those artists who might be commissioned to paint portraits. The Virtuosi of Saint Luke, the arts club Cowper helped found, provided a venue for meeting and discussing works of art, where connoisseurship could be cultivated and personal style developed. Some doctors, like Cheselden, approached their artist friends to learn how to draw, while others taught painters about anatomy so that they might be proficient illustrating medical tomes; some did both. Artists and literati moved in the same circles as elite doctors, "circles in which classical learning was highly valued." Iain Pears has found parallels of another sort between the occupations of painting and medicine: "like painters, doctors were slowly struggling towards social respectability."[117] Moreover, medical men dominate the lists of enthusiastic patrons and collectors of art. Hans Sloane purchased a subscription with an initial payment of one guinea for twelve prints "in claro obscuro" from Elisha Kirkall in 1722, promising to pay another guinea when the prints were delivered.[118] Richard Mead, a sketch of whom by Thomas Birch can be seen in the British Museum Additional Manuscripts, contracted for several portraits of himself and had his bust sculpted by Louis François Roubillac. Mead bought much art for investment purposes, including the Rubens portrait of Dr. Mayerne, a Vesalius attributed to Titian, and Holbein's Erasmus; following the established tradition, "he collected the heads of eminent men."[119] Mead's assembly of Italian pictures and sculpture has been described as an archetype of Augustan Age taste.[120] However, Pears thinks Mead's fabled financial bonanza from art collecting was just that: a fable. He calculates an average annual return on Mead's investment, spread over twenty-five years after the collection was amassed, of under three percent, less than the rate offered by the government. The art-buying activities of a large number of doctors can be traced in the sales catalogues of the period. Christopher Bateman, James Petiver's publisher, specialized in disposing of the libraries and art belonging to wealthy medical men such as Charles Scarburgh, Charles Bernard, and John Woodward.[121]

8.14. John Simon's mezzotint after Peter Paul Rubens' portrait of Sir Theodore Turquet de Mayerne. Reproduced by permission of the Wellcome Library, London.

Not to be outdone by an elite physician like Mead, the empiric William Salmon collected Dutch paintings for cachet.[122] Salmon even wrote on art in his 1672 publication, *Polygraphice or the Arts of Drawing*. Copper plate engravings by William Sherwin and William Vaughan, the latter who acknowledged his artistic debt to Dürer, festoon the pages.[123] Besides the mechanics of art, *Polygraphice* describes ways of representing passions and emotions in portraiture. Later editions added more illustrations, twenty-three pages in the 1692 version, but all ended with an advertisement for Salmon's pills at three shillings a box.[124] Salmon usually included pictures when possible, such as eight leaves of plates in his *Medica Practica* (1692), twenty-four anatomical "sculptures" in *Ars Anatomica* (1714), and 221 illustrations in his *Botanologia* (1710), an herbal from the press of Ichabod Dawks. Salmon's own portrait, affixed to his various volumes, was done many times, including likenesses executed by William Sherwin, one of the first workers in mezzotint, and Michael Vander Gucht, paterfamilias to the artistic brood that supplemented its income by illustrating dozens of medical books.[125]

Medical historians and literary specialists have tended to concentrate their analyses on printed texts stripped of the illustrations that accompanied them. Though these pictures were freighted with messages that audiences of yesteryear could understand, serious scholars largely ignored them as mere visual baubles, "stepchildren" in the history of medicine.[126] Studies of the human body, outlines of herbs, caricatures of medical practitioners, and serious portraits of iatric celebrities ought to be seen for what they are: the visual culture of medicine, a culture that has been obscured by the writing of medical history. Of course, for the Tudor and Stuart centuries, some historians have classified the older forms of mechanical reproduction, such as engravings or etchings, as "works of the imagination," inferior to "the permanent mirror of memory we call photography."[127] Others have felt anxious about interpreting pictorial evidence for fear of distorting its "real" meaning, of not reading it "right." Through these various images, mindful of their intricate nature, we observe the world of early modern medicine across the centuries and, whatever the caveats about the naive viewer or the manipulative nature of the illustrative tradition, medical iconography provides "multiple, simultaneous meanings," all of which can help unlock historical fact and fantasy.[128] Rather than anguish over the problems inherent in the study of graphic evidence, Roy Porter chose to revel in the interplay of word and image, calling the visual and verbal "two sides of the same cultural coin."[129] As evident from the foregoing chapter, medical pictures and the controversy they have generated warrant significantly more than a thousand words.

EPILOGUE

AFTER THE *Rose* CASE: ASSESSING THE IMPACT OF PRINT ON THE MEDICAL REVOLUTION

In 1702, the Court of Queen's Bench ruled that William Rose, a member of the London Society of Apothecaries, had been practicing medicine without permission from the College of Physicians and in violation of law. The presiding judge in the case, Chief Justice John Holt, had previously been an attorney for the College and apparently used his judicial authority to procure a "special verdict" amiable to the physicians.[1] When Queen Anne's government in 1703 allowed a petition for a writ of error to be entered before the House of Lords, the final appellate tribunal in the English system of justice, Rose appealed the lower court's decision. In early 1704 the Lords Justice overturned the foregoing judgment and found that apothecaries had the legal right to visit the sick and prescribe remedies, as long as they charged the patient only for those remedies. Ever since, the *Rose* case has been regarded as a milestone in legitimizing the services of popular practitioners. Consequently, as part of a zero-sum game unfolding in the medical marketplace, historians have argued that the licensing monopoly and professional status of physicians in Augustan London declined.[2] The symbol of establishment medicine in London, the College of Physicians lost its supremacy over practice in the capital and its putative leadership of iatric science. In the words of medical historian Roy Porter, the "Royal College ended the Stuart era enfeebled, and it was to grow ever more cliquy, clubby, and comatose."[3]

The *Rose* case and its corollary jurisdictional battles produced a flurry of published materials before, during, and after adjudication. Printed polemics emanated from all sides of the medical spectrum, and the roots of the conflict went deep into the basic philosophical controversies—political, social, and medical—of late seventeenth-century England. A decade before *Rose*, the Society of Apothecaries had sought an exemption by an act of Parliament for its members from the performance of routine civic offices, claiming that they provided health care to the vast majority of Londoners and could not be spared for minor municipal duties. Leaders of the City reacted angrily with opposition pamphlets, such as *Reasons Humbly Offered against Passing the Bill for Exempting Apothecaries from Serving . . . Parish and Ward Offices*, and the Society responded in kind with brochures of its own.[4] The ultimate success of the apothecaries in obtaining passage of the exemption in early 1695 was a legislative acknowledgment that they were genuine medical professionals. But the battle was hardly over. Because of the Society's impudence towards them, miffed City fathers deliberately united with the furious College Fellows in an attempt to end practice by apothecaries.[5]

However, the College of Physicians was hardly the best-loved institution in London and more of a burden for the City fathers in their political coalition than a succor. The College, the focus of so many published diatribes, had created some of its own public relations problems by keeping the number of approved physicians preposterously small in the burgeoning metropolis. Fellows and licentiates numbered 136 in 1695 within a city of more than half a million inhabitants, and they often kept their patients at arm's length or beyond. Many late Stuart practitioners no longer visited the indisposed in their homes, but met them in coffeehouses or private rooms, scarcely different from the advertising empirics they derided. Some physicians never saw their patients at all, sending surgical emissaries to examine sufferers and report back with observable symptoms. No wonder open defiance of the College's licensing control was widespread; even England's monarchs turned to unlicensed healers, dismissive of the Fellows' expertise.[6] Moreover, bishops began to reassert their traditional prerogative of sanctioning doctors in order to relieve the pressing need for medical men in their dioceses who would be willing to care for the impoverished sick.

Just as the honor of individual physicians suffered from their collective apparent pride, the status of the College had declined over its attempts to curtail the success of foreign doctors who engaged in conjectural medicine, doctors like Johannes Groeneveldt (John Greenfield), a licentiate whose methods irked the College censors. In the mid-1690s, Groeneveldt, one of many Dutch doctors who came to England after the Glorious Revolution, was charged with malpractice by a female patient supported by the College censors; he was committed to Newgate prison for prescribing large doses of cantharides taken with camphor. That he associated with empirics and medical iconoclasts did little to endear him to traditionalists among the Fellows. The charges produced a split in the ranks of the Fellows and made Groeneveldt a sympathetic figure in London. Found not guilty of malpractice by the Court of King's Bench, he brought a countersuit with the Society of Apothecaries against the College and, although the College temporarily had its right to police physicians reaffirmed, its reputation was demolished.[7]

The entire case and its aftermath played itself out in florid print.[8] Having been found guilty of malpractice for using cantharides, Groeneveldt wrote *De tuto cantharidum* in 1698; it was translated in 1706 as *A Treatise of the Safe, Internal Use of Cantharides in the Practice of Physick.* In his preface, he blamed his enemies in the College for bringing him down and fumed over his imprisonment in a "common gaol for thieves and rogues."[9] A sympathetic pamphlet by the pseudonymous Lysiponius Celer attacked the medical competence and common sense of the College officers in their actions against Groeneveldt; Celer was really Groeneveldt. Richard Boulton was paid by the Fellows to refute Celer, but ended up feuding with College President Charles Goodall instead.[10] To add fuel to the fire, Groeneveldt pointed out to the Crown and anyone else who could read that the "law-abiding" censors who prosecuted him had neglected to take oaths of allegiance and supremacy, as required of sitting judges. Why should his persecutors be excused from the penalties they deserved under the statute?[11] A suit came against the censors, and although it eventually died in the House of Lords, the whole Groeneveldt mess besmirched the leadership of the College and provided fodder for humorists. Ned Ward chortled that the Fellows had indicted a man more able in medicine than they, a man whose patient had recovered, because "they hold it a greater crime to cure out of the common method, than it is to kill in it."[12]

Undeterred by setbacks and bolstered by the City's steadfast support, the College Fellows decided to undercut their competitors' claims as caretakers of the indigent by opening a dispensary sponsored by the charity of its members and free to the sick poor. The physicians hoped to demonstrate not only their charity, but also that the druggists had been overcharging and overprescribing their patients.[13] Unanimity was lacking, however, as some of the Fellows felt a dispensary, which surely would further exacerbate relations with the apothecaries, warranted more consideration; moreover, they objected to having the dispensary imposed upon on their munificence and set up in haste. Nonetheless, in August 1695, fifty-seven College subscribers contributed twenty shillings each to the dispensary; the City offered its thanks and suggested ways to promulgate the new enterprise and certify its clients.[14] The venture expanded; ultimately, besides the dispensary located in buildings adjacent to the College in Warwick Lane, the Fellows established two more dispensaries, one in St. Martin's Lane and the other in Gracechurch Street, the first free outpatient clinics in the metropolis.

As a final affront to their adversaries, the College commanded the apothecaries to submit their apprentices for examination by the Fellows and to inspect apothecaries' shops for violations of cleanliness standards. Turning the tables on those who used print to undercut the learned doctors, Dr. Samuel Garth, in *The Dispensary, A Poem*, lampooned the apothecaries' opposition to outpatient rooms and their own filthy establishments. Moreover, Garth, a prominent Whig and Harveian orator at the College, ridiculed certain thinly disguised physicians who contested the dispensary. The six-canto mock-heroic verse went through three editions in a few months, eight in Garth's lifetime, demonstrating popular interest in the dispute over medical dominion between physicians and apothecaries.[15] Publications like *The Dispensary* or the anti-academy tracts by Gideon Harvey, William III's "Physician of the Tower," and by Robert Pitt, Physician to St. Bartholomew's Hospital, delivered opposing opinions to an eager readership searching for ways to measure the legitimacy of those tenets.[16]

Reformers a generation or two before the Dispensary controversy had pushed for publishing medical arcana to enable ordinary citizens to be their own doctors; learned physicians foresaw a diminution of their profession's status if such information were widely available. According to historians of medical print influenced by Habermas, neither forecast proved true. The public sphere of this debate was not a forum where serious medical information was on display at no cost; it was an economic one where hacks and credentialed M.D.'s alike touted their secret recipes in print and urged their purchase. Everyman simply shifted his payments for health care from practitioners to entrepreneurs. Moreover, medical publications, even the comical squabbles among doctors, did not diminish medicine, but rather lent status to the profession. Summing up the impact of print on early modern medical controversies, G. S. Rousseau explains that "daily news and diuretics, politics and pharmacology . . . went hand in hand, adjacent columns in the same broadsides and gazettes." Print culture lent proof that the medical profession was developing beyond a private enterprise into a public one.[17]

Understanding then that the abstract audience for this controversy extended beyond the medical principles involved, the apothecaries and their anti-dispensarian allies struck back with truculent pamphlets attacking the Dispensary and the motives of its physicians.[18] Critics like Joseph Browne charged that private interest and arbitrary monopoly alone inspired the College officers; even Richard Blackmore, a "disaffected Member" of the College struck back in his trenchant *Satyr against Wit*.[19] Physicians became the object of ridicule in the press and were savaged in cartoons. One comic writer described a lively disputation in Hell by resident member-professionals over which was the more hateful, lawyer or doctor; it must have been little consolation to physicians that the lawyers won.[20] Not all of this bad press was spontaneous. The Society of Apothecaries paid Dr. John Badger, a known anti-dispensarian, to castigate the College in print for its disreputable practices. He did so with gusto, having been denied admission to the Fellowship, publishing along with his diatribe the College's "illogical and unjust" statutes in English.[21] No wonder the College Fellows eventually decided to go after a high-ranking apothecary in court and, in early 1701, filed suit against William Rose for practicing physick without a license. Likely as a result of all this inimical attention to the physicians' collective arrogance and their own unseemly public in-fighting, the Fellows forfeited their authorization to oversee the stock of medicines supplied to the army and navy, a substantial loss of power given the importance of the military to affairs of state. In 1702 the Society of Apothecaries won the right to supply medicines to the fleets without supervision of the College.[22]

The decision in the *Rose* case proved that publicity and politics had dovetailed against the College. Citizens who read and those who were read to were of one voice against the Fellows. The finding was an historic one, but it did not cause a leveling of the medical playing field; it simply ratified the changes which had already taken place.[23] The litigation attracted popular notice for years, and while the physicians had their friends in court, the apothecaries had theirs in the legislature. Before long the number of apothecary shops in London had tripled, making all too valid the College's fear of competition. Internecine bickering had taken its toll on the College, whose disarrayed Fellows meted out mutual accusations and resorted to internal directives. The new College charter included emphasis on professional dignity, suitable apparel, and the ethics of consultation.

While the apothecaries prospered from their conspicuous struggle with physicians, there were other shifts in the jurisdictional landscape in the late Stuart era that occurred almost unnoticed by contemporaries and which benefitted English surgeons. Susan Lawrence attributes some of that metamorphosis to the emergence of hospital medicine as a public phenomenon, an "arena for witnessed interactions."[24] She submits that the dual role of hospital men as physicians and surgeons blurred the public distinction between physicians and surgeons and transformed the traditional hierarchy of London's medical occupations. David Harley has suggested that the contraction of medical might and prestige associated with university-educated physicians after 1700 coincided with their ceding the performance of autopsies to surgeons, thereby unknowingly "discarding a great source of power."[25] Regarded as familiar and respectable in England, dissection enabled doctors to advance the science of anatomy; as early as the mid-sixteenth century, the London Barber-Surgeons' Company and the College of Physicians each annually received the bodies of four criminals to dissect. Autopsies, on the other hand, required delicate negotiations with bereaved families willing to surrender the bodies of their loved ones to postmortem examination.[26]

Print surely played a significant part in the waning of physicians' standing on this issue. Several respected physicians had published anatomical works using the results of autopsies; William Harvey employed his postmortem observations in the first English work to use autopsy findings, De Motu Cordis (1628). While initially confidential, the opening up of private patients became accessible to all when publishing anatomists identified the cases.[27] Furthermore, accounts of doctors who seemed too eager to arrange for autopsy to learn more about morbid anatomy aroused popular anxieties. Therefore, by the end of the seventeenth century, doubts cast upon the clinical utility of morbid anatomy to therapeutics and criticism of the motives of the anatomists led to the withdrawal of physicians from forensic medicine. Moreover, some doctors, perhaps in the pursuit of professional gentility, eschewed dissection altogether as hazardous and disgusting. Hence, surgeons assumed the task of performing autopsies when coroners' juries ordered postmortems and testified as expert witnesses in trials, further alienating physic from surgery and inhibiting the development of pathological anatomy.[28]

Another development simultaneous to the legal problems of English physicians was the shift of intellectual leadership in scientific research from the College of Physicians to the Royal Society.[29] The true scientists in the Royal

Society suffered from the well-meaning amateurs who brought discredit onto the group by pursuing absurd speculations during the first twenty-five years of its existence, but the entrance of Isaac Newton into the Society's Fellowship changed all that. Some have even pinpointed the date of maturation of the Society to 1687 and its sponsorship of the publication of Newton's *Principia*.[30] Newton became the Society President in 1703, while talk of the *Rose* case still burbled through London's professional circles. He immediately reestablished close connections with the court and talked Prince George, Queen Anne's consort, into joining the Society; Newton also arranged for the purchase of a permanent home for the Fellows at Crane Court, where they stayed until 1780.

Ironically, it was Hans Sloane, a prominent Dispensarian in the College of Physicians and later its President, who brought order to the administration of the Society as its Secretary from 1693 to 1712. He invited correspondence from foreign scientists and sponsored several for membership. Sloane also succeeded in restoring the financial health of the Society. And unlike the Collegiate Fellows, who kept their annals unpublished and private, the Fellows of the Royal Society blazoned their activities in their *Transactions*, suspended between 1687 and 1691, but resumed thereafter with Sloane as editor for sixteen years.[31] Evidence of heightened contemporary interest in the Royal Society includes a new edition in 1702 of Thomas Sprat's 1667 *History of the Royal Society*, published collections of reprinted papers documenting the Fellows' experiments, and essays in the *Tatler* and the *Spectator*.[32] Recipients of the pluses and minuses of fame, the F.R.S. had stolen the spotlight from the F.R.C.P.

Several scholars of the post-*Rose* era in medicine believe that not much had really changed with the victory of the apothecaries. Harold Cook says that the case settled little, merely ratifying what was already in the air.[33] Andrew Wear likewise points out the continuities in medicine, asserting that patterns which appeared prior to 1700 merely deepened. Middle class disdain for folk medicine and its oral tradition, demonstrable in the Tudor era, intensified during the Stuart regime, in part due to the impact of print culture, which elevated the authority of books over hearsay, and in part because those practices were associated with common people, not because they were inherently less rational.[34] Susan Lawrence concurs with the characterization of the medical marketplace as open and undifferentiated. Aristocrats saw learned physicians and irregulars; they also dosed themselves with medicines made in their own kitchens when so inclined. The middling sort of people went to licensed surgeons, but they also bought elixirs in shops and had their barbers bleed them. At a bookseller's, Latin medical texts shared shelf space with vernacular medical manuals and recipe books; customers who wanted access to both surely never thought anything was amiss.[35]

Despite these dispassionate scholarly pronouncements, the worlds of medicine and print collided in early modern England, and from the repercussions came changes in some things. Medicine had become demotic and disjoined, its elite university-educated leadership no longer served by surgeons and apoth-

ecaries, but in competition with them. Those same learned doctors, cut off
from the segments of society most likely to take up medicine, had to vie for
patients and prominence with practitioners from nonconformist institutions
and with remedy-dealing charlatans.[36] A medical marketplace, now so often
surmised, broadened from the earliest publication of a few traditional recipes
and therapies in Tudor times to an avalanche of lively theoretical and jurisdictional altercations in the Stuart century. The popularization of medicine both
reflected political development in England and affected it as well, underscor-
ing the growing public awareness of issues vitally important to ordinary citizens. Through print, medical ideas could be easily transmitted for further
discussion among the literate and the illiterate throughout the country. Print
lent credence to those ideas and, as Joseph Addison remarked, intensified "those
thoughts which arise and disappear in the mind of man, transmitting them to
the last periods of time. . . ."[37] Without the press, medical debates would have
remained private and the results a foregone conclusion. Obversely, the medical controversies of early modern England fueled at least a portion of the growth
in publishing, providing some sense of the progress of knowledge that leads to
truth. The bookmen and women of the sixteenth and seventeenth centuries,
whether motivated by principle or profit, wittingly or unwittingly promoted
the print and pills that symbolized the maturation of the press and of medicine.

NOTES

Notes for Chapter 1

1. Andrew Wear, *Knowledge and Practice in English Medicine, 1550–1680* (Cambridge: Cambridge University Press, 2000), 35.

2. Owsei Temkin, *Galenism: Rise and Decline of a Medical Philosophy* (Ithaca, N.Y.: Cornell University Press, 1973), 91. Galen's influence was even greater in the Islamic East, but Renaissance scholars felt they had liberated Galen from his Arab followers when the first edition of his collected works appeared in Greek in 1525; ibid., 125–26.

3. For more on medical care in Galenism, see F. Kudlien and R. J. Durling, eds., *Galen's Method of Healing* (Leiden: Brill, 1991); and Don Bates, ed., *Knowledge and the Scholarly Medical Traditions* (Cambridge: Cambridge University Press, 1995).

4. John Archer, *Everyman His Own Doctor* (London: Peter Lillicrap, 1671), 34.

5. For Linacre, see Francis Maddison, Margaret Pelling, and Charles Webster, *Essays on the Life and Work of Thomas Linacre* (Oxford: Clarendon Press, 1977); C. Donald O'Malley, *English Medical Humanists* (Lawrence: University of Kansas Press, 1965). For Caius, see Vivian Nutton, *John Caius and the Manuscripts of Galen* (Cambridge: Cambridge Philological Society, 1987); and Nutton, "John Caius and the Linacre Tradition," *Medical History* 23 (1979): 373–91.

6. Quoted in C. Donald O'Malley, "English Medical Literature in the Sixteenth Century," in *Scientific Literature in Sixteenth and Seventeenth Century England* (Los Angeles: William Andrews Clark Library, 1961), 3. See also Peter Murray Jones, "Reading Medicine in Tudor Cambridge," in *History of Medical Education in Britain*, ed. Vivian Nutton and Roy Porter (Amsterdam: Rodopi, 1995), 156–57.

7. Andrew Wear finds the College Galenists "part of a general European movement that aimed to improve medicine and make it safer": Wear, *Knowledge and Practice*, 36. For more on the influence of court physicians on official medical policy, see Elizabeth Lane Furdell, *The Royal Doctors: Medical Personnel at the Tudor and Stuart Courts* (Rochester, N.Y.: University of Rochester Press, 2001).

8. Only 98 M.D.'s and 22 M.B.'s were granted at Cambridge for the entire sixteenth century, and during the last four decades, only two students per year graduated as M.B. or M.D.: Jones, "Reading Medicine in Tudor Cambridge," 158.

9. John Stow, *Annales of England* (London: G. Bishop, 1605), 1020, cited in Barrett L. Beer, *Tudor England Observed: The World of John Stow* (Stroud, England: Sutton, 1998), 51. Stow was unsympathetic, damning healers who "never trained up in reading or practice of physicke and chirurgerie."

10. Margaret Pelling, "Knowledge Common and Acquired: The Education of Unlicensed Medical Practitioners in Early Modern London," in *History of Medical Education in Britain*, ed. Vivian Nutton and Roy Porter (Amsterdam: Rodopi, 1995), 253; Ronald C. Sawyer, "Friends or Foes? Doctors and Their Patients in Early Modern England," in *History of the Doctor-Patient Relationship*, ed. Yosio Kawakita, Shizu Sakai, and Yasuo Otsuka (Tokyo: Ishiyaku EuroAmerica, 1995), 34. Clerical wives often practiced medicine, too.

11. O'Malley, "English Medical Literature in the Sixteenth Century," 3; Paul Slack, "Hospitals, Workhouses and the Relief of the Poor in Early Modern London," in *Health Care and Poor Relief in Protestant Europe, 1500–1700*, ed. Ole Peter Grell and Andrew Cunningham (London: Routledge, 1997), 235–36.

12. Stow, *Annales of England*, quoted in Beer, *Tudor England Observed*, 50–53. Using Stow's figures, Beer calculates a mortality figure of 8 percent for the 1548 crisis and 24 percent for the epidemic of 1563.

13. Paul Slack, *The Impact of Plague in Tudor and Stuart England* (London: Routledge and Kegan Paul, 1985), 14–16, 145–51.

14. Ole Peter Grell, *Paracelsus: The Man and His Reputation, His Ideas and Their Transformation* (Leiden: Brill, 1998), 8.

15. Ole Peter Grell and Andrew Cunningham, "The Counter-Reformation and Welfare Provision in Southern Europe," in *Health Care and Poor Relief in Counter-Reformation Europe*, ed. Ole Peter Grell and Andrew Cunningham with Jon Arrizabalaga (London: Routledge, 1999), 3.

16. Ibid., 16.

17. Hugh Trevor-Roper, *Renaissance Essays* (Chicago: University of Chicago Press, 1985), 150.

18. Temkin, *Galenism*, 131.

19. Before Paracelsus, the twelfth-century, Cordoba-born philosopher Averroës (Ibn Roshd in Arabic) criticized Galen's insistence on bleeding until the patient fainted: Temkin, *Galenism*, 121.

20. Charles Webster, *From Paracelsus to Newton* (Cambridge: Cambridge University Press, 1982). Webster says that French Paracelsianism was at its height between 1610 and 1650, English Paracelsianism after 1650. See also Eric Maple, *Magic, Medicine and Quackery* (S. Brunswick, N.J.: A. S. Barnes, 1968), 74; Trevor-Roper, *Renaissance Essays*, 156–57.

21. Allen Debus, *The English Paracelsians* (London: Oldbourne, 1965), 30, 157.

22. Maple, *Magic, Medicine, and Quackery*, 72.

23. Quoted in *Paracelsus: Selected Writings*, ed. Jolande Jacobi (Princeton, N.J.: Princeton University Press, 1951), 49.

24. Like Galen, Paracelsus thought that the stomach was of prime importance, but his descriptions of the digestive process radically departed from Galenic theory; see Francis McKee, "The Paracelsian Kitchen," in *Paracelsus*, ed. Ole Peter Grell (Leiden: Brill, 1998), 293–308.

25. Roy Porter and G. S. Rousseau, *Gout: The Patrician Malady* (New Haven, Conn.: Yale University Press, 1998), 25. Paracelsus offered no therapies, however, for tartarous diseases.

26. Temkin points out that Galen had faulted the physicians of his time for their avarice and lack of devotion to truth; Paracelsus also manifest scorn for greedy doctors: Temkin, *Galenism*, 130–31.

27. Jones, "Reading Medicine in Tudor Cambridge," 155, 159, 164. Jones demonstrates that medical books were of interest to many readers besides physicians and that one could obtain the latest medical publications from the continent in Cambridge from 1530 onwards; also see his "Book Ownership and the Lay Culture of Medicine in Tudor Cambridge," in *The Task of Healing: Medicine, Religion and Gender in England and The Netherlands, 1450–1800*, ed. Hilary Marland and Margaret Pelling (Rotterdam: Erasmus, 1996), 49–68.

28. For Paracelsus' life, see Walter Pagel, *Paracelsus: An Introduction to Philosophical Medicine in the Era of the Renaissance* (Basel: New York: S. Karger, 1958); for his publications, see Trevor-Roper, *Renaissance Essays*, 149–99.

29. Trevor-Roper, *Renaissance Essays*, 159. Joan Lane points out, however, that some London surgeons did very well; of seven listed there in 1696 one was described as a "gentlemen" and two were worth more than £600 each: Joan Lane, *Apprenticeship in England, 1600–1914* (Boulder, Colo.: Westview Press, 1996), 132.

30. William Birken, "The Social Problem of the English Physician in the Early Seventeenth Century," *Medical History* 31 (1987): 205. Given the number of physicians deriving from clerical families, the College's disregard for the healing clergy is notable. Birken suggests that the early seventeenth-century College decree refusing admittance to ministers deliberately separated the two callings for the exclusive benefit of the medical profession: ibid., 207.

31. Jeffrey L. Berlant, *Profession and Monopoly* (Berkeley: University of California Press, 1975), 141.

32. O'Malley, "English Medical Literature in the Sixteenth Century," 2.

33. Three to four medical books were published in England during each year of Elizabeth I's reign: Paul Slack, *The Impact of Plague in Tudor and Stuart England* (London: Routledge and Kegan Paul, 1985), 22–50.

34. Annals of the College of Physicians, vol. 1, f. 22a, Library of the Royal College of Physicians, London (hereafter LRCP). The author thanks the Librarian of the Royal College of Physicians for permission to quote from the unpublished Annals. For more on Geynes, see William

Munk, *Roll of the Royal College of Physicians*, 2 vols. (London: Longman, Green and Roberts, 1861), 1:62–63.

35. After 1585, those who finished their degrees at Oxford or Cambridge in less than normal time paid double fees; Annals of the College of Physicians, vol. 2, f. 46a, LRCP.

36. Debus, *English Paracelsians*, 24, 57, 62.

37. Hugh Trevor-Roper, "The Court Physician and Paracelsianism," in *Medicine in the Courts of Europe, 1500–1838*, ed. Vivian Nutton (London: Routledge, 1990), 90–91.

38. Charles Webster, "Alchemical and Paracelsian Medicine," in *Health, Medicine and Mortality in the Sixteenth Century*, ed. Charles Webster (Cambridge: Cambridge University Press, 1979), 330. Though some of her courtiers championed the new medicine, Queen Elizabeth I "clung to established ways": Trevor-Roper, "Court Physician and Paracelsianism," 91. Sir George Clark wrote that "until the statutes were revised in 1601 the corporate fidelity of the College to Galen was unimpaired": George Clark, *A History of the Royal College of Physicians*, 2 vols. (Oxford: Clarendon Press, 1964) 1:165.

39. Elizabeth I's surgeon and Barber-Surgeons' Master, George Baker, outlined the middle path between Galenism and Paracelsianism, choosing the former over the latter, but still advocating chemical therapy: Debus, *The English Paracelsians*, 56.

40. Evelyn recorded the experience in his *Diary*, vol. 3, ed. E. S. deBeer (Oxford: Oxford University Press, 1955), 336. See also Pyarali M. Rattansi, "The Helmontian-Galenist Controversy in Restoration England," *Ambix* 12 (1964): 11; and Leslie Matthews, *The Royal Apothecaries* (London: Wellcome Medical Library, 1967), 112–13.

41. For more on Raleigh the chemist, see Charles Nicholl, *The Creature in the Map* (Chicago: University of Chicago Press, 1997), 278–87.

42. Clark, *Royal College of Physicians* 1:160–61; Harold J. Cook, *The Decline of the Old Medical Regime in Stuart London* (Ithaca, N.Y.: Cornell University Press, 1986), 97.

43. Debus, *English Paracelsians*, 24. Many renowned continental physicians converted quickly to Paracelsianism; these included Petrus Severinus, doctor to the king of Denmark, and Vesalius' teacher, Winter von Andernach. See also Trevor-Roper, *Renaissance Essays*, 160, 178.

44. John Aikin, quoted in Randolph Vigne, "Mayerne and his Successors: Some Huguenot Physicians under the Stuarts," *Journal of the Royal College of Physicians of London* 20/3 (July 1986): 222.

45. Theodore Mayerne, *Medicinal Counsels or Advices* (London: N. Ponder, 1677), 36–38. Antiquarian Samuel Clippingdale theorized that Shakespeare's depiction of Dr. Butts was meant to offend Mayerne. See Clippingdale, "Sir William Butt, M.D.: A Local Link with Shakespeare," *West London Medical Journal* (July 1916): 7.

46. Mayerne, quoted in Anne Somerset, *Unnatural Murder: Poison at the Court of James I* (London: Weidenfeld and Nicolson, 1997), 169.

47. See J. L. Turk and Elizabeth Allen, "Bleeding and Cupping," *Annals of the Royal College of Surgeons* 65/2 (March 1983): 128–29.

48. Munk, *Roll* 1: 164; Jessie Dobson, "The Royal Dentists," *Annals of the Royal College of Surgeons* 46 (1970): 284.

49. Norman Moore, *History of the Study of Medicine in the British Isles* (Oxford: Clarendon Press, 1908), 123. The other two are Francis Glisson and Thomas Sydenham. See also Brian Nance, *Turquet de Mayerne as Baroque Physician* (Amsterdam: Ridopi, 2001).

50. Pyarali M. Rattansi, "Paracelsus and the Puritan Revolution," *Ambix* 11 (1963): 24. See also Randolph Vigne, "Mayerne and His Successors," *Journal of the Royal College of Physicians of London* 20 (1986): 222–26; and Harold J. Cook, "Policing the Health of London: The College of Physicians and the Early Stuart Monarchy," *Social History of Medicine* 2 (1989): 1–33.

51. Debus, *English Paracelsians*, 176, 181; Rattansi, "Paracelsus and the Puritan Revolution," 24. For more on van Helmont, see Walter Pagel, *From Paracelsus to Van Helmont*, ed. Marianne Winder (London: Variorum Reprints, 1986).

52. Allen Debus, *The Chemical Philosophy: Paracelsian Science and Medicine in the Sixteenth and Seventeenth Centuries*, 2 vols. (New York: Science History Publications, 1977), 2: 303–4, 310–11.

53. Ibid., 2: 359.

54. Just as Paracelsians had dismissed Galenism as a relic of the dying past, so Francis Bacon likewise condemned the metaphysical system of Paracelsians as archaic and Paracelsus himself as a proposterous magus: Trevor-Roper, *Renaissance Essays*, 186.

55. See Antonio Clericuzio, "From van Helmont to Boyle: A Study of the Transmission of Helmontian Chemical and Medical Theories in Seventeenth-Century England," *British Journal for the History of Science* 26 (1993): 303–35.

56. Grell and Cunningham, "The Reformation and Changes in Welfare Provision in Early Modern Northern Europe," 34–35. Women often worked in hospitals, specializing in treatment for "scald head," ringworm of the scalp: A. L. Wyman, "The Surgeoness: The Female Practitioner of Surgery," *Medical History* 28 (1984): 30.

57. Petty's proposals can be found in *Advice of W. P. to Mr. Samuel Hartlib for the Advancement of Some Particular Parts of Learning* (London: n.p., 1648). See also Charles Webster, "English Medical Reformers of the Puritan Revolution," *Ambix* 14 (1967): 23–24; and Cook, *Decline of the Old Medical Regime*, 110–11.

58. Geoffrey Holmes, *Augustan England: Professions, State and Society, 1680–1730* (London: George Allen and Unwin, 1982), 200–201.

59. Temkin, *Galenism*, 135–36; Wear, *Knowledge and Practice*, 3.

60. Quoted in George Newman, "Thomas Sydenham, Reformer of English Medicine," *Interpreters of Nature: Essays* (Freeport, N.Y.: Books for Libraries, 1968), 29. See also Donald G. Bates, "Thomas Sydenham and the Medical Meaning of 'Method,'" *Bulletin of the History of Medicine* 51 (1977): 324–38; and Andrew Cunningham, "Thomas Sydenham: Epidemics, Experiment and the 'Good Old Cause,'" in *The Medical Revolution of the Seventeenth Century*, ed. Roger French and Andrew Wear (Cambridge: Cambridge University Press, 1989), 164–90. L. J. Rather, however, denies that Sydenham should be called "the English Hippocrates": see Rather, "Pathology at Mid-Century," in *Medicine in Seventeenth-Century England*, ed. Allen G. Debus (Berkeley: University of California Press, 1974), 103.

61. For more on Sydenham, see Kenneth Dewhurst, *Dr. Thomas Sydenham* (Berkeley: University of California Press, 1966); and Donald G. Bates, "Sydenham and Social History," *Society of Social History of Medicine Bulletin* 27 (1980): 27–29.

62. Phyllis Allen, "Medical Education in Seventeenth Century England," *Journal of the History of Medicine and Allied Sciences* 1 (1946): 119. See also Robert G. Frank, Jr., "Science, Medicine and the Universities of Early Modern England," *History of Science* 11 (1973): 194–216; and A.H.T. Robb, "Medical Education at Oxford and Cambridge Prior to 1850," in *The Evolution of Medical Education in Britain*, ed. F.N.L. Poynter (London: Pitman Medical Publishing, 1966), 19–52; Anita Guerrini, "Chemistry Teaching at Oxford and Cambridge, circa 1700," in *Alchemy and Chemistry in the Sixteenth and Seventeenth Centuries*, ed. Piyo Rattansi and Antonio Clericuzio (Dordrecht: Kluwer Academic Publishers, 1994), 183–99.

63. Robert Latham, ed., *The Shorter Pepys* (Berkeley: University of California Press, 1985), 193 (4 May 1662). On this occasion Pepys paid five shillings to be bled sixteen ounces.

64. Quoted in Jonathan Israel, "Dutch Influence on Urban Planning, Health Care and Poor Relief in the North Sea and Baltic Regions of Europe," in *Health Care and Poor Relief in Protestant Europe, 1500–1700*, ed. Andrew Cunningham and Ole Peter Grell (London: Routledge, 1997), 76.

65. Rattansi, "Paracelsus and the Puritan Revolution," 6 n. See also Harold J. Cook, "The New Philosophy and Medicine in Seventeenth-Century England," in *Reappraisals of the Scientific Revolution*, ed. David C. Lindberg and Robert S. Westman (Cambridge: Cambridge University Press, 1990), 397–436.

66. Quoted in Holmes, *Augustan England*, 207.

67. Ibid., 166, 188.

68. Charles Webster, "William Harvey and the Crisis of Medicine in Jacobean England," in *William Harvey and His Age*, ed. Jerome J. Bylebyl (Baltimore, Md.: Johns Hopkins University Press, 1979), 6. Ironically, the College later employed Harvey as a principal lobbiest in its effort to control surgeons and apothecaries: ibid., 9. See also Harold J. Cook, "Against Common Right and

Reason: The College of Physicians versus Dr. Thomas Bonham," *American Journal of Legal History* 29 (1985): 301–22.

69. Margaret Pelling, "Knowledge Common and Acquired," 251; and Pelling "Thoroughly Resented: Older Women and the Medical Role in Early Modern London," in *Women, Science and Medicine, 1500–1700*, ed. Lynette Hunter and Sarah Hutton (Stroud, England: Sutton, 1997), 70. Pelling notes that the College Annals are fragmentary for the Elizabethan period.

70. Lindsay Sharp, "The Royal College of Physicians and Interregnum Politics," *Medical History* 19 (1975): 107–28. See also William Joseph Birken, "The Royal College of Physicians of London and Its Support of the Parliamentary Cause in the English Civil War," *Journal of British Studies* 23 (1983): 47–62; and Harold J. Cook, "The Society of Chemical Physicians, the New Philosophy, and the Restoration Court," *Bulletin of the History of Medicine* 61 (1987): 61–77.

71. See Leslie G. Matthews, "Italian Charlatans in England," *Pharmaceutical Historian* 9 (1979): 2–5.

72. Rattansi, "Paracelsus and the Puritan Revolution," 6 n. Rattansi counts 186 members of the Royal College in all categories.

73. John Simon, *English Sanitary Institutions*, 2nd ed. (London: John Murray, 1897), 70.

74. The Surgeons finally broke away from their barber colleagues in 1745: for more on the surgeons' guild, see R. Theodore Beck, *The Cutting Edge: The Early History of the Surgeons of London* (London: Lund Humphries, 1974); and Jessie Dobson and R. Milnes Walker, *Barbers and Barber-Surgeons of London* (London: Blackwell, 1979).

75. R. R. James, "Licences to Practice Medicine and Surgery Issued by the Archbishop of Canterbury," *Janus* 41 (1936): 97–106.

76. John Hatchet, *A Detection and Querimonie of the Daily Enormities and Abuses Committed in Physick*, quoted in O'Malley, "English Medical Literature in the Sixteenth Century," 7.

77. O'Malley, "English Medical Literature in the Sixteenth Century," 15. For more on the careers of Vicary and Caius, see Furdell, *Royal Doctors*, 32–34, 45–47.

78. Quoted in O'Malley, "English Medical Literature in the Sixteenth Century," 16.

79. John Stow, *Survey of London* (New York: Dutton, 1912), 69, 330; and Andrea Carlino, *Books of the Body*, trans. John Tedeschi and Anne C. Tedeschi (Chicago: University of Chicago Press, 1994), 86. William Clowes praised Forster in *A Prooued Practice for All Young Chirurgians* (London: Thomas Orwyn, 1588), 46.

80. Sawyer, "Friends or Foes?" 33, 42.

81. See, for instance in *The Shorter Pepys*, 6 October 1663 (painful urination); 24 May 1663 and 17 November 1663 (constipation); 27 July 1663 (hemorrhoids); 1 June 1664 and 7–8 March 1665 (kidney stone). Pepys also consulted Hollier on behalf of others.

82. Thomas Dekker, *The Wonderful Yeare* (1603) in *The Plague Tracts of Thomas Dekker*, ed. F. P. Wilson (Oxford: Clarendon, 1925), 36.

83. Richard Wiseman, *Several Chirurgical Treatises* (London: Flesher and Macock, 1676); and his *Charisma Basilicon* (London: Thomas Newcomb, 1684). See also Louis Bakay, "Richard Wiseman, Royalist Surgeon of the English Civil War," *Surgical Neurology* 27 (1987): 415–18; and Furdell, *Royal Doctors*, 159–62, 179–81.

84. Slack, "Hospitals, Workhouses and the Relief of the Poor," 236. Slack points out that the initiative for the united royal hospitals came from prolonged debates among London aldermen and common councillors.

85. Munk, *Roll* 2:35. For Sloane, see Maarten Ultee, "Hans Sloane, Scientist," *British Library Journal* 14 (1988): 1–20.

86. The Act of 1542 quoted in Wyman, "The Surgeoness," 27.

87. Charles Bernard served Queen Anne as serjeant-surgeon and was Master of the Barber-Surgeons' Company; his older brother was Francis Bernard, James II's physician-in-ordinary and one of the most prosperous apothecaries of his time: Sidney Young, *Annals of the Barber-Surgeons of London* (London: Blades, East and Blades, 1890), 563; Furdell, *Royal Doctors*, 219–20, 243–44; and Matthews, *Royal Apothecaries*, 116.

88. Holmes, *Augustan England*, 213, 232.

89. W.S.C. Copeman, *The Apothecaries of London, 1617–1967* (London: Pergamon, 1967), ix.

90. For more on the formation and development of the apothecaries' guild, see Cecil Wall, H. Charles Cameron, and E. Ashworth Underwood, *A History of the Worshipful Society of Apothecaries of London, vol. 1: 1617–1815* (London: Oxford University Press, 1963), 9–12, 41–57.

91. Holmes, *Augustan England*, 190–91. Blackmore, one of the most successful men of the medical profession, served William III and Anne; Radcliffe, also consulted by monarchs, emphasized symptom observation; and Sloane, knighted like Blackmore for his services, left his botanical garden in Chelsea to the Apothecaries' Society: Munk, *Roll* 1:467; 1:455; 1:460. See also Harry M. Solomon, *Sir Richard Blackmore* (Boston: Twayne, 1980); R. Campbell Hone, *The Life of Dr. John Radcliffe* (London: Faber and Faber, 1950); and G. R. deBeer, *Sir Hans Sloane and the British Museum* (London: Oxford University Press, 1953).

92. Matthews, *Royal Apothecaries*, 98–100; and Furdell, *Royal Doctors*, 114–15. An account of de Laune's life can be found in F.N.L Poynter, "Gideon de Laune and His Family Circle," *Wellcome History of Medicine Public Lecture Series*, No. 2 (London: Wellcome Library, 1965).

93. Rudolph E. Siegel and F.N.L. Poynter, "Robert Talbor, Charles II, and Cinchona," *Medical History* 6 (1962): 82–85.

94. Holmes, *Augustan England*, 227. Daniel Malthus, apothecary to Thomas Sydenham, reported on Queen Anne's health to his mentor while he prepared drugs for the royal family: Matthews, *Royal Apothecaries*, 140–41.

95. James St. Amand, royal apothecary from 1679 to 1688, represented St. Ives in 1685–87 and stood as a Tory at Steyning, West Sussex, in 1710; James Chase, apothecary to the Person under William III and Anne, represented Marlow, Buckinghamshire, in 1701 and was re-elected the following year: Matthews, *Royal Apothecaries*, 118–20; 106–7.

96. Peter Ackroyd, *London: The Biography* (London: Chatto and Windus, 2000), 210.

97. Robert Pitt, *The Antidote or the Preservative of Health and Life* (London: 1704), quoted in Holmes, *Augustan England*, 191.

98. Cook, *Decline of the Old Medical Regime*, 99–100.

99. Webster, "English Medical Reformers of the Puritan Revolution," 19–20.

100. Quotation from Goddard in Clark, *Royal College of Physicians*, 343.

101. See Frank H. Ellis, "The Background of the London Dispensary," *Journal of the History of Medicine and Allied Sciences* 20 (1965): 197–212.

102. Wyman, "The Surgeoness," 27–28.

103. James Primrose, *Popular Errours or the Errours of the People in Physick*, trans. Robert Wittie (London: Nicholas Bourne, 1651). Primrose, who attempted to refute the findings of William Harvey, was the grandson of James I's serjeant-surgeon, Gilbert Primrose.

104. Quoted in David Noble, *World without Women: The Christian Clerical Culture of Western Science* (New York: Knopf, 1992), 188. See also Margaret Wertheim, *Pythagoras' Trousers: God, Physics, and the Gender Wars* (New York: Times Books, 1995); and Jeanne Achterberg, *Woman as Healer* (Boston: Shambhala, 1990). Achterberg argues that the collapse of feminine wisdom in the healing arts was completed when Enlightenment scientists developed a methodology that lauded the masculine attributes of reason and objectivity.

105. Matthews, *Royal Apothecaries*, 102, 137–38.

106. Furdell, *Royal Doctors*, 172–73. See also J. H. Aveling, *The Chamberlens and the Midwifery Forceps* (London: Churchill, 1882); and his "A Huguenot Surgeon," *Proceedings of the Huguenot Society of London* 17 (1942–43): 70–71.

107. Furdell, *Royal Doctors*, 206–9, 241–43.

108. For government-sponsored medical changes, see Harold J. Cook, "Living in Revolutionary Times: Medical Change under William and Mary," in *Patronage and Institutions: Science, Technology and Medicine at the European Court, 1500–1750*, ed. Bruce T. Moran (Rochester, N.Y.: Boydell Press, 1991), 111–35; and Cook, "Practical Medicine and the British Armed Forces after the 'Glorious Revolution,'" *Medical History* 34 (1990): 1–26.

109. BL C112, fol. 9 (77), British Library.

110. Roy Porter, *Quacks: Fakers and Charlatans in English Medicine* (Stroud, England: Tempus, 2000), 118.

111. Ackroyd, *London*, 208–9.
112. Holmes, *Augustan England*, 167, 309.

Notes for Chapter 2

1. Roy Porter, *Disease, Medicine and Society in England, 1550–1860* (London: Macmillan, 1987), 44. Medical historians use "empiric" to denote a person who lacks theoretical training, emphasizing instead practical experience or observation; contemporaries used it to mean "quack."

2. For the controversy over whether or not the causal force in the Renaissance is printing technology or the people using it, see Elizabeth Eisenstein, *The Printing Press as an Agent of Change: Communications and Cultural Transformations in Early Modern Europe*, 2 vols. (Cambridge: Cambridge University Press, 1979); and Peter F. McNally, ed., *The Advent of Printing: Historians of Science Respond to Elizabeth Eisenstein's "The Printing Press as an Agent of Change"* (Montreal: McGill University, 1987).

3. William Eamon, *Science and the Secrets of Nature* (Princeton, N.J.: Princeton University Press, 1994), 126.

4. Owen Gingerich, "Copernicus and the Impact of Printing," *Vistas in Astronomy* 17 (1975): 201–18; Stillman Drake, "Early Science and the Printed Book: The Spread of Science beyond the Universities," *Renaissance and Reformation* 6 (1970): 43–52; and Eisenstein, *Printing Press*, 2:520.

5. Elizabeth L. Eisenstein, "Some Conjectures about the Impact of Printing on Western Society and Thought," *Journal of Modern History* 40 (1968): 7–8. For more on the popular appropriation of knowledge through print, see Roger Chartier, *The Cultural Uses of Print in Early Modern Europe*, translated by Lydia G. Cochrane (Princeton, N.J.: Princeton University Press, 1987).

6. Allan Chapman, "Astrological Medicine," in *Health, Medicine and Mortality in Sixteenth-Century England*, ed. Charles Webster (Cambridge: Cambridge University Press, 1979), 277. To identify almanac makers, Chapman used Donald Goddard Wing, *Short-Title Catalogue of Books Printed in England*, 2nd ed., 3 vols. (New York: Modern Language Association, 1994).

7. A copy of *Prognostications*, an almanac for 1537, is in the British Museum. Andrew Boorde, *Introduction and Dyetary*, ed. F. J. Furnivall (London: Trubner, 1871); Andrew Boorde, *The Pryncyples of Astronomye* (London: Robert Copeland, 1547), preface. For more on Boorde, a colorful Henrician priest-physician, see Furdell, *Royal Doctors*, 28–30.

8. Bernard Capp, *English Almanacs, 1500–1800: Astrology and the Popular Press* (Ithaca, N.Y.: Cornell University Press, 1979), 21, 207; Munk, *Roll*, 1:187.

9. Geoffrey Keynes, *The Life of William Harvey* (Oxford: Clarendon Press, 1966), 439.

10. Richard Saunders, *Astrological Judgment and the Practice of Physick* (London: Thomas Sawbridge, 1677); Joseph Blagrave, *Astrological Practice of Physick* (London: Obadiah Blagrave, 1671), sig. Bv.

11. For a discussion of late-sixteenth-century astrological botany, see Agnes R. Arber, *Herbals, Their Origin and Evolution, 1470–1670*, 2nd ed. (Cambridge: Cambridge University Press, 1953).

12. William Caxton himself published medical pieces, such as *The Gouernayle of Helthe* in 1489, an anonymous treatise reprinted by Wynken de Worde in quarto: K. F. Russell, "A Check List of Medical Books Published in English before 1600," *Bulletin of the History of Medicine* 23 (1949): 925, 936.

13. Andrew Boorde, *The Breviary of Helthe* (London: Wyllyam Middleton, 1547). During his lifetime, Boorde's other publishers were Robert Wyer and William Powell. For the herbals in our time frame, see Eleanour Sinclair Rohde, *The Old English Herbals* (New York: Dover, 1971), 203–19.

14. Ibid., 168–69. For a vibrant examination of the plants and herbs used by Nicholas Culpeper, see David Potterton, ed., *Culpeper's Color Herbal* (New York: Sterling, 1983).

15. Quoted in Rohde, *Old English Herbals*, 85. Ever practical, Turner introduced lucerne or alfalfa into Britain: *Dictionary of National Biography* (hereafter *DNB*), ed. Leslie Stephen and Sidney Lee, 66 vols., (New York: Macmillan, 1885–1901).

16. William Bullein, *A Newe Booke entitled The Government of Health* (London: John Day, 1558), fol. xxxiir [*sic*]. Gabriel Frende added a bonus to his zodiacal man, showing the veins commonly used in phlebotomy, so that surgeons would know where to cut: Capp, *English Almanacs*, 205.

17. Ibid, 105.

18. See John Parkinson, *Garden of Pleasant Flowers*, ed. Alfred Hyatt (London: T. N. Foulis, 1904).

19. Leslie G. Matthews. *The Royal Apothecaries* (London: Wellcome Medical Library, 1967), 92.

20. Arnold of Villanova, *Defence of Age and Recovery of Youth* (1540). The full Latin text of the piece was published in Oxford fifty years later.

21. Annals of the College of Physicians, 7 November 1595, cited in Webster, "Alchemical and Paracelsian Medicine," 326.

22. John Hester, *These Oiles, Waters, Extractions, or Essences, Saltes and Other Compositions* (1588), quoted in ibid.

23. Paul Slack, "Mirrors of Health and Treasures of Poor Men: The Uses of the Vernacular Medical Literature of Tudor England," in *Health, Medicine and Mortality in the Sixteenth Century*, ed. Charles Webster (Cambridge: Cambridge University Press, 1979), 237–73; Peter M. Jones, "Book Ownership and the Lay Culture of Medicine in Tudor Cambridge," in *The Task of Healing*, ed. Hilary Marland and Margaret Pelling (Rotterdam: Erasmus Press, 1996), 49–68.

24. Jürgen Habermas, *The Structural Transformation of the Public Sphere*, trans. Thomas Burger and Frederick Lawrence (Cambridge, Mass.: M.I.T. Press, 1989), 41.

25. For a discussion of critiques of Habermas, see Dagmar Freist, *Governed by Opinion: Politics, Religion and the Dynamics of Communication in Stuart London, 1637–1645* (London: Tauris Academic Studies, 1997), 13–22.

26. Though he does not make the medical leap that I do, David Zaret does distinguish a religious sphere of interest, emphasizing the nexus joining religious debate, print culture, and politics. See Zaret, *The Origins of Democratic Culture* (Princeton, N.J.: Princeton University Press, 2000), 169–73.

27. David Cressy, *Literacy and the Social Order* (Cambridge: Cambridge University Press, 1980), 145. See also R. A. Houston, *Literacy in Early Modern England* (London: Longman, 1988); and for what marginalia and other notations tell us, the exhibition catalogue for *The Reader Revealed*, ed. Sabrina Alcorn Baron (Washington, D.C.: Folger Library, 2001).

28. Christopher Brooks, "Professions, Ideology and the Middling Sort in the Late Sixteenth and Early Seventeenth Centuries," in *The Middling Sort of People: Culture, Society and Politics in England, 1550–1800*, ed. Jonathan Barry and Christopher Brooks (London: Macmillan, 1994), 117–23.

29. A trio of historians scoured the accounts of Tudor Cambridge bookseller Garrett Godfrey and put together a list of buyers and recipients of books for a six-year period. Although Godfrey's clientele was more educated than typical in Henrician towns, it is noteworthy nonetheless that many invoices contain medical book purchases, especially Hippocrates and Galen. See Elizabeth Leedham-Green, D. E. Rhodes, and F. H. Stubbings, *Garrett Godfrey's Accounts* (Cambridge: Cambridge Bibliographical Society, 1992), 2–87, 119–64.

30. Russell, "Check List of Medical Books," 924, 945.

31. Christopher Baker printed the first quarto edition; subsequent reprints came from "the deputies of Christopher Baker" in 1592–93.

32. M. A. Shaaber, *Some Forerunners of the Newspaper in England, 1476–1622* (New York: Octagon Books, 1966), 161–62; F. P. Wilson, *The Plague in Shakespeare's London* (Oxford: Clarendon Press, 1927), 197. Wilson says that the threepence charge for a plague bill in 1626 was probably for a yearly reckoning, the contents of which Stansby was forbidden to divulge under pain of £100 fine: ibid., 201. Richard Hodgkinson printed the yearly bill for 1629, but later bills are without imprint.

33. Since 75% of the cost of printed matter came from the paper used, shorter works were

always the cheapest: Tessa Watt, *Cheap Print and Popular Piety, 1550–1640* (Cambridge: Cambridge University Press, 1991), 1.

34. Ibid., 5–6.

35. John Securis, *A Detection and Querimonie of the Daily Enormities and Abuses Commited in Physick* (London: Thomas Marsh, 1655), quoted in Andrew Wear, "Medicine in Early Modern England," in *The Popularization of Medicine, 1650–1850,* ed. Roy Porter (London: Routledge, 1992), 23.

36. James Primrose, *Popular Errours* (London: W. Wilson, 1651). Not all of Primrose's assertions were valid; he also contradicted William Harvey's circulation of the blood.

37. Securis, quoted in Andrew Wear, *Knowledge and Practice in English Medicine, 1550–1680* (Cambridge: Cambridge University Press, 2000), 42.

38. John Caius, *A Counseil against the Sweat* (London: Richard Grafton, 1552), 6

39. D. R. Woolf says that the neglect of oral sources was due to increasing availability of printed material. See his "The 'Common Voice': History, Folklore and Oral Tradition in Early Modern England," *Past and Present* 120 (1988): 26–52.

40. Wear, *Knowledge and Practice,* 40–41; Charles Webster, *The Great Instauration* (New York: Holmes and Meier, 1975), 267. Seventeenth-century authors like John Milton and Isaac Newton sought a Europe-wide audience by writing in Latin.

41. Thomas Elyot, *Castel of Helth* (London, 1580), sig. A 4r, quoted in Wear, "Medicine in Early Modern England," 23. Editions after the original 1534 printing came out in 1539, 1541, 1561, and 1580, remaining popular until the end of the century: *DNB.*

42. Nicholas Culpeper, *Culpeper's School of Physick* (London: N. Brook, 1659), preface. Culpeper, however, was critical of popular knowledge of medicine and supported the physician's knowledge of the properties of herbs: Wear, *Knowledge and Practice,* 61 n37. The Counter-Reformation Catholic Church had reacted to Neoplatonic attacks on its authority by placing all of Paracelsus' works on the Index of forbidden books in 1599: Trevor-Roper, *Renaissance Essays* (Chicago: University of Chicago Press, 1985), 173.

43. Eisenstein, *Printing Press* 1:272–77.

44. The term bookseller in the Tudor-Stuart period could encompass a variety of roles which have since become distinct, such as the activity of a modern publisher. Similarly, printers in early modern England usually sold books and sometimes commissioned and distributed them. The Stationers' Company accommodated liverymen from all categories—publisher, printer, seller—within the book trade. Hence, I will use the nomenclature interchangeably unless differentiation is necessary to understand a particular issue or individual.

45. Elizabeth Armstrong, "English Purchases of Printed Books from the Continent, 1465–1526," *English Historical Review* 94 (1979): 276, 278 n2. Armstrong indicates that John Argentine, physician-provost of King's College, Cambridge, left a personal medical library of printed books from abroad: ibid., 284.

46. Quoted in W. W. Greg, *Some Aspects and Problems of London Publishing between 1550 and 1650* (Oxford: Clarendon Press, 1956), 2.

47. Ibid., 3.

48. Greg points out that guilds of Writers of Court Hand and Text Hand and of Limners existed as early as 1357; they joined in 1403 to petition the London Court of Aldermen for regulation of their craft and that successful petition "virtually marks the foundation of the Stationers' Company:" Greg, *Some Aspects and Problems,* 1. Most of the London Stationers were natives of the capital: see C. Y. Ferdinand, "Towards a Demography of the Stationers' Company, 1601–1700," *Journal of the Printing Historical Society* 21 (1992): 51–69.

49. Cyprian Blagden, "The 'Company' of Printers," *Studies in Bibliography* 13 (1960): 4. Blagden cites a 1628 request to Parliament appealing for help in the printers' struggle with bookseller dominance in the organization. The path to "freedom" and a place in the London livery normally followed apprenticeship and the attainment of one's twenty-fourth birthday.

50. For more on the origin of copyrights, see John Feather, *Publishing, Piracy and Politics: An Historical Study of Copyright in Britain* (London: Mansell, 1994), 10–36.

51. The advantages of being a liveryman included a vote in City elections, the right to keep two apprentices, and a place in the company's leadership queue. Cyprian Blagden, "The Stationers' Company in the Civil War Period," *The Library* 5th ser., 13 (1958): 1–17.

52. Blagden counts upwards of 500 tickets printed for a full company meeting in 1645: Ibid., 3.

53. See Sheila Lambert, "State Control of the Press in Theory and Practice: The Role of the Stationers' Company before 1640," in *Censorship and Control of Print in England and France, 1600–1910*, ed. Robin Myers and Michael Harris (Winchester, England: St. Paul's Bibliographies, 1992), 1–32.

54. Ibid., 12. Greg points out that fees were paid for certain licenses, especially those given out by Charles I's Master of the Revels for the printing of plays: Greg, *Some Aspects and Problems*, 106.

55. Feather, *Publishing, Piracy and Politics*, 38–39.

56. Blanche B. Elliott, *A History of English Advertising* (London: Business Publications Limited, 1962), 25.

57. Carey Bliss used Donald Wing's *Short-Title Catalogue of English Books* as the basis for his calculations, and counted nearly 77,000 entries for 1641–1700. Bliss blames an underappreciation of English printing productivity on the celebrity of Dutch printing houses:Carey Bliss, *Some Aspects of Seventeenth Century English Printing* (Los Angeles: University of California Press, 1965), 5–8.

58. Greg, *Some Aspects and Problems*, 35–39, 49. For more on the proprietary rights of stationers, see Adrian Johns, *The Nature of the Book* (Chicago: University of Chicago Press, 1998), 213–30.

59. Blagden says that Cole was never a licensed printer, but cites him in a 1660 list drawn up by disgruntled journeymen of "master printers" working in 1660; Henry Plomer refers to Cole as a bookseller and printer: see Blagden, "The 'Company' of Printers," 6 n. 9; Henry R. Plomer, *Dictionary of the Booksellers and Printers Who Were at Work in England, Scotland and Ireland from 1641 to 1667* (London: Bibliographical Society, 1907), 48.

60. Johns, *Nature of the Book*, 218. Johns seems to have arrived at his negative impression of Cole from fiery Puritan divine Thomas Edwards, who attacked tolerant Independents like Cole from the pulpit with implacable violence, and from Olav Thulesius, author of a substandard work on Culpeper; see Edwards, *Gangraena* (London: R. Smith, 1646) and Thulesius, *Nicholas Culpeper* (New York: St. Martin's Press, 1992).

61. The Copyright Act of 1710 abolished perpetual ownership of literary property and established the policy by which authors and publishers ultimately acquired control; it was not until 1774, however, that the House of Lords upheld the limitation of copyright written into the law. For more on literary property and the effect of the Copyright Act, see William Zachs, *The First John Murray and the Late Eighteenth-Century London Book Trade* (Oxford: Oxford University Press, 1998), 52–56.

62. Mary Rhinelander McCarl, "Publishing the Works of Nicholas Culpeper," *Canadian Bulletin for the History of Medicine* 13 (1996): 226. I thank Mrs. McCarl for her scholarly generosity and personal counsel tallying the Cole titles and deciphering his will.

63. F.N.L. Poynter, "Nicholas Culpeper and His Books," *Journal of Medical History* 17 (1962): 152–67. Though critics like Culpeper used the press to attack physicians, soon they denounced both the College and the Stationers for restrictionist trade.

64. Professor of Pharmacognosy E. J. Shellard calls Culpeper's *Herbal* "a poor man's dispensatory," and, despite the price and literacy needed to acquire its contents, the book proved hugely popular: David Potterton, ed., *Culpeper's Color Herbal*, foreword by E. J. Shellard (New York: Sterling Publishing, 1983), 6.

65. McCarl, "Publishing the Works of Nicholas Culpeper," 232. McCarl theorizes that Culpeper had worked in Cole's print shop where his knowledge of Latin was recognized and put to use translating the *Pharmacopoeia*: ibid., 232.

66. Cyprian Blagden cites a 1661 petition by Cole to the House of Lords attesting to that expenditure; see Blagden, "The 'Company' of Printers," 6 n. 9. Also McCarl, "Publishing the Works of Nicholas Culpeper," 230; and Johns, *Nature of the Book*, 218.

67. *DNB*; see also Jonathan Sanderson, "Nicholas Culpeper and the Book Trade: Print and Promotion of Vernacular Medical Knowledge, 1649–65," Ph.D. diss., University of Leeds, 1999.

68. McCarl notes that Cole registered seven new Culpeper translations in August 1654: McCarl, "Publishing the Works of Nicholas Culpeper," 238. Graeme Tobyn suggests that other Culpeper titles, if they really existed, may have perished in the Great Fire of London in 1666: Graeme Tobyn, *Culpeper's Medicine* (Shaftesbury, U.K.: Element, 1997), 28.

69. F.N.L. Poynter, "Nicholas Culpeper and the Paracelsians," in *Science, Medicine and Society in the Renaissance*, ed. Allen G. Debus, 2 vols., (New York: Science History Publications, 1972) 1: 202, 219. Poynter agrees with Cole that Culpeper did temper his truculent anti-Galenic views if not his anti-elitism.

70. Alice Culpeper, *Mrs. Culpeper's Information, Vindication and Testimony concerning Her Husband's Books to be Published after His Death*, quoted in Nicholas Culpeper, *The English Physitian Enlarged* (London: Peter Cole, 1653), C8; Tobyn, *Culpeper's Medicine*, 29. McCarl posits that the deal struck between Mrs. Culpeper and Peter Cole was mutually beneficial: Cole got the corroboration he wanted and the widow gained free advertising space for a new elixir: McCarl, "Publishing the Works of Nicholas Culpeper," 239.

71. McCarl, "Publishing the Works of Nicholas Culpeper," 226. Adrian Johns charges that whatever confusion remains over Culpeper's output is the result of "Cole's notoriety upon the authorial credit," rather than anything done by Brook, whom he does not even mention: Johns, *Nature of the Book*, 228. Tobyn, by contrast, blames Brook for the mess and upholds the legitimacy of Cole's imprints: Tobyn, *Culpeper's Medicine*, 29, 251 n. 69.

72. Francis Anthony, an experienced chemical practitioner, often treated diseases with gold and mercury, and was summoned before the College of Physicians for the first of many times in 1600 for using aurum potabile. The Fellows later suspected that the death of theologian Thomas Sanderson, who paid Anthony twenty shillings for the medicine and forty shillings for the essence of gold, had been hastened by aurum potabile: Charles Webster, "William Harvey and the Crisis of Medicine," in *William Harvey and His Age*, ed. Jerome J. Bylebyl (Baltimore, Md.: Johns Hopkins University Press, 1979), 12. Matthew Gwinne, professor of medicine at Gresham College, wrote against Anthony as the College's advocate; his book appended commendatory verses by eminent Fellows: Clark, *Royal College of Physicians* 1:202–3.

73. Anonymous, *Culpeper Revived from the Grave* (Spitalfields: n.p., 1655), 2. Obadiah Blagrave succeeded to Brook's registered titles.

74. Ibid., 5–6; Poynter, "Nicholas Culpeper and the Paracelsians," 213. Bookseller George Eversden, whose shop from 1656 to 1665 was in St. Paul's Churchyard, actually published the treatise, his only Culpeper production.

75. Poynter finds it ironic that Cole authenticates Culpeper's alchemical work with drinkable gold while simultaneously accentuating his return to Galenism: Poynter, "Culpeper and the Paracelsians," 214; *Mr. Culpeper's Ghost*, 5–10.

76. Blagden, "The 'Company' of Printers," 6 n. 9. This is the subject of Cole's petition (27 July 1661) to the House of Lords, to which no notice was taken.

77. Peter Elmer, "Medicine, Religion and the Puritan Revolution," in *The Medical Revolution of the Seventeenth Century*, ed. Roger French and Andrew Wear (Cambridge: Cambridge University Press, 1989), 21 n; Plomer, *Dictionary 1641–1667*, 34–35, 49.

78. Johns, *Nature of the Book*, 218–19 n. 97; Poynter, "Culpeper and the Paracelsians," 213. Cole continued to produce Culpeper books until the year of his death; George Sawbridge and John Streater took over Cole's titles: McCarl, "Publishing the Works of Nicholas Culpeper," 255 n. 6.

79. For all references to Cole's will, see PROB 11/318 (formerly PCC 153. Hyde), Public Record Office, London. Cole left lands and tenements in his native Suffolk to James Cole, "my brother's second son," his coexecutor, and fellow printer, and he bequeathed "leases, many goods and chattel," presumably including the two London printing shops, to three children of his brother, Edward. He gave Elizabeth Ridley, the youngest daughter of a deceased friend and comrade in bookselling, £200 to be paid in full within a year after Cole's demise, and to Ursula Parry and her children he left £250 "to be so secured that her husband may not spend it." The money to fund

Mrs. Parry derived from two bonds, the value of which Cole knew to the shilling, entered into by William Streaton, a man from Kent, who was instructed to pay up all that was due at the Stationers' office door. Cole bestowed £50 on his other coexecutor, haberdasher William Marsh.

80. Of course, it is also possible that Cole had the plague in late 1665 and saved himself further agony. Just nine days after Cole's death, Samuel Pepys attributed an early winter increase in the contagion to unseasonably warm weather: Latham and Matthews, eds., *Pepys Diary* 6:328 (Dec. 13, 1665). See also E. S. de Beer, ed., *The Diary of John Evelyn*, 6 vols. (Oxford: Clarendon Press, 1955) 3:425 (Dec. 10, 1665).

81. Cole's suicide is recorded in State Papers 44/22, p. 328, Public Record Office, London.

82. See Giles Mandelbrote, "From the Warehouse to the Counting-House: Booksellers and Bookshops in Late Seventeenth-Century London," in *A Genius for Letters: Booksellers and Bookselling from the Sixteenth to the Twentieth Centuries*, ed. Robin Myers and Michael Harris (New Castle, Del.: Oak Knoll Press, 1995), 49–84.

83. Streater quoted in Johns, *Nature of the Book*, 276. For the hazards of printing during the 1640s, see Blagden, "Stationers' Company in the Civil War Period," 8–14.

84. For more on Böhme and his re-evaluation of divine gender, see B. J. Gibbons, *Gender in Mystical and Occult Thought: Behmenism and Its Development in England* (Cambridge: Cambridge University Press, 1996).

85. Blagden, "The 'Company' of Printers," 17 n. 11. Johns proclaims Streater insolvent along with Moses Pitt, Francis Smith, and Cole: *Nature of the Book*, 221 n. 105. Smith, a foremost opposition publisher during Charles II's reign, faced the constant threat of searches of his premises and prosecution by the government for his effronteries; he was imprisoned on forty-one occasions. See Timothy Crist, "Francis Smith and the Opposition Press in England, 1660–1688" (unpublished Ph.D. diss., University of Cambridge, 1977).

86. For instance, Streater produced John Smith's *Compleat Practice of Physick* (London: J. Streater, 1656). That same year, he also put out James Harrington's classic of republican literature, *The Commonwealth of Oceana*.

87. For more on the intricacies of Streater's warfare with the Stationers, see Johns, *Nature of the Book*, 266–323.

88. Leona Rostenberg, "Moses Pitt, Publisher and Purveyor of Mathematical Books," in her *The Library of Robert Hooke: The Scientific Book Trade of Restoration England* (Santa Monica, Calif.: Modoc Press, 1987), 27.

89. Michael Harris, "Moses Pitt and Insolvency in the London Book Trade in the Late Seventeenth Century," in *Economics of the British Book Trade 1605–1939*, ed. Robin Myers and Michael Harris (Cambridge: Cambridge University Press, 1985), 180. Rostenberg notes that the production costs of mathematical texts included particular figures and diagrams cut for the text as well as specialized type: Rostenberg, "Moses Pitt, Publisher and Purveyor," 28.

90. Harris, "Moses Pitt and Insolvency," 185.

91. Ibid., 200–201.

92. For more on these cases, see H. R. Plomer, *A Dictionary of the Printers and Booksellers Who Were at Work in England, Scotland, and Ireland from 1668 to 1725* (Oxford: Oxford Bibliographical Society, 1922).

93. Joseph Hindmarsh's titles sold from his shop in Cornhill include Richard Griffith, *A la Mode Phlebotomy No Good Fashion* (1680), *The English Remedy* by Robert Talbor (1682), and *The Works of Ambrose Paré* (1690); from his business in Little Britain, Thomas Sawbridge vended William Salmon's third edition of *Pharmacopoeia Londinensis* in 1685, Salmon's *Systema Medicinale: Complete System of Physick* in 1686, and the seventh edition of *Vade Mecum or A Companion for a Surgeon* by Thomas Brugis in 1690. Bentley also combined with Joshua Phillips, Henry Rhodes, John Taylor, Henry Bonwicke, and Samuel Manship to effect the production of books.

94. Giles Mandelbrote, "Richard Bentley's Copies: The Ownership of Copyrights in the Late Seventeenth Century," in *The Book Trade and Its Customers, 1450–1900*, ed. Arnold Hunt, Giles Mandelbrote, and Alison Shell (New Castle, Del.: Oak Knoll Press, 1997), 55–75. All together fifteen bills to regulate the book trade were introduced in Parliament between 1695 and 1714;

royal assent to an imprecise new Act was obtained in 1710: Feather, *Publishing, Piracy and Politics*, 51.

95. P. M. Handover, *Printing in London* (London: George Allen and Unwin, 1960), 65. Ellic Howe also puts the number of printers at sixty, based on the Stationers' Calendars of Masters and Apprentices; he comments that nearly as many bookbinders were members of the Company, as well as dozens of miscellaneous tradesmen, an indication that by mid-seventeenth century the professional exclusivity of the London craft guilds had broken down: Ellic Howe, *A List of London Bookbinders, 1648–1815* (London: London Bibliographic Society, 1950), xii–xiii.

96. Sometimes called the Press Act, the statute's full title is: An Act for preventing the frequent Abuses in printing seditious . . . Books . . . and for regulating of Printing and Printing Presses. For the continued role of the guild in censorship, see Cyprian Blagden, *The Stationers' Company: A History, 1403–1959* (Stanford, Calif.: Stanford University Press, 1977); and Marjorie Plant, *The English Book Trade*, 3rd ed. (London: George Allen and Unwin, 1974).

97. W. Carew Hazlitt, *The Livery Companies of the City of London* (New York: Benjamin Blom, 1892), 627; Johns, *Nature of the Book*, 131–32.

98. Feather, *Publishing, Piracy and Politics*, 49.

99. Inventories of Sawbridge's property, mostly investments in the book trade, show him to be a very wealthy man when he died in July 1681; his estate was valued at £11,000, plus a further £15,000 owed him at his death. Sawbridge's widow in 1683 paid the Stationers £158 that a committee investigating his Cambridge swindle had decided was due to the Company. For more on the episode, see Blagden, *The Stationers' Company*; and Mandelbrote, "From the Warehouse to the Counting House." Despite his misappropriation of English Stock monies, Sawbridge left a reputation in the trade that prompted John Dunton to describe him as 'the greatest bookseller that has been in England for many years': John Dunton, *The Life and Errors of John Dunton* (London: S. Malthus, 1705), 291.

100. *To the Honourable Members, Assembled in Parliament*, cited in Feather, *Publishing, Piracy and Politics*, 54.

101. John Feather, *A History of British Publishing* (London: Routledge, 1988), 62.

Notes for Chapter 3

1. See Roy Porter, ed., *The Popularization of Medicine, 1650–1850* (New York: Routledge, 1992) and Lucinda McCray Beier, *Sufferers and Healers* (London: Routledge and Kegan Paul, 1987).

2. John Archer, *Every Man His Own Doctor* (London: Peter Lillicrap, 1671). Archer, never licensed by the College of Physicians but named "chemical physician" to Charles II's court in 1671, sold nostrums and advertised his inventions. See also Roy Porter, *Health for Sale: Quackery in England, 1660–1850* (Manchester: Manchester University Press, 1989).

3. However, printers did not always publish works with which they agreed. In the allegiance controversy that followed the Revolution of 1688, several Whig publishers put out Tory pamphlets and vice versa. Mark Goldie, "The Revolution of 1689 and the Structure of Political Argument," *Bulletin of Research in the Humanities* 93 (1980): 492–94. Although the printers of Jacobite literature are harder to identify as they usually omitted their colophons from publications, Joseph Hindmarsh, William Canon, and William Anderton are noteworthy. Anderton, the most prominent Jacobite printer, was executed for treason in 1694; Hindmarsh published four medical books—inexpensive, popular works in English.

4. Collins quoted in Leona Rostenberg, "Moses Pitt, Publisher and Purveyor of Mathematical Books," in Rostenberg, *The Library of Robert Hooke: The Scientific Book Trade of Restoration England* (Santa Monica, Calif.: Modoc Press, 1989).

5. A .W. Pollard and G. R. Redgrave, *A Short Title Catalogue of Books Printed in England, Scotland, Ireland . . .1475–1640*, 2nd ed., 2 vols. (London: Bibliographial Society, 1976); Donald Wing, *Short Title Catalogue of Books Printed in England, Scotland, Ireland . . .* , *1641–1700*, 2nd ed., 3 vols. (New York: Modern Language Association, 1994); and Edward Arber, ed., *The Term Catalogues*,

1668–1709 (and Easter Term of 1711), 3 vols. (New York: Johnson Reprint, 1965). London printer Robert Clavell originally compiled the catalogue. It is not a list of all books printed in England during those years, since advertising fees had to be paid to Clavell for inclusion in the inventory, but it does provide additional information for this study.

6. Porter, *Disease, Medicine and Society*, 46.

7. Among those cautioning restraint in categorizing certain types of publications for the exclusive use of particular classes of people are Watt, *Cheap Print and Popular Piety*, 261; Johns, *Nature of the Book*, 384–85; and Sandra Clark, *The Elizabethan Pamphleteers: Popular Moralistic Pamphlets, 1580–1640* (Rutherford, N.J.: Fairleigh Dickinson University Press, 1983), 21.

8. Wear, *Knowledge and Practice*, 41.

9. See Keith Thomas, "The Meaning of Literacy in Early Modern England," in *The Written Word: Literacy in Transition*, ed. Gerd Bauman (Oxford: Clarendon Press, 1986), 99; and Derek Nuttall, "English Printers and Their Typefaces, 1600–1700," in *Aspects of Printing from 1600*, ed. Robin Myers and Michael Harris (Oxford: Oxford Polytechnic, 1987), 30–48.

10. Kevin Sharpe, *Reading Revolutions: The Politics of Reading in Early Modern England* (New Haven, Conn.: Yale University Press, 2000), 51.

11. Cited in K. F. Russell, *British Anatomy, 1525–1800*, 2nd ed. (Winchester, England: St. Paul's Bibliographies, 1987), xvii. Woodcuts on the title page shows two gruesome cranial surgeries involving large screws trepanning men's skulls.

12. Ibid., xviii, 73.

13. Ibid., xxi. Russell also notes the printing of four fugitive sheets (see chapter eight).

14. A number of printed syllabi from the anatomy lectures given before the Barber-Surgeons' Company are extant: see ibid., 186–89.

15. Annals of the Royal College of Physicians of London, 3 April 1615, LRCP.

16. Jaggard's wife and son Isaac succeeded him in the prosperous family enterprise in 1623; publishing the first folio of Shakespeare's works was among the last ventures of William Jaggard. Richard Cotes was later the official printer for the City of London (1642–53) and his wife Ellen continued the business after his death; in 1668 she had three presses, two apprentices, and nine pressmen: Plomer, *Dictionary 1641–1667*, 52.

17. Russell, *British Anatomy*, 161.

18. Ibid., 162.

19. Ibid., plate 567.

20. Munk (*Roll* 1:193) errs, saying it was James Moleyns who treated Cromwell. Edward's father, James, died in 1639; Edward's son, also James, became surgeon to the Stuart household in 1680 and surgeon-in-ordinary to James II in 1685. He trephined the skull of Prince Rupert, a Stuart cousin, in 1667. See G.C.R. Morris, "Which Molins Treated Cromwell for the Stone and Did Not Prescribe for Pepys?" *Medical History* 26 (1982): 429–35; Graham Martin, "Prince Rupert and the Surgeons," *History Today* 40 (December 1990): 41.

21. Annals of the College of Physicians, vol. 3, f. 166a, LRCP; Munk, *Roll* 1:193. George C. Peachey adds that Moleyns asked for a drink after working on Cromwell, was taken to the wine cellar, and toasted the health of Charles Stuart: see Peachey, "Thomas Trapham—Cromwell's Surgeon—and Others," *Proceedings of the Royal Society of Medicine* 24 (1931): 1442.

22. Plomer, *Dictionary 1641–1667*, 74.

23. The "newly revised" edition of *Myotoma* (London: Abel Roper, 1676) included Charles Scarburgh's "Syllabus Musculorum," never before published but credited to the author. Another rendering appeared from the presses of William Rogers in 1680.

24. Russell, *British Anatomy*, xxix.

25. For more on Robert White, see Malcolm C. Salaman, *The Old Engravers of England* (London: Cassell and Company, 1907), 56–59.

26. Plomer, *Dictionary 1641–1667*, 136.

27. *Medicaster medicatus* also rebutted the work of William Salmon, a quack whom the Tory Yonge, as a Fellow of both the College of Physicians and the Royal Society, would have disdained: *DNB*.

28. James Yonge, *Medicaster medicatus or Remedy for the Itch of Scribbling* (London: Gabriel Kunholt, 1685); and *Observations in Chyrurgery and Anatomy* (London: R. Wilde, 1687). Kunholt sold patent medicines from his shops in London and Oxford.

29. Jennifer B. Lee and Miriam Mandelbaum, *Seeing Is Believing* (New York: New York Public Library, 1999), 45–46. Fabrici's work, *De venarum ostiolis*, was published in 1603; Bauhin's *Theatrum Anatomicum* came out in 1614.

30. Russell, *British Anatomy*, xxiii.

31. Plomer, *Dictionary 1641–1667*, 2–3, 75–76, 123, 158. The book business was precarious in many ways; Fletcher got into trouble in 1668 with his father, Miles Fletcher, for illegally printing law books. Roycroft had a spectacular career printing gorgeous Bibles and editions of the classics; he even was Charles II's printer for Oriental languages and held a share in the King's Printing House. But his business and that of James Allestry were destroyed in the Fire of London.

32. Leona Rostenberg, "John Martyn, 'Printer to the Royal Society,'" in Rostenberg, *The Library of Robert Hooke: The Scientific Book Trade of Restoration England* (Santa Monica, Calif.: Modoc Press, 1989), 13–25.

33. The others named for whom the work was printed are Thomas Dring, Charles Harper, Joseph Leigh; Robert Clavell is named as the seller at the Peacock in St. Paul's Churchyard.

34. For the early history of the Royal Society, see Margery Purver, *The Royal Society: Concept and Creation* (Cambridge, Mass.: M.I.T. Press, 1967).

35. The press of Lawrence Sadler and Robert Beaumont, partners in Little Britain, issued Glisson's *De rachitide sive morbo puerili* in 1650 in octavo. Sadler died of plague in 1664 at the Hague.

36. Charles Webster, *The Great Instauration: Science, Medicine and Reform, 1626–1660* (New York: Holmes and Meier, 1975), 318.

37. *DNB*. Beale, who styled himself a "phylomathist," saw his work come into print for the Stationers' Company as part of its monopoly on almanacs.

38. Webster, *Great Instauration*, 53.

39. Goddard, physician to the army of Parliament, is also said to have made the first English telescope: Munk, *Roll* 1:240.

40. Russell, *British Anatomy*, xxxiii.

41. For a modern edition, see Robert Burton, *Anatomy of Melancholy*, ed. Floyd Dell and Paul Jordan-Smith (New York: Tudor Pub. Co., 1955).

42. Webster, *Great Instauration*, 44–45.

43. Webster warns against connecting the two disparate groups: ibid., 58.

44. Ibid., 67–77.

45. Ibid., 1.

46. Nicholas Culpeper, *A Physicall Directory* (London: Peter Cole, 1649), sig. A1r.

47. This was a second charter, the first issued in 1662.

48. Webster, *Great Instauration*, 94. T.P.R. Laslett goes so far as to call the Royal Society "to a surprising extent the work of the English medical profession": Laslett, "The Foundation of the Royal Society and the Medical Profession in England," *British Medical Journal* 2, no. 5193 (1960): 165–69.

49. Sydenham obtained licentiate status from the College in 1663; his M.D. from Cambridge was issued in 1676.

50. Other London publishers who handled Boyle's oeuvre include the most important bookseller of the Restoration era, Henry Herringman, who was Dryden's publisher and held a share in the King's Printing House, and William Cademan, the latter famed according to Plomer for publishing good literature in the 1670s and 1680s from his shop in the Strand: Henry R. Plomer et al., *Dictionaries of the Printers and Booksellers Who Were at Work in England, Scotland and Ireland, 1557–1775* (London: Bibliographical Society, 1977), 62, 96.

51. Boyle may have reserved his most candid comments about the medical establishment because he was not himself a member: see Barbara B. Kaplan, *"Divulging Useful Truths in Physick": The Medical Agenda of Robert Boyle* (Baltimore, Md.: Johns Hopkins University Press, 1993); and Michael Hunter, "Boyle versus the Galenists: A Suppressed Critique of Seventeenth Century Medical Practice and Its Significance," *Medical History* 41 (1997): 322–61.

52. Quoted in Lawrence M. Principe, *The Aspiring Adept: Robert Boyle and His Alchemical Quest* (Princeton, N.J.: Princeton University Press, 1998), 47.

53. Hunter, "Boyle versus the Galenists," 326. While Barbara Kaplan theorized that Boyle preferred a peaceful medical world, Hunter believes that he deliberately suppressed his more belligerent appraisal of elite physicians because he feared their hostility: ibid., 341.

54. George Castle, *The Chymical Galenist* (London: Henry Twyford, 1667), 6, 16–17.

55. Hunter, "Boyle versus the Galenists," 327.

56. Principe, *Aspiring Adept*, 187. Chrysopoeia and argyropoeia, seventeenth-century terms, denote the transmutation of base metals into noble ones, gold and silver respectively.

57. *Methodus curandi febres* (1666) appeared in a second edition the following year as *Observationes medicae*, this time dedicated to Robert Mapletoft, M.D., Sydenham's partner in medical practice and the man who introduced him to John Locke.

58. Andrew Cunningham, "Thomas Sydenham: Epidemics, Experiment and the 'Good Old Cause,'" in *The Medical Revolution of the Seventeenth Century*, ed. Roger French and Andrew Wear (Cambridge: Cambridge University Press, 1989), 165.

59. Ibid., 171–73.

60. R. G. Latham, ed., *The Works of Thomas Sydenham*, 2 vols. (London: Sydenham Society, 1848) 1:11–24. Ever practical, Sydenham suggested that a vice-physician might assist in the record-keeping that an observant clinician engaged in.

61. Patrick Romanell, *John Locke and Medicine* (Buffalo, N,Y,: Prometheus Books, 1984), 27.

62. Peter Laslett, "Introduction," in John Locke, *Two Treatises of Government*, ed. Laslett (Cambridge: Cambridge University Press, 2000), 86. Laslett credits Dugald Stewart with first having stressed the importance of Locke's medical training on his philosophy.

63. Quoted in ibid., 23.

64. Locke's journal for 26 June 1681 quoted in ibid., 85.

65. Locke also worked in Holland under the assumed name Dr. van der Linden. He said he preferred voluntary exile abroad rather than "intolerance at home": quoted in Romanell, *John Locke and Medicine*, 38.

66. Ibid., 75.

67. Ibid., 88. See also Latham, *Works of Sydenham*, 1:24. Thomas Basset, a dealer in law books, published some of Locke's works, but his principal publishing house was that of Awnsham and John Churchill.

68. Partridge specialized in astrological books along with his partner, Humphrey Blunden; John Sherley and Thomas Underhill also produced some of Lilly's astrological works.

69. Robert Latham, ed., *The Shorter Pepys* (Berkeley: University of California Press, 1985), 14 June 1667, 792. Pepys would have also chortled over an earlier stunt of Lilly's, a 1644 plan to dig up the Westminster Abbey cloister with the king's clockmaker, Davy Ramsey, searching for treasure found with "Mosaical rods": *DNB*.

70. *Legends no Histories* was an attempt to refute Thomas Sprat's history of the Royal Society. Joseph Glanvill replied to Stubbe in a 212–page tome, defending the Society and calling Stubbe a hypocrite: *A Prefatory Answer to Mr. Henry Stubbe* (London: J. Collins, 1671), title page.

71. Davis also published the works of Robert Boyle.

72. Annals of the College, vol. 3, fols. 121b–122b; 129b; 139b (30 May, 25 June, 4 July 1632), LRCP.

73. Primrose eventually got a license to practice, paid £8 plus other fees, and relocated to Hull: Charles Webster, "William Harvey and the Crisis of Medicine," in *William Harvey and His Age*, ed. Jerome J. Bylebyl (Baltimore, Md.: Johns Hopkins University Press, 1979), 6.

74. Perhaps out of jealousy, Clarke also feuded with Dr. Laurence Wright, Oliver Cromwell's favorite physician, who had a neighboring practice, and emerged the victor from this quarrel: Munk, *Roll* 1:181.

75. Despite his lack of bona fide medical credentials, Nedham wrote *Medela medicinae* (London: Richard Lowndes, 1665), a 516–page tome. The piece attracted several printed refutations.

76. Henry Stubbe, *The Plus Ultra Reduced to a Non Plus* (London: printed for the author, 1670), 77–94, 111–12. Besides Harvey, Stubbe attacked Joseph Glanville, a defender of the Royal Society.

77. Robert G. Frank, Jr., "The Image of Harvey in Commonwealth and Restoration England," in *William Harvey and His Age*, ed. Jerome J. Bylebyl (Baltimore, Md.: Johns Hopkins University Press, 1979), 130–34. Frank points out that the "uncompromisingly professional" library Harvey bequeathed to the College, sadly lost in the Great Fire, further enhanced his image: ibid., 114–15.

78. Webster, "William Harvey," 3–4.

79. Harold J. Cook, "Physicians and the New Philosophy: Henry Stubbe and the Virtuosi-Physicians," in *The Medical Revolution of the Seventeenth Century*, ed. Roger French and Andrew Wear (Cambridge: Cambridge University Press, 1989), 246–48.

80. See, for instance, Richard Foster Jones, *Ancients and Moderns: A Study of the Rise of the Scientific Movement in Seventeenth-Century England* (Berkeley: University of California Press, 1965), 238, 244–63; R. H. Syfret, "Some Early Critics of the Royal Society," *Notes and Records of the Royal Society* 8 (1950): 20–64.

81. See Jim Jacob, *Henry Stubbe: Radical Protestantism and the Early Enlightenment* (Cambridge: Cambridge University Press, 1983).

82. For an earlier mapping of the stores there, see Peter Blayney, *The Bookshops in Paul's Cross Churchyard* (London: Bibliographic Society, 1990).

83. Seven of the first ten Smith medical imprints were written in Latin (1684–90), but only three of the last ten he produced with Walford (1705–7).

84. For more on Bate see Munk, *Roll* 1:228 and my entry on him in the *New Dictionary of National Biography* (Oxford: Oxford University Press, forthcoming 2004).

85. For more on Sydenham, see Kenneth Dewhurst, *Dr. Thomas Sydenham* (Berkeley: University of California Press, 1966).

86. Munk, *Roll* 1:423.

87. For more on Colbatch, published medical entrepreneurialism, and its effect on the London medical establishment, see Harold J. Cook, "Sir John Colbatch and Augustan Medicine," *Annals of Science* 47 (1990): 475–505.

88. Plomer, *Dictionary 1641–1667*, 16.

89. F.N.L. Poynter, "The First English Medical Journal," *British Medical Journal* 2 (1948): 307–8. Two earlier publications, the *Philosophical Transactions* of the Royal Society—the first English scientific periodical, and the *Weekly Memorials*—the first English abstracting journal, had some medical information, about 15 to 30 percent of their content respectively. See Fielding H. Garrison, "The Medical and Scientific Periodicals of the Seventeenth and Eighteenth Centuries," *Bulletin of the Institute for the History of Medicine* 5 (1934): 285–342.

90. *Medicina Curiosa*, No. 1 (17 June 1684), British Library.

91. Roy Porter commented that "hardly anything has been written about this journal." See his "Medical Journalism in Britain to 1800," in *Medical Journals and Medical Knowledge*, ed. W. F. Bynum, Stephen Lock, and Roy Porter (London: Routledge, 1992).

92. De Blegny, whose "Englished" books were sold in London by Thomas Burrell, a neighbor of Basset's in Fleet Street, published the first French medical journal, *Les Nouvelles Descouvertes sur Toutes les Parties de la Medecine* (1679–84). See D.A. Kronick, "Nicholas de Blegny, Medical Journalist," *Bulletin of the Cleveland Medical Library* 7 (1960): 47–56.

93. *Medicina Curiosa*, number 2 (23 October 1684), British Library. See also Eric Colman, "The First English Medical Journal: *Medicina Curiosa*," *Lancet* 354 (1999): 324–26.

94. Although Clavell worked as an agent for Tory publisher Roger L'Estrange, he got into trouble for printing Dutch propaganda in 1688. Goldie, "Revolution of 1689," 494.

95. Quoted in Laslett, "Introduction," 7. Locke had particular difficulties bringing *Two Treatises of Government* to press.

96. The first newspaper advertisement for a medicine appeared in *Mercurius Publicus* in November 1652, but handbills and pamphlets vaunted the virtues of patent medicines as much as a

century earlier. For more, see Juanita Burnby, "Pharmaceutical Advertising in the 17th and 18th Centuries," *European Journal of Marketing* 22, 4 (1988): 24–40.

97. For more on William's intentions, see Harold J. Cook, "Practical Medicine and the British Armed Forces after the 'Glorious Revolution,'" *Medical History* 35 (1990): 1–26. Dr. Welwood also served on the Commission for the Sick, Wounded, and Prisoners of War: Elizabeth Lane Furdell, *James Welwood: Physician to the Glorious Revolution* (Conshohocken, Penn.: Combined Books, 1998), 179–80.

98. Dunton, *Life and Errors,* 292. Allen's first issue came from the press of John White and was republished in Dublin in 1686 by Andrew Crook and Samuel Helsham before making its London appearance the following year. See R. A. Cohen, Introduction, in Charles Allen, *Operator for the Teeth* (London: Dawsons, 1969), iii.

99. Max Geshwind reflects on Allen's obscure legacy and the absence of his name in other British dental books that followed Allen's: Max Geshwind, "William Salmon, Quack-Doctor and Writer of Seventeenth Century London," *Bulletin of the History of Dentistry* 43, 2 (1995): 76.

100. Quoted in ibid., 76.

101. *Shorter Pepys,* 13 October 1663, 312–13.

102. The Churchills were described as "universalists" by Plomer, and Goldie refers to the political pragmatism of some prominent publishers, including the Churchills, as "promiscuous." Goldie, "Revolution of 1689," 494.

Notes for Chapter 4

1. Robert K. Merton, *Science, Technology and Society in Seventeenth Century England* (New York: Fertig, 1970), xviii. Steven Shapin, arguing that Merton has been misunderstood, nonetheless acknowledges the source of popular and scholarly identification of the nexus between Puritanism and science as Merton. See Shapin, "Understanding the Merton Thesis," *Isis* 79 (1988): 594–605.

2. Allen G. Debus, "Guintherius, Libavius and Sennert: The Chemical Compromise in Early Modern Medicine," in *Science, Medicine and Society in the Renaissance,* ed. Allen G. Debus, 2 vols. (New York: Science History Publications, 1972) 1:162. See also Allen G. Debus, *The English Paracelsians* (London: Oldbourne, 1965), 49–85; and Paul H. Kocher, "Paracelsian Medicine in England: The First Thirty Years," *Journal of the History of Medicine* 2 (1947): 451–80.

3. *All's Well That Ends Well* is cited as evidence of Shakespeare's perspicacity in Charles Webster, "Alchemical and Paracelsian Medicine," in *Health, Medicine and Mortality in the Sixteenth Century,* ed. Charles Webster (Cambridge: Cambridge University Press, 1979), 323.

4. Ibid., 317–19, 329. Joining Webster in this 1960s thesis was P. M. Rattansi, "Paracelsus and the Puritan Revolution," *Ambix* 11 (1963): 23–32; and P. M. Rattansi, "The Helmontian-Galenist Controversy in Restoration England," *Ambix* 12 (1964): 1–23. For a critique of Webster, see Peter Elmer, "Medicine, Religion, and the Puritan Revolution," in *The Medical Revolution in the Seventeenth Century,* ed. Roger French and Andrew Wear (Cambridge: Cambridge University Press, 1989), 10–45.

5. Trevor-Roper, *Historical Essays,* 177–78.

6. Elmer, "Medicine, Religion and the Puritan Revolution," 10–12. Margaret and J. R. Jacob posit that liberal Anglicanism actually provided the link to inventive science: see their "Anglican Origins of Modern Science," *Isis* 71 (1980): 251–67.

7. Andrew Wear, "Religious Belief and Medicine in Early Modern England," in *The Task of Healing: Medicine, Religion and Gender in England and the Netherlands, 1450–1800,* ed. Hilary Marland and Margaret Pelling (Rotterdam: Erasmus, 1996), 146; William Birken, "The Dissenting Tradition in English Medicine of the Seventeenth and Eighteenth Centuries," *Medical History* 39 (1995): 212–13.

8. Ole Peter Grell, "Plague, Prayer and Physic: Helmontian Medicine in Restoration England," in *Religio Medici: Medicine and Religion in Seventeenth Century England,* ed. O. P. Grell and Andrew Cunningham (Aldershot, England: Scolar Press, 1996), 205.

9. See David Harley, "Medical Metaphors in English Moral Theology," *Journal of the History of Medicine* 48 (1993): 396–435.

10. Eustace F. Bosanquet, *Early Printed Almanacks and Prognostications* (London: Bibliographical Society, 1917), 2–4.

11. Ibid., 188–92.

12. *DNB.*

13. Bosanquet, *English Printed Alamancs*, 5.

14. Boorde, *Breuiary of Helthe*, fol. A4v–A5r.

15. Bosanquet, *English Printed Almanacks*, 27.

16. *Pepys Diary*, 10 October 1666.

17. Mother Shipton's four-page *Mercurius Propheticus* appeared in 1643 with no printer identified. No evidence of her existence can be found, and the first reference to her at all is in 1641: *DNB*. According to Plomer, Harper printed mainly ballads, broadsides, political tracts, and sermons; the Irish-born Head is known for books of jests and the play, *The English Rogue*: see Plomer, *Dictionary 1641–1667*, 90, 94–95.

18. Oliver Lawson-Dick, ed., *Aubrey's Brief Lives* (London: Mariner, 1992), 217. Sir Richard Napier also obtained an ecclesiastical certificate (his from the bishop of Lincoln) to practice medicine, but did manage to procure an M.D. from Oxford nine years later, in 1642.

19. Alan Macfarlane, *The Family Life of Ralph Josselin* (New York: Norton, 1970), 172–74.

20. William Birken, "The Dissenting Tradition in English Medicine," 206, 209.

21. Elmer, "Medicine, Religion, and the Puritan Revolution," 26–27.

22. Plomer, *Dictionary 1641–1667*, 56–57. Earlier, unauthorized Latin versions of *Religio Medici* came out of continental print shops including Francis Hack of Leiden; Nathaniel Ekins, "licenser of pedlars and petty chapmen" put out Browne's *Pseudodoxia epidemica* in 1659.

23. Gordon Wolstenholme, ed., *Royal College of Physicians: Portraits* (London: Churchill, 1964), 88.

24. William Clowes, *Brief and Necessarie Treatise* (London: T. Cadman, 1585), 45v–46r.

25. Robert Burton, *Anatomy of Melancholy*, ed. F. Dell and P. Jordan-Smith (New York: Tudor, 1983), 385. Satan might, however, be held at bay by patriotism; Burton thought gazing at England's nascent Empire helped to diminish melancholy: Malcolm C. Salaman, *The Old Engravers of England* (Philadelphia: Lippincott, 1907), 3.

26. Quoted in Robert G. Frank, Jr., "Thomas Willis and His Circle: Brain and Mind in Seventeenth-Century Medicine," in *Languages of Psyche: Mind and Body in Enlightenment Thought*, ed. G. S. Rousseau (Berkeley: University of California Press, 1990), 118.

27. P. M. Rattansi, "Paracelsus and the Puritan Revolution."

28. Wear, "Religious Beliefs and Medicine," 155.

29. William Perkins, *The Works of . . . Mr. William Perkins* (London: John Legatt, 1616), 505. Some writers described Satan as a physician from whom witches and sorcerers derived their power. See Wear, "Religious Beliefs and Medicine," 168 n. 47.

30. The quote is from Ecclesiasticus 37:10, cited in Wear, "Religious Beliefs and Medicine," 158.

31. Ibid., 162–63.

32. Grell, "Plague, Prayer and Physic," 204.

33. George Thomson, *Galeno-Pale*, quoted in Charles Webster, "The Helmontian George Thomson and William Harvey," *Medical History* 15 (1971): 156.

34. Gouge's publisher was Edward Brewster.

35. Harold J. Cook, "Institutional Structures and Personal Belief in the London College of Physicians," in *Religio Medici: Medicine and Religion in Seventeenth Century England*, edited by O. P. Grell and Andrew Cunningham (Aldershot, U.K.: Scolar Press, 1996), 91.

36. John R. Guy, "The Episcopal Licensing of Physicians, Surgeons and Midwives," *Bulletin of the History of Medicine* 56 (1982): 529–33.

37. For the context of this famous phrase, see Mark Curtis, "The Hampton Court Conference and Its Aftermath, *History* 46 (1961): 1–16.

38. Cook, "Institutional Structures and Personal Belief," 94, 110.

39. Ibid., 94.

40. William Birken, "The Puritan Connections of Sir Edward Alston, President of the Royal College of Physicians, 1655–1666," *Medical History* 18 (1974): 370–74. Despite making a case for a Puritan takeover of the College by the 1640s, Birken acknowledges that the bond of upholding professional medical standards superseded partisan allegiance.

41. For the definitive work on the College's political descent, see Harold J. Cook, *The Decline of the Old Medical Regime in Stuart London* (Ithaca, N.Y.: Cornell University Press, 1986).

42. Charles Webster, "English Medical Reformers of the Puritan Revolution," *Ambix* 14 (1967): 17–22; Jonathan Scott, *England's Troubles* (Cambridge: Cambridge University Press, 2000), 254.

43. Webster, *Great Instauration,* 112–15.

44. David A. Reid, "Science and Pedagogy in the Dissenting Academies of Enlightenment Britain," Ph.D. diss. (University of Wisconsin–Madison, 1999), 49. For a definition of this category, see Margaret T. Hunt, *The Middling Sort: Commerce, Gender, and the Family in England, 1680–1780* (Berkeley: University of California Press, 1996), 15–21.

45. The Fellows of the College came from "non-gentle, plebeian, or clerical" ancestry: William Birken, "The Social Problem of the English Physician in the Early Seventeenth Century," *Medical History* 31 (1987): 205.

46. Reid, "Science and Pedagogy," 70. At least 38 sons of ejected or Dissenting ministers entered the medical profession during the late Stuart period.

47. Ellen Cotes printed Starkey's work. She was the widow of Richard Cotes and employed three presses, two apprentices, and nine pressmen: Plomer, *Dictionary 1641–1667,* 52. For more on Starkey and his ilk, see Webster, *The Great Instauration,* 273–88.

48. Noah Biggs, *Chymiatrophilos, mataeotechnia medicinae praxeos* (London: Edward Blackmore, 1650). See also Allen G. Debus, "Paracelsian Medicine: Noah Biggs and the Problem of Reform," in *Medicine in Seventeenth Century England,* ed. Allen G. Debus (Berkeley: University of California Press, 1974). The sniping rival chemist was William Johnson, himself the author of *Lexicon cymicum* (London: William Nealand, 1651).

49. Charles Webster, *Samuel Hartlib and the Advancement of Learning* (Cambridge: Cambridge University Press, 1970), 65–66. For implications on political discourse, see David Zaret, "Religion, Science and Printing in the Public Spheres in Seventeenth-Century England," in *Habermas and the Public Sphere,* ed. Craig Calhoun (Cambridge, Mass.: MIT Press, 1997), 212–35.

50. Webster, "English Medical Reformers," 39. For more on the connection between religion, the press, and Caroline government, see Thomas O'Malley, "Religion and the Newspaper Press, 1660–1685: A Study of the *London Gazette,*" in *The Press in English Society from the Seventeeth to Nineteenth Centuries,* ed. Michael Harris and Alan Lee (Rutherford, N.J.: Fairleigh Dickinson University Press, 1986), 25–46.

51. Grell, "Plague, Prayer and Physic," 208–9. Sheldon granted a license to practice medicine to William Lilly, called the "English Merlin" for his prophetical almanacs. A half-hearted Parliamentarian during the Civil War, Lilly often found himself after the Restoration accused of causing the calamities he predicted, like the Fire of 1666. He had influential friends like Elias Ashmole, who recommended his medical practice to Sheldon: *DNB.*

52. For more on them, see J. H. Aveling, *The Chamberlens and the Midwifery Forceps* (London: Churchill, 1882), 30–124; and "A Huguenot Surgeon," *Proceedings of the Huguenot Society of London* 17 (1942–43): 70–71.

53. Annals of the Royal College of Physicians, 10 and 24 January, 21 February 1617, LRCP.

54. Webster, "William Harvey and the Crisis of Medicine," 7. Webster mixes the troubles of the Chamberlen brothers, Peters elder and younger, into one Petrine case, when actually both of them had run-ins with the College of Physicians: for clarification, see Clark, *History of the Royal College of Physicians,* 1:236–38; *DNB.*

55. The Chamberlen-Delaune nexus, likely arising from their common French Huguenot origins, proved multifarious. Peter the younger was wed to Sara Delaune; Gideon Delaune, a royal apothecary, married Judith Chamberlen; and Paul Delaune, through the influence of Master Mercer Thomas Chamberlen, garnered an appointment at Gresham College.

56. Annals of the College of Physicians, vol. 3, f. 83b, LRCP.

57. Annals of the College of Physicians, vol. 3, fols. 144a–145a; vol. 4, f. 15b, LRCP; Peter Chamberlen, *A Voice in Rhama* (London: John Marshall, 1646). In the pamphlet, Chamberlen identifies himself as "one of His Majesty's physicians extraordinary."

58. Because of the coins given to the sick, records about the healing rituals of Henry VII and Henry VIII would have been kept in the Almonery books, now lost. Henry VII started the practice of giving a gold coin to those whom he touched. Edward VI touched occasionally, despite his disdain for superstitious images and idolatrous practices. Ironically, he contracted the virulent pulmonary form of tuberculosis. Marc Bloch, *The Royal Touch* (London: Routledge, 1973), 181, 189; Thomas M. Daniel, *Captain of Death: The Story of Tuberculosis* (Rochester, N.Y.: University of Rochester Press, 1997), 24. See also Keith Thomas, *Religion and the Decline of Magic* (New York: Penguin, 1985), 227–35.

59. Henry Hills was the Catholic printer who put out James's proclamation; at the time of the 1688 revolution, his printing house at Blackfriars and its contents were destroyed by an angry mob: Plomer et al., *Dictionaries 1557–1775*, 154–55.

60. Carolly Erickson, *Bloody Mary* (Garden City, N.Y.: Doubleday, 1978), 443.

61. Quoted in Bloch, *Royal Touch*, 182. Bloch noted that the coin's inscription had been "O Christ, Redeemer, save us by Thy cross" until Mary Tudor's reign.

62. Bloch, *Royal Touch*, 190.

63. Edward Allde published Clowes' *Artificiall Cure of the Struma* in 1602.

64. Bloch points out that "not a single genuine cramp ring has come down to us" and that ensuing generations doubted their secret virtues: *Royal Touch*, 190.

65. *Basilikon Doron*, James's essay on kingship, can be found in *King James VI and I: The Political Writings*, ed. Johann P. Somerville (Cambridge: Cambridge University Press, 1994).

66. Steven Shapin, *A Social History of Truth: Civility and Science in Seventeenth-Century England* (Chicago: University of Chicago Press, 1994), 200.

67. Bloch, *Royal Touch*, 191–92; Roger Lockyer, *James VI and I* (London: Longman, 1998), 202.

68. Bloch mentions sermons by Archbishop of Canterbury William Sancroft, pamphlets by John Bird, and an argument in favor of the royal touch for many ailments by one of the king's surgeons, John Browne: Bloch, *Royal Touch*, 211. Robert Boyle also lauded the efficacy of touching: see Raymond Crawfurd, *The King's Evil* (Oxford: Oxford University Press, 1911).

69. See Richard Wiseman, *Severall Chirurgicall Treatises* (London: printed by E. Flesher and John Macock, 1676), a 550–page opus dedicated to Charles II that deals with, among many other things, the King's Evil, and the best contemporary account, *Charisma Basilicon* (London: Thomas Newcomb for Samuel Lowndes, 1684) by John Browne, who enumerates 92,107 touched between 1660 and 1682.

70. J. C. Sainty and R. O. Bucholz, *Officials of the Royal Household, 1660–1837, Part One: Department of the Lord Chamberlain* (London: Institute of Historical Research, 1997), 84. Hugh Chamberlen had no medical degree until 1689, and that by *comitiis regiis*. Even though he was a royal doctor, Fellow of the Royal Society, and an acclaimed man-midwife, the College of Physicians refused to admit him until 1694; in fact, the Fellows were asked to consider a complaint against him in 1688 for causing the death of a pregnant woman to whom he administered four vomits, four purges, and three bleedings of eight ounces each. The latter was a powerful hydragogue, cathartic, and emmenagogue made from black hellebore. Mrs. Wilmer miscarried, experienced horrible diarrhea, and died. The College found Hugh Chamberlen guilty of malpractice and fined him £10: Annals of the College of Physicians, vol. 5, fols. 82b–83a, LRCP. Notwithstanding these incidents, Chamberlen continued in royal service to James II's queen and was summoned to attend her in 1688, but got there too late. Hugh Chamberlen's brother, Paul, was a quack who invented an anodyne necklace for children's teeth and women in labor.

71. William Walwyn, *A Touch-Stone for Physick* (London: J. Winter, 1667), 47–48. *Spirits Moderated* was published by J(ohn) C(lowes) for sale by William Larner. *Physick for Families* was published by J. Winter in 1669 for sale by Robert Horn; later editions appeared in 1674, 1681 and

1696. For more on Walwyn's medical tracts, see *The Writings of William Walwyn*, ed. Jack R. MeMichael and Barbara Taft (Athens: University of Georgia Press, 1989), 455–523.

72. See, for instance, Webster, *Great Instauration*.

73. Roy Porter, *Disease, Medicine and Society in England, 1550–1860* (London: Macmillan, 1987), 46.

74. See Harold J. Cook, "Physicians and the New Philosophy: Henry Stubbe and the Virtuosi-Physicians," in *The Medical Revolution of the Seventeenth Century*, ed. Roger French and Andrew Wear (Cambridge: Cambridge University Press, 1989), 246–71.

75. That charter gave the College full police powers over London medicine and added many new Fellows, some Catholic like the new king, others Nonconformists whom James tried to cultivate. The Glorious Revolution in 1688 threw the College's jurisdiction into confusion.

76. Thomas O'Dowde, *The Poor Man's Physician*, 3rd ed. (London: n.p., 1665). However, in an atmosphere less congenial to the charitable social attitudes of medico-religious reformers, that assembly quickly disintegrated.

77. Harold J. Cook, "The Society of Chemical Physicians, the New Philosophy, and the Restoration Court," *Bulletin of the History of Medicine* 61 (1987): 67–69. Cook suggests that because O'Dowde cast himself as a chemical physician, King Charles, a dabbler in chemistry, supported O'Dowde's claims; moreover, Charles issued royal licenses to a number of foreign quacks during this same period. See Leslie G. Matthews, "Licensed Mountebanks in Britain," *Journal of the History of Medicine* 19 (1964): 30–45.

78. For Sheldon's anti-Nonconformist tactics as Bishop of London, see Paul Seaward, "Gilbert Sheldon, the London Vestries, and the Defence of the Church," in *The Politics of Religion in Restoration England*, ed. Tim Harris, Paul Seaward, and Mark Goldie (Oxford: Basil Blackwell, 1990).

79. The 1662 Act of Uniformity restored to bishops their licensing privilege; they retained that right for another century, though the law itself was not repealed until 1948. Guy, "Episcopal Licensing of Physicians, Surgeons and Midwives," 541–42.

80. Mark Goldie found a similar lack of consistency in the allegiance controversy publications that followed the "Glorious Revolution." Several prominent Whig publishers put out Tory pamphlets and vice versa. Mark Goldie, "The Revolution of 1689 and the Structure of Political Argument," *Bulletin of Research in the Humanities* 93 (1980): 492–94.

81. John Archer, *Every Man His Own Doctor* (London: Peter Lillicrap, 1671). Archer, never licensed by the College of Physicians but named "chemical physician" to Charles II's court in 1671, sold nostrums and advertised his inventions. The government arrested Peter Lillicrap for seditious printing in 1662 and again in the mid-1670s: Richard Greaves, *Enemies under His Feet: Radicals and Nonconformists in Britain, 1664–1677* (Stanford, Calif.: Stanford University Press, 1990), 162, 228.

82. Bookman John Dunton reported that Darby "goes to heaven with the Anabaptists": John Dunton, *The Life and Errors of John Dunton* (London: S. Malthus, 1705), 247. See also Greaves, *Enemies under His Feet*, 168, 175, 179.

83. John Schroeder, *The Compleat Chymical Dispensatory in Five Books*, Englished by William Rowland, (London: John Darby, 1669).

84. François Mauriceau, *The Diseases of Women with Child and in Child-Bed*, 2nd ed. (London: John Darby, 1683).

85. Thomas Nevett, *A Treatise of Consumptions*, 2nd ed. (London: John Astwood, 1697).

86. Plomer, *Dictionary 1641–1667*, 92; Greaves, *Enemies under His Feet*, 173.

87. Leona Rostenberg, "Book Stalls of Duck Lane and Moorfields," in *The Library of Robert Hooke: The Scientific Book Trade of Restoration England* (Santa Monica, Calif.: Modoc Press, 1989), 49–65.

88. William Eamon points out that eventually some of the chemical physicians backed away from disseminating certain kinds of knowledge and that the Fellows of the Royal Society, ostensibly dedicated to public science, waxed ambivalent about divulging their secrets: Eamon, *Science and the Secrets of Nature* (Princeton, N.J.: Princeton University Press, 1994), 344.

89. Dunton, *Life and Errors*, 281.

90. Ibid., 216.

91. Women were quite active in London publishing, owing to the unusual acceptance of the widows and daughters of pressmen by the Stationers' Company. See Paula McDowell, *The Women of Grub Street: Press, Politics and Gender in the London Literary Marketplace* (Oxford: Clarendon Press, 1998).

92. Hindmarsh, thoroughly loyal to the Stuarts, was accused in 1680 of producing *The Presbyterians' Paternoster and Ten Commandments*, an anti-presbyterian piece by Thomas Asheden, purportedly published by "Tom Tell-Truth" in Westminster: Plomer, *Dictionaries 1557–1775*, 156–57.

93. Nicolas de Blegny, *The English Remedy or Talbor's Wonderful Secret for Cureing of Agues and Feavers* (London: Joseph Hindmarsh, 1682). Talbor had sold his "secret" to Louis XIV, who had it printed in French for his subjects. Hindmarsh had it "Englished" for his customers. For more on cinchona and its impact on the struggle for medical supremacy, see Rudolph E. Siegel and F.N.L. Poynter, "Robert Talbor, Charles II and Cinchona," *Medical History* 6 (1962): 82–85.

94. Grell, "Plague, Prayer and Physic," 205. For more on the phenomenon of secularization in English life, see C. John Sommerville, *The Secularization of Early Modern England* (New York: Oxford University Press, 1992).

95. See Eamon Duffy, "Valentine Greatrakes, the Irish Stroker: Miracle, Science and Orthodoxy in Restoration England," *Studies in Church History* 17 (1981): 251–73. Benjamin Harris, an ardent Protestant and critic of "popish" government, published Mrs. Fanshawe's claim to heal in 1681.

96. Anne's touching engendered patriotic enthusiasm, particularly among the Tories, who applauded the rebirth of regal protocol. Jonathan Swift, Tory propagandist and Anne's speechwriter, lauded the efficacy of the royal hand and denounced the excesses of skepticism in the souls of those who denied the truth of the matter. For more, see Furdell, *Royal Doctors*, passim.

97. Sommerville, *Secularization of Early Modern England*, 157.

98. Cook, "Institutional Structures and Personal Belief," 105; Mary Douglas, "The Construction of the Physician: A Cultural Approach to Medical Fashions," in *The Healing Bond: The Patient-Practitioner Relationship and Therapeutic Responsibility*, ed. Susan Budd and Ursula Sharma (London: Routledge, 1994), 25.

99. Thomas, *Religion and the Decline of Magic*, 790.

Notes for Chapter 5

1. See, for instance, David Noble, *World without Women: The Christian Clerical Culture of Western Science* (New York: Knopf, 1992) and Margaret Wertheim, *Pythagoras' Trousers: God, Physics, and the Gender Wars* (New York: Times Books, 1995). Jeanne Achterberg argues that the collapse of feminine wisdom in the healing arts was completed when Enlightenment scientists developed a methodology that lauded the masculine attributes of reason and objectivity. See Achterberg's *Woman as Healer* (Boston: Shambhala, 1990).

2. A number of scholars early in the development of women's studies sought to chronicle the lives of women and science and medicine from the ancient world to the present. Typical of that effort are Margaret Alic, *Hypatia's Heritage: The History of Women in Science from Antiquity through the Nineteenth Century* (Boston: Beacon Press, 1986) and Marilyn Bailey Ogilvie, *Women in Science: Antiquity through the Nineteenth Century* (Cambridge, Mass.: MIT Press, 1986). More recent work has criticized those attempts to shape women's ventures to meet male standards of accomplishment, thereby obscuring a genuine understanding of their careers. See Londa Schiebinger, *Nature's Body: Gender in the Making of Modern Science* (Boston: Beacon Press, 1995) and Lilian R. Furst, ed., *Women Healers and Physicians* (Lexington: University Press of Kentucky, 1997).

3. Sarah Hutton takes issue with this feminist critique of science, especially the interpretations of Baconian science by Evelyn Fox Keller, as a misreading of textual metaphors. See Hutton's "The Riddle of the Sphinx: Francis Bacon and the Emblems of Science," in *Women, Science and Medicine, 1500–1700,* ed. Lynette Hunter and Sarah Hutton (Stroud, England: Sutton Publishing, 1997), 7–28.

4. Although it was the ancient custom of London that the widows of livery company freemen became freewomen, few females were apprenticed or admitted by patrimony. Some London livery companies, like the Stationers, recognized the rights of daughters and widows to take apprentices and obtain loans, but the Barber-Surgeons and the Apothecaries did not.

5. C.R.B. Barrett, *History of the Society of the Apothecaries of London* (London: E. Stock, 1905), 64.

6. J. H. Bloom and R. R. James, *Medical Practitioners, 1529–1725* (Cambridge: Cambridge University Press, 1935), 11. For a full portrait of a seventeenth-century midwife, see Adrian Wilson, "Memorial of Eleanor Willughby," in *Women, Science and Medicine, 1500–1700,* ed. Lynette Hunter and Sarah Hutton (Stroud, England: Sutton Publishing, 1997), 138–77.

7. Nicholas Culpeper, *Directory for Midwives* (London: Peter Cole, 1651). The guide was reprinted several times, including a 1671 edition to correct "gross errors." The Rüff text was printed in England by Edward Griffin II for Simon Burton and sold by Thomas Alchorn, an unusual separation of the often comingled jobs of printer, publisher, and vendor.

8. Antonia Fraser, *The Weaker Vessel* (New York: Knopf, 1984), 447.

9. Thomas R. Forbes, "The Regulation of English Midwives in the Sixteenth and Seventeenth Centuries," *Medical History* 8 (1961): 241. For more on Cellier and six other Tudor-Stuart era women in health care, see Charlotte F. Otten, *English Women's Views: 1540–1700* (Miami: Florida International University Press, 1992).

10. See Jean Donnison, *Midwives and Medical Men: A History of Inter-Professional Rivalries and Women's Rights* (London: Heinemann, 1977). For a provocative take on the effeminate image of physicians and apothecaries, as well as the "danger [they faced] of being seen as too much part of the female world," see Margaret Pelling, "Compromised by Gender: The Role of the Male Medical Practitioner in Early Modern England," in *The Task of Healing: Medicine, Religion and Gender in England and the Netherlands, 1450–1800,* ed. Hilary Marland and Margaret Pelling (Rotterdam: Erasmus, 1996), 101–33.

11. Hugh Chamberlen, *Diseases of Women with Child and in Child-Bed* (London: John Darby, 1672).

12. The publishing tandem of Darby and Billingsley printed and sold Sharp's tome. Jane Sharp's 418–page manual went through several editions and modern reprints exist; see *The Midwives Book* (New York: Garland, 1985). Sharp advocated use of the eagle-stone, a hollow stone or fossil sometimes found in eagles' nests, "held near the privy parts to draw out the child and after burthen"; the stone could also be worn during pregnancy to prevent miscarriage. Her recommendation was echoed by apothecary Richard Andrews, who in correspondence with Margaret Cavendish, Duchess of Newcastle, prescribed this regimen for childbirth: "Tie an eagle-stone around your thigh to make labor easier, drink a powder of cassia, saffron, and borax to hasten labour, and drink cinnamon water." Historical Manuscripts Commission, *Thirteenth Report: The Manuscripts of His Grace, the Duke of Portland,* 4 vols. (London: HMSO, 1891), Appendix, Pt. 2, 123.

13. Mrs. Nihell in her *Treatise on the Art of Midwifery* (London: A. Morley, 1760) argued that in ordinary circumstances, midwifery should be confined to women practitioners: John Glaister, *Doctor William Smellie and His Contemporaries* (Glasgow: James Maclehose, 1894), 299.

14. For excerpts from the diary and commentary, see Rachell Weigall, "An Elizabethan Gentlewoman: The Journal of Lady Mildmay," *Quarterly Review* 215 (1911): 119–36. For an overview of gentlewomen and medicine, see Lynette Hunter, "Women and Domestic Medicine," in *Women, Science and Medicine, 1500–1700,* edited by Lynette Hunter and Sarah Hutton (Stroud, U.K.: Sutton Publishing, 1997), 89–107.

15. The green sickness or chlorosis was anemia. In her *Choice Manuall of Rare and Select Secrets in Physick and Chirurgerie* (London: W[illiam] J[arvis], 1653), which went through nineteen editions, the Countess advised mixing the sifted powder with rhubarb, taking it three times daily, and walking after the morning dosage. See the excerpt relating to the powder in Charlotte F. Otten, ed., *English Women's Voices, 1540–1800* (Miami: Florida International University Press, 1992), 184.

16. Patricia Phillips, *The Scientific Lady*, (New York: St. Martin's Press, 1990), 106.

17. Webster, *Great Instauration*, 255. Mrs. Ray's son was the naturalist, John Ray.

18. The derisive phrase, from a seventeenth-century Stafford apothecary, is quoted in Dorothy Porter and Roy Porter, *Patient's Progress: Doctors and Doctoring in Eighteenth-Century England* (Stanford: Stanford University Press, 1989), 24–25.

19. *The Family Physitian* was printed in 1696 by Henry Hills Jr., who in 1689 had succeeded to his father's share in the King's Printing House.

20. See the *Diary of Lady Margaret Hoby*, ed. Dorothy Meads (London: Routledge, 1930), *The Household Book of Lady Grisell Baillie* (Edinburgh: Scottish History Society, 1911), and Christina Hole, *The English Housewife in the Seventeenth Century* (London: Chatto and Windus, 1953). Lucinda Beier discusses Hoby as a case study of the woman healer in *Sufferers and Healers: The Experience of Illness in Seventeenth Century England* (London: Routledge and Kegan Paul, 1987).

21. An ardent anti-Papist, Harris repeatedly got into trouble with the authorities during the feverish days of the Popish plot; he was fined and pilloried over the 1681 printing of *A Protestant Petition*. Harris subsequently emigrated to Massachusetts, but ran afoul of the law there when he attempted to publish the first American newspaper, *The New England Primer*. He eventually returned to London in 1695 and resumed his career as a printer and seller: Plomer et al., *Dictionaries 1557–1775*, 144–45.

22. Margaret Pelling, "Thoroughly Resented? Older Women and the Medical Role in Early Modern London," in *Women, Science and Medicine, 1500–1700*, ed. Lynette Hunter and Sarah Hutton (Stroud, England: Sutton, 1997), 70–71. Pelling points out that the College had more difficulty accepting the practices of younger women than those of older ones.

23. Barberry used to be given as a cathartic for jaundice on account of the yellow color of its inner bark, a clear example of the so-called Doctrine of Signatures. The author thanks Dr. Walter Sneader and Micaela Sullivan-Fowler for this information.

24. Annals of the Royal College of Physicians, vol. 2, fols. 172b, 173a, and 6b, LRCP.

25. Ibid., fols. 158b and 182a, LRCP.

26. Ibid., fols. 69b, 72b, and 73a, LRCP. Eventually the College came to favor incorporation of examined midwives under the Fellows' supervision, but their endorsement bogged down in controversy: ibid., vol. 3, fol. 27a. See also Audrey Eccles, *Obstetrics and Gynaecology in Tudor and Stuart England* (London: Croom Helm, 1982), 67–70.

27. Both queens were Protestant daughters of English women and their rivals were not. (Elizabeth's Catholic half-sister, Mary I, was called a "Spanish Tudor;" Anne's Catholic half-brother, James, was the son of Mary of Modena.) By healing their scrofulous subjects a century apart, Elizabeth and Anne demonstrated their mystical legitimacy and genuine nationalism at a touch. Anne was the last monarch to do so. See Raymond Crawfurd, *The King's Evil* (Oxford: Clarendon Press, 1911).

28. Hunter, "Women and Domestic Medicine," 93.

29. Title page of *The Queen's Closet Opened*, transcribed by W. M. (London: Nathaniel Brook, 1655).

30. Lynette Hunter, "Sisters of the Royal Society: The Circle of Katherine Jones, Lady Ranelagh," in *Women, Science and Medicine, 1500–1700*, ed. Lynette Hunter and Sarah Hutton (Stroud, England: Sutton, 1997), 179–80. Lady Alethea's book, containing secret cures for "all sorts of infirmities," was printed for three London booksellers: Henry Twyford, Gabriell Bedell, and Nathaniel Ekins.

31. Quoted in Meads, *Diary of Lady Margaret Hoby*, 57–58.

32. A photograph of the "Great Picture" can be seen in Barbara Kiefer Lewalski, *Writing Women in Jacobean England* (Cambridge, Mass.: Harvard University Press, 1993), 124.

33. Lucy Hutchinson, *The Memoirs of Colonel Hutchinson* (London: J. M. Dent, 1965), 144. Her father was Sir Allen Apsley, Governor of the Tower of London, who saw to his daughter's meticulous education.

34. John Loftis, ed., *The Memoirs of Anne, Lady Halkett and Ann, Lady Fanshawe* (Oxford: Clarendon Press, 1979), 55–58; *The Autobiography of Lady Anne Halkett* (London: Camden Society, 1875), 62–67; and Otten, *English Women's Voices,* 177.

35. Simon Patrick was the licensing bishop for Elizabeth Strudwicke: Cap. I/3/1, West Sussex Record Office, Chichester.

36. Doreen A. Evenden, "Gender Differences in the Licensing and Practice of Female and Male Surgeons in Early Modern England," *Medical History* 42 (1998): 198–99. The York Barber-Surgeons' guild included women, such as Isabell Warwicke, apprenticed in 1572: R. A. Cohen, Introduction, in Charles Allen, *Operator for the Teeth* (London: Dawsons, 1969), iii.

37. Evenden, "Licensing and Practice of Female and Male Surgeons," 207.

38. Evenden calls Pernell "Elizabeth Penell [sic]" on some occasions and "Jane" on others: ibid., 209, 213. Pernell's testimonial, cited in Evenden, is twelve pages in length and in the Lambeth Palace Library, VX 1A/10/223.

39. A. L. Wyman, "The Surgeoness: The Female Practitioner of Surgery, 1400–1800," *Medical History* 28 (1984): 28, 36–37. See also Deborah Simonton, "Apprenticeship: Training and Gender in Eighteenth-Century England," in *Markets and Manufacture in Early Industrial Europe,* ed. Maxine Berg (New York: Routledge, 1991).

40. Lawson-Dick, *Aubrey's Brief Lives,* 161. John Aubrey reported that the men surgeons "envy and hate her." Mrs. Holder's husband was William Holder, canon of St. Paul's and Fellow of the Royal Society.

41. Maureen Bell, George Parfitt, and Simon Shepherd, eds., *Biographical Dictionary of English Women Writers, 1580–1720* (Boston: G. K. Hall and Company, 1990), 115.

42. *The Womans Almanack for . . . 1688,* quoted in ibid., 107. John Streater printed Jinner's almanacs for the Company of Stationers and John Miller did the honors for Holden's.

43. Ibid., 151.

44. For the varied world of metropolitan relicts, see Caroline M. Barron and Anne F. Sutton, eds., *Medieval London Widows, 1300–1500* (London: Hambledon Press, 1994).

45. Evenden, "Licensing and Practice of Female and Male Surgeons," 201; Amy Erickson, Introduction, in Alice Clark, *The Working Life of Women in the Seventeenth Century,* 4th ed. (London: Routledge, 1992), xxxii–xxxiii.

46. Stephen Pumfrey, "Who Did the Work? Experimental Philosophy and Public Demonstrators in Augustan England," *British Journal of the History of Science* 28 (1995): 133. The exclusion of women from public experimental science was exacerbated by the rise of paid professionals like Robert Hooke, by 1664 the Royal Society's Curator of Experiments: ibid., 135.

47. For more on Cavendish and her circle, see Frances Harris, "Living in the Neighbourhood of Science," and Sarah Hutton, "Anne Conway, Margaret Cavendish and Seventeenth-Century Scientific Thought," both in *Women, Science and Medicine, 1500–1700,* ed. Lynette Hunter and Sarah Hutton (Stroud, U.K.: Sutton Publishing, 1997), 198–217; 218–34.

48. Robert Latham, ed., *The Shorter Pepys* (Berkeley: University of California Press, 1985), 780–81. See also Sara Heller Mendelson, *The Mental World of Stuart Women: Three Studies* (Amherst: University of Massachusetts, 1987), 12–61; Wertheim, *Pythagoras' Trousers,* 102–3.

49. See the Epistle Dedicatory to "The Two Most Famous Universities of England," in *Philosophical and Physical Opinions,* 2nd ed. (London: William Wilson, 1663).

50. Thomas Vicary, *The Surgion's Directorie for Young Practitioners in Anatomie, Wounds and Cures* (London: printed by Thomas Fawcett and sold by James Nuthall, 1651); Leonard Sowerby, *The Ladies Dispensatory* (London: Robert Ibbitson, 1652).

51. Gervase Markham, *The English House-Wife* (London: George Sawbridge, 1675), 4, 35, 43.

The first version came out as *Countrey Contentments in Two Books*; part two was *The English House-Wife* (London: R. Jackson, 1615).

52. Gerald Dennis Meyer, *The Scientific Lady in England, 1650–1760* (Berkeley: University of California Press, 1955), 51–59. Dunton's success with the biweekly mercury and its successor, *The Athenian Oracle*, led in 1704 to the long-lived *Ladies' Diary*, a yearly almanac, and to a semiweekly sheet begun in 1718 called *The Free-Thinker*: ibid., 65.

53. Quoted in ibid., 78.

54. Ibid., 81–93. Meyer notes that scientific books and instruments were available from a number of London entrepreneurs, particularly at the shop of John Newbery.

55. Hunter, "Sisters of the Royal Society," 182–83.

56. Bathsua Makin, *An Essay to Revive the Antient Education of Gentlewomen* (London: 1673), quoted in Rob Iliffe and Frances Willmoth, "Astronomy and the Domestic Sphere," in *Women, Science and Medicine 1500–1700*, ed. Lynette Hunter and Sarah Hutton (Stroud, England: Sutton, 1997), 238. See also Phillips, *Scientific Lady*, 33–43; Vivian Salmon, "Bathsua Makin: A Pioneer Linguist and Feminist in Seventeenth-Century England," in *Neuere Forschungen zur Wortbildung und Historiographie der Linguistik*, ed. Brigitta Asbach-Schnitker and Johannes Roggenhofer (Tübingen: Tübinger Beiträge zur Linguistik, 1987).

57. *Mediatrix* was published in 1675 in octavo and sold by Henry Broome and John Leete. See the excerpt in Otten, *English Women's Voices*, 193–96.

58. Richard Jugge put out the 1565 edition of Rösslin, R. Watkins the 1598 version.

59. David Loades, *Mary Tudor* (Oxford: Basil Blackwell, 1989), 330. Loades points out that two Oxford colleges, Trinity and St. John's, were founded by private initiative during Mary's reign, as well as numerous schools, some by the queen herself and others by charity-minded subjects.

60. Annals of the Royal College of Physicians, vol. 2, fol. 7b, LRCP. A literary exposition of Margaret Kennix's story can be found in William Kerwin, "Where Have You Gone, Margaret Kennix: Seeking the Tradition of Healing Women in English Renaissance Drama," in *Women Healers and Physicians*, ed. Lilian R. Furst (Lexington: University Press of Kentucky, 1997), 93–113. Kerwin, not having consulted the College Annals, decries the "paucity of the historical record" and pronounces that "the outcome of this story is unknown:" ibid., 94–95.

61. Annals of the Royal College of Physicians, vol. 3, fol. 2b, LRCP. The Fellows fined her fifty-one shillings and imprisoned her for practicing medicine without a license.

62. Quoted in Gale E. Christianson, *In the Presence of the Creator: Isaac Newton and His Times* (New York: The Free Press, 1984), 483.

63. Ibid., 447–49; 486–91.

64. Eric Jameson, *The Natural History of Quackery* (Springfield, Ill.: C. C. Thomas, 1961), 80–81. Jonathan Swift wrote to Stella that at least Read "made good punch and served it in golden vessels." Quoted in *DNB*.

65. Nicholas Orme and Margaret Webster, *The English Hospital* (New Haven, Conn.: Yale University Press, 1995), 139, 141, 165.

66. Webster, *Great Instauration*, 40.

67. Orme and Webster, *English Hospital*, 182, 186–87, 226.

68. Peter Earle, refuting earlier scholarship by Alice Clark, points out that in the late seventeenth century "few widows carried on their husband's trade after his death" and that the great majority of them did "women's work": Peter Earle, "The Female Labour Market in London in the Late Seventeenth and Early Eighteenth Centuries," *Economic History Review* 2nd ser., 42 (1989): 339; Alice Clark, *The Working Life of Women in the Seventeenth Century* (London: Routledge, 1919), 10, 235. See also B. A. Holderness, "Widows in Pre-Industrial Society," in *Land, Kinship and Life-Cycle*, ed. R. M. Smith (Cambridge: Cambridge University Press, 1984), 423–42.

69. R. B. McKerrow, ed., *A Dictionary of Printers and Booksellers in England, Scotland, Ireland, and of Foreign Printers of English Books, 1557–1640* (London: Bibliographical Society, 1968), 6; see also R. B. McKerrow, "Edward Allde as a Typical Trade Printer," *The Library* 4th ser., 10 (1929): 121–62. McKerrow lists Mrs. Allde as a bookseller, but imprints clearly state that she printed books: *Five Centuries of Women Book Artists*, 7.

70. *Five Centuries of Women Book Artists*, 6. For continental comparisons, see Susan V. Lenkey, "Printers' Wives in the Age of Humanism," in *Gutenberg-Jahrbuch* (Mainz: Verlag de Gutenberg Gesellschaft, 1975), 331–37.

71. Paula McDowell, *The Women of Grub Street: Press, Politics, and Gender in the London Literary Marketplace, 1678–1730* (Oxford: Clarendon Press, 1998), 11, 15.

72. McKerrow, *Dictionary 1557–1640*, 182–83.

73. Allport and Thomas Dawks published François de Saint Andre's *Chymical Disceptations* in 1689, but "most of the finest books of the time [were] the work of the Bowyer press:" Plomer et al., *Dictionaries 1557–1775*, 44–45. For percentages of the imprints attributed to book trade families, see Giles Mandelbrote, "From the Warehouse to the Counting House: Booksellers and Bookshops in Late Seventeenth-Century London," in *A Genius for Letters*, ed. Robin Myers and Michael Harris (New Castle, Del.: Oak Knoll Press, 1995), 78.

74. Frances Hamill, "Some Unconventional Women before 1800: Printers, Booksellers, and Collectors," *Papers of the Bibliographic Society of America* 49 (1955): 304–6. Among the earliest "true-born" female English printers she identifies were Elisabeth Pickering Redman (fl. 1539), Katherine Hertford and Joan Sutton in the 1560s, and Joanne Jugge (fl. 1579).

75. Hannah Barker, *Newspapers, Politics and English Society, 1695–1855* (New York: Longman, 2000), 100; Maureen Bell, "Women in the London Book Trade 1557–1700," *Leipziger Jahrbuch zur Buchgeschichte* 6 (1996): 14, 24–25. Bell acknowledges that most of these 300 or so women were active after 1640: Bell, Parfitt, and Shepherd, *Biographical Dictionary*, 288.

76. Lists of the Company's master printers for 1668, 1675, 1686, and 1705 include several females, mostly widows of liverymen: Michael Treadwell, "A List of English Master Printers," *The Library* 6th ser., 4 (1982): 57–61; Hannah Barker, "Women, Work, and the Industrial Revolution: Female Involvement in the English Printing Trades," in *Gender in Eighteenth-Century England*, ed. Hannah Barker and Elaine Chalus (London: Longman, 1998), 99. Compare the problems faced by women in the Barber-Surgeons' guild: Evenden, "Licensing and Practice of Female and Male Surgeons," 201–2.

77. Martha Driver, "Women Printers and the Page, 1477–1541," in *Gutenberg-Jahrbuch* (Mainz: Verlag de Gutenberg-Gesellschaft, 1998), 140.

78. Bell, "Women in the London Book Trade," 15.

79. Hamill, "Some Unconventional Women," 305–6. Hamill notes that an apprentice became a master printer if he married into a licensed business.

80. Richard Grassby reports that five guilds in early Tudor London specifically excluded women, and only a handful of girls actually apprenticed; Grassby, *The Business Community of Seventeenth-Century England* (Cambridge: Cambridge University Press, 1995), 150, 318. See also Mary Prior, "Women and the Urban Economy, 1500–1800," in *Women in English Society, 1500–1800*, ed. Mary Prior (London: Methuen, 1985), 103; Judith M. Bennett, *Ale, Beer, and Brewsters in England* (Oxford: Oxford University Press, 1996), 62–64, 68, 71; and Lorna Weatherill, "A Possession of One's Own: Women and Consumer Behavior in England, 1660–1740," *Journal of British Studies* 25 (1986): 148.

81. *Five Centuries of Women Book Artists*, 8.

82. McKerrow, *Dictionary 1557–1640*, 271–72. Jacklin Vautrollier, a Huguenot fugitive from France, took out letters of denization with her first husband in 1562, probably five years before Richard Field was even born. Her son Manasses, a stationer and bookbinder, opened his first shop in 1587, and therefore was likely a contemporary of his stepfather.

83. Amy Louise Erickson, *Women and Property in Early Modern England* (London: Routledge, 1993), 157. Erickson has found that between 63 and 89 percent of married men named their wives either sole or joint executrix; wealthy men, however, were less likely to do so.

84. Erickson remarks on the high incidence of single women, particularly widows, in seventeenth-century England: see her Introduction, xxxv, and *Women and Property*, 225. Barker recounts several instances of married women in the book trade working independently of their husbands: Barker, "Women, Work and the Industrial Revolution," 99.

85. Driver, "Women Printers and the Page," 139.

86. Driver notices that Pickering uses the emphatic identification of the book's maker, "by me," when she refers to herself by her first name or when she employs her maiden name: ibid., 151.

87. *Five Centuries of Women Book Artists: Printers and Engravers, 1478–1984* (Urbana-Champaign: University of Illinois, 1992), 5–6. The exhibit from which this catalogue derives displayed one of the titles printed by Elizabeth Pickering, a 1541 issue of the Magna Carta.

88. Driver reports that Middleton used Pickering's title pages and ornaments and reproduced exactly several of her copies: ibid., 151.

89. Young, *Annals of the Barber-Surgeons,* 536; Fielding Garrison, *Introduction to the History of Medicine,* 4th ed. (Philadelphia: W. B. Saunders, 1929), 227.

90. D. F. McKenzie, *Stationers' Company Apprentices 1605–1640* (Charlottesville: Bibliographical Society of the University of Virginia, 1961), 16; *Stationers' Company Apprentices, 1641–1700* (Oxford: Oxford Bibliographical Society, 1974), 68.

91. Businesses run by females were not necessarily minor. Widow Mary Simmons presided over large premises with thirteen hearths in Aldersgate Street from 1656 to 1667. Another remarkable business was run by Anne Maxwell, printer near Baynard's Castle from 1665 to 1676. The widow of David Maxwell, she had two presses, three compositors, three pressmen, but no apprentices. See Plomer, *Dictionary 1641–1667,* 164, 125.

92. Mary Clark took seven apprentices between 1681 and 1686: McKenzie, *Stationers' Company Apprentices, 1641–1700,* 32.

93. Other categories besides politics and religion included almanacs (8.1%), literature and music (11.5%), and biography and history (4.9%): Judith E. Gardner, "Women in the Book Trade, 1641–1700," in *Gutenberg-Jahrbuch* (Mainz: Verlag der Gutenberg-Gesellschaft, 1978), 346.

94. Notable female printers in Augustan Age London would include Sarah Malthus, Dorman Newman's daughter and the widow of printer Thomas Malthus; Sarah Passenger, widow of Thomas; and Hannah Sawbridge, widow of George. Henry Plomer reports on nearly a hundred women in the book trade for this period throughout Britain, most of them in London, but he did not include them all. Clearly, more research needs to be done on this topic.

95. Charles Webster, "English Medical Reformers of the Puritan Revolution," *Ambix* 14 (1967): 18. See also Jonathan Sanderson, "Nicholas Culpeper and the Book Trade: Print and Promotion of Vernacular Medical Knowledge, 1649–65," Ph.D. thesis, University of Leeds, 1999.

96. Elizabeth Grey, Countess of Kent, *A Choice Manual or Rare and Select Secrets in Physick and Chyrurgery* (London: G[ertrude] D[awson], 1653). Included in later editions were "exquisite ways of preserving, conserving, and candying" and information on Gascon powder and *lapis contra yarvam.* Between 1649 and 1666 Maureen Bell counts eighty-eight imprints of Mrs. Dawson, whose shop employed six apprentices: Bell, "Women in the English Book Trade," 34.

97. Peter Isaac, "Pills and Print," in *Medicine, Mortality and the Book Trade,* ed. Robin Myers and Michael Harris (New Castle, Del.: Oak Knoll Press, 1998), 25.

98. Maureen Bell, "Hannah Allen and the Development of a Puritan Publishing Business, 1646–51," *Publishing History* 26 (1989), 45; Plomer, *Dictionary 1641–1667,* 170; and Plomer, *Dictionary 1668–1725,* 163. For medical advertising by women, see Patricia Crawford, "Printed Advertisements for Women Medical Practitioners in London, 1670–1710," *Society for the Social History of Medicine Bulletin* 35 (1984): 66–70.

99. Dunton, *Life and Errors,* 230; BL Harley 5931 (93). Dunton's publisher for this book was Sarah Malthus and later, down on his luck, he worked as a hireling for Sarah Popping and Ann Dodd.

100. Dunton, *Life and Errors,* 213.

101. Paula McDowell asserts that while there was some private solidarity among women in the book trade, distaff workers could not "organize for their protection and advancement on an institutional level": McDowell, *Women of Grub Street,* 95. Susannah Miller married bookseller William Laycock, who carried on her father's tradition of handling quality volumes. In 1710 Charles Tooker prepared a sale catalogue of the Miller collection, said to date from 1600, with a dedicatory epistle by Laycock.

102. For more on the Sawbridge matter, see Cyprian Blagden, *The Stationers' Company: A History* (London: George Allen and Unwin, 1960).

103. Printed on affordable octavos, Culpeper's *The English Physician Enlarged* was sold at Thomas Malthus's shop in the Poultry.

104. Like *The English House-Wife*, *A Way to Get Wealth* went through multiple editions, some of the earlier ones published by John Harrison, twelve in total by the time of George Sawbridge's issue of the tome in 1668, thirty years after Markham's death.

105. PROB 11/382, ff.53r-54v; PROB 6/56, f.89r, Public Record Office, London. Blagden erroneously reported in his history of the Stationers' Company that Mrs. Sawbridge died intestate, but her will meticulously lays out the distribution of a huge estate to a son (who also died in 1686) and four daughters. She was not alone in compiling a fortune from print; Thomas Guy made enough money as a publisher and investor to found Guy's Hospital, opened in 1726.

106. The quotation is usually attributed to Sydenham, based on his opinion in *Observationes medicae*, published in 1676, but may in fact be John Locke's; Robert L. Martensen, "'Habit of Reason': Anatomy and Anglicanism in Restoration England," *Bulletin of the History of Medicine* 66 (1992): 533 n99. For more on Sydenham, see Kenneth Dewhurst, *Dr. Thomas Sydenham* (Berkeley: University of California Press, 1966).

107. The preface from the fourth edition (1708), quoted in Isaac, "Pills and Print," 29. The British Library's first copy is dated 1714, published by Richard Wilkin.

108. She married John Darby and continued in the trade, successfully organizing an arcane chain of distribution for Darby's opposition pamphlets designed to protect him from prosecution for seditious printing. Bell, "Women in the English Book Trade," 27.

109. Maureen Bell, "'Her Usual Practices': The Later Career of Elizabeth Calvert," *Publishing History* 35 (1994): 51. Another female printer of almanacs was Mary Roberts. She put out John Partridge's *Merlinus liberatus*, an almanac for 1706.

110. Michael Treadwell speculates that the Bennets' shop was a "sort of mother house for a small group of Catholic printers:" Treadwell, "London Printers and Printing Houses in 1705," *Publishing History* 7 (1980): 13.

111. Dunton, *Life and Errors*, 223.

112. Hamill, "Some Unconventional Women," 309–10.

113. My finding that no consistent pattern in medical publishing existed among London bookmen and women when factoring in political, religious, or jurisdictional preferences echoes that of Mark Goldie in the partisan arena of the "Glorious Revolution." See his seminal article, "The Revolution of 1689 and the Structure of Political Argument," *Bulletin of Research in the Humanities* 83 (1980): 473–564.

114. McDowell, *Women of Grub Street*, 5–6.

115. Richard Cust, "News and Politics in Early Seventeenth-Century England," *Past and Present* 112 (1986): 87, 90. Cust concludes that the Whig historians were correct in their assessment that news roiled political waters.

116. Andrew Wear argues that most medical publishing was cross-cultural: Wear, *Knowledge and Practice*, 7.

117. Bennett, *Ale, Beer, and Brewsters*, 152; Barker, "Women, Work and the Industrial Revolution," 84.

118. Margaret R. Hunt, *The Middling Sort: Commerce, Gender, and the Family in England, 1680–1780* (Berkeley: University of California Press, 1996), 133. However, these late eighteenth-century businesswomen may not have been in the Stationers' Company.

119. H. R. Plomer, et al., *Dictionary of the Printers and Booksellers Who Were at Work in England, Scotland and Ireland, 1726–1775* (Oxford: Oxford Bibliographical Society, 1932); Ian Maxted, *The London Book Trades 1775–1800* (Old Woking, England: Dawson, 1977), cited in C. J. Mitchell, "Women in the Eighteenth-Century Book Trades," in *Writers, Books and Trade*, ed. O. M. Brack Jr. (New York: AMS Press, 1994), 31. For comparison of distaff apprentice numbers, see McKenzie, *Stationers' Company Apprentices, 1641–1700* and *1701–1800* (Oxford: Oxford Bibliographical Society, 1979).

120. That same census put at 2,035 the number of female booksellers and bookbinders, a figure, however, that includes employers and employed; 8,873 men claimed the occupation: J. Ramsay

MacDonald, ed., "Women in the Printing Trades," in *The English Working Class*, ed. Standish Meacham (New York: Garland, 1980), 17.

121. McDowell, *Women of Grub Street*, 30, 117. Felicity Hunt has affirmed that women "had always been considered marginal" in the trade, but that "mechanization and the growth of unions provided new arenas for industrial antagonism between male and female workers": Felicity Hunt, "The London Trade in the Printing and Binding of Books," *Women's Studies International Forum* 6 (1983): 517.

Notes for Chapter 6

1. The *Spectator* (#28), 2 April 1711.

2. Cecil A. Meadows, *Trade Signs and Their Origin* (London: Routledge and Kegan Paul, 1957), 114–19.

3. Juanita Burnby, "Pharmaceutical Advertisement in the Seventeenth and Eighteenth Centuries," *European Journal of Marketing* 22/4 (1988): 29.

4. C. Paul Christianson, *Memorials of the Book Trade in Medieval London* (Cambridge: D. S. Brewer, 1987), 1–2, 17–19. The Bridge House records supply extensive data about members of the trade and contain extensive artifacts.

5. Margaret Spufford, *Small Books and Pleasant Histories* (Cambridge: Cambridge University Press, 1981), 111–12.

6. Peter Blayney has found no evidence that transitory stalls existed after 1600 in St. Paul's Churchyard: Peter W. M. Blayney, *The Bookshops in Paul's Cross Churchyard* (London: Bibliographical Society, 1990), 11.

7. Blayney, *Bookshops in Paul's Cross*, 10–11.

8. The *Spectator* (#403), 12 June 1712.

9. Blanche B. Elliott, *A History of English Advertising* (London: Business Publications Limited, 1962), 11.

10. Daniel Defoe, *The Complete English Tradesman* (London: C. Rivington, 1726), 98–100.

11. Blayney, *Bookshops in Paul's Cross*, 5, 18–19.

12. Christianson, *Memorials of the Book Trade*, 48–53.

13. Blayney, *Bookshops in Paul's Cross*, 13–17.

14. *The Reader Revealed*, ed. Sabrina Alcorn Baron (Washington, D.C.: Folger Shakepeare Library, 2001), 122; McKerrow, *Dictionary 1557–1640*, 24, 256; Plomer, *Dictionary 1641–1667*, 12, 144, 155–56.

15. Blayney takes issue with Cyprian Blagden's identification of the early hall (before 1554) as on the west side of Milk Street: Blayney, *Bookshops in Paul's Cross*, 95; Blagden, *The Stationers' Company*, 224–25.

16. Nashe quoted in Johns, *Nature of the Book*, 67; Earle quoted in Jean-Christophe Agnew, *Worlds Apart: The Market and Theatre in Anglo-American Thought, 1550–1750* (Cambridge: Cambridge University Press, 1986), 86–87.

17. Richard Flecknoe, *Miscellania* (London: T. R., 1653), 140.

18. Johns, *Nature of the Book*, 68.

19. The *Spectator* (#10), 12 March 1711. For commentary by Steele on coffeehouses, see *The Spectator* (#49), 26 April 1711 and (#50), 28 August 1711.

20. Johns, *Nature of the Book*, 66–67; 600.

21. John Brewer, *The Pleasures of the Imagination: English Culture in the Eighteenth Century* (New York: Farrar, Straus and Giroux, 1997), 36.

22. *London Encyclopaedia*, 618. The Poultry was famed for its great number of taverns.

23. For more on the "Long Shop" and the Alldes, see Henry R. Plomer, "The Long Shop in the Poultry, *Bibliographica* 2 (1896): 61–80; and R. B. McKerrow, "Edward Allde as a Typical Trade Printer," *The Library*, 4th ser., no. 2 (Sept. 1929): 121–62; and McKerrow, *Dictionary 1557–1640*, 6, 231–32.

24. R. T. Gunther, "The Diary of Robert Hooke," *Early Science in Oxford* 10 (1935): 223.

25. T. F. Reddaway, *The Rebuilding of London after the Great Fire* (London: Edward Arnold, 1951), 37, 293–94. For discussion and diagrams of cuts to widen the Poultry and Grocers' Alley made from existing plots of land, see Peter Mills and John Oliver, *Survey of Building Sites in the City of London after the Great Fire of 1666*, 5 vols. (London: London Topographical Society, 1962–67) 1: xxiii; 4: 21, 38, 74v, 88v, and 122.

26. Johns, *Nature of the Book*, 124.

27. Cited in Giles Mandelbrote, "From the Warehouse to the Counting-House: Booksellers and Bookshops in Late Seventeenth-Century London," in *A Genius for Letters: Booksellers and Bookselling from the Sixteenth to the Twentieth Centuries*, ed. Robin Myers and Michael Harris (New Castle, Del.: Oak Knoll Press, 1995), 50. See also Johns, *Nature of the Book*, 69–71.

28. For a catalogue raisonné, see Alexander Globe, *Peter Stent, London Printseller 1642–1665* (Vancouver: University of British Columbia Press, 1985).

29. Timothy Clayton, *The English Print, 1688–1802* (New Haven, Conn.: Yale University Press, 1997), 7; Sarah Tyacke, *London Map-Sellers, 1660–1720* (Tring, England: Map Collector Publications, 1978), xxi.

30. Brewer, *Pleasures of the Imagination*, 164–66.

31. For more on the Kit-Kat Club, which flourished between 1696 and 1720, and other discriminating groups, see Brewer, *Pleasures of the Imagination*, 41–50.

32. Dunton, *Life and Errors*, 239. Dunton had a shop located in the Poultry at the sign of the Raven.

33. Grassby, *Business Community of Seventeenth-Century England*, 237.

34. Dunton, *Life and Errors*, 87.

35. Johns, *Nature of the Book*, 76.

36. D. F. McKenzie, ed., *Stationers' Company Apprentices, 1641–1700* (Oxford: Oxford Bibliographical Society, 1974), 120, 126. For traditional practices in the early printing industry, see John Rule, "Against Innovation?: Custom and Resistance in the Workplace," in *Popular Culture in England, c. 1500–1800*, ed. Tim Harris (New York: St. Martin's Press, 1995), 170–71.

37. D. J. McKitterick, *A History of Cambridge University Press: Printing and the Book Trade in Cambridge, 1534–1698* (Cambridge: Cambridge University Press, 1992), 268; Michael Clapham, "Printing," in *A History of Technology*, ed. Charles Singer et al., 3 vols., (Oxford: Clarendon Press, 1957) 3:404. Clapham reminds us that average printing in 1700 was debased in quality and should not be compared to the 300 or so sheets a day which earlier printers were proud to have created.

38. Joseph Moxon, *Mechanic Exercises on the Whole Art of Printing* (London: Printed for Joseph Moxon on the Westside of Fleet-Ditch at the Sign of the Atlas, 1683–84), facsimile reprint, ed. H. Davis and H. Carter, 2nd ed. (London: Oxford University Press, 1962).

39. Plomer, *Dictionary 1641–1667*, 134. James Moxon sometimes published with his brother.

40. D. F. McKenzie, *Cambridge University Press, 1696–1712: A Bibliographical Study*, 2 vols. (Cambridge: Cambridge University Press, 1966) 1:18.

41. Moxon, *Mechanic Exercises*, 45.

42. According to Moxon's drawings, the Blaeu press used an iron hose, not a wooden one, had different catches for the bar, and the height of the gallows was adjustable. See the images in Johns, *Nature of the Book*, 86.

43. Johns, *Nature of the Book*, 87. Moxon's sketch of a compositor's cases is on *ibid.*, 86.

44. Moxon, *Mechanic Exercises*, 246–47. For more on proofing, see Percy Simpson, *Proof-Reading in the Sixteenth, Seventeenth and Eighteenth Centuries* (Oxford: Oxford University Press, 1970).

45. W. W. Greg, *A Companion to Arber* (Oxford: Clarendon Press, 1967), 142. I thank Ian Gadd for this reference.

46. Michael Harris, "Printers' Diseases," in *Medicine, Mortality, and the Book Trade*, ed. Robin Myers and Michael Harris (New Castle, Del.: Oak Knoll Press, 1998), 2–3.

47. Things only got worse in the trade. Printers' death rates in the 1850s were twice that of

agricultural workers and their levels of mortality induced by consumption double that of equivalent age groups in all of London: Harris, "Printers' Diseases," 5.

48. Thomas Oliver, "Lead and Its Compounds," in *Dangerous Trades*, ed. Thomas Oliver (London: E. P. Dutton, 1902), 151.

49. Johns, *Nature of the Book*, 111. Coffee was not the only beverage quaffed at coffeehouses. Customers ordered hot chocolate, wine, brandy, and punch, all served from a small bar in the main room.

50. Mark Knights, *Politics and Public Opinion in Crisis, 1678–81* (Cambridge: Cambridge University Press, 1994), 172–73; and *The Character of a Coffee-House* (London: J. Edwin, 1673), 1, cited in Johns, *Nature of the Book*, 111.

51. Brewer, *Pleasures of the Imagination*, 183.

52. For more on the coffeehouse phenomenon, see Alison Olson, "Coffee House Lobbying," *History Today* 41 (Jan. 1991): 35–42; R. B. Walker, "The Newspaper Press in the Reign of William III," *Historical Journal* 17 (1974): 702; Peter Clark and Paul Slack, *English Towns in Transition, 1500–1700* (Oxford: Oxford University Press, 1976), 74; John and Linda Pelzer, 'The Coffee Houses of Augustan London," *History Today* 32 (Oct. 1982): 40–48; and Steve Pincus, "Coffee Politicians Does Create," *Journal of Modern History* 67 (1995): 807–35. Johns dismisses without documentation the notion that by custom if not law, women were excluded from the premises: *Nature of the Book*, 112.

53. Brought to England in 1652, chocolate enlivened menus thereafter; the Cocoa Tree Chocolate House came into existence in the 1690s. Garraway's started up in 1669 as an auction house, probably with fur sales for the Hudson's Bay Company, and within a decade Thomas Garraway sold and retailed tea there for £10 a pound. Garraway's was also famous for cherry wine, sherry, and punch: *London Encyclopaedia*, 187, 303, 332, 714.

54. Quoted in Johns, *Nature of the Book*, 113. The 1675 proclamation closing London's coffeehouses had to be withdrawn a few days after it was issued due to general public outcry. Charles II had underestimated the attachment Londoners had for their favorite hangouts.

55. Dunton, *Life and Errors*, 70.

56. Johns, *Nature of the Book*, 109–11.

57. Paul J. Voss, "Books for Sale: Advertising and Patronage in Late Elizabethan England," *Sixteenth Century Journal* (1998); Marjorie Plant, *The English Book Trade*, 3rd ed. (London: George Allen and Unwin, 1974), 248. For a discussion of shopping and the interior space of shops, see Elizabeth Kowaleski-Wallace, *Consuming Subjects* (New York: Columbia University Press, 1997), 75–82.

58. David Cressy, "Literacy in Context: Meaning and Measurement in Early Modern England," in *The Consumption of Culture, 1600–1800*, ed. Ann Bermingham and John Brewer (London: Routledge, 1995), 307, 310, 314.

59. Richard Baxter, *A Christian Directory* (London: Robert White, 1673), 548, 582.

60. Margaret R. Hunt, *The Middling Sort: Commerce, Gender and the Family in England, 1680–1780* (Berkeley: University of California Press, 1996), 85. See also David Cressy, *Literacy and the Social Order: Reading and Writing in Tudor and Stuart England* Cambridge: Cambridge University Press, 1980), 176–77; Peter Earle, "The Female Labour Market in London in the Late Seventeenth and Early Eighteenth Centuries," *Economic History Review* (2nd series) 42 (1989): 335; and Jonathan Barry, "Literacy and Literature in Popular Culture," in *Popular Culture in England, c. 1500–1800*, ed. Tim Harris (New York: St. Martin's Press, 1995), 80.

61. Susan R. Suleiman, Introduction, in *The Reader in the Text: Essays on Audience and Interpretation*, edited by Suleiman and Inge Crosman (Princeton, N.J.: Princeton University Press, 1980), 3–4.

62. James Raven, Helen Small, and Naomi Tadmor, eds., Introduction, in *The Practice and Representation of Reading in England* (Cambridge: Cambridge University Press, 1996), 5–7.

63. Lorna Weatherill, "The Meaning of Consumer Behaviour in Late Seventeenth-and Early

Eighteenth-Century England," in *Comsumption and the World of Goods,* ed. John Brewer and Roy Porter (London: Routledge, 1993), 207.

64. Lorna Mui and Hoh-cheung Mui, *Shops and Shopkeeping in Eighteenth Century England* (London: Routledge, 1989), 40. See also James Carrier, *Gifts and Commodities* (London: Routledge, 1995), chapter 3. Carrier compares the earliest reasonable statistics from a government survey of 1769, which showed that for England and Wales as a whole there were 43.3 people per shop and 30 per shop for London, with a United States survey from 1840 finding about 290 people per shop.

65. *Shorter Pepys,* 493 (1 June 1665); 706 (24 December 1666). With the increased production of print, many publishers accumulated large inventories stored in a separate facility. In the 1660s Charles Tias had 90,000 books in his London warehouse ready to be dispatched to booksellers: Craig Muldrew, *The Economy of Obligation: The Culture of Credit and Social Relations in Early Modern England* (New York: St. Martin's Press, 1998), 19.

66. Grassby, *Business Community of Seventeenth-Century England,* 63.

67. Ibid., 165.

68. *Case of the Inhabitants of the Town and Parish of Croyden* (London: n.p., 1673) 2, 8–9, cited in Johns, *Nature of the Book,* 140; Peter Earle, *City Full of People* (London: Methuen, 1994), 66. For more on shoplifting, see Richard Head, *The Canting Academy* (London: F. Leach, 1673), 53, 106; for transported prisoners, see Abbot E. Smith, *Colonists in Bondage: White Servitude and Convict Labor in America, 1607–1776* (Chapel Hill: University of North Carolina Press, 1947).

69. Rostenberg, "John Martyn," 20. Rostenberg calls Martyn "the outstanding publisher and bookseller of Restoration science": ibid.,25.

70. Arber, *Term Catalogues* 2:642.

71. Dunton, *Life and Errors,* 214.

72. *Shorter Pepys,* 651 (13 August 1666).

73. Ibid., 778 (27 May 1667); 586 (19 February 1666). See also Plomer, *Dictionary 1641–1667,* 141.

74. Stow quoted in Steve Rappaport, *Worlds within Worlds: Structures of Life in Sixteenth-Century London* (Cambridge: Cambridge University Press, 1989), 84.

75. Plant, *English Book Trade,* 52–56.

76. Weatherill, "Meaning of Consumer Behaviour," 219, 223.

77. Cressy, *Literacy and the Social Order,* 49.

78. Lorna Weatherill, *Consumer Behaviour and Material Culture in Britain, 1660–1760* London: Routledge, 1988), 44–47.

79. Weatherill, "Meaning of Consumer Behaviour," 225.

80. Joyce Ellis, "On the Town: Women in Augustan England," *History Today* 45 (December 1995): 22. For more on women as readers in the Augustan Age, see Kathryn Shevelow, *Women and Print Culture* (London: Routledge, 1989), 27–37; Hunt, *Middling Sort,* 85.

81. Distribution by hawkers did not necessarily indicate that a publication was aimed at the literate poor. Some newspapers distributed on the streets appealed principally to politicians and the professional class. Applying the Flesch Reading scale to the *Current Intelligence* and the *London Gazette,* B. I. Diamond has determined that both publications focused on a highly literate category of Londoners, roughly equivalent to those with a ninth-or tenth-grade education today. Standard writing in the United States in the 1990s equated approximately to the seventh-grade level. The author thanks Professor Diamond for use of his unpublished manuscript, "A Lively Presenter of News: Henry Muddiman, the *Current Intelligence* and Its Rival, the *London Gazette,* in Restoration England," presented at the Southern Conference on British Studies, Atlanta 1997.

82. Joan Thirsk, *Economic Policy and Projects: The Development of a Consumer Society in Early Modern England* (Oxford: Clarendon Press, 1978), 123–24; Barry, "Literacy and Literature," 80–81. Besides publishers catering to the wealthy and the literate poor, the industry also satisfied "every part of bourgeois society:" self-improvement books, political ephemera, periodicals, literary magazines, and the novel, complete with middle class hero or heroine. Peter Earle, *The Making of the English Middle Class* (Berkeley: University of California Press, 1989), 10.

83. Brewer, *Pleasure of the Imagination*, 174.

84. For more on the precarious life of the professional writer, see Earle, *Making of the English Middle Class*, 74–75. Earle calls the "demi-monde" of writers and printers, a "raffish section of London society." For the generation after Newman, see Pat Rogers, *Grub Street* (London: Methuen, 1972) and Pat Rogers, "The Writer and Society," in *The Eighteenth Century*, ed. Pat Rogers (New York: Holmes and Meier, 1978).

85. Edmund Coote, *The English Schoolmaster* (London: A. Maxwell, 1670), quoted in *Reader Revealed*, 25.

86. Evidently, reading black letter was a more basic skill than reading roman: Keith Thomas in "The Meaning of Literacy in Early Modern England" discusses the notion of "black letter literacy." See *The Written Word: Literacy in Transition*, ed. Gerd Bauman (Oxford: Oxford University Press, 1986), 99; *Reader Revealed*, 26.

87. McKerrow, *Edward Allde*, 134.

88. Peter Isaac, "Pills and Print," in *Medicine, Mortality and the Book Trade*, ed. Robin Myers and Michael Harris (New Castle, Del.: Oak Knoll Press, 1998), 39. The earliest examples given by Isaac for a bookman who arranged the manufacturing, advertising, and distribution of panaceas are in the 1720s.

89. She also points out that these distinctions may have been more in the mind of the physician than in the patient: Mary E. Fissell, *Patients, Power, and the Poor in Eighteenth-Century Bristol* (Cambridge: Cambridge University Press, 1991), 44.

90. Roy Porter, *Health for Sale: Quackery in England, 1650–1850* (Manchester: Manchester University Press, 1989), 142.

91. Harold J. Cook, "Sir John Colbatch and Augustan Medicine: Experimentalism, Character and Entrepreneurialism," *Annals of Science* 47 (1990): 478.

92. William Cowper, "An Account of Some Experiments Lately Made on Dogs and of the Effects of Mr. John Colbatch's Styptic on Humane Bodies," *Philosophical Transactions of the Royal Society* 18/208 (February 1693/94): 42.

93. Ibid., 44.

94. Cook, "Sir John Colbatch," 483–84.

95. Colbatch, *Some Farther Considerations concerning Alkali and Acid* (London: Brown, 1696), quoted in Cook, "Sir John Colbatch," 486.

96. An advertisement from *The Post Man* (20–23 March 1697), cited in Cook, "Sir John Colbatch," 487 n. 64.

97. See Richard Boulton, *An Examination of John Colbatch and His Treatise of the Gout* (London: Thomas Bennett, 1699). Boulton also was hired to attack Johannes Groeneveldt; see the epilogue.

98. Coward's book was put out by Timothy Childe, who stocked his author's tinctura sanitatis for interested customers.

99. John Colbatch, *Novum Lumen Chirurgicum* (London: Daniel Brown, 1695), 81. See William Cole, *A Physico-Medical Essay concerning Apoplexies*, 2nd ed. (London: Daniel Brown, 1692). Cole likely introduced Colbatch to Brown: Cook, "Sir John Colbatch," 484 n. 43, 487 n. 63.

100. Ebenezer Tracy, *A Discourse on Balsam de Chili in Curing Most Diseases in Human Bodies* (London: Tracy, 1696). Evidently, John Stuart, a stationer in Tracy's neighborhood on London Bridge, also sold a balsam of chili in competition with Tracy: Plomer et al., *Dictionaries 1557–1775*, 294.

101. Plant, *English Book Trade*, 248.

Notes for Chapter 7

1. Paul J. Voss persuasively takes issue with the conventional assumption that advertising developed in the mid-seventeenth century. See his "Books for Sale: Advertising and Patronage in Late Elizabethan England," *Sixteenth Century Journal* 29 (1998): 733–57; see also Blanche B. Elliott, *A History of English Advertising* (London: Business Publications Limited, 1962), 24.

2. See Juanita Burnby, "Pharmaceutical Advertisement in the Seventeenth and Eighteenth Centuries," *European Journal of Marketing* 22/4 (1988): 24–40.

3. Quoted in Elliott, *History of English Advertising,* 39–40.

4. R. B. Walker, "Advertising in London Newspapers, 1650–1750," *Business History* 15 (1973): 113; The *Newes* quoted in Elliott, *History of English Advertising,* 49.

5. These separate sheets were the *City Mercury* and the *Weekly Advertisements,* licensed only for that commercial purpose. Anthony Smith, *The Newspaper: An International History* (London: Thames and Hudson, 1979), 44; James Playsted Wood, *The Story of Advertising* (New York: Ronald Press, 1957), 31. Walker says the *Gazette* eventually "unbent so far as to allow occasional insertions" by physicians: Walker, "Advertising in London Newspapers," 113.

6. P. M. Handover, *Printing in London* (London: G. Allen and Unwin: 1960), 20–21; Smith, *Newspaper,* 44. For a specialized look at what one group of enterprising Londoners advertised in the *Gazette,* see Sarah Tyacke, *London Map-Sellers, 1660–1720* (Tring, England: Map Collectors Publications, 1978).

7. Walker, "Advertising in London Newspapers," 114.

8. *Domestick Intelligence* 10 July 1679. Walker compared Harris's paper to the *Gazette* and found twenty-eight medical ads in the *Domestick Intelligence* to one for the *Gazette*: Walker, "Advertising in London Newspapers," 115.

9. Ibid., 118. Houghton recommended his periodical in March 1692 and continued to publish it in weekly folios until September 1703.

10. Wood, *Story of Advertising,* 33; Walker, "Advertising in London Newspapers," 118, 121; and C. John Sommerville, *The News Revolution in England* (New York: Oxford University Press, 1996), 14, 54. For the evolution of British advertising, see Elliott, *History of English Advertising,* and T. R. Nevett, *Advertising in Britain* (London: Heinemann, 1982). The importance of periodicity to advertising and to other aspects of journalism should not be underestimated.

11. Lawrence Lewis, *The Advertisements of "The Spectator"* (Boston: Houghton Mifflin, 1909), 2, 62–71. The Tories chuckled over their success bringing down the Whig press, especially the "impertinent" *Spectator*: see Jonathan Swift, *Journal to Stella* (Oxford: Clarendon Press, 1948), Letter 39 (17 January 1712), Letter 49 (1 July 1712), and Letter 51 (7 August 1712).

12. By the reign of George I, larger establishments vested printers with the responsibility of receiving and setting ads. James Sutherland, *The Restoration Newspaper and Its Development* (Cambridge: Cambridge University Press, 1986), 216–17. Sutherland notes that putting printers or their apprentices in charge of advertising led to occasional trouble.

13. For more on the complicated and contentious relationships of the publishing world, see Johns, *Nature of the Book,* and John Feather, *A History of British Publishing* (London: Croom Helm, 1988).

14. See Bennett Woodcroft, *Subject-Matter Index of Patents of Invention,* 2 vols. (London: Queen's Printing Office, 1854).

15. Juanita Burnby reminds us that most patent medicines had some therapeutic value and bore resemblance to "official" drugs in the pharmacopoeias of the day: Burnby, "Pharmaceutical Advertisement," 38.

16. Elizabeth Lane Furdell, "Grub Street Commerce: Advertisements and Politics in the Early Modern British Press," *The Historian* 63 (2000): 35–52. For more on the array of proprietary medicines, see Roy Porter, *Quacks: Fakers and Charlatans in England Medicine* (Stroud, U.K: Tempus, 2000).

17. *Mercurius Reformatus,* 11 December 1689.

18. Ibid.

19. Ibid., 7 May 1690.

20. Ibid., 24 September 1690.

21. *The Spectator,* 22 October 1711, 10 October 1712, and 20 July 1711.

22. *Mercurius Reformatus,* 14 August 1689.

23. *The Spectator,* 13 May 1711. Stoughton claimed to have also put notices in *The Postman, The Tatler,* and *Courant.*

24. Houghton's *Collection*, 17 November 1693, quoted in Walker, "Advertising in London Newspapers," 127.

25. *Mercurius Reformatus*, 24 July 1690.

26. Ibid., 29 January 1690.

27. See Furdell, *The Royal Doctors*.

28. W. A. Jackson, "Grana Angelica: Patrick Anderson and the True Scots Pill," *Pharmaceutical Historian* 17 (1987): 2. Juanita Burnby disagrees with William A. Jackson on this "first" and deems the earliest medicine patented Nehemiah Grew's "Salt of Purging Water," Epsom Salts, in 1698: Burnby, "Pharmaceutical Advertisement," 37.

29. Printed in Jackson, "Grana Angelica," 4. The broadside is No. 911, John Rylands University Library of Manchester. Jackson traced the rights to Weir's widow, son, and daughter. Upon Weir's daughter's death in 1770, the pills became the property of her nephew and his family until 1837.

30. *London Gazette*, 8–11 March 1707; *Observator*, 4–8 September 1708. Jackson found such a wooden pillbox bearing Isabella Inglish's seal at an antiques fair: Jackson, "Grana Angelica," 2.

31. *Observator*, 4–8 September 1708.

32. *The Flying Post*, January 1706; *The Female Tatler*, October-December 1709.

33. Quoted in Francis Doherty, *A Study in Eighteenth-Century Advertising Methods* (Lewiston, N.Y.: Edwin Mellon Press, 1992), 23.

34. Quoted in Doherty, *Study in Eighteenth-Century Advertising Methods*, 431–32.

35. *Mercurius Reformatus*, 11 December 1689. Groeneveldt had good reason to Anglicize his name; see pp. 189–90.

36. *The Spectator*, 14 April 1712, reprinted in Lewis, *The Advertisements of "The Spectator,"* 274–75. "Greenfield" accused another lithotomist, a "pretender to that difficult operation for cutting for the stone," of declaring him dead.

37. Maureen Bell, George Parfitt, and Simon Shepherd, eds., *Biographical Dictionary of English Women Writers, 1580–1720* (Boston: G. K. Hall and Company, 1990), 173. Searl's father was Samuel Searl.

38. *Athenian Gazette* (later *Athenian Mercury*) 12/9 (21 November 1693); BL Harley 5931 (89), British Library. For more on the commercials of female healers, see Patricia Crawford, "Printed Advertisements for Women Medical Practitioners in London, 1670–1710," *Society for the Social History of Medicine Bulletin* 35 (1984): 66–70.

39. *The Tatler*, #55 (13–16 August, 1709).

40. Timothy Childe, *A Full and True Account of a Miraculous Cure of a Young Man in Newington* (London: Elizabeth Holt, 1709). Childe, a bookseller and printer, also wrote tracts castigating religious nonconformists.

41. For instance, Grant's ad in *The London Gazette*, 28 September 1710. See also Leslie G. Matthews, "Licensed Mountebanks in Britain," *Journal of the History of Medicine* 19 (1964): 30–45.

42. Mary Rhinelander McCarl, "Publishing the Works of Nicholas Culpeper," *Canadian Bulletin for the History of Medicine* 13 (1996): 242–43.

43. Eisenstein, *Printing Press*, 1:52. Peter Blayney has argued, however, that the publisher's imprint and location was intended to inform retailers where they could obtain books wholesale. Retail information for customers was only incidental. See Blayney, "The Publication of Playbooks," in *A New History of Early English Drama*, ed. John D. Cox and David Scott Kastan (New York: Columbia University Press, 1997), 390.

44. Marjorie Plant, *The English Book Trade*, 3rd ed. (London: George Allen and Unwin, 1974), 248, 251.

45. John Alden, "Pills and Publishing: Some Notes on the English Book Trade, 1600–1715," *The Library*, 5th ser., 7 (1952): 21; Burnby, "Pharmaceutical Advertisement," 35.

46. Peter Isaac, "Pills and Print," in *Medicine, Mortality and the Book Trade*, ed. Robin Myers and Michael Harris (New Castle, Del.: Oak Knoll Press, 1998), 31.

47. Culpeper's advertisement, quoted in Graeme Tobyn, *Culpeper's Medicine* (Shaftesbury, England: Element, 1997), 30–31. Culpeper's *Treatise of Aurum Potabile* (London: G. Eversden, 1656) discusses hermetic philosophy.

48. For Sarah Gardiner's "No Cure, No Money," see BL Harley 5931 (79); Isabella Inglish's handbill, No. 622 at the Society of Antiquaries, is reprinted in Jackson, "Grana Angelica," 3; Mrs. Gill's poster is BL 551.a.32 (184).

49. BL Harley 5931 (110). You could obtain the drops, with printed directions, for five shillings a bottle at several perfumeries in town.

50. BL C.112.f.9; BL 551.a.32; and BL Harley 5931, British Library.

51. John Keevil, "Coffeehouse Cures," *Journal of the History of Medicine and Allied Sciences* 9 (1954): 193. The Russell broadsheet, formerly held by the Society of Apothecaries, sold at Sotheby's in 1953.

52. BL 551.a.32 (21); BL C.112.f.9 (128).

53. BL Harley 5931 (89).

54. BL Harley 5931 (219) is an exception to the lack of printing identification; it was printed for D. M. in 1677.

55. David Zaret, *Origins of Democratic Culture* (Princeton, N.J.: Princeton University Press, 2000), 136–37. For the "corner press," see David Landau and Peter Parshall, *The Renaissance Print* (New Haven, Conn.: Yale University Press, 1994), 219–31.

56. Doherty, *Study in Eighteenth Century Advertising Methods*, 374–76.

57. BL 551.d.19 (55); BL 551.a.32 (27) and (141); BL 551.a.32 (218). For contemporary comment on James, see Dunton, *Life and Errors*, 252–53. James's widow wrote *Mrs. James's Advice to All Printers in General* in 1725. For more on the Jameses, see Paula McDowell, *The Women of Grub Street* (Oxford: Clarendon Press, 1998), 33–34, 47–49, 130–31.

58. For Larkin: BL 551.a.32 (18); Dunton, *Life and Errors*, 245, 250, 441. For Gardiner: BL 551.a.32 (213); Plomer et al., *Dictionaries 1557–1775*, 103.

59. *The Athenian Gazette* 2 (1693): preface, quoted in McDowell, *Women of Grub Street*, 25. For print distribution networks and the part played by women in selling cheap published materials, see McDowell, *Women of Grub Street*, 25–27, 55–62, 81–91; and Margaret Hunt, "Hawkers, Bawlers, and Mercuries: Women and the London Press in the Early Enlightenment," *Women and History* 9 (1984): 41–68.

60. *The London Gazette*, 7 August 1679, quoted in Sean Shesgreen, *The Criers and Hawkers of London* (Stanford, Calif.: Stanford University Press, 1990), 186.

61. These are Daniel Defoe's descriptions from *Journal of the Plague Year* (New York: Signet, 1960), 37–38.

62. Ned Ward, *The London Spy*, ed. Kenneth Fenwick (London: Folio Society, 1955), 134–35.

63. BL 551.a.32 (33); Keevil, "Coffeehouse Cures," 192; and Defoe, *Journal of the Plague Year*, quoted in Ackroyd, *London*, 207.

64. Isaac, "Pills and Print," 28.

65. BL C.112.f.9 (436).

66. BL 551.a.32 (191); BL C.112.f.9 (9).

67. Harold J. Cook, *Trials of an Ordinary Doctor: Johannes Groenvelt in Seventeenth-Century England* (Baltimore, Md.: Johns Hopkins University Press, 1994), 135–48. In the mid-1690s, the College charged Groenvelt (sometimes Groeneveldt or Greenfield), one of the many Dutch physicians who had come to England after the "Glorious Revolution," with malpractice and had him committed to Newgate prison. Behind their contempt for Groenvelt was aversion to his marketing techniques.

68. BL 551.a.32 (186).

69. She also claimed through her powers to have helped a woman whose wedding ring was stolen and a young pregnant woman obtain £50 from "the party that got it:" BL Harley 5931 (216).

70. BL C.112. f.9 (34).

71. BL Harley 5931 (89) and BL Harley 5931 (94).

72. BL Harley 5931 (104), side A; BL C.112.f.9 (140).

73. BL C.112.f.9 (125).

74. BL 551.a.32 (49); BL C.112.f.9 (61); and BL C.112.f.9 (138), side B.

75. BL 551.a.32 (123).

76. BL Harley 5931 (218).

77. Elliott, *History of English Advertising,* 49. Elliott cites Lord Crawford's *Collection of English Broadsides,* Nos. 89–99, and quotes William Page's bill, No. 96 in the series.

78. BL Harley 5931 (217).

79. BL 551.a.32 (88).

80. BL 551.a.32 (9); BL C.112.f.9 (179).

81. Porter, *Quacks,* 172; *DNB.*

82. Quoted in C. R. Hone, *The Life of Dr. John Radcliffe* (London: Faber and Faber, 1950), 71. One could get the elixir at Lloyd's Coffeehouse, Lombard Street, for a shilling a bottle.

83. William Read, *A Short But Exact Account of All the Diseases Incident to the Eyes,* 2nd ed. (London: n.p., 1710); for Addison's judgment of Read, see Porter, *Quacks,* 58; for the Swift comment, see *DNB.*

84. Quoted in Eric Maple, *Magic, Medicine and Quackery* (S. Brunswick, N.J.: A. S. Barnes, 1968), 111.

85. Historian C. D. O'Malley, quoted in Eric Sangwine, "The Private Libraries of Tudor Doctors," *Journal of the History of Medicine and Allied Sciences* 33 (1978): 170 n.2.

86. See Margaret Pelling, "Knowledge Common and Acquired: The Education of Unlicensed Medical Practitioners in Early Modern England," in *The History of Medical Education in Britain,* ed. Vivian Nutton and Roy Porter (Amsterdam: Ridopi Press, 1995), 250–79.

87. John Henry, "Doctors and Healers: Popular Culture and the Medical Profession," in *Science, Culture and Popular Belief in Renaissance Europe,* ed. Stephen Pumfrey, Paolo Rossi, and Maurice Slawinski (Manchester: Manchester University Press, 1991), 210.

88. Barbara Howard Traister, *The Notorious Astrological Physician of London: Works and Days of Simon Forman* (Chicago: University of Chicago Press, 2001), 123–24. Traister notes that Forman composed a number of other works and prepared them for print, but only *The Groundes of Longitude* appeared.

89. Ibid., 51, 80.

90. *DNB.*

91. Ackroyd, *London,* 208–9; Porter, *Quacks,* 84.

92. George Hartman, *The Family Physician* (London: Richard Wellington, 1690), 422–23.

93. BL 551.a.32 (116).

94. BL 551.a.32 (188) lists 27 names of parents and children who made use of his "virtuous necklace."

95. BL 551.a.32 (39), side A; BL Harley 5931 (123).

96. BL 551.a.32 (199), side A.

97. BL C.112.f.9 (26), side A; BL 551.a.32 (71), side A.

98. BL C.112.f.9 (61), side B.

99. BL C.112.f.9 (37).

100. Kevin P. Siena, "The 'Foul Disease' and Privacy: The Effects of Venereal Disease and Patient Demand on the Medical Marketplace of Early Modern London," *Bulletin for the History of Medicine* 75 (2001): 211. I thank Prof. Siena for providing me with an advance copy of his article and some of the advertisements on which it was based.

101. *St. James's Evening Post,* 23 September 1718, quoted in Walker, "Advertising in London Newspapers," 127.

102. BL Harley 5931 (98); BL C.112.f.9 (105).

103. BL Harley 5931 (226).

104. BL Harley 5931 (121).

Notes for Chapter 8

1. The German title is *New Kreüterbüch* (Basle: Durch M. Isingrin, 1543). See Frederick G. Meyer, *The Great Herbal of Leonhart Fuchs* (Stanford, Calif.: Stanford University Press, 1999).

2. Cited in John Crellin, "Herbalism," in *Medicine: A History of Healing,* ed, Roy Porter (New York: Marlowe, 1997), 76.

3. Driver, "Women Printers and the Page," 144. See also Martha Driver, "Nuns as Patrons, Artists, Readers: Bridgettine Woodcuts in Printed Books Produced for the English Market," in *Art into Life*, ed. Carol Garrett Fisher and Kathleen L. Scott (East Lansing: Michigan State University Press, 1995).

4. David T. Bird, "The Illustration of Anatomical Atlases during the Hand-Press Era," *Journal of Audiovisual Media in Medicine* 10 (1987): 91.

5. Quoted in Eleanour Sinclair Rohde, *The Old English Herbals* (New York: Dover, 1971), 169.

6. Ibid., 82–83.

7. Quoted in Crellin, "Herbalism," 77.

8. Rohde, *Old English Herbals*, 103. Norton, three times Master of the Stationers' Company and a London alderman, wore all the book trade's hats: printer, publisher, and seller: *DNB*.

9. Ibid., 93, 104.

10. *Paradisi* came from the presses of Londoners Humphrey Lownes and Robert Young, the latter "an important member of the Company of Stationers" who was King's printer in Scotland from 1632 and manager of an Irish printing office established by the Stationers: Plomer, *Dictionary 1641–1667*, 199.

11. Quoted in Rohde, *Old English Herbals*, 145. Thomas Cotes was *Theatrum*'s publisher.

12. William Thomas Stern, "Horticulture and Botany," in *The Age of William III and Mary II: Power, Politics and Patronage*, ed. Robert P. Maccubbin and Martha Hamilton-Phillips (Williamsburg, Va.: College of William and Mary, 1989) 185. Samuel Smith and Benjamin Walford, partners at the Prince's Arms in St. Paul's Churchyard and booksellers to the Royal Society, published the *Historia*. Dunton called Walford "a very ingenious man who knew books extraordinary well": Dunton, *Life and Errors*, 207.

13. Volume one indicates that it was printed by Mary Clark for Henry Faithorne and the Royal Society, but the ubiquitous Samuel Smith and Benjamin Watford published the other volumes.

14. "Catalogue of the Exhibition," in *The Age of William III and Mary II: Power, Politics and Patronage*, ed. Robert P. Maccubbin and Martha Hamilton-Phillips (Williamsburg, Va.: College of William and Mary, 1989), 405.

15. Joseph Strutt calls Nicholls "a very indifferent engraver" whose etchings of shells were good, but whose representations of the human body were "below all criticism": Strutt, *Biographical Dictionary of All Engravers*, 2 vols. (Geneva: Minkoff Reprints, 1972) 2:183.

16. Quoted in Capp, *English Almanacs*, 205. Frende's almanacs carried ornamental borders and were printed for the Stationers' Company.

17. Carolyn Nelson, "English Newspapers and Periodicals," in *The Age of William III and Mary II: Power, Politics and Patronage*, ed. Robert P. Maccubbin and Martha Hamilton-Phillips (Williamsburg, Va.: College of William and Mary, 1989), 368.

18. William Schupbach, *The Iconographic Collections of the Wellcome Institute for the History Of Medicine* (London: Wellcome Institute, 1989), 14–15.

19. Lithography, surface printing using stone slabs, became practicable by 1798. For discussion of the types of print families—relief, intaglio, and planographic, see Bamber Gascoigne, *How to Identify Prints* (New York: Thames and Hudson, 1986), 5–18.

20. Clapham, "Printing," 409; Bird, "Illustration of Anatomical Atlases," 92. Normally, intaglio plates were printed on separate leaves, hence the term "plates" for illustrations not incorporated into the text.

21. Giles Barber, "Thomas Linacre: A Bibliographical Survey of His Works," in *Essays on the Life and Work of Thomas Linacre*, ed. Francis Maddison, Margaret Pelling, and Charles Webster (Oxford: Clarendon Press, 1977), 312–13. The Paris publisher was Simon de Colines.

22. Malcolm C. Salaman, *The Old Engravers of England* (London: Cassell and Company, 1907), 23 and the plate facing 24. Salaman reports, however, that Payne squandered his successes with idle dissipation and drunkenness.

23. Nicholas Bourne, twice Master of the Stationers, produced *The Surgeon's Mate*; Plomer records that Bourne handled mainly theological works and that he would not allow his shop to sell play-books: *Dictionary 1641–1667*, 29.

24. Stern, "Horticulture and Botany," 184.

25. Harold J. Cook, "The Medical Profession in London," in *The Age of William III and Mary II: Power, Politics and Patronage*, ed. Robert P. Maccubbin and Martha Hamilton-Phillips (Williamsburg, Va.: College of William and Mary, 1989), 192. This vista appeared in *Pharmacopoea Batheana*, the Dutch-language edition published in 1698 by Jan ten Hoorn in Amsterdam.

26. K. F. Russell, *British Anatomy: 1525–1800*, 2nd ed. (Winchester, England: St. Paul's Bibliographies, 1987), xvii.

27. Andrea Carlino, *Books of the Body: Anatomical Ritual and Renaissance Learning*, trans. John Tedeschi and Anne C. Tedeschi (Chicago: University of Chicago Press, 1994), 1. Vesalius' biographer, C. D. O'Malley, concludes that despite the many errors in the *Fabrica*, its "contribution . . . was far greater than that made by any previous book": Charles D. O'Malley, *Andreas Vesalius of Brussels, 1514–1564* (Berekely: University of California Press, 1965), 181.

28. The frontispiece of the book supposedly shows Calcar at a public dissection, sitting in the first row of the gallery just behind Vesalius. He holds a tablet, drawing from the cadaver on the dissecting table. L. G. Audette, "Stylism in Anatomical Illustration from the Sixteenth to the Twentieth Centuries," *Journal of Biocommunication* 6/1 (1979): 26.

29. J. B. Saunders and Charles D. O'Malley, *The Illustrations from the Works of Andreas Vesalius* (New York: Dover, 1973), 25. I thank Elizabeth Eisenstein for this reference. See also O'Malley, *Andreas Vesalius*, 184–85, and *The Epitome of Andreas Vesalius* (Cambridge: M.I.T. Press, 1969).

30. Geminus' project provided a text for surgical studies by the newly united Barber-Surgeons' Company, permitted four corpses of executed felons per year for dissection by an Act of 1540. There is a fine portrait of Henry VIII in the first edition. K. B. Roberts and J.D.W. Tomlinson, *The Fabric of the Body: European Traditions of Anatomical Illustration* (Oxford: Clarendon Press, 1992), 141.

31. O'Malley, *Andreas Vesalius*, 127, 184.

32. The English version of *Compendiosa* brags that the first edition, published by John Herford, was "notably well accepted and hath dooen muche good . . . in foren parties," but one written in the vernacular would be even more useful and profitable: quoted in ibid., 141.

33. O'Malley, "English Medical Literature in the Sixteenth Century," 15. Bird disagrees, calling the Geminus effort "crude translations of the woodcut medium [which] do not demonstrate the full potential of line engraving": see his "Illustration of Anatomical Atlases," 93. See also Salaman, *Old Engravers*, 2–3, and for Geminus as one of five pioneers in the making of scientific implements, Gerard L'E. Turner, *Elizabethan Instrument Makers* (Oxford: Oxford University Press, 2001).

34. Jean Paul Richter, *The Literary Works of Leonardo da Vinci*, 2 vols. (Berkeley: University of California Press, 1977) 2:393.

35. Rubens' anatomical sheets, and those made by his assistant, reveal the artist's mastery of muscle anatomy, but they are not live figures and were drawn from flayed torsos. Mimi Cazort, Monique Kornell, and K. B. Roberts, *The Ingenious Machine of Nature: Four Centuries of Art and Anatomy* (Ottawa: National Gallery of Canada, 1996), 180–81.

36. Joseph M. Levine, *Between the Ancients and the Moderns* (New Haven, Conn.: Yale University Press, 1999), 176.

37. Christine A. Kenney, "A Historical Review of the Illustrations of the Circle of Willis from Antiquity to 1664," *Journal of Biocommunication* 25/2 (1998): 31. Kenney thinks Wren deliberately simplified the sketch, omitting some blood vessels in order to emphasize the circular configuration of the arteries.

38. William Carleton Gibson, "The Bio-Medical Pursuits of Christopher Wren," *Medical History* 14 (1970): 336, 340. Willis acknowledged Wren's figures of the brain and skull, and may also have been indebted to physician Richard Lower for diagraming the autonomic nervous system in the neck and thorax: Roberts and Tomlinson, *Fabric of the Body*, 400.

39. Zachary Cope, *William Cheselden, 1688–1752* (Edinburgh: Livingstone, 1953), facing page 16.

40. William Cheselden, *Anatomy of the Humane Body* (London: Nathaniel Cliff, David Jackson, and William Innys, 1713). Gerard Vander Gucht was the eldest son and pupil of Antwerp

native Michael Vander Gucht, who came to London in 1690. Gerard, who lived in Grosvenor Square, also dealt in pictures for an elite clientele. After his death, his inventory was sold at auction, probably to benefit the "thirty to forty children" he begat: *DNB*. See also *Catalogue of the Pictures, Bronzes, Marble Busts . . . of the late Mr. Gerard Vandergucht* (London: n.p., 1677).

41. The document transferring the copyright to Hitch and Dodsley can be seen at the Royal College of Surgeons and in Russell, *British Anatomy*, plate 164.

42. Published in 1723 by John Osborn, the *Treatise* contained seventeen leaves of plates. Of 213 patients whom Cheselden cut for the stone at St. Thomas' Hospital, he lost less than ten percent; of 105 patients under ten years of age, only three died, "deservedly claimed as remarkable results." Zachary Cope, "William Cheselden Tercentenary," *Annals of the Royal College of Surgeons of England* 71 (1989): 27.

43. John Douglas should not be confused with his brother, Cheselden's good friend Dr. James Douglas, who as a court physician helped procure an appointment for Cheselden as surgeon to George II's Queen Caroline; Cope, "Cheselden Tercentenary," 27.

44. Viewing an eclipse of the sun in January 1544, Reinerus Frisuis Gemma (*De Radio Astronomico et Geometrico Liber*, Antwerp: 1545) described and illustrated its application for this purpose; Robert Ollerenshaw, "The Camera Obscura in Medical Illustration," *British Journal of Photography* 23 Sept. 1977, 816.

45. William Cheselden, *Osteographia or the Anatomy of Bones* (London: W. Bowyer, 1733), preface. The work was issued with two sets of plates: one printed before the lettering of the plates was added, the other including the letters corresponding to the descriptions of the figures. See K. F. Russell, "Osteographia of W. Cheselden," *Bulletin of the History of Medicine* 28 (1954): 32–49; M. A. Sanders, "William Cheselden: Anatomist, Surgeon, and Medical Illustrator," *Spine* 24 (1999): 2282–89.

46. Bird, "Illustration of Anatomical Atlases," 93.

47. Cheselden and Thornhill, quoted in Cazort et al, *Ingenious Machine*, 191. See also Roberts and Tomlinson, *Fabric of the Body*, 423–45. Strutt, however, dismisses Gerard Vander Gucht as having done "no work of any material consequence": Strutt, *Dictionary of Engravers* 1:356.

48. K. B. Roberts, "Bidloo, Cowper and Plagiarism of Anatomical Illustrations," *Canadian Social History of Medicine Newsletter*, September 1970, 7–10. The original Dutch title of Bidloo's work can be seen when examined by transmitted light underneath the paper pasted on the cartouche: Russell, *British Anatomy*, plate 211.

49. Jessie Dobson, "The Royal Dentists," *Annals of the Royal College of Surgeons* 46 (1970): 285; Conrad Gysel, "Dental Aspects of Bidloo's 'Anatomy,'" *Medical Hygiene* 44 (1986): 2212–13. "Fair water" is a generic term for pleasant-smelling and tasting waters, probably flavored with lavender or balsamint, and used here as a mouthwash.

50. Cazort et al., *Ingenious Machine*, 34–35; Bird, "Illustration of Anatomical Atlases," 93. For more on Blooteling, see Strutt, *Dictionary of Engravers* 1:107–8; Salaman, *Old Engravers*, 68–71. For Lairesse, see Roberts and Tomlinson, *Fabric of the Body*, 311–12.

51. Cook, "Medical Profession in London," 188. The *Anatomy* came from the Oxford printing house of Samuel Smith and Benjamin Walford.

52. Some scholars have argued that the controversy over the borrowed illustrations has obscured the prescience of Cowper's scientific text. See Robert F. Buckman Jr., and J. William Futrell, "William Cowper," *Surgery* 99 (1986): 587–88.

53. G. A. Lindeboom, "Cowper's Brutale 'Plagiaat' van Bidloo's Anatomische Atlas," *Nederlands Tijdschrift voor Geneeskunde* 126/41 (1982): 1878–82. I wish to thank Mrs. Letty Jolly of Neptune Beach, Florida, for her translation of this article from the Dutch. Cowper's *Eucharistia* was bound within the translation of his *Glandularum Quarundam*, called *An Account of Two Glands* (London: Samuel Smith and Benjamin Walford, 1702), 19–72.

54. He presented to the members his findings that the nerves are not hollow, nor do they contain fluid, but consist of fibers.

55. Cowper's gland or the bulbourethral gland is either of the two glands embedded in the substance of the sphincter of the male urethra.

56. Cazort et al., *Ingenious Machine*, 59, 187. Busy entrepreneurs Samuel Smith and Benjamin Walford published the works by Ridley and Drake.

57. For more on Cowper and Colbatch, see chapter 6. For Colbatch and medical entrepreneurialism, see Harold J. Cook, "Sir John Colbatch and Augustan Medicine," *Annals of Science* 47 (1990): 475–505.

58. Samuel Smith and Benjamin Walford also published *Myotomia*.

59. Buckman and William Futrell, "William Cowper," 589.

60. Plomer calls Knaplock "one of the chief London publishers of his time . . . (who) held shares in the most important books." The Innyses, père et fils, were leading booksellers and had Clarendon's *History of the Rebellion*, Strype's *Life of Archbishop Whitgift*, and Newton's works printed for them: Plomer et al., *Dictionaries 1557–1775*, 167–68, 180–81.

61. Cazort et al., *Ingenious Machine*, 187–88.

62. Russell, *British Anatomy*, xxi; and his "Check List of Medical Books," 939.

63. Martin Kemp and Marina Wallace, *Spectacular Bodies: The Art and Science of the Human Body from Leonardo to Now* (Berkeley: University of California Press, 2000), 35; Andrea Carlino, *Paper Bodies: A Catalogue of Anatomical Fugitive Sheets, 1538–1687* (London: Wellcome Institute, 1999), 61. Since they were meant to be cut out and glued on, very few of the pages with these forms survive. The author thanks William Eamon, Katharine Donahue, and Sachiko Kusukawa for this information.

64. Carlino, *Paper Bodies*, 3.

65. Simon Schaffer, "Regeneration," in *Science Incarnate—Historical Embodiments of Natural Knowledge*, ed. Christopher Lawrence and Steven Shapin (Chicago: University of Chicago Press, 1998), 87. For more on Newman, see Elizabeth Lane Furdell, "'At the King's Arms in the Poultry': The Bookshop Emporium of Dorman Newman," *London Journal* 23/2 (1998): 1–20.

66. Roy Porter, *Bodies Politic: Disease, Death and Doctors in Britain, 1650–1900* (Ithaca, N.Y.: Cornell University Press, 2001), 26. Porter tells of the comments made by a Swiss visitor who noted that all the patent medicine ads that were repeated endlessly in the papers produced a drug-like fascination.

67. See Roy Porter, "Laymen, Doctors and Medical Knowledge in the Eighteenth Century: The Evidence of the *Gentleman's Magazine*," in *Patients and Practitioners: Lay Perceptions of Medicine in Pre-Industrial Society*, ed. Roy Porter (Cambridge: Cambridge University Press, 1985), 283–314.

68. *The Spectator*, 24 March 1711.

69. "Loe here a woman comes in charitie, to see the sicke and brings her remedie." But the intervening angel "leads the physitian and guides his hand, approves his art, and what he doth must stand": James Primrose, *Popular Errours or the Errours of the People in Physick* (London: Nicholas Bourne, 1651), frontispiece.

70. Porter, *Quacks*, 14, 16, 25, 95. Though undated, these cartoons seem to belong to the Augustan age, roughly 1670–1720.

71. Sean Shesgreen, ed., *The Criers and Hawkers of London* (Stanford, Calif.: Stanford University Press, 1990), 204–5. The quack pictured may be Hans Buling: Cook, "Medical Profession in London," 186.

72. For eighteenth-century medical ridicule, see Mortimer Frank, "Caricature in Medicine," *Bulletin of the Society of Medical History of Chicago* 1 (1911): 46–57.

73. Wolfgang Born, "The Nature and History of Medical Caricature," *Ciba Symposia* 6 (1944–45): 1910–24. Even Dürer doodled a physician inspecting urine in the margins of a prayer book belonging to the Emperor Maximilian: ibid., 1913.

74. Cook, "Medical Profession," 190. Sam Briscoe published the four-volume Brown work of satirical poems and prose. He may have had reasons of his own to humiliate Blackmore, as the "Satyr against Wit" complained of the immorality of London's theatrical productions and Briscoe

published numerous plays: Plomer et al., *Dictionaries, 1557–1775*, 50. For a more respectful rendering of Blackmore by John Closterman, see Gordon Wolstenholme, ed., *Royal College of Physicians: Portraits* (London: Churchill, 1964), 64–65 (hereafter *Portraits I*).

75. Quoted in Porter, *Bodies Politic*, 174. See also Christopher Lawrence, "Medical Minds, Surgical Bodies: Corporeality and the Doctors," in *Science Incarnate—Historical Embodiments of Natural Knowledge*, ed. Christopher Lawrence and Steven Shapin (Chicago: University of Chicago Press, 1998), 156–201.

76. Cheselden served as one of the Wardens of the new Company of Surgeons and helped design the first Surgeons' Hall. Cheselden's portrait by his good friend and neighbor Jonathan Richardson, successor to Swedish painter Michael Dahl as the portraitist of choice among the elite, still bedecks the Royal College of Surgeons: Cope, "Cheselden Tercentenary," 26; *DNB*.

77. Quoted in Porter, *Quacks*, 15.

78. *DNB*; Munk, *Roll*, 2:35. Munk says Turner was disenfranchised from the surgeons.

79. For more on the commemorative function of portraiture, see Louise Lippincott, "Expanding on Portraiture: The Market, the Public, and the Hierarchy of Genres in Eighteenth-Century Britain," in *The Consumption of Culture 1600–1800*, ed. Ann Bermingham and John Brewer (London: Routledge, 1995), 80–85.

80. John Securis, *A Detection and Querimonie of the Daily Enormities and Abuses Committed in Physick* (London: Thomas Marshe, 1566; Norwood, N.J.: Johnson Reprints, 1976), Aiii-Aiv.

81. Maureen Hill, "An Iconography of Thomas Linacre," *Essays on the Life and Work of Thomas Linacre*, ed. Francis Maddison, Margaret Pelling, and Charles Webster (Oxford: Clarendon Press, 1977), 356–57.

82. See Ann Hoffman, *Lives of the Tudor Age* (New York: Harper and Row, 1977), 301; David Piper, "Take the Face of a Physician," in Gordon Wolstenholme and John F. Kerslake, *Portraits: The Royal College of Physicians, Catalogue II* (Amsterdam: Elsevier, 1977), 25–49 (hereafter *Portraits II*).

83. The canvas is known as the "Fuller Maitland" portrait, named for the previous owner.

84. From the portrait, Chambre appears to have lost most of his teeth: Piper, "Take the Face of a Physician," in *Portraits II*, 28. The Holbein original is in the Kunsthistorische Museum in Vienna. For more on limning and Peter Oliver, see Roy Strong, *The English Renaissance Miniature* (London: Thames and Hudson, 1984).

85. Ludmilla Jordanova, *Defining Features: Scientific and Medical Portraits, 1660–2000* (London: Reaktion Books, 2000), 30–31.

86. Wolstenholme, *Portraits I*, 204–5.

87. An oil on canvas portrait of Glisson in the Royal College of Physicians is often attributed to Faithorne because of its similarity to the engraving, but the facial expression is different; moreover, Faithorne was not known to have worked in oils: Wolstenholme, *Portraits I*, 184–85.

88. *DNB*. In 1680 Beale painted a scarlet and fur bedecked Dr. William Croone, whose work was frequently issued in continental editions of Thomas Willis' books. The Sydenham portrait hangs in the National Portrait Gallery, London, and the Croone is at the Royal College of Physicians: Wolstenholme, *Portraits I*, 144–45.

89. Wolstenholme, *Portraits I*, 90–91, 130–31, 376–77.

90. *DNB*.

91. *DNB*; Salaman, *Old Engravers*, 34–44. Strutt praises Faithorne's artistry in a variety of genres: Strutt, *Dictionary of Engravers* 1:283–84. Another famous portrait of Edmund King, done about 1680 and in the Royal College of Physicians, is by Peter Lely; in it, a bust of Hippocrates peers approvingly at Dr. King: Wolstenholme, *Portraits I*, 252–53.

92. Porter, *Quacks*, 67, C1. Greatrakes was born in Affane on 14 Feb. 1629 and died there in 1683.

93. Nathaniel Brook, Culpeper's nemesis, published the queen's book, transcribed by W.M., "one of her late servants," in 1655. See Lynette Hunter, "Women and Domestic Medicine: Lady

Experimenters, 1570–1620," in *Women, Science and Medicine 1500–1700*, ed. Lynette Hunter and Sarah Hutton (Stroud, U.K.: Sutton, 1997), 94.

94. A trio of London booksellers underwrote the Countess's 1655 tome: Henry Twyford, Gabriell Bedell, and Nathaniel Ekins.

95. Hunter, "Women and Domestic Medicine," 94, 104.

96. Timothy Clayton, *The English Print 1688–1802* (New Haven, Conn.: Yale University Press, 1997), 117.

97. Jordanova, *Defining Features*, 27–33, 74; *DNB*.

98. Cook, "The Medical Profession in London," 189.

99. Narcissus Luttrell, *A Brief Historical Relation of State Affairs 1678–1714*, 6 vols. (Oxford: Oxford University Press, 1857) 4:310. See also Campbell R. Hone, *Life of Dr. John Radcliffe* (London: Faber and Faber, 1950).

100. See Edward Strother, ed., *Pharmacopoeia Radcliffeanae* (London: C. Rivington, 1716). The anti-intellectual Radcliffe left a fortune to build the famous Radcliffe Camera at Oxford University, prompting Samuel Garth to retort that "for Radcliffe to found a library was about as logical as if a eunuch should found a seraglio:" quoted in Otto Beckman, *A Pictorial History of Medicine* (Springfield, Ill.: Thomas, 1956), 192.

101. The second edition (1699) of *The Dispensary* contained plates by Michael Vander Gucht illustrating the mock-epic. For more on Garth, see Richard I. Cook, *Sir Samuel Garth* (Boston: Twayne, 1980). For the Kneller self-portrait, see Kemp and Wallace, *Spectacular Bodies*, 75.

102. Porter, *Bodies Politic*, 138.

103. For more on the outrageous Woodward, see Joseph M. Levine, *Doctor Woodward's Shield: History, Science and Satire in Augustan England* (Ithaca, N.Y.: Cornell University Press, 1977).

104. Jordanova, *Defining Features*, 27; Benedict Nicolson, *Treasures of the London Foundling Hospital* (Oxford: Clarendon Press, 1972).

105. Jordanova, *Defining Features*, 26; *DNB*. Jordanova insists that Mead did not like the Pond portrait.

106. The pamphlet was *The Cornuter of 75, being a Genuine Narrative of the Life, Adventures, and Amours of Don Ricardo Honeywater*: cited in Porter, *Bodies Politic*, 138; Laurence Sterne, *The Life and Opinions of Tristram Shandy*, ed. Graham Petrie (Harmondsworth, England: Penguin, 1967), 43.

107. See William MacMichael, *The Gold-Headed Cane* (London: Longmans, 1884). Mead, who took in £7000 annually in receipts, acquired the cane from Radcliffe; he also got Radcliffe's practice and Covent Garden house.

108. Jordanova, *Defining Features*, 43.

109. Clark, *Royal College of Physicians* 1:85. The union of the Barber-Surgeons lasted until 1745, when the surgeons separated to form their own organization.

110. Christopher Lloyd and Simon Thurley, *Henry VIII: Images of a Tudor King* (London: Phaidon, 1995), 68. The panel is in the Barber-Surgeons' Hall, London.

111. Thomas Sprat, *History of the Royal Society of London* (London: Thomas Roycroft for J. Martyn and J. Allestry, 1667). Engravers were paid a flat fee for their work, and an eminent artist like Hollar might command £50, but to cut costs printsellers usually employed engravers of the second rank; Clayton, *English Print*, 21. For more on Hollar, see Strutt, *Dictionary of Engravers* 2:25–27; Salaman, *Old Engravers*, 46–52.

112. Twenty of the Lely "beauties" reside at Hampton Court.

113. Quoted in Clayton, *English Print*, 62–63.

114. Wolstenholme and Kerslake, *Portraits II*, 8. The picture is marked Rowlandson and pupils, suggesting a dating around 1800; see T.G.H. Drake, "The Medical Caricatures of Thomas Rowlandson," *Bulletin of the History of Medicine* 12 (1942): 323–35.

115. The Stukeley engraving is in the Guildhall Library London and is reproduced in Cook, "Medical Profession in London," 191.

116. *DNB*. Kirkall did many engravings for Stukeley's books.

117. Jordanova, *Defining Features*, 27; Iain Pears, *The Discovery of Painting: The Growth and*

Interest in the Arts in England, 1680–1768 (New Haven, Conn.: Yale University Press, 1988), 110, 250 n. 19. Pears notes the symbiotic relationship established between art and medicine at the Foundling Hospital, which used the first public exhibition of art to generate joint publicity. See also Benedict Nicolson, *The Treasures of the Foundling Hospital* (Oxford: Clarendon Press, 1972), 20–32.

118. Clayton, *English Print*, 55. The advance served to pay off the engravers and covered the cost of printing; establishing how many people would buy the prints made the operation more efficient.

119. Mary Webster, "The Taste of an Augustan Collector: The Collection of Dr. Richard Mead—I," *Country Life* 148 (January 29, 1970): 249.

120. Mary Webster, "The Taste of an Augustan Collector: The Collection of Dr. Richard Mead—II," *Country Life* 148 (September 24, 1970): 765.

121. Pears, *Discovery of Painting,* 104, 110, 165. Also see the series of sale catalogues compiled by Richard Houlditch for the Victoria and Albert Museum. For more on Mead, see R. H. Meade, *In the Sunshine of Life* (Philadelphia: Dorrance, 1974.); *DNB*.

122. Salmon's extensive library was sold at auction in 1713–14 by Thomas Ballard, bookseller; see *Biblioteca Salmoneana* (London: Ballard, 1713), a catalogue of the sale.

123. Vaughan produced a book on drawing, limning and the art of painting, published by Thomas Jenner in 1660.

124. *DNB*; William Salmon, *Polygraphice or the Arts of Drawing* (London: Richard Jones, 1672). The 5th edition (1685) came from the presses of Passinger and Sawbridge, but Salmon published with many London sellers including Dawks, Randal Taylor, and E. Brewster.

125. William Sherwin did the portraits of many royal and noble personalities, but Strutt says his mezzotints were "exceedingly bad": Strutt, *Dictionary of Engravers* 2:316; Salaman, *Old Engravers,* 65–66. Michael Vander Gucht devised title pages, portraits, and illustrations for London's booksellers, all engraved with the burin; his sons, by contrast, produced etchings: ibid., 2:355–56; *DNB*.

126. Sander Gilman, *Picturing Health and Illness: Images of Identity and Difference* (Baltimore, Md.: Johns Hopkins University Press, 1995), 9. See also Francis Haskell, *History and Images: Art and the Interpretation of the Past* (New Haven, Conn.: Yale University Press, 1993).

127. Joel-Peter Witkin, *Masterpieces of Medical Photography* (Pasadena, Calif.: Twelvetrees Press, 1987), 1.

128. Gilman, *Picturing Health and Illness,* 19.

129. Porter, *Bodies Politic,* 10.

Notes for Epilogue

1. Trial documents quoted in Cecil Wall, H. Charles Cameron, and E. Ashworth Underwood, *History of the Worshipful Society of Apothecaries of London: Vol. 1, 1617–1815* (London: Oxford University Press, 1963), 133.

2. For this view of the *Rose* case, see Penelope Hunting, *A History of the Society of the Apothecaries* (London: Society of Apothecaries, 1998), passim; Juanita Burnby, *A Study of the English Apothecary from 1660 to 1760,* Medical History Supplements, No. 3 (London: Wellcome Institute, 1983), 9; Roy Porter and Dorothy Porter, "The Rise of the English Drugs Industry," *Medical History* 33 (1989): 280; and Lester S. King, *The Medical World of the Eighteenth Century* (Chicago: University of Chicago Press, 1958), 18–22.

3. Porter, *Bodies Politic,* 139.

4. *Reasons Humbly Offered against Passing the Bill, for Exempting Apothecaries from Serving . . . Parish and Ward Offices* (London: n.p., 1694). For the apothecaries' legislative strategy and response to their opponents, see *Reasons on Behalf of the Apothecaries Bill . . . in Answer to the City of London's Petition* (London: n.p., 1694); *The Apothecaries' Reply to the City's Printed Reasons against Their Bill* (London: n.p., 1694).

5. For more on the brouhaha, see Cook, *Decline of the Old Medical Regime*, 228–32.

6. Queen Anne often consulted John Shadwell, unlicensed by the College until 1712 but a member of the Royal Society and prosperous anyway. She also consulted Roger Grant, a quack oculist from Wapping, and knighted the itinerant tailor William Read, who advertised his cures in *The Tatler*: Furdell, *The Royal Doctors*, 232–33.

7. See Harold J. Cook, *Trials of an Ordinary Doctor* (Baltimore, Md.: Johns Hopkins University Press, 1994).

8. Pompous doctors were often the butt of literary jokes, and the insults intensified throughout the early modern period. See Paul G. Brewster, "Physician and Surgeon As Depicted in 16th and 17th Century English Literature," *Osiris* 14 (1962): 13–32. Brewster highlights the foibles of professional jargon, disagreements over diagnoses, unsavory medicines, and exorbitant fees ridiculed in print.

9. Johannes Groenevelt, *De tuto cantharidum in medicina usu interno* (London: J.H. for John Taylor, 1698), preface.

10. Lysiponius Celer, *The Late Censors Deservedly Censured: And Their Spurious Litter of Libels against Dr.Greenfield and Others, Justly Expos'd to Contempt* (London: printed for the author, 1698); Richard Boulton, *Letter to Dr. Charles Goodall* (London: A. Baldwin, 1699). Boulton also belittled John Colbatch in print at the Fellows' behest.

11. Groenevelt, *Reasons Humbly Offer'd . . . Why Thomas Burwell . . . [et al] . . . should not be excused from the penalty of the Act of 25 Car. II* (London: n.p., 1700).

12. Ned Ward, *London Spy*, 98–99.

13. See Frank H. Ellis, "The Background of the London Dispensary," *Journal of the History of Medicine* 20 (1965): 197–212; Albert Rosenberg, "The London Dispensary for the Sick Poor," *Journal of the History of Medicine* 14 (1959): 41–56.

14. Annals of the Royal College of Physicians, 6: 217–21, 223–27, LRCP. The College officers used dissention over the dispensary to impose greater discipline on the recalcitrant Fellows who objected to the authority and politics of the association. See ibid., 7: 12–14.

15. For more on Garth, see C. C. Booth, "Sir Samuel Garth, F.R.S.: The Dispensary Poet," *Notes and Records of the Royal Society of London* 40 (1986): 125–45.

16. Gideon Harvey, *Conclave of Physicians* (London: James Partridge, 1683); Robert Pitt, *The Craft and Frauds of Physick Expos'd* (London: Timothy Childe, 1702). James Partridge is sometimes referred to as "Stationer to Prince George of Denmark," Queen Anne's husband, and he published many medical works: Plomer, *Dictionary 1668–1725*, 232.

17. G. S. Rousseau, "'Stung into Action . . .': Medicine, Professionalism and the News," in *Newspapers and Society in Early Modern Britain*, ed. Joad Raymond (London: Cass, 1999), 177, 180–81.

18. William Salmon, *A Rebuke to the Authors of a Blew-Book Called The State of Physick in London* (London: Elizabeth Whitlock, 1698).

19. Joseph Browne, *The Modern Practice of Physick Vindicated* (London: Nicholas Cox, 1703); Richard Blackmore, *A Satyr against Wit* (London: Samuel Crouch, 1700).

20. Richard Burrage, *Hell in an Uproar* (London: n.p., 1700).

21. John Badger, *The Case between Doctor John Badger and the Colledge of Physicians* (London: n.p., 1693).

22. For Queen Anne's contract with the Apothecaries, see *Calendar of Treasury Books, 1702* 1:34–35.

23. Irvine Louden, *Medical Care and the General Practitioner* (Oxford: Oxford University Press, 1986), 22–23; Harold J. Cook, "The Rose Case Reconsidered: Physicians, Apothecaries, and the Law in Augustan England," *Journal of the History of Medicine and Allied Sciences* 45 (1990): 554–55.

24. Susan Lawrence, *Charitable Knowledge: Hospital Pupils and Practitioners in Eighteenth Century London* (Cambridge: Cambridge University Press, 1996), 23.

25. David Harley, "Political Post-Mortems and Morbid Anatomy in Seventeenth-Century England," *Social History of Medicine* 7 (1994): 27.

26. See Andrew Cunningham, "Kinds of Anatomy," *Medical History* 19 (1975): 1–19.

27. Thomas Willis, for instance, discusses the autopsy of Dr. Henry Hammond in *Two Discourses concerning the Soul of Brutes*, trans. S. Pordage (London: T. Dring, 1683), 224–25.

28. Harley, "Political Post-Mortems," 26.

29. See Harold J. Cook, "The New Philosophy and Medicine in Seventeenth-Century England," in *Reappraisals of the Scientific Revolution*, ed. D. C. Lindberg and R. S. Westman (Cambridge: CUP, 1990), 397–436.

30. Dorothy Stimson, *Scientists and Amateurs: A History of the Royal Society* (New York: Greenwood Press, 1968), 97. Both Christopher Wren and Samuel Pepys served as President, but from 1670 to 1685 the Society's leadership was generally weak.

31. The College Fellows finally got into print in 1767 with a three-volume series, *Medical Transactions Published by the College of Physicians in London*, superseded in 1785 by the annual *Medical Transactions Published by the Royal College of Physicians*.

32. Of course, the *Tatler* and *Spectator* pieces poked fun at the F.R.S., but the mere presence of articles about the Society's affairs demonstrates their newsworthiness. Joseph Addison himself was interested in scientific matters and improvements in natural knowledge, erudite business clearly in the public domain. See *Tatler* 15 (1709), 236; and *Spectator* 262 (1711).

33. Cook, "Rose Case Reconsidered," 550.

34. Lawrence, *Charitable Knowledge*, 8; see also Mary Fissell, "Readers, Texts and Context: Vernacular Medical Works in Early Modern England," in *Popularization of Medicine, 1650–1850*, ed. Roy Porter (London: Routledge, 1992), 72–96.

35. Lawrence, *Charitable Knowledge*, 336.

36. Margaret Pelling, "Medical Practice in Early Modern England: Trade or Profession?" in *The Professions in Early Modern England*, ed. Wilfred Prest (London: Croom Helm, 1987), 118.

37. *The Spectator*, 10 Sept. 1711.

BIBLIOGRAPHY

Unpublished Primary Sources

Additional Manuscripts. British Library, London.

Annals of the Royal College of Physicians. Library of the Royal College of Physicians, London.

Collections of Medical Advertisements (C.112, f.9; 551.a.32; and Harley 5931). British Library, London.

Egerton Manuscripts. British Library, London.

Harley Manuscripts. British Library, London

Lansdowne Manuscripts. British Library, London.

Registered Copy Wills, Prerogative Court of Canterbury. Public Record Office, London.

Sloane Manuscripts. British Library, London.

Published Primary Sources

Allen, Charles. *Operator for the Teeth*. Introduction by R. A. Cohen. London: Dawsons, 1969.

Arber, Edward, ed. *The Term Catalogues, 1668–1709*. 3 vols. New York: Johnson Reprint Corp., 1965.

Archer, John. *Every Man His Own Doctor*. London: Peter Lillicrap, 1671.

Badger, John. *The Case between Doctor John Badger and the College of Physicians*. London: n.p., 1693.

Baillie, Lady Grisell. *The Household Book of Lady Grisell Baillie*. Edinburgh: Scottish History Society, 1911.

Baker, George. *The Nature and Property of Quicksilver*. London: T. Cadman, 1585.

———. *New Jewell of Health*. London: Henrie Denham, 1576.

Bate, George. *Pharmacopoea Batheana*. Amsterdam: Jan ten Hoorn, 1698.

Baxter, Richard. *A Christian Directory*. London: Robert White, 1673.

Blackmore, Richard. *A Satyr against Wit*. London: Samuel Crouch, 1700.

Blagrave, Joseph. *Astrological Practice of Physick*. London: Obadiah Blagrave, 1671.

Boorde, Andrew. *The Book of Berdes*. London: n.p., 1547.

———. *Brevarie of Helth*. London: Wylliam Middleton, 1547.

———. *Introduction and Dyetary with Barnes in the Defence of the Berde*. Ed. F. J. Furnivall. London: Trubner, 1870.

———. *The Pryncyples of Astronomye*. London: Robert Copeland, 1547.

Boulton, Richard. *An Examination of John Colbatch and His Treatise of the Gout*. London: Thomas Bennett, 1699.

————. *Letter to Dr. Charles Goodall*. London: A. Baldwin, 1699.

Brian, Thomas. *The Piss-Prophet*. London: R. Thrale, 1637.

Browne, John. *Charisma Basilicon*. London: Samuel Lowndes, 1684.

Browne, Joseph. *The Modern Practice of Physick Vindicated*. London: Nicholas Cox, 1703.

Browne, Thomas. *Religio Medici*. London: Printed for Andrew Crooks, 1643.

————. *Works of Thomas Browne*. 4 vols. London: Sam Briscoe, 1707.

Bullein, William. *A Newe Booke entitled The Government of Health*. London: John Day, 1558.

Burrage, Richard. *Hell in an Uproar*. London: n.p., 1700.

Burton, Robert. *Anatomy of Melancholy*. Edited by Floyd Dell and Paul Jordan-Smith. New York: Tudor Publishing, 1955.

Caius, John. *A Counseil against the Sweat*. London: Richard Grafton, 1552.

Castle, George. *The Chymical Galenist*. London: 1667.

Catalogue of the Pictures, Bronzes, Marble Busts . . . of the late Mr. Gerard Vandergucht. London: n.p., 1677.

Celer, Lysiponius. *The Late Censors Deservedly Censured*. London: Printed for the Author, 1698.

Chamberlen, Hugh. *Diseases of Women with Child and in Child-bed*. London: John Darby, 1672.

Chamberlen, Peter. *A Voice in Rhama*. London: John Marshall, 1646.

Cheselden, William. *Anatomy of the Human Body*. London: N. Cliff, D. Jackson, and W. Innys, 1713.

————. *Osteographia or the Anatomy of the Bones*. London: William Bowyer, 1733.

Child, Timothy. *A Full and True Account of a Miraculous Cure of a Young Man in Newington*. London: Elizabeth Holt, 1709.

Clowes, William. *Brief and Necessarie Treatise*. London: 1585.

————. *A Prooued Practice for All Young Chirurgians*. London: Thomas Orwyn, 1588.

————. *Treatise on the King's Evil*. London: n.p., 1602.

Colbatch, John. *Novum Lumen Chirurgicum or the New Light on Chirurgery*. London: Daniel Brown, 1695.

Cole, William. *A Physico-Medical Essay concerning Apoplexies*. 2nd ed. London: Daniel Brown, 1692.

Cowper, William. "An Account of Some Experiments Lately Made on Dogs and of the Effects of Mr. John Colbatch's Styptic on Humane Bodies." *Philosophical Transactions of the Royal Society* 18/208 (February 1693/94).

————. *Eucharistia*. London: Smith and Walford, 1702.

————. *Myotomia Reformata*. London: Smith and Walford, 1694.

Culpeper, Nicholas. *Culpeper's School of Physick*. London: N. Brook, 1659.

————. *Directory for Midwives*. London: Peter Cole, 1651.

————. *The English Physitian Enlarged*. London: Peter Cole, 1653.

————. *A Physicall Directory*. London: Peter Cole, 1649.

————. *Treatise of Aurum Potabile*. London: G. Eversden, 1656.

Culpeper Revived from the Grave. Spitalfields, n.p., 1655.

de Blegny, Nicolas. *The English Remedy or Talbor's Wonderful Secret for Cureing of Agues and Feavers*. London: Joseph Hindmarsh, 1682.

Defoe, Daniel. *The Complete English Tradesman*. London: C. Rivington, 1726.

Dekker, Thomas. *The Plague Tracts of Thomas Dekker*. Edited by F. P. Wilson. Oxford: Clarendon Press, 1925.

Dunton, John. *Life and Errors of John Dunton*. London: S. Malthus, 1705.

Edwards, Thomas. *Gangraena*. London: R. Smith, 1646.

Evelyn, John. *The Diary of John Evelyn*. Edited by John Bowle. Oxford: Oxford University Press, 1985.

Flying Post.

Flecknoe, Richard. *Miscellania*. London: T.R., 1653.

Garth, Samuel. *The Dispensary*. London: 1699.

Gerard, John. *Herball*. London: John Norton, 1597.

Glanvill, Joseph. *A Prefatory Answer to Mr. Henry Stubbe*. London: J. Collins, 1671.

Grey, Elizabeth (Countess of Kent). *Choice Manuall of Rare and Select Secrets in Physick and Chirurgerie*. London: William Jarvis, 1653.

Groeneveldt, Johannes. *De tuto cantharidum in medicina usu interno*. London: J.H. for John Taylor, 1698.

————. *Reasons Humbly Offer'd . . . Why Thomas Burwell . . . Should Not Be Excused from the Penalty of the Act of 25 Car. II*. London: n.p., 1700.

Halkett, Anne. *The Autobiography of Lady Anne Halkett*. London: Camden Society, 1875.

Hartman, George. *The Family Physician*. London: Richard Wellington, 1690.

Harvey, Gideon. *Conclave of Physicians*. London: James Partridge, 1683.

Henrietta Maria, Queen of England. *The Queen's Closet Opened*. London: Nathaniel Brook, 1655.

Hoby, Margaret. *Diary of Lady Margaret Hoby*. Edited by Dorothy Meads. London: Routledge, 1930.

James VI and I, King. Basilikon Doron. In *King James VI and I: The Political Writings*, ed. Johann P. Somerville (Cambridge: Cambridge University Press, 1994).

Loftis, John, ed. *The Memoirs of Anne, Lady Halkett and Ann, Lady Fanshawe*. Oxford: Clarendon Press, 1979.

London Gazette.

Markham, Gervase. *The English House-Wife*. London: George Sawbridge, 1675.

————. *A Way to Get Wealth*. London: George Sawbridge, 1668.

Mauriceau, François. *The Diseases of Women with Child and in Child-Bed*. London: John Darby, 1683.

Mayerne, Theodore. *Medical Counsels or Advices*. London: N. Ponder, 1677.

Medicina Curiosa.

Mercurius Reformatus.

Moxon, Joseph. *Mechanic Exercises on the Whole Art of Printing*. London: Printed for Joseph Moxon, 1683–84.

Nedham, Marchamont. *Medela medicinae*. London: Richard Lowndes, 1665.

Nevett, Thomas. *A Treatise of Consumptions*. 2nd ed. London: John Astwood, 1697.

Nihell, Elizabeth. *Treatise on the Art of Midwifery*. London: A. Morley, 1760.

Observator.

O'Dowde, Thomas. *The Poor Man's Physician*. 3d. ed. London: n.p., 1665.

Paracelsus. *Paracelsus: Selected Writings*. Edited by Jolande Jacobi. Princeton, N.J.: Princeton University Press, 1951.

Parkinson, John. *Garden of Pleasant Flowers*. Edited by Alfred Hyatt. London: T. Foulis, 1904.

———. *Theatrum Botanicum*. London: Thomas Cotes, 1640.

Pepys, Samuel. *The Shorter Pepys*. Edited by Robert Latham. Berkeley: University of California Press, 1985.

Perkins, William. *The Works of Mr. William Perkins*. London: 1616.

Petty, William. *Advice of W. P. to Mr. Samuel Hartlib for the Advancement of Some Particular Parts of Learning*. London: n.p., 1648.

Pitt, Robert. *The Craft and Frauds of Physick Expos'd*. London: Timothy Childe, 1702.

Primrose, James. *Popular Errours or the Errours of People in Physick*. London: Nicholas Bourne, 1651.

Ray, John. *Historia Plantarum*. London: Smith and Walford, 1686.

Read, William. *A Short But Exact Account of All the Diseases Incident to the Eyes*. 2nd ed. London: n.p., 1710.

Salmon, William. *Polygraphice or the Arts of Drawing*. London: Richard Jones, 1672.

———. *A Rebuke to the Authors of a Blew-Book called The State of Physick in London*. London: Elizabeth Whitlock, 1698.

Saunders, Richard. *Astrological Judgment and the Practice of Physick*. London: Thomas Sawbridge, 1677.

Schroeder, John. *The Compleat Chymical Dispensatory in Five Books*. London: John Darby, 1669.

Securis, John. *A Detection and Querimonie of the Daily Enormities and Abuses Committed in Physick*. London: Thomas Marshe, 1566; Norwood, N.J. Johnson Reprints, 1976.

Sharp, Jane. *The Midwives Book*. New York: Garland, 1985.

Smith, John. *Compleat Practice of Physick*. London: J. Streater, 1656.

Sprat, Thomas. *History of the Royal Society*. London: Thomas Roycroft for J. Martyn and J. Allestry, 1667.

Steele, Richard and Joseph Addison. *Selections from* The Tatler *and* The Spectator. Edited by Angus Ross. New York: Penguin, 1988.

Stow, John. *The Survey of London*. London: J. M. Dent, 1912.

Strother, Edward, ed. *Pharmacopoeia Radcliffeanae*. London: C. Rivington, 1716.

Stubbe, Henry. *Legends no Histories*. London: printed for the author, 1670.

———. *The Plus Ultra Reduced to a Non Plus*. London: printed for the author, 1670.

Swift, Jonathan. *Journal to Stella*. 2 vols. Oxford: Clarendon Press, 1948.

Sydenham, Thomas. *The Works of Thomas Sydenham*. Edited by R. G. Latham. 2 vols. London: Sydenham Society, 1848.

Tracy, Ebenezer. *A Discourse on Balsam de Chili in curing Most Diseases in Human Bodies*. London: Ebenezer Tracy, 1696.

Vicary, Thomas. *The Surgion's Directorie for Young Practitioners in Anatomie, Wounds and Cures*. London: Thomas Fawcett, 1651.

Walwyn, William. *A Touch-Stone for Physick*. London: J. Winter, 1667.

———. *The Writings of William Walwyn*. Edited by Jack R. McMichael and Barbara Taft. Athens: University of Georgia Press, 1989.

Ward, Edward. *The London Spy*. Edited by Kenneth Fenwick. London: Folio Society, 1955.

Willis, Thomas. *Cerebri Anatome*. London: Thomas Roycroft for Joseph Martyn and James Allestry, 1664.

———. *Two Discourses concerning the Soul of Brutes*. London: 1683.

Wiseman, Richard. *Chrisma Basilicon*. London: Thomas Newcomb, 1684.

———. *Several Chirurgical Treatises*. London: Flesher and Macock, 1676.

Woodall, John. *The Surgeon's Mate*. London: Nicholas Bourne, 1639.

Yonge, James. *Medicaster medicatus or Remedy for the Itch of Scribbling*. London: Gabriel Kunholt, 1685.

———. *Observations in Chyrurgery and Anatomy*. London: R. Wilde, 1687.

Published Secondary Sources

Achterberg, Jeanne. *Woman as Healer*. Boston: Shambhala, 1990.

Ackroyd, Peter. *London: The Biography*. London: Chatto and Windus, 2000.

Adburgham, Alison. *Shopping in Style*. London: Thames and Hudson, 1979.

———. *Women in Print: Writing Women and Women's Magazines from the Restoration to the Accession of Victoria*. London: George Allen and Unwin, 1972.

Agnew, Jean-Christophe. *Worlds Apart: The Market and Theatre in Anglo-American Thought, 1550–1750*. Cambridge: Cambridge University Press, 1986.

Alden, John. "Pills and Publishing: Some Notes on the English Book Trade, 1600–1715." *The Library*, 5th ser., 7 (1952): 21–37.

Allen, Phyllis. "Medical Education in Seventeenth-Century England." *Journal of the History of Medicine and Allied Sciences* 1 (1946): 115–43.

Allison, Antony F. *Titles of English Books*. 2 vols. Hamden, Conn.: Archon Books, 1976.

Amussen, Susan, and Mark A. Kishlansky, eds. *Political Culture and Cultural Politics in Early Modern England*. Manchester: Manchester University Press, 1995.

Arber, Agnes. *Herbals, Their Origins and Evolution*. Cambridge: Cambridge University Press, 1912.

Archer, Ian. "The London Lobbies in the Later Sixteenth Century." *Historical Journal* 31 (1988): 17–44.

———. *The Pursuit of Stability: Social Relations in Elizabethan London.* Cambridge: Cambridge University Press, 1991.

Armstrong, Elizabeth. "English Purchases of Printed Books from the Continent, 1465–1526." *English Historical Review* 94 (1979): 268–90.

Arnold, Kevin. *Picturing the Body.* London: Wellcome Trust, 1993.

Arrizabalaga, Jon, John Henderson, and Roger French. *The Great Pox: The French Disease in Renaissance Europe.* New Haven, Conn.: Yale University Press, 1997.

Ashton, Robert. "Samuel Pepys's London." *London Journal* 11/1 (1985): 75–87.

Audette, Louis G. "Stylism in Anatomical Illustration from the Sixteenth to the Twentieth Centuries." *Journal of Biomedical Communication* 6 (1979): 24–29.

Aveling, J. H. *The Chamberlens and the Midwifery Forceps.* London: Churchill, 1882.

Barker, Hannah. *Newspapers, Politics and English Society, 1695–1855.* New York: Longman, 2000.

———. "Women, Work, and the Industrial Revolution: Female Involvement in the English Printing Trades." In *Gender in Eighteenth-Century England,* edited by Hannah Barker and Elaine Chalus. London: Longman, 1998.

Baron, Sabrina Alcorn, ed. *The Reader Revealed.* Washington, D.C.: Folger Shakespeare Library, 2001.

Barrett, C.R.B. *History of the Society of Apothecaries of London.* London: E. Stock, 1905.

Barron, Caroline M., and Anne F. Sutton, eds. *Medieval London Widows, 1300–1500.* London: Hambledon Press, 1994.

Bates, Donald G. "Thomas Sydenham and the Medical Meaning of 'Method.'" *Bulletin of the History of Medicine* 51 (1977): 324–38.

Beck, R. Theodore. *The Cutting Edge: Early History of the Surgeons of London.* London: Lund Humphries, 1974.

Beer, Barrett L. *Tudor England Observed: The World of John Stow.* Stroud, England: Sutton, 1998.

Beier, A. L., and R. Finlay, eds. *London 1500–1700.* New York: Longman, 1986.

Beier, Lucinda McCray. *Sufferers and Healers: The Experience of Illness in Seventeenth Century England.* London: Routledge and Kegan Paul, 1987.

Bell, Maureen. "Hannah Allen and the Devlopment of a Puritan Publishing Business, 1646–51." *Publishing History* 26 (1989): 5–66.

———. "'Her Usual Practices': The Later Career of Elizabeth Calvert," *Publishing History* 35 (1994): 5–64.

———. "Women in the English Book Trade, 1557–1700." *Leipziger Jahrbuch zur Buchgeschichte* 6 (1996): 13–45.

Bell, Maureen, George Parfitt, and Simon Shepherd, eds. *Biographical Dictionary of English Women Writers, 1580–1720.* Boston: G. K. Hall, 1990.

Bennett, Judith M. *Ale, Beer, and Brewsters in England*. Oxford: Oxford University Press, 1996.

Berlant, Jeffrey L. *Profession and Monopoly*. Berkeley: University of California Press, 1975.

Bermingham, Ann, and John Brewer, eds. *The Consumption of Culture, 1600–1800*. London: Routledge, 1995.

Berry, Helen. "An Early Coffee House Periodical and Its Readers: The *Athenian Mercury*, 1691–1697." *London Journal* 25/1 (2000): 14–33.

Bird, David T. "The Illustration of Anatomical Atlases during the Hand-Press Era." *Journal of Audiovisual Media in Medicine* 10 (1987): 90–96.

Birken, William. "The Dissenting Tradition in English Medicine of the Seventeenth and Eighteenth Centuries." *Medical History* 39 (1995): 197–218.

———. "The Royal College of Physicians of London and Its Support of the Parliamentary Cause in the English Civil War." *Journal of British Studies* 23 (1983): 47–62.

———. "The Social Problem of the English Physician in the Early Seventeenth Century." *Medical History* 31 (1987): 201–16.

Blagden, Cyprian. "The 'Company' of Printers." *Studies in Bibliography* 13 (1960): 3–15.

———. *The Stationers' Company: A History*. Stanford, Calif.: Stanford University Press, 1977.

———. "The Stationers' Company in the Civil War Period." *The Library*, 5th ser., 13 (1958): 1–17.

Blayney, Peter W. M. *The Bookshops in St. Paul's Cross Churchyard*. London: Bibliographical Society, 1990.

———. "The Publication of Playbooks." In *A New History of Early English Drama*, edited by John D. Cox and David Scott Kasten. New York: Columbia University Press, 1997.

Bliss, Carey. *Some Aspects of Seventeenth Century English Printing*. Los Angeles: University of California Press, 1965.

Bloch, Marc. *The Royal Touch*. London: Routledge, 1973.

Bloom, J. H., and R. R. James. *Medical Practitioners, 1529–1725*. Cambridge: Cambridge University Press, 1935.

Blumenfeld-Kosinski, Renate. *Not of Woman Born: Representations of Caesarean Birth in Medieval and Renaissance Culture*. Ithaca, N.Y.: Cornell University Press, 1990.

Booth, C. C. "Sir Samuel Garth, F.R.S.: The Dispensary Poet." *Notes and Records of the Royal Society of London* 40 (1986): 125–45.

Born, Wolfgang. "The Nature and History of Medical Caricature." *Ciba Symposia* 6 (1944–45): 1910–24.

Bosanquet, Eustace F. *English Printed Almanacks and Prognostications*. London: Chiswick Press, 1917.

Brewer, John. *The Pleasures of the Imagination: English Culture in the Eighteenth Century*. New York: Farrar, Straus and Giroux, 1997.

Brewster, Paul G. "Physician and Surgeon as Depicted in 16th and 17th Century English Literature." *Osiris* 14 (1962): 13–32.

Brooks, Christopher. "Professions, Ideology and the Middling Sort in the Late Sixteenth and Early Seventeenth Centuries." In *The Middling Sort of People: Culture, Society and Politics in England, 1550–1800*, edited by Jonathan Barry and Christopher Brooks, 113–40. London: Macmillan, 1994.

Brown, Theodore M. "The College of Physicians and the Acceptance of Iatromechanism in England, 1665–1695." *Bulletin of the History of Medicine* 44 (1970): 12–30.

Buckman, Robert F. Jr., and J. William Futrell. "William Cowper." *Surgery* 99 (1986): 587–88.

Burnby, Juanita. "Pharmaceutical Advertisement in the Seventeenth and Eighteenth Centuries." *European Journal of Marketing* 22/4 (1988): 24–40.

———. *A Study of the English Apothecary from 1660 to 1760*. London: Wellcome Institute, 1983.

Burtt, Shelley. *Virtue Transformed: Political Argument in England, 1688–1740*. Cambridge: Cambridge University Press, 1992.

Bylebyl, Jerome, ed. *William Harvey and His Age*. Baltimore: Johns Hopkins University Press, 1979.

Bynum, W. F., and Roy Porter, eds. *Medical Fringe and Medical Orthodoxy*. London: Croom Helm, 1987.

Capp, Bernard. *English Almanacs, 1500–1800: Astrology and the Popular Press*. Ithaca, N.Y.: Cornell University Press, 1979.

Carlino, Andrea. *Books of the Body: Anatomical Ritual and Renaissance Learning*. Chicago: University of Chicago Press, 1999.

———. *Paper Bodies: A Catalogue of Anatomical Fugitive Sheets, 1538–1687*. London: Wellcome Institute, 1999.

Carr, Gregg. *Residence and Social Status: The Development of Seventeenth-Century London*. New York: Garland, 1990.

Carrier, James. *Gifts and Commodities*. London: Routledge, 1995.

Cazort, Mimi, Monique Kornell, and K. B. Roberts. *The Ingenious Machine of Nature: Four Centuries of Art and Anatomy*. Ottawa: National Gallery of Canada, 1996.

Champion, J.A.I., ed. *Epidemic Disease in London*. London: Centre for Metropolitan History, 1993.

———. *London's Dreaded Visitation*. London: Centre for Metropolitan History, 1995.

Chartier, Roger. *The Cultural Uses of Print in Early Modern France*. Princeton, N.J.: Princeton University Press, 1987.

Christianson, C. Paul. *Memorials of the Book Trade in Medieval London*. Cambridge: D. S. Brewer, 1987.

Christianson, Gale E. *In the Presence of the Creator: Isaac Newton and His Times*. New York: Free Press, 1984.

Clapham, Michael. "Printing." In *A History of Technology*, edited by Charles Singer et al., 3:377–411. Oxford: Clarendon Press, 1957.

Clark, Alice. *Working Life of Women in the Seventeenth Century*. 4th ed. London: Routledge, 1992.

Clark, George N. *History of the Royal College of Physicians.* 2 vols. Oxford: Clarendon Press, 1964.

Clark, Peter, and Paul Slack. *English Towns in Transition 1500–1700.* Oxford: Oxford University Press, 1976.

Clark, Sandra. *The Elizabethan Pamphleteers: Popular Moralistic Pamphlets, 1580–1640.* Rutherford, N.J.: Fairleigh Dickinson University Press, 1983.

Clayton, Timothy. *The English Print, 1688–1802.* New Haven, Conn.: Yale University Press, 1997.

Clericuzio, Antonio. "From van Helmont to Boyle: A Study of the Transmission of Helmontian Chemical and Medical Theories in Seventeenth-Century England." *British Journal for the History of Science* 26 (1993): 303–35.

Colman, Eric. "The First English Medical Journal: *Medicina Curiosa.*" *Lancet* 354 (1999): 324–26.

Cook, Harold J. "Against Common Right and Reason: The College of Physicians versus Dr. Thomas Bonham." *American Journal of Legal History* 29 (1985): 301–22.

———. *Decline of the Old Medical Regime in Stuart London.* Ithaca, N.Y.: Cornell University Press, 1986.

———. "Living in Revolutionary Times: Medical Change under William and Mary." In *Patronage and Institutions: Science, Technology and Medicine at the European Court,* edited by Bruce T. Moran. Rochester, N.Y.: Boydell Press, 1991.

———. "The New Philosophy and Medicine in Seventeenth-Century England." In *Reappraisals of the Scientific Revolution,* edited by David C. Lindberg and Robert S. Westman, 397–436. Cambridge: Cambridge University Press, 1990.

———. "Policing the Health of London: The College of Physicians and the Early Stuart Monarchy." *Social History of Medicine* 2 (1989): 1–33.

———. "Practical Medicine and the British Armed Forces after the 'Glorious Revolution.'" *Medical History* 35 (1990): 1–26.

———. "The Rose Case Reconsidered: Physicians, Apothecaries and the Law in Augustan England." *Journal of the History of Medicine and Allied Sciences* 454 (1990): 527–55.

———. "Sir John Colbatch and Augustan Medicine." *Annals of Science* 47 (1990): 475–505.

———. "The Society of Chemical Physicians, the New Philosophy, and the Restoration Court." *Bulletin of the History of Medicine* 61 (1987): 61–77.

———. *The Trials of an Ordinary Doctor.* Baltimore, Md.: Johns Hopkins University Press, 1994.

Cook, Joanna. *Surgical Illustrations in Sixteenth Century Printed Books.* London: Wellcome Institute, 1999.

Cook, Richard I. *Sir Samuel Garth.* Boston: Twayne, 1980.

Cope, Zachary. *William Cheselden, 1688–1752.* Edinburgh: Livingtone, 1953.

———. "William Cheselden Tercentenary." *Annals of the Royal College of Surgeons of England* 71 (1989): 26–29.

Copeman, W.S.C. *The Apothecaries of London 1617-1967*. London: Pergamon, 1967.

———. *Doctors and Disease in Tudor Times*. London: Dawson's, 1960.

Corbett, Margery and Ronald Lightbown. *The Comely Frontispiece*. London: Routledge and Kegan Paul, 1979.

Crawford, Patricia. "Printed Advertisements for Women Medical Practitioners in London, 1670–1710." *Society for the Social History of Medicine Bulletin* 35 (1984): 66–70.

Crawfurd, Raymond. *The King's Evil*. Oxford: Oxford University Press, 1911.

Creighton, Charles. *A History of Epidemics in Britain*. 2d ed., 2 vols. Cambridge: Cambridge University Press, 1891.

Cressy, David. *Literacy and the Social Order: Reading and Writing in Tudor and Stuart England*. Cambridge: Cambridge University Press, 1980.

Crist, Timothy. "Francis Smith and the Opposition Press in England, 1660–1688." Ph.D. diss. University of Cambridge, 1977.

Cunningham, Andrew. *The Anatomical Renaissance* (Aldershot, England: Scholar Press, 1997.

———. "Kinds of Anatomy." *Medical History* 10 (1975): 1–19.

———. *Medicine and the Reformation*. London: Routledge, 1993.

Darrington, Susan. *History of Medical Illustrations at St. Bartholomew's Hospital*. London: St. Bartholomew's Hospital Medical College, 1991.

Davies, C.S.L. *Peace, Print and Protestantism, 1450–1558*. London: Paladin, 1990.

Debus, Allen G. *The Chemical Philosophy: Paracelsian Science and Medicine in the Sixteenth and Seventeenth Centuries*. 2 vols. New York: Science History Publications, 1977.

———. *The English Paracelsians*. London: Oldbourne, 1965.

———. "The Paracesian Compromise in Elizabethan England." *Ambix* 8 (1960): 71–97.

———. *Science, Medicine and Society in the Renaissance*. 2 vols. New York: Science History Publications, 1972.

Debus, Allen G., ed. *Medicine in Seventeenth Century England*. Berkeley: University of California Press, 1974.

Dewhurst, Kenneth. *Dr. Thomas Sydenham*. Berkeley: University of California Press, 1966.

———. *Thomas Willis's Oxford Lectures*. Oxford: Sandford Publications, 1980.

Dictionary of National Biography, edited by Leslie Stephen and Sidney Lee. 22 vols. New York: Macmillan, 1885–1903.

Dictionary of National Biography Supplement: Corrections and Additions. Boston: G. K. Hall, 1966.

Digby, Anne. *Making a Medical Living*. Cambridge: Cambridge University Press, 1994.

Dobson, Jessie. "The Royal Dentists." *Annals of the Royal College of Surgeons* 46 (1970): 277–91.

Dobson, Jessie, and R. Milnes Walker. *Barbers and Barber-Surgeons of London.* London: Blackwell, 1979.

Dobson, Mary. *Contours of Death and Disease in Early Modern England.* Cambridge: Cambridge University Press, 1995.

Doherty, Francis. *A Study in Eighteenth-Century Advertising Methods: The Anodyne Necklace.* Lewiston, N.Y.: Edwin Mellen Press, 1992.

Donegan, Jane B. *Women and Men Midwives.* Westport, Conn.: Greenwood Press, 1978.

Donnison, Jean. *Midwives and Medical Men: A History of Inter-Professional Rivalries and Women's Rights.* London: Heinemann, 1977.

Douglas, Mary. "The Construction of the Physician: A Cultural Approach to Medical Fashions." In *The Healing Bond: The Patient-Practitioner Relationship and Therapeutic Responsibility,* edited by Susan Budd and Ursula Sharma. London: Routledge, 1994.

Drake, Stillman. "Early Science and the Printed Book: The Spread of Science beyond the Universities." *Renaissance and Reformation* 6 (1970): 43–52.

Drake, T.G.H. "The Medical Caricatures of Thomas Rowlandson." *Bulletin of the History of Medicine* 12 (1942): 323–35.

Driver, Martha. "Nuns as Patrons, Artists, Readers: Bridgettine Woodcuts in Printed Books Produced for the English Market." In *Art into Life,* edited by Carol Garrett Fisher and Kathleen L. Scott. East Lansing: Michigan State University Press, 1995.

———. "Women Printers and the Page, 1477–1541." In *Gutenberg-Jahrbuch.* Mainz: Verlag der Gutenberg-Gesellschaft, 1998. 139–53.

Duff, E. Gordon. *A Century of the English Book Trade.* London: Bibliographic Society, 1948.

Duffy, Eamon. "Valentine Greatrakes, the Irish Stroker: Miracle, Science and Orthodoxy in Restoration England." *Studies in Church History* 17 (1981): 251–73.

Duran-Reynals, M. L. *The Fever-Bark Tree.* Garden City, N.Y.: Doubleday, 1946.

Eamon, William. *Science and the Secrets of Nature.* Princeton, N.J.: Princeton University Press, 1994.

Earle, Peter. *A City Full of People: Men and Women of London, 1650–1750.* London: Methuen, 1994.

———. "The Female Labour Market in London in the Late Seventeenth and Early Eighteenth Centuries." *Economic History Review,* 2nd ser., 42 (1989): 328–53.

———. *The Making of the English Middle Class.* Berkeley: University of California Press, 1989.

Eccles, Audrey. *Obstetrics and Gynaecology in Tudor and Stuart England.* London: Croom Helm, 1982.

Eisenstein, Elizabeth. *The Printing Press as an Agent of Change: Communications and Cultural Transformations in Early Modern Europe.* 2 vols. Cambridge: Cambridge University Press, 1979.

————. *The Printing Revolution in Early Modern Europe*. Cambridge: Cambridge University Press, 1983.

————. "Some Conjectures about the Impact of Printing on Western Society and Thought." *Journal of Modern History* 40 (1968): 7–29.

Elliott, Blanche B. *A History of English Advertising*. London: Business Publications Limited, 1962.

Ellis, Aytoun. *The Penny Universities: A History of the Coffee-Houses*. London: Secker and Warburg, 1956.

Ellis, Frank. "The Background of the London Dispensary." *Journal of the History of Medicine* 20 (1965): 197–212.

Ellis, Joyce. "On the Town: Women in Augustan England." *History Today* 45 (Dec. 1995): 20-27.

Erdmann, Axel. *My Gracious Silence: Women in the Mirror of 16th Century Printing in Western Europe*. Lucerne: Gilhofer and Ranschburg, 1999.

Erickson, Amy Louise. *Women and Property in Early Modern England*. London: Routledge, 1993.

Evenden, Doreen A. "Gender Differences in the Licensing and Practice of Female and Male Surgeons in Early Modern England." *Medical History* 42 (1998): 194–216.

Feather, John. *A History of British Publishing*. London: Croom Helm, 1988.

————. *Publishing, Piracy and Politics: An Historical Study of Copyright in Britain*. London: Mansell, 1994.

Ferdinand, C. Y. "Towards a Demography of the Stationers' Company, 1601–1700." *Journal of the Printing Historical Society* 21 (1992): 51–69.

Fissell, Mary E. *Patients, Power, and the Poor in Eighteenth-Century Bristol*. Cambridge: Cambridge University Press, 1991.

————. "Readers, Texts and Context: Vernacular Medical Works in Early Modern England." In *The Popularization of Medicine, 1650–1850*, edited by Roy Porter. London: Routledge, 1992.

Five Centuries of Women Book Artists: Printers and Engravers, 1478–1984; An Exhibit of Their Works in the Collection of the University of Illinois Rare Book and Spceial Collections Library. Urbana-Champaign: University of Illinois, 1992.

Forbes, Thomas R. "The Regulation of English Midwives in the Sixteenth and Seventeenth Centuries." *Medical History* 8 (1961): 352–62.

Ford, Brian. *Images of Science: History of Scientific Illustration*. London: British Library, 1992.

Ford, Wyn. "The Problem of Literacy in Early Modern England." *History* 78 (1993): 22–37.

Frank, Joseph. *The Beginnings of the English Newspaper, 1620–1660*. Cambridge, Mass.: Harvard University Press, 1961.

Frank, Mortimer. "Caricature in Medicine." *Bulletin of the Society of Medical History of Chicago* 1 (1911): 46–57.

Frank, Robert G. Jr. "Science, Medicine and the Universities of Early Modern England." *History of Science* 11 (1973): 194–216; 239–69.

———. "Thomas Willis and His Circle: Brain and Mind in Seventeenth-Century Medicine." In *Languages of Psyche: Mind and Body in Enlightenment Thought*, edited by G. S. Rousseau, 107–46. Berkeley: University of California Press, 1990.

Fraser, Antonia. *The Weaker Vessel*. New York: Knopf, 1984.

French, Peter. *John Dee*. London: Ark, 1987.

French, Roger, and Andrew Wear, eds. *British Medicine in an Age of Reform*. London: Routledge, 1991.

———. *The Medical Revolution of the Seventeenth Century*. Cambridge: Cambridge University Press, 1989.

Freist, Dagmar. *Governed by Opinion: Politics, Religion and the Dynamics of Communication in Stuart London 1637-1645*. London: Tauris Academic Studies, 1997.

Furdell, Elizabeth Lane. "'At the King's Arms in the Poultrey': The Bookshop Emporium of Dorman Newman, 1670–1694." *London Journal* 23/2 (1998): 1–20.

———. "Grub Street Commerce: Advertisements and Politics in the Early Modern British Press." *The Historian* 63 (2000): 35–52.

———. *James Welwood: Physician to the Glorious Revolution*. Conshohocken, Penn.: Combined Publishing, 1998.

———. *The Royal Doctors: Medical Personnel at the Tudor and Stuart Courts*. Rochester, N.Y.: University of Rochester Press, 2001.

Gardner, Judith E. "Women in the Book Trade, 1641–1700: A Preliminary Survey." In *Gutenberg-Jahrbuch*. Mainz: Verlag der Gutenberg-Gesellschaft, 1978. 343–46.

Garrison, Fielding. *Introduction to the History of Medicine*. 4th ed. Philadelphia: W. B. Saunders, 1929.

———. "The Medical and Scientific Periodicals of the Seventeenth and Eighteenth Centuries." *Bulletin of the the Institute of the History of Medicine* 2 (1934): 285–343.

———. "Medicine in *The Tatler, The Spectator*, and *The Guardian*." *Bulletin of the Institute for the History of Medicine* 2 (1934): 477–503.

Gascoigne, Bamber. *How to Identify Prints*. New York: Thames and Hudson, 1986.

Geneva, Ann. *Astrology and the Seventeenth Century Mind*. Manchester: Manchester University Press, 1995.

Geshwind, Max. "William Salmon, Quack-Doctor and Writer of Seventeenth Century London." *Bulletin of the History of Dentistry* 43/2 (1995): 76.

Gibbons, B. J. *Gender in Mystical and Occult Thought: Behmenism and Its Development in England*. Cambrdige: Cambridge University Press, 1996.

Gibson, William Carleton. "The Bio-Medical Pursuits of Christopher Wren." *Medical History* 14 (1970): 331–41.

Gilman, Sander L. *Picturing Health and Illness: Images of Identity and Difference*. Baltimore: Johns Hopkins University Press, 1995.

Gingerich, Owen. "Copernicus and the Impact of Printing." *Vistas in Astronomy* 17 (1975): 201–18.

Globe, Alexander. *Peter Stent, London Printseller, 1642–1665*. Vancouver: University of British Columbia Press, 1985.

Goldie, Mark. "The Revolution of 1689 and the Structure of Political Argument." *Bulletin of Research in the Humanities* 83 (1980): 473–564.

Grafton, Anthony. "The Importance of Being Printed." *Journal of Interdisciplinary History* 11 (1980): 265–86.

———. *New Worlds, Ancient Texts: The Power of Tradition and the Shock of Discovery*. Cambridge, Mass.: Harvard University Press, 1992.

Grassby, Richard. *The Business Community of Seventeenth-Century England*. Cambridge: Cambridge University Press, 1995.

Greaves, Richard. *Enemies under His Feet: Radicals and Nonconformists in Britain, 1664–1677*. Stanford, Calif.: Stanford University Press, 1990.

Greg, W. W. *Some Aspects and Problems of London Publishing between 1550 and 1650*. Oxford: Clarendon Press, 1956.

Grell, Ole Peter, ed. *Paracelsus: The Man and His Reputation, His Ideas and Their Transformation*. Leiden: Brill, 1998.

Grell, Ole Peter, and Andrew Cunningham, eds. *Health Care and Poor Relief in Protestant Europe, 1500–1700*. London: Routledge, 1997.

———. *Religio Medici: Medicine and Religion in Seventeenth-Century England*. Aldershot, England: Scolar Press, 1996.

Guerrini, Anita. "Chemistry Teaching at Oxford and Cambridge, circa 1700." In *Alchemy and Chemistry in the Sixteenth and Seventeenth Centuries*, edited by Piyo Rattansi and Antonio Clericuzio. Dordrecht: Kluwer Academic Publishers, 1994.

Gunther, R. T. *Early Science in Oxford*. 14 vols. "The Diary of Robert Hooke" in vol. 10, *The Life and Work of Robert Hooke, Pt. 4*. Oxford: Printed for the Author, 1935.

Guy, John R. "The Episcopal Licensing of Physicians, Surgeons, and Midwives." *Bulletin of the History of Medicine* 56 (1982): 529–33.

Gysel, Conrad. "Dental Aspects of Bidloo's Anatomy." *Medical Hygiene* 44 (1986): 2212–13.

Habermas, Jürgen. *The Structural Transformation of the Public Sphere*. Translated by Thomas Burger and Frederick Lawrence. Cambridge, Mass.: M.I.T. Press, 1989.

Hamburger, Philip. "Seditious Libel." *Stanford Law Review* 37 (1985): 661–720.

Hambridge, Roger A. "Epiricomany or an Infatuation in Favor of Empiricism or Quackery." In *Literature, Science and Medicine*, edited by Serge Soupel and Roger A. Hambridge. Los Angeles: University of California Press, 1982.

Hamill, Frances. "Some Unconventional Women before 1800: Printers, Booksellers, and Collectors." *Papers of the Bibliographical Society of America* 49 (1955): 300–314.

Handover, P. M. *Printing in London from 1476 to Modern Times*. London: George Allen and Unwin, 1960.

Hansen, Julie. *Physician's Art: Representations of Art and Medicine.* Durham, N.C.: Duke University Medical College Library, 1999.

Harding, Vanessa. "Mortality and the Mental Map of London: Richard Smyth's *Obituary.*" In *Medicine, Mortality and the Book Trade,* edited by Robin Myers and Michael Harris. New Castle, Del.: Oak Knoll Press, 1998.

Harley, David. "Medical Metaphors in English Moral Theology." *Journal of the History of Medicine* 48 (1993): 396–435.

———. "Political Post-Mortems and Morbid Anatomy in Seventeenth-Century England." *Social History of Medicine* 7 (1994): 1–28.

Harris, Michael. "Moses Pitt and Insolvency in the London Booktrade in the Late-Seventeenth Century." In *The Economics of the British Book Trade, 1605–1937,* edited by Robin Myers and Michael Harris. Cambridge: Cambridge University Press, 1985.

———. "The Structure, Ownership and Control of the Press, 1620–1780." In *Newspaper History,* edited by George Boyce, James Curran, and Pauline Wingate. London: Constable, 1978.

Harris, Michael and Alan Lee, eds. *The Press in English Society from the Seventeenth to the Nineteenth Centuries.* Rutherford, N.J.: Fairleigh Dickinson University Press, 1986.

Harris, Tim, ed. *Popular Culture in England, 1500–1800.* New York: St. Martin's, 1995.

Hazlitt, W. Carew. *The Livery Companies of the City of London.* New York: Benjamin Blom, 1892.

Henry, John. "Doctors and Healers: Popular Culture and the Medical Profession." In *Science, Culture and Popular Belief in Renaissance Europe,* edited by Stephen Pumfrey, Paolo Rossi, and Maurice Slawinski. Manchester: Manchester University Press, 1991.

———. "The Scientific Revolution in England." In *The Scientific Revolution in National Context,* edited by Roy Porter and Mikulas Teich. New York: Cambridge University Press, 1992.

Herrlinger, Robert. *History of Medical Illustration.* London: Pitman Medical Press, 1970.

Hill, Christopher. *Change and Continuity in Seventeenth-Century England.* Rev. ed. New Haven, Conn.: Yale University Press, 1991.

Hirsch, Rudolf. *Printing Selling and Reading, 1450-1550.* 2nd printing. Wiesbaden: Otto Harrassowitz, 1974.

Holderness, B. A. "Widows in Pre-Industrial Society." In *Land, Kinship and Life-Cycle,* edited by R. M. Smith. Cambridge: Cambridge University Press, 1984.

Holloway, S.W.F. "The Apothecaries' Act, 1815: A Reinterpretation. Part I: The Origins of the Act." *Medical History* 10 (1966): 107–29; "Part II: The Consequences of the Act." *Medical History* 10 (1966): 221–36.

Hole, Christina. *The English Housewife in the Seventeenth Century.* London: Chatto and Windus, 1953.

Holmes, Geoffrey S. *Augustan England: Professions, State and Society, 1680–1730*. London: George Allen and Unwin, 1982.

Hone, C. R. *The Life of Dr. John Radcliffe*. London: Faber and Faber, 1950.

Horden, John. "'In the Savoy': John Nutt and His Family." *Publishing History* 24 (1988): 5–26.

Houston, R. A. *Literacy in Early Modern England*. London: Longman, 1998.

Howe, Ellic. *List of London Bookbinders, 1648–1815*. London: Bibliographical Society, 1950.

Hunt, Felicity. "The London Trade in the Printing and Binding of Books." *Women's Studies International Forum* 6 (1983): 517–24.

Hunt, Margaret. "Hawkers, Bawlers, and Mercuries: Women and the London Press in the Early Enlightenment." *Women and History* 9 (1984): 41–68.

———. *The Middling Sort: Commerce, Gender and the Family in England, 1680–1780*. Berkeley: University of California Press, 1996.

Hunter, Lynette, and Sarah Hutton, eds. *Women, Science and Medicine 1500–1700*. Stroud, England: Sutton, 1997.

Hunter, Michael. "Boyle versus the Galenists: A Suppressed Critique of Seventeenth-Century Medical Practice and Its Significance." *Medical History* 41 (1997): 322–61.

Hunting, Penelope. *A History of the Society of Apothecaries*. London: Society of Apothecaries, 1998.

Isaac, Peter. "Pills and Print." In *Medicine, Mortality and the Book Trade*, edited by Robin Myers and Michael Harris. New Castle, Del.: Oak Knoll Press, 1998.

Jacob, Jim. *Henry Stubbe: Radical Protestantism and the Early Enlightenment*. Cambridge: Cambridge University Press, 1983.

Jacob, Margaret, and J. R. Jacob. "Anglican Origins of Modern Science." *Isis* 71 (1980): 251–67.

Jackson, W. A. "Grana Angelica: Patrick Anderson and the True Scots Pill." *Pharmaceutical Historian* 17 (1987): 1–5.

James, R. R. "Licenses to Practice Medicine and Surgery Issued by the Archbishop of Canterbury." *Janus* 41 (1936): 97–106.

Jameson, Eric. *The Natural History of Quackery*. Springfield, Ill.: C. C. Thomas, 1961.

Jewson, N.D. "Medical Knowledge and the Patronage System." *Sociology* 8/3 (1974): 369–85.

Johns, Adrian. *The Nature of the Book: Print and Knowledge in the Making*. Chicago: University of Chicago Press, 1998.

Jones, Gordon W. "A Relic of the Golden Age of Quackery: What Read Wrote." *Bulletin of the History of Medicine* 37 (1963): 226–38.

Jones, Peter Murray. "Reading Medicine in Tudor Cambridge." In *History of Medical Education in Britain*, edited by Vivian Nutton and Roy Porter. Amsterdam: Ridopi, 1995.

Jones, Richard Foster. *Ancients and Moderns: A Study of the Rise of the Scientific Movement in Seventeenth-Century England*. 1975.

Jordanova, Ludmilla. *Defining Features: Scientific and Medical Portraits, 1660–2000*. London: Reaktion Books, 2000.

Kaplan, Barbara Beigun. *"Divulging of Useful Truths in Physick": The Medical Agenda of Robert Boyle*. Baltimore, Md.: Johns Hopkins University Press, 1993.

Kearney, Hugh. *Scholars and Gentlemen: Universities and Society in Pre-Industrial Britain, 1500–1700*. Ithaca, N.Y.: Cornell University Press, 1970.

Keeble, N. H. *The Literary Culture of Nonconformity in Later Seventeenth-Century England*. Athens: University of Georgia Press, 1987.

Keevil, John. "Coffeehouse Cures." *Journal of the History of Medicine and Allied Sciences* 9 (1954): 191–95.

Kemp, Martin, and Marina Wallace. *Spectacular Bodies: The Art and Science of the Human Body from Leonardo to Now*. Berkeley: University of California Press, 2000.

Kenney, Christine A. "A Historial Review of the Illustrations of the Circle of Willis." *Journal of Biocommunication* 25/2 (1998): 26–31.

Kerwin, William. "Where Have You Gone, Margaret Kennix?" In *Women Healers and Physicians*, edited by Lilian R. Furst. Lexington: University Press of Kentucky, 1997.

Knights, Mark. *Politics and Public Opinion in Crisis, 1678–81*. Cambridge: Cambridge University Press, 1994.

Kocher, Paul H. "Paracelsian Medicine in England: The First Thirty Years." *Journal of the History of Medicine* 2 (1947): 451–80.

Kowaleski-Wallace, Elizabeth. *Consuming Subjects*. New York: Columbia University Press, 1997.

Kronick, D. A. "Nicholas de Blegny, Medical Journalist." *Bulletin of the Cleveland Medical Library* 7 (1960): 47–56.

Lambert, Sheila. "State Control of the Press in Theory and Practice: The Role of the Stationers' Company before 1640." In *Censorship and Control of Print in England and France, 1600–1910*, edited by Robin Myers and Michael Harris. Winchester, England: St. Paul's Bibliographies, 1992.

Landau, David, and Peter Parshall. *The Renaissance Print*. New Haven, Conn.: Yale University Press, 1994.

Lane, Joan. *Apprenticeship in England, 1600–1914*. Boulder, Colo.: Westview Press, 1996.

Laslett, T.P.R. "The Foundations of the Royal Society and the Medical Profession in England." *British Medical Journal* 2/5193 (1960): 165–69.

———. Introduction. In *Two Treatises of Government*, edited by Peter Laslett. Cambridge: Cambridge University Press, 2000.

Laurence, Anne. *Women in England, 1500–1760*. New York: St. Martin's, 1994.

Lawler, John. "Dr. Bernard's Library." In *Book Auctions in England in the Seventeenth Century*. London: E. Stock, 1898.

Lawrence, Christopher, and Steven Shapin, eds. *Science Incarnate: Historical Embodiments of Natural Knowledge*. Chicago: University of Chicago Press, 1998.

Lawrence, Susan C. *Charitable Knowledge: Hospitals and Practitioners in Eighteenth-Century London*. Cambridge: Cambridge University Press, 1996.

Lawson-Dick, Oliver, ed. *Aubrey's Brief Lives*. London: Mandarin, 1992.

Lee, Jennifer B., and Miriam Mandlebaum. *Seeing Is Believing*. New York: New York Public Library, 1999.

Leedham-Green, Elizabeth, D. E. Rhodes, and F. H. Stubbings. *Garrett Godfrey's Accounts*. Cambridge: Cambridge Bibliographic Society, 1992.

Lenkey, Susan V. "Printers' Wives in the Age of Humanism." In *Gutenberg-Jahrbuch*. Mainz: Gutenberg-Gesellshaft, 1975.

Levine, Joseph M. *Between the Ancients and the Moderns*. New Haven, Conn.: Yale University Press, 1999.

———. *Doctor Woodward's Shield: History, Science and Satire in Augustan England*. Ithaca, N.Y.: Cornell University Press, 1977.

Lewalski, Barbara Kiefer. *Writing Women in Jacobean England*. Cambridge, Mass.: Harvard University Press, 1993.

Lewis, Lawrence. *The Advertisements of "The Spectator."* Boston: Houghton Mifflin, 1909.

Lillywhite, Bryant. *London Coffee Houses*. London: George Allen and Unwin, 1963.

Lindeboom, G. A. "Cowper's Brutal 'Plagiaat' van Bidloo's Anatomische Atlas." *Nederlands Tijdschrift voor Geneeskunde* 126/41 (1982): 1878–82.

Lippincott, Louise. "Expanding on Portraiture." In *The Consumption of Culture 1600–1800*, edited by Ann Bermingham and John Brewer. London: Routledge, 1995.

Lord, Alexandra. "The Great Arcana of the Deity." *Bulletin for the History of Medicine* 73 (1999): 38–63.

Louden, Irvine. *Medical Care and the General Practitioner*. Oxford: Oxford University Press, 1986.

Luborsky, Ruth S., and Elizabeth M. Ingram. *A Guide to English Illustrated Books, 1536–1603*. 2 vols. Tempe, Az.: Medieval and Renaissance Texts, 1998.

Maccubbin, Robert P., and Martha Hamilton-Phillips, eds. *The Age of William III and Mary II: Power, Politics and Patronage*. Williamsburg, Va.: College of William and Mary, 1989.

MacDonald, J. Ramsay, ed. *Women in the Printing Trades*. In *The English Working Class*, edited by Standish Meacham. New York: Garland, 1980.

Macfarlane, Alan. *The Family Life of Ralph Josselin*. New York: W. W. Norton, 1970.

MacKinney, Loren C., and Thomas Herndon. *Medical Illustrations in Medieval Manuscripts*. Berkeley: University of California Press, 1965.

Maddison, Francis, Margaret Pelling and Charles Webster, eds. *Essays on the Life and Work of Thomas Linacre*. Oxford: Clarendon Press, 1977.

Mandelbrote, Giles. "From the Warehouse to the Counting-House: Booksellers and Bookshops in Late Seventeenth Century London." In *A Genius for Letters: Booksellers and Bookselling from the Sixteenth to the Twentieth Centu-

ries, edited by Robin Myers and Michael Harris. New Castle, Del.: Oak Knoll Press, 1995.

———. "Richard Bentley's Copies: The Ownership of Copyrights in the Late Seventeenth Century." In *The Book Trade and Its Customers*, edited by Arnold Hunt, G. Mandelbrote, and Alison Shell. New Castle, Del.: Oak Knoll Press, 1997.

Manley, Lawrence. *Literature and Culture in Early Modern London*. Cambridge: Cambridge University Press, 1995.

Maple, Eric. *Magic, Medicine and Quackery*. S. Brunswick, N.J.: A. S. Barnes, 1968.

Marland, Hilary, and Margaret Pelling, eds. *The Task of Healing: Medicine, Religion and Gender in England and the Netherlands, 1450–1800*. Rotterdam: Erasmus, 1996.

Martensen, Robert L. "'Habit of Reason': Anatomy and Anglicanism in Restoration England." *Bulletin of the History of Medicine* 66 (1992): 511–35.

Martin, Graham. "Prince Rupert and the Surgeons." *History Today* 40 (December 1990): 38–43.

Matthews, Leslie G. "Italian Charlatans in England." *Pharmaceutical Historian* 9 (1979): 2–5.

———. "Licensed Mountebanks in Britain." *Journal of the History of Medicine* 19 (1964): 30–45.

———. *The Royal Apothecaries*. London: Wellcome Medical Library, 1967.

McCarl, Mary Rhinelander. "Publishing the Works of Nicholas Culpeper, Astrological Herbalist and Translator of Latin Medical Works in Seventeenth-Century London." *Canadian Bulletin for the History of Medicine* 13 (1996): 225–76.

McDowell, Paula. *The Women of Grub Street: Press, Politics, and Gender in the London Literary Marketplace, 1678–1730*. Oxford: Clarendon Press, 1998.

McKenzie, D. F. *Cambridge University Press, 1696–1712: A Bibliographical Study*. Cambridge: Cambridge University Press, 1966.

———. "A List of Printers' Apprentices, 1605–1640." *Studies in Bibliography* 13 (1960): 109–31.

———. *The London Book Trade in the Later Seventeenth Century*. Sandars Lectures. Cambridge: Cambridge University Press, 1976.

———. *Stationers' Company Apprentices, 1605–1640*. Charlottesville, Va.: Bibliographical Society of the University of Virginia, 1961.

———. *Stationers' Company Apprentices, 1641–1700*. Oxford: Oxford Bibliographical Society, 1974.

———. *Stationers' Company Apprentices, 1701–1800*. Oxford: Oxford Bibliographical Society, 1978.

McKerrow, R. B., ed. *A Dictionary of Printers and Booksellers in England, Scotland and Ireland, and of Foreign Printers of English Books, 1557–1640*. London: Bibliographial Society, 1968.

———. "Edward Allde as a Typical Trade Printer." *The Library*, 4th ser., 10 (1929): 121–62.

McKitterick, D. J. *A History of Cambridge University Press: Printing and the Book Trade in Cambridge, 1534–1698.* Cambridge: Cambridge University Press, 1992.

McNally, Peter F., ed. *The Advent of Printing: Historians of Science Respond to Elizabeth Eisenstein's "The Printing Press as an Agent of Change."* Montreal: McGill University, 1987.

Meadows, Cecil. *Trade Signs and Their Origins.* London: Routledge and Paul, 1957.

Mendelson, Sara Heller. *The Mental World of Stuart Women: Three Studies.* Amherst: University of Massachusetts Press, 1987.

Merton, Robert K. *Science, Technology and Society in Seventeenth Century England.* New York: Howard Fertig, 1970.

Meyer, Frederick G. *The Great Herbal of Leonhart Fuchs.* Stanford, Calif.: Stanford University Press, 1999.

Meyer, Gerald Dennis. *The Scientific Lady in England, 1650–1760.* Berkeley: University of California Press, 1955.

Mills, Peter, and John Oliver. *Survey of Building Sites in the City of London after the Great Fire.* 5 vols. London: Topographical Society, 1962.

Mitchell, C. J. "Women in the Eighteenth-Century Book Trades." In *Writers, Books and Trade*, edited by O. M. Brack Jr., 25–75. New York: AMS Press, 1994.

Moe, Harald. *The Art of Anatomical Illustration in the Renaissance and Baroque.* Copenhagen: Rhodos, 1995.

Moore, Norman. *History of the Study of Medicine in the British Isles.* Oxford: Clarendon Press, 1908.

Morris, G.C.R. "Which Molins Treated Cromwell for the Stone and Did Not Prescribe for Pepys?" *Medical History* 26 (1982): 429–35.

Morrison, Paul G. *Index of Printers, Publishers and Booksellers in Donald Wing's Short-Title Catalogue.* Charlottesville: University of Virginia Press, 1955.

Mui, Lorna, and Hoh-cheung Mui. *Shops and Shopkeeping in Eighteenth Century England.* London: Routledge, 1989.

Muldrew, Craig. *The Economy of Obligation: The Culture of Credit and Social Relations in Early Modern england.* New York: St. Martin's Press, 1998.

Munk, William. *Roll of the Royal College of Physicians.* 2 vols. London: Longman, Green and Roberts, 1861.

Myers, Robin, and Michael Harris, eds. *Medicine, Mortality and the Book Trade.* New Castle, Del.: Oak Knoll Press, 1998.

——. *The Stationers' Company and the Book Trade, 1550–1990.* New Castle, Del.: Oak Knoll Press, 1997.

Nagy, Doreen Evenden. *Popular Medicine in Seventeenth Century England.* Bowling Green, Ohio: Bowling Green State University Popular Press, 1988.

Nance, Brian. *Turquet de Mayerne as Baroque Physician.* Amsterdam: Ridopi, 2001.

Nevett, T.R. *Advertising in Britain.* London: Heinemann, 1982.

Nevitt, Marcus. "Women in the Business of Revolutionary News." In *News, Newspapers and Society in Early Modern Britain*, edited by Joad Raymond. London: Cass, 1999.

Newman, George. "Thomas Sydenham, Reformer of English Medicine." In *Interpreters of Nature: Essays.* Freeport, N.Y.: Books for Libraries, 1968.

Noble, David. *World without Women: The Christian Clerical Culture of Western Science.* New York: Knopf, 1992.

Nuttall, Derek. "English Printers and Their Typefaces, 1600–1700." In *Aspects of Printing from 1600*, edited by Robin Myers and Michael Harris, 30–48. Oxford: Oxford Polytechnic, 1987.

Nutton, Vivian. "Humanist Surgery." In *The Medical Renaissance of the Sixteenth Century*, edited by A. Wear, R. K. French, and I. M. Lonie. Cambridge: Cambridge University Press, 1985.

———. "John Caius and the Linacre Tradition." *Medical History* 23 (1979): 373–91.

Nutton, Vivian, and Roy Porter, eds. *The History of Medical Education in Britain.* Amsterdam: Rodopi, 1995.

Oliver, Thomas. "Lead and Its Compounds." In *Dangerous Trades*, edited by Thomas Oliver. London: E. P. Dutton, 1902.

Ollerenshaw, Robert. "The Camera Obscura in Medical Illustration." *British Journal of Photography*, 23 September 1977: 815–16.

Olson, Alison. "Coffee House Lobbying." *History Today* 41 (Jan. 1991): 35–42.

O'Malley, Charles Donald. *Andreas Vesalius of Brussels, 1514–1564.* Berkeley: University of California Press, 1965.

———. "English Medical Literature in the Sixteenth Century." In *Scientific Literature in Sixteenth and Seventeenth Century England.* Los Angeles: William Andrews Clark Memorial Library, 1961.

O'Malley, Thomas. "Religion and the Newspaper Press, 1660–1685: A Study of the *London Gazette.*" In *The Press in English Society from the Seventeenth to the Nineteenth Centuries*, edited by Michael Harris and Alan Lee. Rutherford, N.J.: Fairleigh Dickinson University Press, 1986.

Orme, Nicholas, and Margaret Webster. *The English Hospital.* New Haven, Conn.: Yale University Press, 1995.

Otten, Charlotte F. *English Women's Views, 1540–1700.* Miami: Florida International University Press, 1992.

Pagel, Walter. *From Paracelsus to van Helmont*, edited by Marianne Winder. London: Variorum Reprints, 1986.

Parks, Stephen. *John Dunton and the English Book Trade.* New York: Garland, 1976.

Payne, Leonard. "A Plagiarist Plagiarised." *Journal of the Royal College of Physicians of London* 19/1 (1985): 44–47.

Peachey, George C. "Thomas Trapham—Cromwell's Surgeon—and Others." *Proceedings of the Royal Society of Medicine* 24 (1931): 1441–49.

Pears, Iain. *The Discovery of Painting: The Growth of Interest in the Arts in England, 1680–1768.* New Haven, Conn.: Yale University Press, 1988.

Pelling, Margaret. *The Common Lot: Sickness, Medical Occupations and the Urban Poor in Early Modern England.* London: Longman, 1998.

———. "Knowledge Common and Acquired: The Education of Unlicensed Medical Practitioners in Early Modern London." In *History of Medical Education in Britain*, edited by Vivian Nutton and Roy Porter. Amsterdam: Ridopi, 1995.

Pelzer, John, and Linda Pelzer. "The Coffee Houses of Augustan London." *History Today* 32 (Oct. 1982): 40–48.

Phillips, Patricia. *The Scientific Lady*. New York: St. Martin's Press, 1990.

Pincus, Steve. "Coffee Politicians Does Create." *Journal of Modern History* 67 (1995): 807–35.

Plant, Marjorie. *The English Book Trade*. 3d ed. London: George Allen and Unwin, 1974.

Plomer, Henry R. *A Dictionary of the Booksellers and Printers Who Were at Work in England, Scotland and Ireland from 1641 to 1667*. London: Bibliographical Society, 1907.

———. "The Long Shop in the Poultry." *Bibliographica* 2 (1896): 61–80.

———. *A Dictionary of the Printers and Booksellers Who Were at Work in England, Scotland, and Ireland from 1668 to 1725*. Oxford: Oxford Bibliographical Society, 1922.

Plomer, Henry R., et al. *Dictionaries of the Printers and Booksellers Who Were at Work in England, Scotland and Ireland 1557–1775*. London: Bibliographical Society, 1977.

———. *Dictionary of the Printers and Booksellers Who Were at Work in England, Scotland and Ireland 1726–1775*. Oxford: Oxford Bibliographical Society, 1932.

Pointon, Marcia. *Hanging the Head: Portraiture and Social Formation in Eighteenth-Century England*. New Haven, Conn.: Yale University Press, 1993.

Pollard, A. W., and G. R. Redgrave. *Short-Title Catalogue of Books Printed in England, Scotland and Ireland, 1475–1640*. 2nd ed. 2 vols. London: Bibliographical Society, 1976.

Pollard, A. W. and G. R. Redgrave, eds. *A Short-Title Catalogue of Books Printed in England, Scotland and Ireland and of English Books Printed Abroad 1475–1640*. Vol. 3: *A Printers and Publishers Index* by Katherine F. Pantzer. London: The Bibliographical Society, 1991.

Porter, Dorothy, and Porter, Roy, eds. *Doctors, Politics and Society: Historical Essays*. Amsterdam: Rodopi, 1993.

Porter, Roy. *Bodies Politic: Disease, Death and Doctors in Britain, 1650–1900*. Ithaca, N.Y.: Cornell University Press, 2001.

———. *Disease, Medicine and Society in England 1550–1860*. London: Macmillan, 1987.

———. *Health for Sale: Quackery in England 1660–1850*. Manchester: Manchester University Press, 1989.

———. "Lay Medical Knowledge in the Eighteenth Century: The Evidence of the *Gentleman's Magazine*." *Medical History* 29 (1985): 138–68.

———. "Medical Journalism in Britain to 1800." In *Medical Journals and Medi-*

cal Knowledge, edited by W. F. Bynum, Stephen Lock, and Roy Porter. London: Routledge, 1992.

———. "The Patient in England, 1660–1800." In *Medicine in Society*, edited by Andrew Wear. Cambridge: Cambridge University Press, 1992.

———. *Patient's Progress: Doctors and Doctoring in Eighteenth-Century England.* Stanford, Calif.: Stanford University Press, 1989.

———. *Patients and Practitioners.* Cambridge: Cambridge University Press, 1985.

———. *Quacks: Fakers and Charlatans in English Medicine.* Stroud, England: Tempus, 2000.

———, ed. *Medicine: A History of Healing.* New York: Marlowe, 1997.

———, ed. *The Popularization of Medicine 1650–1850.* New York: Routledge, 1992.

Porter, Roy, and Dorothy Porter. "The Rise of the English Drugs Industry: The Role of Thomas Corbyn." *Medical History* 33 (1989): 277–95.

Porter, Roy, and G. S. Rousseau. *Gout: The Patrician Malady.* New Haven, Conn.: Yale University Press, 1998.

Porter, Roy, and Andrew Wear, eds. *Problems and Methods in the History of Medicine.* London: Croom Helm, 1987.

Power, D'Arcy, ed. *British Masters of Medicine.* Freeport, N.Y.: Books for Libraries, 1969.

Poynter, F.N.L. *The Evolution of Medical Education in Britain.* London: Pitman Medical Publishing Company, 1966.

———. "The First English Medical Journal." *British Medical Journal* 2 (1948): 307–8.

———. "Gideon de Laune and His Family Circle." In *Wellcome History of Medicine Public Lecture Series*, No. 2. London: Wellcome Library, 1965.

———. "Nicholas Culpeper and His Books." *Journal of Medical History* 17 (1962): 152–67.

———. "Nicholas Culpeper and the Paracelsians." In *Science, Medicine and Society in the Renaissance*, edited by Allen G. Debus. 2 vols. New York: Science History Publications, 1972.

Prest, Wilfred, ed. *The Professions in Early Modern England.* London: Croom Helm, 1987.

Principe, Lawrence. *The Aspiring Adept: Robert Boyle and His Alchemical Quest.* Princeton, N.J.: Princeton University Press, 1998.

Prior, Mary, ed. *Women in English Society, 1500–1800.* New York: Methuen, 1985.

Pumfrey, Stephen. "Who Did the Work? Experimental Philosophy and Public Demonstrators in Augustan England." *British Journal of the History of Science* 28 (1995): 131–56.

Purver, Margery. *The Royal Society: Concept and Creation.* Cambridge, Mass.: M.I.T. Press, 1967.

Pyle, Cynthia. "Art as Science: Scientific Illustration, 1490–1670." *Endeavor* 24/2 (2000): 69–75.

Rappaport, Steve. *Worlds within Worlds: Structures of Life in Sixteenth-Century London.* Cambridge: Cambridge University Press, 1989.

Rattansi, Pyrali M. "The Helmontian-Galenist Controversy in Restoration England." *Ambix* 12 (1964): 1–23.

———. "Paracelsus and the Puritan Revolution." *Ambix* 11 (1963): 24–32.

Raven, James, Helen Small, and Naomi Tadmore, eds. *The Practice and Representation of Reading in England.* Cambridge: Cambridge University Press, 1996.

Reay, Barry. *Popular Cultures in England, 1550–1750.* London: Longman, 1998.

Reddaway, T. F. *The Rebuilding of London after the Great Fire.* London: Edward Arnold, 1951.

Reid, David A. "Science and Pedagogy in the Dissenting Academies of Enlightenment Britain." Ph.D. diss. University of Wisconsin–Madison, 1999.

Richter, Jean Paul. *The Literary Works of Leonardo da Vinci.* 2 vols. Berkeley: University of California Press, 1977.

Roberts, K. B. "Bidloo, Cowper and Plagiarism of Anatomical Illustrations." *Canadian Social History of Medicine Newsletter* September 1970: 7–10.

Roberts, K. B., and J.D.W. Tomlinson. *The Fabric of the Body: European Traditions of Anatomical Illustration.* Oxford: Clarendon Press, 1992.

Roberts, R. S. "The Personnel and Practice of Medicine in Tudor and Stuart England. Part 1: The Provinces." *Medical History* 6 (1962): 363–82.

———. "The Personnel and Practice of Medicine in Tudor and Stuart England. Part 2: London." *Medical History* 8 (1964): 217–34.

Roberts, W. "Bookselling in the Poultry." *City Press* 34, no. 2386 (16 August 1890).

Rogers, Pat. *Grub Street.* London: Methuen, 1972.

———. "Readers, Books and Patrons." In *The New Pelican Guide to English Literature,* edited by Boris Ford. Vol. 4, 214–27. Harmondsworth, England: Penguin-Pelican, 1982.

———. "The Writer and Society." In *The Eighteenth Century,* edited by Pat Rogers. New York: Holmes and Meier, 1978.

Rohde, Eleanour Sinclair. *The Old English Herbals.* New York: Dover, 1971.

Romanell, Patrick. *John Locke and Medicine.* Buffalo, N.Y.: Prometheus Books, 1984.

Rosenberg, Albert. "The London Dispensary for the Sick Poor." *Journal of the History of Medicine* 14 (1959): 41–56.

Rostenberg, Leona. *The Library of Robert Hooke: The Scientific Book Trade of Restoration England.* Santa Monica, Cal.: Modoc Press, 1989.

———. *Literary, Politial, Scientific, Religious and Legal Publishing, Printing and Bookselling in England, 1551–1700.* 2 vols. New York: Burt Franklin, 1965.

———. "Richard and Anne Baldwin, Whig Patriot Publishers." *Papers of the Bibliographical Society of America* 47 (1953): 1–42.

Rousseau, G. S. "'Stung into Action . . .': Medicine, Professionalism and the News." In *Newspapers and Society in Early Modern Britain,* edited by Joad Raymond. London: Cass, 1999.

Rule, John. "Against Innovation? Custom and Resistance in the Workplace."
In *Popular Culture in England, c. 1500–1800*, edited by Tim Harris. New
York: St. Martin's Press, 1995.

Russell, Kenneth Fitzpatrick. "A Bibliography of Anatomical Books Published
in English before 1800." *Bulletin of the History of Medicine* 23 (1949): 268–
306.

———. *British Anatomy 1525–1800*. 2nd ed. Winchester, England: St. Paul's
Bibliographies, 1987.

———. "A Check-list of Medical Books Published in English before 1600."
Bulletin of the History of Medicine 21 (1947): 922–58.

———. "John Browne, 1642–1702." *Bulletin of the History of Medicine* 33/5
(1959): 393–414; 33/6 (1959): 503–22.

———. "Osteographia of W. Cheselden." *Bulletin of the History of Medicine* 28
(1954): 32–49.

Salaman, Malcolm C. *The Old Engravers of England*. London: Cassell and Company, 1907.

Salmon, Vivian. "Bathsua Makin: A Pioneer Linguist and Feminist in Seven-
teenth-Century England." In *Neuere Forschungen zur Wortbildung und
Historiographie der Linguistik*, edited by Brigitte Asbach-Schnitker and
Johannes Roggenhofer. Tübinger Beiträge zur Linguistick, 284. Tübingen:
G. Narr, 1987.

Sanders, M.A. "William Cheselden: Anatomist, Surgeon, and Medical Illustrator." *Spine* 24 (1999): 2282–89.

Sanderson, Jonathan. "Nicholas Culpeper and the Book Trade: Print and the
Promotion of Vernacular Medical Knowledge, 1649–65." Ph.D. diss. University of Leeds, 1999.

Sangwine, Eric. "The Private Libraries of Tudor Doctors." *Journal of the History
of Medicine and Allied Sciences*. 33 (1978): 167–84.

Saunders, J. B., and C. D. O'Malley. *Illustrations from the Works of Andreas
Vesalius*. New York: Dover, 1970.

Sawday, Jonathan. *The Body Emblazoned*. London: Routledge, 1995.

Sawyer, R. C. "Friends or Foes? Doctors and Their Patients in Early Modern
England." In *History of the Doctor-Patient Relationship*, edited by Yosio
Kawakita, Shizu Sakai, and Yasuo Otsuka, 31–53. Tokyo: Ishiyaku
EuroAmerica, 1995.

Schaffer, Simon. "The Glorious Revolution and Medicine in Britain and the
Netherlands." *Notes and Records of the Royal Society of London* 43 (1989):
167–90.

Schneller, Beverly. "Using Newspaper Advertisements to Study the Book
Trade." In *Writers, Books and Trade*, edited by O. M. Brack Jr., 123–43. New
York: AMS Press, 1994.

Schupbach, William. *The Iconographic Collections at the Wellcome Institute for
the History of Medicine*. London: Wellcome Institute for the History of Medicine, 1989.

————. *The Paradox of Rembrandt's 'Anatomy of Dr. Tulp.'* London: Wellcome Institute for the History of Medicine, 1982.

Seaward, Paul. "Gilbert Sheldon, the London Vestries, and the Defence of the Church." In *The Politics of Religion in Restoration England*, edited by TimHarris, Paul Seaward, and Mark Goldie. Oxford: Basil Blackwell, 1990.

Shaaber, M. A. *Some Forerunners of the Newspaper in England, 1476–1622.* New York: Octagon Books, 1966.

Shapin, Steven. *A Social History of Truth: Civility and Science in Seventeeth-Century England.* Chicago: University of Chicago Press, 1994.

————. "Understanding the Merton Thesis." *Isis* 79 (1988): 594–605.

Sharp, Lindsay. "The Royal College of Physicians and Interregnum Politics." *Medical History* 19 (1975): 107–28.

Sharpe, Kevin. *Reading Revolutions: The Politics of Reading in Early Modern England.* New Haven, Conn.: Yale University Press, 2000.

Sharpe, Kevin, and Stephen Zwicker, eds. *Politics of Discourse:The Literature and History of Sevententh-Century England.* Berkeley: University of California Press, 1987.

Shesgreen, Sean, ed. *The Criers and Hawkers of London*, Stanford, Calif.: Stanford University Press, 1990.

Shevelow, Katherine. *Women and Print Culture.* London: Routledge, 1989.

Siegel, Rudolph E. and F.N.L. Poynter. "Robert Talbor, Charles II, and Cinchona." *Medical History* 6 (1962): 82–85.

Siena, Kevin P. "The 'Foul Disease' and Privacy: The Effects of Venereal Disease and Patient Demand on the Medical Marketplace in Early Modern London." *Bulletin for the History of Medicine* 75 (2001): 199–224.

Simon, John. *English Sanitary Institutions.* 2nd ed. London: John Murray, 1897.

Simonton, Deborah. "Apprenticeship: Training and Gender in Eighteenth-Century England." In *Markets and Manufacture in Early Industrial Europe*, edited by Maxine Berg. New York: Routledge, 1991.

Simpson, Percy. *Proof-Reading in the Sixteenth, Seventeenth and Eighteenth Centuries.* Oxford: Oxford University Press, 1970.

Slack, Paul. "Hospitals, Workhouses and the Relief of the Poor in Early Modern London." In *Health Care and Poor Relief in Protestant Europe, 1500–1700*, edited by Ole Peter Grell and Andrew Cunningham. London: Routledge, 1997.

————. *The Impact of Plague in Tudor and Stuart England.* London: Routledge and Kegan Paul, 1985.

Smith, Anthony. *The Newspaper: An International History.* London: Thames and Hudson, 1979.

Smith, Hilda. "Gynecology and Ideology in Seventeenth-Century England." In *Liberating Women's History*, edited by Berenice A. Carroll. Urbana: University of Illinois Press, 1976.

Smith, Margaret M. *The Title Page.* New Castle, Del.: Oak Knoll Press, 2000.

Sommerville, C. John. *The News Revolution in England.* New York: Oxford University Press, 1996.

————. *The Secularlization of Early Modern England.* New York: Oxford University Press, 1992.

Spufford, Margaret. *Small Books and Pleasant Histories: Popular Fiction and Its Readership in Seventeenth Century England.* Cambridge: Cambridge University Press, 1981.

Stevenson, Lloyd G. "New Diseases of the Seventeenth Century." *Bulletin of the History of Medicine* 39 (1965): 1–21.

Stimson, Dorothy. *Scientists and Amateurs: A History of the Royal Society.* New York: Greenwood Press, 1968.

Strutt, Joseph. *Biographical Dictionary of All Engravers.* 2 vols. Geneva: Minkoff Reprints, 1972.

Suleiman, Susan, and Inge Crosman, eds. *The Reader in the Text: Essays on Audience and Interpretation.* Princeton, N.J.: Princeton University Press, 1980.

Sutherland, James. *The Restoration Newspaper and Its Development.* Cambridge: Cambridge University Press, 1986.

Temkin, Owsei. *Galenism: Rise and Decline of a Medical Philosophy.* Ithaca, N.Y.: Cornell University Press, 1973.

Thirsk, Joan. *Economic Policy and Projects: The Development of a Consumer Society in Early Modern England.* Oxford: Clarendon Press, 1978.

Thomas, Keith. "The Meaning of Literacy in Early Modern England." In *The Written Word: Literacy in Transition*, edited by Gerd Baumann, 97–131. Oxford: Clarendon Press, 1986.

————. *Religion and the Decline of Magic.* New York: Scribners, 1971.

Thompson, C.J.S. *The Quacks of Old London.* London: Brentano, 1928.

Thorndike, Lynn. "Newness and Novelty in Seventeenth-Century Science and Medicine." In *Roots of Scientific Thought*, edited by P. P. Wiener and A. Noland. New York: Basic Books, 1957.

Thornton, John L., and Carole Reeves. *Medical Book Illustration.* Cambridge: Oleander Press, 1983.

Thulesius, Olav. *Nicholas Culpeper: English Physician and Astrologer.* New York: St. Martin's Press, 1992.

Tobyn, Graeme. *Culpeper's Medicine.* Shaftesbury, England: Element, 1997.

Traister, Barbara Howard. *The Notorious Astrological Physician of London: Works and Days of Simon Forman.* Chicago: University of Chicago Press, 2001.

Treadwell, Michael. "Lists of Master Printers: The Size of the London Printing Trade, 1637–1723." In *Aspects of Printing from 1600*, edited by Robin Myers and Michael Harris. Gosport, England: Oxford Polytechnic Press, 1987.

————. "London Printers and Printing Houses in 1705." *Publishing History* 7 (1980): 5–44.

————. "London Trade Publishers, 1675–1750." *The Library*, 6th ser. 4 (1982): 99–134.

Trevor-Roper, Hugh. "The Court Physician and Paracelsianism." In *Medicine at the Courts of Europe, 1500–1837*, edited by Vivian Nutton. London: Routledge, 1990.

————. *Religion, the Reformation and Social Change*. London: Macmillan, 1972.

————. *Renaissance Essays*. Chicago: University of Chicago Press, 1985.

Turk, J. L., and Elizabeth Allen. "Bleeding and Cupping." *Annals of the Royal College of Surgeons* 65/2 (March 1983): 128–29.

Tyacke, Sarah. *London Map-Sellers 1660–1720*. Tring, England: Map Collector Publications, 1978.

Ultee, Maarten. "Hans Sloane, Scientist." *British Library Journal* 14 (1988): 1–20.

Underwood, E. A., ed. *Science, Medicine, and History*. London: Oxford University Press, 1953.

Vickers, Brian, ed. *Occult and Scientific Mentalities in the Renaissance*. Cambridge: Cambridge University Press, 1984.

Vigne, Randolph. "Mayerne and His Successors." *Journal of the Royal College of Physicians of London* 20/3 (1986): 222–26.

Voss, Paul. "Books for Sale: Advertising and Patronage in Late Elizabethan England." *Sixteenth Century Journal* 29 (1998): 733–57.

Walker, R. B. "Advertising in London Newspapers, 1650–1750." *Business History* 15 (1973): 112–30.

————. "The Newspaper Press in the Reign of William III." *Historical Journal* 17 (1974): 691–709.

Wall, Cecil. *History of the Surgeons Company*. London: Oxford University Press, 1937.

————. *The London Apothecaries*. London: Apothecaries Hall, 1955.

Wall, Cecil, H., Charles Cameron, and E. Ashworth Underwood. *History of the Worshipful Society of Apothecaries of London: Vol. 1: 1617–1815*. London: Oxford University Press, 1963.

Walsh, Elizabeth, et al. *Yesterday's News: Seventeenth Century English Broadsides and Newsbooks*. Washington, D.C.: Folger Library, 1996.

Watt, Tessa. *Cheap Print and Popular Piety, 1550–1640*. Cambridge: Cambridge University Press, 1994.

Wear, Andrew. *Knowledge and Practice in Early English Medicine*. Cambridge: Cambridge University Press, 2000.

————. *Medicine in Society*. Cambridge: Cambridge University Press, 1992.

————. "Puritan Perceptions of Illness in Seventeenth Century England." In *Patients and Practitioners*, edited by Roy Porter. Cambridge: Cambridge University Press, 1985.

Wear, Andrew, Roger French, and Iain Lonie, eds. *The Medical Renaissance of the Sixteenth Century*. Cambridge: Cambridge University Press, 1985.

Weatherill, Lorna. *Consumer Behaviour and Material Culture in Britain, 1660–1760*. London: Methuen, 1988.

————. "The Meaning of Consumer Behaviour in Late Seventeenth-and Early Eighteenth-Century England." In *Comsumption and the World of Goods*, ed. John Brewer and Roy Porter (London: Routledge, 1993).

————. "A Possession of One's Own: Women and Consumer Behavior in England, 1660–1740." *Journal of British Studies* 25 (1986): 131–56.

Webster, Charles. "The College of Physicians: 'Solomon's House' in Commonwealth England." *Bulletin of the History of Medicine* 41 (1967): 393–412.

————. "English Medical Reformers of the Puritan Revolution." *Ambix* 14 (1967): 17–22.

————. *From Paracelsus to Newton: Magic and the Making of Modern Science.* Cambridge: Cambridge University Press, 1982.

————. *The Great Instauration: Science, Medicine and Reform, 1626–1660.* New York: Holmes and Meier, 1975.

————, ed. *Health, Medicine and Mortality in the Sixteenth Century.* Cambridge: Cambridge University Press, 1979.

————, ed. *Samuel Hartlib and the Advancement of Learning.* Cambridge: Cambridge University Press, 1970.

Webster, Mary. "The Taste of an Augustan Collector." *Country Life* 148 (January 29, 1970): 249–51; (September 24, 1970): 765–67.

Weigel, Rachell. "An Elizabethan Gentlewoman: The Journal of Lady Mildmay." *Quarterly Review* 215 (1911): 119–36.

Wertheim, Margaret. *Pythagoras' Trousers: God, Physics, and the Gender Wars.* New York: Times Books, 1995.

Whitteridge, Gweneth. "Anatomical Illustration in the Sixteenth and Seventeenth Centuries." *Transactions of the Medical Society of London* 104 (1987–88): 71–80.

Wilson, F. P. *The Plague in Shakespeare's London.* Oxford: Clarendon Press, 1927.

Wing, Donald. *Short-Title Catalogue of Books Printed in England, Scotland, Ireland, Wales, and British America, and of English Books Printed in Other Countries, 1641–1700.* 3 vols. New York: Modern Language Association, 1972.

Wing, Donald. *Short Title Catalogue of Books Printed in England, Scotland, Ireland, Wales . . . 1641–1700.* 3 vols. 2nd ed. New York: Modern Language Association, 1994.

Wolstenholme, Gordon, ed. *The Royal College of Physicians of London: Portraits.* London: Churchill, 1964.

Wolstenholme, Gordon, and John F. Kerslake. *Royal College of Physicians of London: Portraits, Catalogue II.* Amsterdam: Elsevier, 1977.

Wood, James Playsted. *The Story of Advertising.* New York: Ronald Press, 1957.

Woodcroft, Bennett. *Subject-Matter Index of Patents of Invention.* 2 vols. London: Queen's Printing Office, 1854.

Woolf, D. R. "The 'Common Voice': History, Folklore and Oral Tradition in Early Modern England." *Past and Present* 120 (1988): 26–52.

Wyman, A. L. "The Surgeoness: The Female Practitioner of Surgery, 1400–1800." *Medical History* 28 (1984): 22–41.

Young, Sidney. *Annals of the Barber-Surgeons of London.* London: Blades, East, and Blades, 1890.

Zaret, David. *Origins of Democratic Culture: Printing, Petitions and the Public Sphere in Early-Modern England*. Princeton, N.J.: Princeton University Press, 2000.

————. "Religion, Science, and Printing in the Public Spheres in Seventeenth-Century England." In *Habermas and the Public Sphere*, edited by Craig Calhoun. Cambridge, Mass.: M.I.T. Press, 1992. 212–35.

Index